Praise for

THE STADIUM

"In this fascinating work, Guridy takes us from the Colosseum of the Roman Empire to indoor arenas to the Barclays Center in Brooklyn and convincingly demonstrates that these edifices are not only a reflection of their times but have also been instrumental in shaping them." Guridy's discussion of the construction, cost and use of stadiums is an intriguing and ultimately convincing new way to view history and the growth of social movements. Guridy also proves that, despite their ability to contain thousands, stadiums have oftentimes not been havens of inclusion but instruments of exclusion as well as racial and social stratification. Sports fans, history buffs, social movement examiners—not necessarily an expected interest confluence—will find this work illuminating. It is an accessible and thought-provoking effort that every person who has sat in the stands or admired a stadium from afar would be wise to read."

—Eric H. Holder Jr., 82nd attorney general

"Guridy's impressively wide-ranging and lucid history reveals that stadiums have always been about far more than just play. They are, as he shows, 'America's public square': combustible sites of conflict, community, and consumption that embody both reactionary and utopian visions of our society. This is essential reading for anyone who has ever been to a stadium."   —Theresa Runstedtler, author of *Black Ball*

"All of the hallmarks of Guridy's many talents are vividly apparent in *The Stadium*, a deeply researched work that is beautifully shaped with meticulous and engaging detail, all crafted with Guridy's usual flair for writing about sport from an intensely historical perspective. Guridy situates the landscape of America's favorite playing spaces as pathways to understanding some of the most complicated facets of our society, from political maneuverings to activist uprisings, all within the ever-increasing corporate model of the modern sport arena."

—Amy Bass, author of *One Goal*

"When is a stadium not just a stadium? How about when it is a staging ground for protest? Or a site to drum up support for war? Or a publicly funded cudgel of gentrification? In Guridy's new book, he unmasks the power of the stadium and how it is interwoven into our lives whether we are sports fans or not. His concrete and steel protagonist comes to life in ways both exhilarating and terrifying. *The Stadium* is a masterwork of history, journalism, and cultural analysis. A triumph."

—David Zirin, sports editor, the *Nation*

"Guridy has delivered a deep and impactful book that spells out both the complicity the public infrastructure owns in reinforcing the heinous foundations of segregation as well as its long history of serving as a place for protest and change. This book is a terrific reminder that, for all its private billions, the stage of sports has been funded by us, the public. Far from politics being an anomaly in sports, *The Stadium* offers proof that, while we were watching one game, an equally important one was taking place."

—Howard Bryant, author of *Full Dissidence*

"Frank Guridy's *The Stadium* brilliantly reveals how these iconic structures—from the humble beginnings of wooden ballparks to the towering mega-arenas of steel and glass—have served as not only simple spaces for recreation but also as monoliths of institutional power and vibrant public squares for political activism. *The Stadium* unravels and lays bare the complex interplay between play, protest, and politics with pulsating prose and enthralling historical research. A tribute to the tradition of using the sports arena as a platform for justice, Guridy's work is a compelling reminder of the stadium's pivotal role in the ongoing struggle for equality in America—a must-read for anyone fascinated by the intersection of sports, society, and activism."

—Rowan Ricardo Phillips, author of *The Circuit*

THE
STADIUM

THE
STADIUM

AN AMERICAN HISTORY
OF POLITICS,
PROTEST, AND PLAY

FRANK ANDRE GURIDY

BASIC BOOKS
New York

Basic Books
Hachette Book Group
1290 Avenue of the Americas, New York, NY 10104
www.basicbooks.com

Printed in the United States of America

First Edition: August 2024

Published by Basic Books, an imprint of Hachette Book Group, Inc. The Basic Books name and logo is a registered trademark of the Hachette Book Group.

The Hachette Speakers Bureau provides a wide range of authors for speaking events. To find out more, go to hachettespeakersbureau.com or email HachetteSpeakers@hbgusa.com.

Basic Books copies may be purchased in bulk for business, educational, or promotional use. For more information, please contact your local bookseller or the Hachette Book Group Special Markets Department at special.markets@hbgusa.com.

The publisher is not responsible for websites (or their content) that are not owned by the publisher.

Print book interior design by Bart Dawson.

Library of Congress Cataloging-in-Publication Data
Names: Guridy, Frank Andre, author.
Title: The stadium : an American history of politics, protest, and play / Frank A. Guridy.
Description: First edition. | New York : Basic Books, 2024. | Includes bibliographical references and index.
Identifiers: LCCN 2023040319 | ISBN 9781541601451 (hardcover) | ISBN 9781541601475 (ebook)
Subjects: LCSH: Stadiums—Political aspects—United States.
Classification: LCC GV415 .G87 2024 | DDC 796.06/873—dc23/eng/20231214
LC record available at https://lccn.loc.gov/2023040319

ISBNs: 9781541601451 (hardcover), 9781541601475 (ebook)

LSC-C

Printing 1, 2024

CONTENTS

INTRODUCTION

On May 29, 2020, a massive crowd converged from all directions on Barclays Center, the sprawling multipurpose arena that colonizes the corner of Atlantic and Flatbush Avenues in Brooklyn, New York. They got there by bus, subway, commuter train, or on foot. Some braved the traffic and drove in their cars. They were not arriving to attend a Brooklyn Nets NBA game. Nor did they come to attend a Jay-Z concert or to see a boxing match as many New Yorkers have done since the building opened in 2012. They came for another purpose altogether. Like millions of others throughout the world, they had seen the shocking footage of a black man, George Floyd, being callously murdered by a police officer in Minneapolis on May 25, 2020. Taken by seventeen-year-old Darnella Frazier, the video went viral in a matter of days, provoking widespread rage and nationwide protests against police brutality and racial injustice. Days after Floyd's murder, protesters across the country took to the streets to find spaces to grieve and protest police violence. In Brooklyn, demonstrators and activists gravitated to Barclays Center day after day to express their anger and demands for racial justice.[1]

The Barclays Center appears like a gigantic extraterrestrial that landed in the middle of a densely populated New York City neighborhood. Rust-colored panels swoop down and curl around the building to form a circular open-roof canopy that looms over the plaza at the arena's entrance. The displays on the electronic billboard beneath the big baby-blue BARCLAYS CENTER sign on the building's facade give the impression that the structure is owned by the multinational

1

banking corporation. In fact, the building, like most arenas and stadiums in the United States, belongs to the public. It is owned by a public entity, the Empire State Development Authority, which leases the arena to the owners of the Brooklyn Nets—a shell game that enables the team to avoid paying millions of dollars in property taxes.[2] The arena was constructed atop a railyard and a subway stop served by multiple subway lines, buses, and the Long Island Railroad, making it an accessible location for an entertainment venue.

Barclays Center is the centerpiece of a $6 billion development project that included construction of several buildings of market-rate and affordable housing. In the early 2000s, when the development was announced, it purported to regenerate an area that the State of New York had declared blighted. After the state used the power of eminent domain to take and then hand over twenty-two acres of land to the developers, many Brooklynites have viewed the development as a mechanism of gentrification that displaces longtime residents and provides housing and entertainment for affluent fans. For years, locals have mobilized against the project, arguing that it has not produced enough benefits for the community. The arena opened in 2012, but only a fraction of the promised housing development has been completed. Ironically, in spite of this fraught history, Barclays Center, by virtue of its central location, has also turned into an ideal space for outraged citizens to make their voices heard.

On that supercharged day in late May 2020, protesters converged on the plaza under the gigantic canopy that swoops over the arena's entrance. As advertisements for Starbucks coffee, T-Mobile cell phones, Geico insurance, and other companies' products flashed across the massive electronic message board above their heads, the people chanted, they marched, they screamed, they clapped, and they cried. Most in the crowd wore masks to protect themselves from the COVID-19 virus that was killing people daily. They came holding signs with not only the name George Floyd but also the names Sandra Bland, Ahmaud Arbery, Breonna Taylor. Others carried slogans like ABOLISH THE POLICE. They came, well schooled in the repertoire of gestures that have been made popular by the Movement for Black Lives over the past ten years: raising their fists, holding their hands up, and clutching their cell phones to vigilantly document the moment. They were also preparing themselves for the likelihood of police misconduct, and with good reason. In a scene that repeated itself over and over again during the summer of 2020, the peaceful protest turned into violent clashes with police, who walloped demonstrators with batons, doused them with pepper spray, and arrested many of them that night.

Over the course of that summer, and on many nights since 2020, protesters gathered at the Barclays Center plaza. With their bodies they repurposed the arena into a public square, a gathering place to express dissent, an epicenter of activism and community building. Though normal uses of the facility resumed after COVID-19 vaccinations became available, the plaza remained an important gathering place for Brooklyn-based activists. Free jazz concerts were held, voters were registered, and the demands of the community were expressed. "It is a mecca," one protester told the *New York Times* that summer. "This is where everything happens."[3]

Barclays Center, May 29, 2020. *Credit: Angela Weiss/AFP via Getty Images*

The transformation of the Barclays Center plaza into a space of protest and politics might seem to be an instance of the many unprecedented improvisations the COVID-19 pandemic caused and a moment of social and political turmoil. In actuality, since the days of the circus tent and wooden ballpark after the Civil War, stadiums and arenas have been important institutions in American life. Though stadiums have long been identified as sport and entertainment venues, they functioned not just as spaces for recreation but also as deeply political places where Americans from a variety of backgrounds have expressed conflicting aspirations and agendas. Elites have constructed stadiums as monuments to affluence, technological wonder, and exclusivity. Yet, America's marginalized groups have transformed them into venues to express their desires and discontents, and to proclaim a more inclusive vision of American society. The stadium has been America's public square. It is a venue of not just play but also politics and protest.

Stadiums became political spaces because governments have been deeply involved in them—their location, their funding, their use—throughout their history. Buildings initially built by private entrepreneurs for the purposes of sport and entertainment quickly morphed into spaces for political theater. In the early twentieth century, they hosted political conventions. In subsequent decades, politicians approached them as ideal platforms from which to promote their political agendas. By the mid-twentieth century, stadiums fully developed into state institutions when governments took over their primary ownership and management. Stadium construction became state policy for a sports-crazed nation. Even in recent decades, as naming-rights agreements have turned them into corporate billboards and as sports franchises have largely dictated their use, the vast majority of stadiums in the United States, including the Barclays Center in Brooklyn, are in the hands of the public.

Political theater can play out in stadiums because, from the beginning, their role as spaces for recreation was shaped by systems of racial, gender, class, and sexual exclusion. In the United States, more often than not, stadiums were built by and for white men. Because stadiums and arenas proved costly to construct and maintain, especially as they grew larger and more architecturally sophisticated, stadium builders were compelled to broaden the audience they catered to in order to make the venues financially solvent. Herein lies the tension between social inclusion and exclusion that is at the core of stadium history. Buildings that are designed to attract and accommodate large numbers of people are also envisioned as engines of social stratification and exclusion.

The history of the American stadium is the story of a country wrestling with racial, class, gender, and sexual inequalities and how these struggles played out in public. From the late nineteenth to the early twentieth century, stadiums manifested varying degrees of racial, class, and gender segregation, especially in the South, where the stadium functioned as a platform to project and defend the Jim Crow order. When the civil rights, second-wave feminist, and gay liberation movements erupted in the mid-twentieth century, the stadium was a prime location to effectively challenge racism, sexism, and homophobia. Buildings constructed for performances in front of thousands of spectators made ideal environments to showcase for the American public what justice and equality could look like. Since that time, the stadium has continued to be a venue of social and political conflict. The growing reach of corporate control in every aspect of American life, widening class stratification, and movements against racism and other forms of injustice have all had a profound impact on the way the American stadium is experienced and understood.

The stadium has never had a singular meaning or purpose. It is a vessel marked by and filled with society's aspirations and conflicts. The social and political dimensions of the American stadium story should not be surprising because these aspects first appeared in the stadium environment thousands of years ago.

THE SPACES WE NOW CALL STADIUMS ORIGINATED IN THE ANCIENT world. The word *stadium* comes from the Greek *stadion*, which originally referred to a measurement of distance in ancient Greek foot-races (approximately 600 feet). *Stadion* eventually came to describe the rectangular-shaped venues where the footraces took place. Other venues, such as hippodromes, were wider structures used for horse and chariot races. These spaces were sacred sites, where athletic competitions were held to honor the Greek gods. Among the most famous is the Panathenaic Stadium, built in Athens in 330 BC, and the site of the ancient Panathenaic festival. The rectangular structure was later excavated and renovated for the Olympic Games revival in the late nineteenth century.[4]

During the Roman era, stadiums increased in size and became more technologically sophisticated. The Greek hippodrome, built for chariot races, eventually transformed into the circular structure known as the Roman circus. Amphitheaters were larger oval-shaped structures where various kinds of events, the most famous being the bloody spectacles of the gladiatorial games, could be staged. The monumental four-storied Colosseum was the most famous amphitheater. Though these structures have rightly been hailed as architectural marvels, they were also temples embedded in the exploitation and exclusions characteristic of the ancient world. The tiered construction correlated with the class and gender hierarchies of the day: elites sat down lower, closer to the action, whereas the popular classes and women sat higher up. From the ancient world to the present, stadiums have helped stage and preserve social hierarchies.[5]

The collapse of the Roman Empire initiated a long period of decline in stadium building and use in world history. Though ancient pastimes such as chariot racing continued to be held in venues such as the Hippodrome of Constantinople into the time of the Byzantine Empire, most ancient sporting events faded from everyday life, as did the venues where they were performed. During the medieval era, militarized fighting such as jousting and knightly tournaments were typically held in smaller structures or open fields where temporary stands for spectators were built. Still, the histories of venues for sport and recreation during the next two millennia after the large monuments of the Roman era were plundered and demolished are largely unknown.[6]

What we know is that the reemergence of stadiums in world history correlates with urbanization. As industrial urban centers emerged in Europe in the late eighteenth and early nineteenth centuries, the conditions for modern sport and its venues arose. Cities created an environment where larger numbers of people could participate in cricket, horse racing, rugby, and other amusements in front of mass audiences. They were ideal places that fostered the rise of commercialized sport and entertainment. Improved transportation networks, especially the advent of the streetcar and the railway, helped provide an infrastructure that allowed for the spread in popularity of sports. By the 1860s, playing "grounds" and eventually larger structures known as stadiums were built for cricket, rugby, and association football (soccer). In the early twentieth century, the explosive growth of soccer and other sports spawned the building of stadiums across Europe to stage athletic events.[7]

As in Europe, the modern American stadium emerged as industrialization and urbanization created the conditions for the rise of the sport and entertainment industries. The history of the stadium in the United States tends to center on the story of baseball stadiums, often known as "ballparks." Facilities such as Union Grounds in Brooklyn and South End Grounds in Boston were among the earliest ballparks, built in the 1860s and 1870s to provide venues for the rapidly growing sport. Baseball developed a large cross-class constituency of players and fans, who crowded into cheaply built wooden structures erected on the outskirts of rapidly growing cities to watch the athletes play. However, these accommodations were exceedingly dangerous fire traps that could easily burn to the ground with the accidental combination of intense heat and a lit match. Ballpark fires were not uncommon during these years. The short shelf life of ballparks made them de facto temporary facilities. Eventually, local governments developed stringent fire codes and safety standards that compelled the creation of more fire-resistant venues.[8]

Yet, the ballpark story overshadows a more complex and revealing history. Ballparks, however important, were but one kind of venue transforming American social life in the late nineteenth century. The explosion of all sorts of mass entertainments, including the circus, bicycle racing, horse racing, boxing, and football, in addition to baseball, necessitated the construction of different kinds of structures. Before the baseball stadium came the large fabric circus tents that popped up across the country in the decades after 1793, when the British equestrian John Bill Rickets staged the first modern circus in Philadelphia. More than half a century later, by the 1860s and 1870s, prominent circus impresarios such as P. T. Barnum, Adam Forepaugh, and the Ringling brothers, among others, took advantage of the new railroad systems to bring elaborate traveling shows of clowns, muscular acrobats, and exotic animals to rural and urban areas across the country, staging the spectacles under temporary fabric structures with wooden stands for spectators. The large canvas tent, colloquially known as the Big Top, became the iconic image representing the nineteenth-century circus. By the 1880s, the success of the circus served as the main impetus for the construction of permanent indoor arenas such as Madison Square Garden in New York City.[9]

Meanwhile, the spread of prizefighting also drove stadium construction. Critics abhorred the violence of the sport but could not prevent its growing popularity. Because boxing regulations varied from state to state, matches were held, often clandestinely, in a wide variety of places such as gyms and local meeting halls. However, as the sport's fan base grew, in states where the sport was legal, boxing promoters staged bouts outdoors in temporary wooden facilities. Like the circus owners, boxing promoters, including George Lewis "Tex" Rickard, used railway access to bring fans from far and wide to see matches. The most famous boxing match of the era was the Jack Johnson–Jim Jeffries bout Rickard staged on July 4, 1910, in Reno, Nevada. More than twenty thousand fans crowded into temporary wooden stands to see Johnson become the first African American heavyweight champion by defeating the white American Jeffries. Johnson's triumph outraged white supremacist America, but it did little to stop boxing's growth. Eventually, prizefighting moved to permanent indoor venues after boxing impresarios successfully lobbied states like New York to legalize the sport in the 1920s.[10]

Stadiums acquired their monumental qualities, growing larger and featuring architectural designs, in the late nineteenth and early twentieth centuries. They also assumed a permanent quality, transforming from makeshift wooden structures vulnerable to fires to more durable buildings made of concrete and steel. New engineering technologies gave a fresh class of entrepreneurs confidence in the belief that sports could be made profitable in permanent structures. Baseball team owners, including Ben Shibe in Philadelphia and Charles Ebbets in Brooklyn, were among a number of businessmen who built their ballparks by leveraging political connections with local governments to gain access to favorable locations close to mass transportation. A new era in American stadium construction was about to begin.[11]

The advent of concrete and steel construction technology at the turn of the century also made indoor arenas attractive venues for a wide variety of events. The Big Top remained an integral part of the traveling circus, but in big cities it was supplanted by the permanent indoor arena, which had more seating capacity and improved illumination after electric lighting became widely available. Municipal auditoriums and convention halls, early incarnations of indoor arenas, were ideal spaces for political gatherings as well as for ice hockey and ice skating, new forms of entertainment just gaining popularity, especially in the Northeast and Midwest. Eventually, the circus and boxing joined dog shows and horse shows and a host of other events in indoor arenas, where a regular rotation of touring acts brought spectators through the doors for decades to come.

With the exceptions of the boxing arena and the circus tent, most early stadiums and arenas in the United States originally catered to the elite classes. However, the immigrant working classes that flooded into American cities during the late nineteenth and early twentieth centuries quickly transformed stadiums and arenas into mass entertainment spaces. Even when these structures were designed for specific sports or cultural events, they were never simply recreational facilities. The revenue needed to maintain stadiums and arenas meant that they often had to be used for concerts, rallies, and expositions.

Though the American stadium was multiuse from its inception, conceived to house the emerging amusements of the late nineteenth century, during the twentieth century it became more strongly associated with sporting events as the American sports industry grew by leaps and bounds. During the 1910s and 1920s, the ballpark was an institution in cities and towns, and baseball became America's national pastime. The classic concrete and steel ballparks, such as Shibe Park, Forbes Field, Comiskey Park, Tiger Stadium, Fenway Park, and Ebbets Field, were celebrated venues and have been the subjects of much nostalgia and commentary. Smaller facilities were built for an assortment of leagues in the South and the West. Though the majority were privately owned, they aroused local civic pride. But the monumental structures, such as Yankee Stadium and Cleveland's Municipal Stadium, were gigantic edifices designed to be more than ballparks. They were monuments of grandeur that symbolized the making of the modern American city. Osborn Engineering Company, a Cleveland-based firm, dominated stadium design and construction throughout the first half of the twentieth century.[12]

The growing popularity of college football was another impetus for the increase in number of stadiums in the United States. The public's anxiety about the safety of the sport did not stop it from spreading across the country. The opening of Franklin Field at the University of Pennsylvania in 1895 and Harvard Stadium in 1903, as well as other stadiums at elite schools in the Northeast, prompted universities across the country to build their own football facilities to the point that the college football stadium became ubiquitous. Here again, Osborn Engineering played a major role in designing and building many of the fabled college football venues, including Michigan Stadium (1927) and Notre Dame Stadium (1930). Out west, the Rose Bowl in Pasadena, Stanford Stadium, Memorial Stadium in Berkeley, and the Los Angeles Memorial Coliseum were massive bowl-like structures built to house thousands of spectators.[13] A decade later, businessmen in New Orleans, Dallas, and Miami pushed for the construction of large football stadiums to host annual New Year's Day sports carnivals in an effort to generate tourist dollars. The Sugar Bowl in New Orleans, the Cotton Bowl in Dallas, and the Orange Bowl in Miami became New Year's Day traditions that turned these cities into tourist destinations.

As stadiums and arenas became common features of American life, they also became increasingly political. Government officials discovered stadiums' potential for gathering an audience so they could promote their policies and their personalities. Political conventions and rallies were in the regular rotation of events at Madison Square Garden, Chicago Stadium, and other arenas all over the country. US presidents tossing ceremonial first balls at baseball games became a tradition. After "The Star-Spangled Banner" was officially named the US national anthem in 1931, the stadium and the arena increasingly became ideal places to cultivate mass loyalty to the nation. Even though most stadiums were privately owned, they acquired a civic character. Indeed, many arenas of the 1920s were built as war memorials for those who died serving in World War I. Stadium construction became state policy during the New Deal era of the 1930s because stadiums were envisaged as public works projects that provided jobs and public recreational spaces for Americans suffering from the Great Depression. The New Deal era marked the beginning of major public investment in stadium construction, a phenomenon that spread widely in the postwar years.

During the Second World War, these political traditions expanded into ceremonies designed to cultivate loyalty to the Allied cause. Stadiums like the Memorial Coliseum in Los Angeles were used to stage battle reenactments.[14] The stadium became a venue for promoting American nationalism, and though it would remain so for years, at the same time, it served as a venue of protest for insurgent social movements.

Indoor arenas, such as Madison Square Garden, were sites of political turmoil, especially during the Depression years. Socialists, communists, and many other labor activists used the Garden as a massive meeting hall. Not to be outdone, fascist organizations and pro-Hitler and pro-Mussolini groups refashioned the Garden into a venue that resembled the fascist meeting halls of Berlin and Rome. Indeed, as the world drove headlong toward World War II during the 1930s, the struggle over fascism was played out in the American stadium. As in Europe, the American sporting world could not be divorced from politics, as the memorable boxing matches between American Joe Louis and German Max Schmeling in Yankee Stadium vividly illustrated. The stadium became a de facto American public square, where real and symbolic political battles took place, sometimes resulting in violent confrontation. As stadiums and arenas became even more numerous and costly to the public in the decades to come, their very existence became subject to political controversy. Politics became a recurring feature of stadium life.

But, as in the ancient world, the modern stadium replicated social hierarchies and made them more concrete.[15] Throughout the first half of the twentieth century, the American stadium was a Jim Crow and settler colonial institution that catered to white elite and working-class men. Even when performers on the field or the stage were racially integrated, often the spectators in the stands were not. Professional baseball was played by segregated teams in front of fans segregated in the stands. College football, like baseball and other sports, was also defined by the hierarchies of Jim Crow. This was particularly clear in the South, a hotbed for college football. Football stadiums, such as Tulane Stadium in New Orleans, home of the Sugar Bowl New Year's Day classic, not only provided entertainment for the sport's white fan base, but also provided a staging ground to project a twentieth-century version of the Confederate States of America. At the same time, sport and entertainment events held in stadiums perpetuated Native American subordination. Native mascots and team names were extremely popular. What the historian Phil Deloria called "playing Indian" became a pervasive performance tradition at stadiums and arenas all over the United States.[16]

The stadium was a masculine domain, where men were the dominant performers on the field, the writers who described the action off it, and the majority of the fans in the stands. Over time, women were welcomed into the masculinized domain of the stadium, but on designated "Ladies Days." Meanwhile, African Americans created their own sporting and recreational cultures, and more often than not, they were forced to do so in peripheral spaces. During the 1930s, Negro League team owner Gus Greenlee was one of the very few African American entrepreneurs who managed his own stadium for his baseball team, the Pittsburgh Crawfords. The vast majority of black sports teams at all levels had to rent facilities that were under white control.[17]

Stadium construction changed dramatically after World War II. The number of facilities multiplied as the power of professional sports leagues grew. Baseball leagues continued to be popular as professional football, basketball, and hockey leagues pined for facilities for their franchises. Sports leagues found willing partners in America's public officials, who discovered that having sports teams in their communities generated enormous political capital. Tax-exempt municipal bonds— rather than the pockets of team owners—became primary sources of financing for the construction of stadiums and arenas. Building a stadium with public funds could entice a team to a city and generate substantial political capital in an increasingly sports-crazed nation. Beginning in the mid-twentieth century, new concrete structures were constructed to accommodate both football and baseball. Nationalizing professional sports leagues trudged on turf once dominated by college football and regional sports leagues.

It was in the 1950s when the modern "stadium scenario" was born. Cities built stadiums to compete for the attention of monopoly sports leagues. Once a prospective team was identified, sports franchises, politicians, and citizens fought fierce political battles to determine the merits of a stadium project. More often than not, the proponents of stadiums won those battles. Stadium projects regularly exceeded initial cost projections, draining public resources. After a facility was built, architectural critics, the press, and fans would celebrate the beauty and amenities of the new structure, but in a few decades, sometimes sooner, the stadium would be deemed obsolete, and sports franchises would agitate for better stadium deals, driving costs up further. Sometimes team owners would allow their teams to stay; other times they would break the hearts of fans and leave. A franchise relocation transferred the drama of the stadium scenario to another city, where the cycle would start all over again. The stadium was inextricably linked to the whims of the growing professional sports industry. The pattern that originated in this era would replicate itself at a dizzying rate at the turn of the next century.[18]

Like the single-family home, the midcentury stadium was more likely to be constructed in a city's outskirts, where there was automobile access, as a way of catering to an imagined suburban demographic. Yet, contrary to what has often been written about the stadiums of this time, these buildings turned out to be the most democratic structures built in the history of American stadiums. Though they are often derided by today's architectural critics for their modernist aesthetics, at the time, boosters, commentators, and fans celebrated the midcentury stadium for its architectural design. In retrospect, the minimal corporate advertising—usually confined to the scoreboard—illustrates how these venues were conceived to be monuments to local civic identity more than to the local sports franchise. Moreover, their larger seating capacities, affordable ticket prices, minimal security, and multiple uses attracted a cross-class and cross-racial constituency, which reflects a sensibility that stadiums were to be accessible to a wider social demographic than what existed before and what has existed since.[19]

These stadiums, built during the great freedom movements of the era—the civil rights, second-wave feminist, Native American, anti-war, and gay liberation movements—hosted the most diverse groups of performers and spectators in American history. The freedom movements held rallies at these facilities, which helped topple racial and gender barriers at the stadium. Indeed, activists leveraged the fact that these facilities were publicly managed to push their movements into the ballpark. This was when the Jim Crow stadium collapsed, when women fought for the right to get on the playing field and to cover sports in equal working conditions with their male counterparts, and when gays and lesbians asserted their right to exist.

But after three decades of unprecedented social inclusion, this era of public accessibility gave way to a new time when the meaning and function of the American stadium dramatically altered. In the 1990s, the American stadium stood as a symbol of unbridled corporatization. With some exceptions, stadiums were public facilities masquerading as corporate buildings owned by sports franchises. Arenas that were once named after their city, local sports boosters, or veterans began to be named after a dizzying array of ever-changing corporate sponsors. Spaces that housed an array of political events and rallies were remade into apolitical sites of mindless consumption. The prosperity of the decade coupled with the end of the Cold War bolstered arguments businesses, politicians, and economists made that governments were no longer needed to equalize opportunities in American society. Stadiums came to symbolize the infiltration of market values into every aspect of American life.[20]

The stadium-naming-rights deal became standard: municipal governments, which owned these facilities, could not resist the sponsorship dollars that corporations lavished upon them and were happy to trade away the facility's name. Public sports commissions, which had traditionally partnered with sports franchises while also ensuring that stadiums served a public purpose, were widely discredited as corrupt and inefficient. In response, these institutions relinquished their management responsibilities to third-party, private entities. Naming-rights agreements unleashed the total commodification of the stadium. Advertisements were plastered on every inch of visible space, and this corporatization continued unabated for the next three decades. The meaning and function of stadiums changed as they became more commodified.

If stadiums symbolized the triumph of corporate power at the turn of the twenty-first century, they were also reenvisioned as engines of economic revitalization for dormant postindustrial urban centers. Sports franchises argued that stadiums could foster economic development and create jobs, warranting the skyrocketing cost of construction. These structures formed a key component in the gentrification of American cities, the remaking of formerly poor and working-class districts into zones of consumption centered on amenities for newly arrived affluent residents or suburbanites who came into cities to attend sporting events and concerts. When critics cited the substantial body of evidence showing that stadiums had minimal impact on the economic development of surrounding neighborhoods, sports franchises responded by making the structures the center of massive real estate development projects that promised to provide jobs and housing for locals. Reviving the inner city with a new stadium became the latest justification for stadium construction.[21]

Over the next three decades, these arguments became unquestioned orthodoxy as the United States embarked on another stadium construction boom, one that was much larger than the previous booms of the 1920s and 1960s. It was, for all intents and purposes, a veritable stadium- and arena-building orgy. Hundreds of stadiums and arenas were built for professional sports franchises all over the country. They cost more money and occupied more real estate even as seating capacities decreased. What's more, they were products of a new type of urbanism. Stadium architects abandoned concrete structures in favor of decorative glass, brick, and steel designs. Once admired for their modernist aesthetics, midcentury stadiums were now derided as "concrete doughnuts," with sports franchises, like-minded journalists, and architectural critics claiming that they not only were ugly but also failed to satisfy fan bases. The praise for new stadium designs attempted to obscure the astronomical construction costs. Facilities that cost tens of millions of dollars in the 1980s cost more than $1 billion by the early 2020s. Moreover, stadiums and arenas proliferated because sports franchises were no longer willing to share facilities with other teams. At one time, sports franchises did not have the power to demand their own stadiums from public officials, but during the final decades of the twentieth century, the balance of power shifted decisively to sports franchises.

The new stadiums and arenas of the 1990s and beyond took up larger footprints in the landscape, symbolizing the outsized impact of the sports industry in late-twentieth- and early-twenty-first-century America. In a sense, the United States entered a period of conspicuous wealth and inequalities that resembled those of the Gilded Age. But the palaces were no longer built on private property and adorned with towers and statues of Roman goddesses, like Stanford White's Madison Square Garden, built in 1890. Rather, they were constructed on public property for a smaller constituency of affluent corporate fans and decorated with tiers of luxury suites and premium seating that were plastered with advertisements and billboards as far as the eye could see. Commerce and consumption displaced the stadium's historic role as a venue of public recreation and civic engagement.

Though stadiums and arenas might have provided more entertainment options for Americans, after the 1980s, they looked more like monuments to the widening income gaps and racial inequities of a new age of gentrification. Unlike the Gilded Age a century before, few if any sections of these new mega structures were reserved for working-class spectators, who were priced out of the stadium altogether unless they were present as concession workers or security guards. Though team owners and politicians touted stadiums as engines of economic development and revitalization, they became, in fact, resource-sucking money pits that provided poor returns on investment.[22] They were also increasingly segregated and policed by private security forces whose role was to segregate crowds by class more than to provide actual public safety. The freedom movements of the 1960s enabled athletes and performers to knock down the racial barriers that had kept them off the field of play and stage. By the early 2000s, however, they were performing for whiter and more affluent spectators, who at once admired them and resented the fact that they were being paid salaries higher than what they were perceived to deserve. The stadium became a social and political powder keg, even as it continued to be widely perceived as an apolitical place of entertainment.

As the stadium reinforced the social hierarchies of the early twenty-first century in America, its political function was narrowed to hosting carefully choreographed celebrations of militarism. For more than a century, politicians had been using the stadium to promote their agendas, but the terrorist attacks of September 11, 2001, facilitated an unprecedented amplification of a very narrow conception of American patriotism at sporting events. The US government partnered with sports leagues to promote a militarized nationalism designed to solidify support for the War on Terror. Before 9/11, sports teams had already begun to market themselves as pro-military, but the terrorist attacks unleashed a staggering amount of military-themed paraphernalia that enabled them to cash in on American patriotism. Almost immediately, commemorations of those who died on that tragic day were overshadowed by glorifications of first responders, especially police officers.

As the wars in Afghanistan and Iraq raged on for the next two decades, the stadium was converted into a venue for a recurring pep rally for the military. The government and sports leagues reminded Americans again and again that the nation was at war. Standing at attention during performances of "The Star-Spangled Banner" was portrayed as a mandatory act of patriotism. Honoring soldiers fighting abroad morphed into honoring increasingly militarized police forces across the country.[23] The national and local governments successfully manipulated fears of another 9/11 to justify a dramatic expansion of the military and of the police's influence on everyday life. The stadium, the major congregation space in American life, was the place where the United States government reinforced its political agenda during the presidency of George W. Bush. The arrival of Barack Obama to the presidency in 2009 did nothing to stop the beating of war drums at the ballpark. In turn, the militarization of the stadium helped produce a public that was even more intolerant of political dissent.

Two decades of war drums and glorification of law enforcement had created a repressive political environment when the Black Lives Matter movement erupted and spilled over into the American stadium in the early 2010s. The murders of Trayvon Martin by George Zimmerman in Sanford, Florida, and Michael Brown by police officer Darren Wilson in Ferguson, Missouri, and other high-profile incidents of police violence against black Americans, unleashed the twenty-first century's version of the centuries-long Black Freedom struggle. When black athletes inspired by the movement began to take public stands against anti-black violence enacted by the police, the heretofore heroes of post-9/11 America, they were greeted with a fierce counterreaction in stadiums and arenas. This counterreaction was stoked by another consequence of two decades of American war drumming and police glorification—the revival of right-wing politics, galvanized by Donald Trump. Yet, following in the footsteps of previous generations of activists, black athletes Colin Kaepernick, Maya Moore, and a host of others at all levels, along with a smaller number of white allies such as Megan Rapinoe, took their politics into the stadium. They expressed their solidarity with those suffering from police violence and systemic racism by taking a knee, highlighting the issue in press conferences and interviews, and displaying messages of racial justice on their uniforms. These were courageous acts that inspired many others to join the movement for racial justice.[24]

The murder of George Floyd by Minneapolis police officer Derek Chauvin in May 2020 intensified the struggle for racial justice at levels not seen since the 1960s. The explosion of an unprecedented national and international solidarity movement against police violence in the aftermath of Floyd's death convinced even formerly apolitical public figures, athletes included, to make public declarations against systemic racism. Once again, black athletes took the cause of Black Freedom to the stadium, and this time, they successfully pushed back against the repressive political culture of militarism. They demanded that American institutions, including sports leagues, recognize that black lives mattered. Not even Donald Trump's popular brand of fascist demagoguery could stop the powerful protest movement during the summer of 2020. The spell of two decades of militarized patriotism was broken, or so it seemed.

However, sports institutions, like other corporations, responded to calls for racial justice with proclamations of support in the dominant idiom of the twenty-first century: the corporate advertisement. Black Lives Matter–inspired slogans were commodified and watered down and displayed at stadiums and arenas all across the country. Cosmetic changes, such as the public performance of racial reckoning through the promotion of select African Americans to high public and private positions by the government and corporate America, have done little to fundamentally alter the centuries-long phenomenon of systemic racism. American institutions' tepid responses were laid bare by the coup attempt at the US Capitol on January 6, 2021, and the continuing spread of right-wing politics after Trump was voted out of the White House.

Today's era of political polarization resembles the political conflicts that occurred in stadiums and arenas during the 1930s. The upheavals of the past two decades have put to rest the notion that the stadium is merely a space for apolitical entertainment. And yet in the midst of this cauldron of conflict, exacerbated by the COVID-19 crisis, the stadium's historic civic function was once again revived with the advent of stadium voting during the 2020 presidential election. The conversion of stadiums and arenas into polling stations as a response to the racial justice movement and the pandemic was a moment of democratic renewal in the middle of a decades-long period of reactionary politics. It remains to be seen whether these transformations will have lasting effects on the design and use of the American stadium.

THE STADIUM DRAWS UPON FIFTEEN YEARS OF RESEARCH IN ARCHIVES across the United States. It is also based on more than forty years of my observations as a spectator in stadiums and arenas all over the country.

Records of public buildings stored in state and municipal archives and libraries illustrate the enormous amount of resources governments have invested in stadium construction and maintenance. The records of sports franchises and architectural and engineering firms tend to be out of the historian's reach, but information about these sources can be found in the records of public institutions that partnered with them to build and manage stadiums. The centrality of stadium planning and construction in higher educational institutions is documented in university archives around the country. For this book, I relied on the plethora of material left behind by the social movements that changed the United States during the sixties, seventies, and eighties. Records of the National Association for the Advancement of Colored People (NAACP), the Congress of Racial Equality (CORE), Black Power organizations, the LGBTQ movements of the 1980s such as the Gay Games and the AIDS Coalition to Unleash Power (ACT UP), and other organizations reveal the intersection between the worlds of the stadium and the social movement.

As important, this book benefits from the staggering array of digital sources available on the internet. Libraries and archives across the United States have digitized an enormous number of photographs and audiovisual materials. A plethora of sports telecasts, highlight films, documentaries, concert footage, and films of speeches and rallies is now widely available on digital platforms such as YouTube, which opens up endless research possibilities. No longer is the historian enslaved by scant references to, say, crowd behavior in order to understand the impact of spectators in the past. In short, stadiums and arenas are ubiquitous and so are their archives.

The Stadium reveals how an American institution has long served as a space of protest and politics, not just play. The extent to which stadiums are widely seen as homes for protest and politics has changed over the years. Stadiums became increasingly political during the 1920s and 1930s, as political parties and activist groups remade them into meeting halls. From the 1960s to the 1980s, the great freedom movements brought their struggles into the confines of the stadium and transformed American society. However, as stadiums were dressed up as corporate billboards from the 1990s onward, elites and public officials became increasingly intolerant of political dissent, especially in such prominent spaces as American stadiums. The corporatization of stadiums created the illusion that they functioned solely as places of apolitical entertainment and conspicuous consumption. Yet, the US government's efforts to make the stadium into a major platform from which to promote the War on Terror and celebrate law enforcement since 9/11 further politicized the stadium. The polarized political environment has persisted at stadiums and arenas to the present, even as American society moves away from the upheavals of 2020.

This, then, is what this book offers: a people's history of the American stadium. The story shifts between a bird's-eye view of national patterns of stadium construction and usage and up-close, detailed portraits of how these patterns were informed by local dynamics. Each chapter highlights a particular transformative moment when people engaged in ordinary and extraordinary activities in front of tens of thousands of people in a confined space. In these pages, I meditate on the impact of southern marching bands unfurling large Confederate flags while performing "Dixie" in front of eighty thousand spectators—with millions more listening on radio and watching on television—at the Sugar Bowl in New Orleans in the immediate aftermath of the *Brown v. Board of Education* Supreme Court decision. I speculate on the harm done when fans of the Washington Redskins NFL franchise donned headdresses and war paint and sang "Hail to the Redskins" year after year in the federally controlled confines of Robert F. Kennedy Memorial Stadium. But I also highlight the powerful impact a hundred thousand black people chanting Jesse Jackson's "I Am Somebody" litany in the Los Angeles Memorial Coliseum in the summer of 1972 had. In these pages, we'll revisit the moments when Robin Herman, Melissa Ludtke, and dozens of other women sportswriters courageously broke through the barriers erected at press boxes and locker rooms in the face of male hostility. We'll see the power of gay and lesbian athletes and fans performing, cheering and hugging and kissing in the stands of San Francisco's Kezar Stadium during the opening and closing ceremonies of the Gay Games in the 1980s. And we'll remember how contemporary black athletes declared they were unafraid of the entrenched rituals of militarized patriotism by standing up with their words and their bodies against systemic racism and police violence in stadiums named after corporations, whether the American sports fan liked it or not. Finally, we'll see how poll workers and voters overcame their fears of the deadly COVID-19 pandemic and cast votes for democracy in stadiums and arenas during the historic 2020 presidential election. These are the stories that show what the American stadium has been—an institution that has had far more impact than its commonly understood function as a sports facility—and what it might be in the future.

CHAPTER ONE

PALACES OF PLEASURE, ARENAS OF PROTEST

O n the night of June 28, 1924, pandemonium broke out at the stately arena on Madison Avenue and 26th Street in Manhattan. In a deeply divided America, a crowd of over seventeen thousand had crammed into Madison Square Garden for the fourth day of the Democratic National Convention. The country was in the throes of a nativist reaction to mass immigration from eastern and southern Europe that had transformed the demographics of the United States.

Leading the nativist charge was the increasingly powerful Ku Klux Klan. The Klan, in the midst of a rebirth in the 1920s, attracted millions of white men, who donned white hoods and pledged oaths to wage a race and religious war against African Americans, Catholics, and anyone who was not a white Anglo-Saxon Protestant (WASP).[1] The Klan had joined forces with the Prohibitionist movement, arguing that immigrants were corrupting the country with their conspicuous consumption of alcohol. Immigration, Prohibition, and religious freedom were among the top issues in that year's presidential campaign. In this tumultuous political climate, the Democratic Party sought to work out its platform and pick a presidential nominee at the convention held in

New York, a city that, like no other, represented the immigrant threat to WASP America.[2]

The contentious 1924 Democratic National Convention was one of the last major events held at the original Madison Square Garden, on the East Side just north of Madison Square Park, before the arena moved across town. Two later iterations of the Garden—including its current location on West 33rd Street and Seventh Avenue—were built on the West Side. At the time, the arena was famous for staging dog shows and circus acts. Indeed, that summer Ringling Bros. and Barnum & Bailey Circus had just left town as the convention delegates arrived in the spruced-up Garden. By the 1920s, the Garden had been repurposed as a political meeting hall. The political struggles of the age turned the building that had been known as the "palace of pleasure" into an arena of protest. At the Democratic convention, the sounds of the cheering and jeering crowd blaring from the loudspeakers would have been deafening to convention goers as well as to the thousands more who listened on the radio. Though the smell of circus animals was still fresh, thousands crammed into the old building to battle for their vision of America. The animals were gone, but the spirit of the circus remained in town.

The front-runners for the Democratic Party's nomination were Alfred E. Smith, the son of Irish immigrants and the governor of New York, and William McAdoo, a Georgia-born lawyer and former secretary of the Treasury. What was at stake was much more than a party's pick to run for the presidency. It was a struggle between competing visions of the United States: immigrant America versus nativist America. "Wet" America versus Prohibitionist "dry" America. Catholic and Jewish America versus Protestant America. Smith represented the forces of immigrant America, while McAdoo symbolized Klanish WASP America.

A key sticking point for the convention's delegates was whether the party would adopt a resolution condemning the Klan for interfering with religious liberty and "limit[ing] the civic rights of any citizen or body of citizens because of religion, birthplace, or racial origin."

Delegates from the southern and western parts of the country argued that singling out the Klan would further divide the party and they instead pushed for a generic statement standing for religious freedom. Many northern delegates, especially those from New York, insisted that Democrats denounce the Klan directly by name.[3]

Over the course of five hours on the night of June 28 and into the early morning hours of June 29, delegates listened to speeches for and against the anti-Klan resolution, and they debated and fought with each other. The tense atmosphere was intensified by a shocking speech given by Andrew Erwin, a delegate from Georgia, the birthplace of the Klan. Rather than adhere to the position of his fellow southerners, this son of a Confederate officer and member of the southern plantocracy deviated from the white supremacist script when he characterized the Klan as "the most destructive force in America today." Erwin stunned the crowd when he insisted that the Georgian "who does not take a stand against this hooded menace, which prowls, in the darkness, that dares not show its face, is not worthy of his ancestry." As he implored the convention to adopt the anti-Klan resolution, the crowd erupted in jeers and cheers. Members of the New York delegation hoisted Erwin on their shoulders and carried him around the meeting hall. After hours of debating, speechifying, cheering, and jeering, the anti-Klan resolution lost by one vote.[4]

It was a surreal moment in a bitterly contested political convention that would last sixteen exhausting days, the longest in US political history. McAdoo and Smith supporters bludgeoned each other for days thereafter to no avail. Neither generated the necessary support from two-thirds of the delegates to win the nomination. The dwindling numbers of delegates were finally forced to settle on John W. Davis, a compromise candidate from West Virginia. The battle over the party's nomination ultimately was for naught because Davis was soundly beaten by Republican nominee Calvin Coolidge in the presidential election later that year.[5]

The political convulsions that took place during the 1924 Democratic National Convention at Madison Square Garden illustrate how modern stadiums and arenas have served multiple purposes from their earliest incarnations. Buildings that were originally imagined as entertainment venues to stage the emerging amusements of the late nineteenth century became centers of political theater during the opening decades of the twentieth. Mass entertainment venues became venues for mass politics. During the 1920s, political rallies and speeches were recurring spectacles in the increasingly ubiquitous buildings. Indoor arenas and outdoor stadiums served as meeting halls where major political battles were fought. From the Roaring Twenties into the Great Depression years of the 1930s, scenes of conflict like what happened at the Garden during the Democratic National Convention gave way to more ferocious political battles. The screaming, the booing, and the fisticuffs that marked the 1924 convention paled in comparison to what would transpire a decade later, when immigrant-inspired radical labor and Communist organizers violently clashed with Far Right activists.

THE POLITICAL BATTLES OF THE 1920S AND 1930S AT MADISON SQUARE Garden were rooted in New York's long-standing connections to Europe, which were forged after the conquest and colonization of the Lenape people. New York emerged as a commercial hub in the seventeenth century, when it was a colonial territory under Dutch and British rule. Goods and people circulated through the city for centuries, but the era of rapid industrialization and urbanization in the nineteenth century further transformed New York City into the leading financial and commercial center in the country. Its growth was furthered especially by dramatic improvements in transportation and communication networks facilitated by the opening of the Erie Canal in Upstate New York, by the expansion of the railway networks, and by the advent of steamship travel. Fueled by commodity trading from all directions, especially Europe, the Caribbean, and the US interior, New York became the dominant commercial hub in the country.[6]

In this period, Manhattan was the epicenter of the rapid changes unleashed by industrialization and urbanization. It was the heyday of the wealthy robber barons, who sought to create a political, economic, and social order in their own image. They made the city into a showcase of their newfound wealth, prominently displaying their mansions and other forms of conspicuous consumption. This was when the millions of immigrants arriving from Europe and other parts of the Americas transformed the United States. Though they initially did not have the resources to participate in the American stadium scene, by the turn of the twentieth century it was these immigrants and their children who saw the performative stage of the ballpark and the arena as a vehicle of upward mobility and a place to demand their rightful position in US society.[7]

All these conditions created a favorable environment for a new class of sports and entertainment entrepreneurs to tap into the densely populated city as a market. There was the emerging wealthy class of industrialists and a working class of native white people, formerly enslaved black people, and a rapidly growing European immigrant population comprising Germans, Irish, and eastern and southern Europeans. Though elites were initially the primary constituency of the budding sports industry, other amusements such as the circus and prizefighting found a fertile base among the city's laboring majority.[8]

Madison Square Park was a central congregation space for New Yorkers in the nineteenth and early twentieth centuries. Since the inauguration of the park in 1847, well-heeled Gothamites enjoyed strolling around the square and taking in the neighborhood's delights: the theater, the shopping, and the dining. Surrounded by stately buildings, hotels, and entertainment venues, the square was a focal point in the city and country as Manhattan expanded northward and grew into the culture capital of America. The park was a popular place for politicians and international dignitaries to drum up support for their causes. It was also one of the areas where the city's nineteenth-century amusement and sporting culture took shape. Indeed, some of the earliest forms of baseball were played in the park: in 1845, the New York Knickerbockers Club played one of the first versions of the game in the United States.[9]

The apocryphal Knickerbocker story is one starting point for the history of the American stadium that commences with the games at Madison Square Park and evolves into the emergence of baseball ballparks in the years after the Civil War. Manhattan's rapid development in the mid-nineteenth century, however, forced the baseball scene to move to the city's outskirts. By the 1860s, ballparks such as Union Grounds in Brooklyn and Elysian Fields in Hoboken, New Jersey, were some of the earliest stadiums in the United States. Baseball developed a large cross-class constituency of players and fans who crowded into cheaply built wooden structures. Yet the baseball-centric version of this story obscures the rise of other types of venues that were equally impactful on the history of the American stadium.[10]

Madison Square Park's role in shaping the American stadium begins with a cultural phenomenon that was as impactful as baseball— the circus. Throughout the nineteenth century, traveling shows of clowns, acrobats, animals, and ever-changing casts of "curiosities" toured the country relentlessly after the equestrian John Bill Rickets brought this cultural practice to the United States from Europe. Even before the rise of the baseball stadium, large tents popped up all over the country to house the circus while it was in town. The circus had ambiguous meanings that at once reinforced and disrupted the social hierarchies of the day. While it showed men and women in nontraditional gender roles performing acrobatic feats, it also portrayed nonwhite and other perceived "backward" peoples in a grotesque and racist manner. Circuses also involved the routine abusive treatment of animals. Still, the spectacle was enormously popular across a broad swath of Americans throughout the century.[11]

The circus performance space was characterized by a circular enclosure on the floor (the ring) surrounded by wooden stands. In the 1820s, the ring was installed under a large canvas tent, which became known as the Big Top. In the 1860s, P. T. Barnum, one of the more prominent circus impresarios and the man who promoted himself as America's greatest showman, utilized the new railroad networks to transport elaborate shows of clowns, muscular acrobats, and exotic animals to rural and urban areas across the country. By the mid-1870s, Barnum was ready to launch his hippodrome show, a new performance venture loosely inspired by the ancient Roman races, and he needed the right venue to stage it. He found it in an abandoned railroad depot on the northeast corner of Madison Square Park in New York.[12]

The fact that Barnum zeroed in on an abandoned railroad depot is not as surprising as it may seem. In this era access to the railroads was central to planning the location of stadiums and arenas. The country's rail system facilitated the rise in popularity of baseball and the growth of other culture industries, including the circus, because it provided an accessible form of transportation not only for performers but also for the audience. In the case of Madison Square Park, the railroad provided the necessary infrastructure to support a new entertainment center in 1871. In 1832, the New York and Harlem Railroad had built a depot on 26th Street stretching between Fourth (now Park) and Madison Avenues. The structure was designed to accommodate horses, railroad cars, and passengers. Because steam-powered locomotives spewing cinder all over the city streets and into the homes of residents was not ideal for a rapidly growing urban environment, a city ordinance mandated that railroad cars had to be drawn by horse south of 42nd Street, the more densely populated part of the island. Soon after the railroad magnate Cornelius "Commodore" Vanderbilt consolidated his control over the New York Central and the Hudson Lines in 1870, he built a new uptown rail depot at 42nd Street, the edifice that eventually became Grand Central Terminal. In the 1870s, when the building's role as a transport depot was over, a new purpose was about to emerge.[13]

It was at that point that P. T. Barnum planned to bring his circus act to Madison Square Park. In 1873, he leased the old depot from the commodore and quickly set it up as the new showplace in a neighborhood filled with other entertainment options. The great showman tore down part of the depot and built a twenty-eight-foot-high wall around the entire block, from Madison to Fourth Avenue, and installed an oval-shaped ring as a stage for his circus. The venue became his latest version of the Big Top, the "largest tent ever seen," according to the *New York Times*. Underneath, he set up rows of wooden seats for spectators. He dubbed the new facility the Grand Roman Hippodrome.[14]

On opening night, April 27, 1874, massive crowds surrounded the venue and spilled out onto the streets. After the doors opened at eight o'clock and the crowd was finally let in, they were treated to vintage Barnumesque exoticism. They witnessed six women riding English Thoroughbreds, three women driving two horses each in a Roman chariot race, and a chariot race between four-horse teams. They saw an exciting exhibition in which performers playing Comanche Indians and Mexicans lassoed Texan cattle, another horse race with English jockeys, and a hurdle race of women on fast horses.[15] The show transported New Yorkers to the ancient world and to the American frontier without asking them to leave their seats. The representations of

P. T. Barnum's Grand Roman Hippodrome. *Credit: The New York Public Library*

cowboys and Indians illustrates how Barnum's show, like many circus acts of the era, both entertained spectators and perpetuated powerful myths that projected white Americans as civilizers of the American West.

Barnum's Grand Roman Hippodrome was the first site of Madison Square Garden, which became known as the "world's most famous arena." The Hippodrome initiated a pattern that subsequent stadium builders would emulate. They drew upon the image of sport and leisure in the ancient Greco-Roman world to project their own aspirations for monumentality in the modern era. Stadium builders liked to imagine themselves inspired by ancient structures such as the iconic Roman Colosseum. To be a modern American was to play and spectate in the manner of the glorious civilizations of the past. Decades later, whether it was Roy Hofheinz, who dubbed the Houston Astrodome the "Eighth Wonder of the World," or Jack Kent Cooke, who christened his arena "the Forum," twentieth-century stadium builders modeled their modern facilities after ancient imperial structures. Barnum's Hippodrome of the 1870s established a tradition that only became more pronounced as stadiums and arenas gained size and technological sophistication during the twentieth century.[16]

P. T. Barnum was the first of many impresarios who envisioned the place that became known as Madison Square Garden as a headline and profit generator. Like others after him, he relied on the labor of performers, both human and animal, for fame and fortune. Despite its spectacular debut, however, the Hippodrome did not last long. The old showman confronted a predicament that would bedevil subsequent sport and entertainment venue builders for more than a century afterward: How to make an entertainment venue solvent? Barnum failed to do so. Erecting and disassembling temporary circus tents for a traveling circus show for audiences across the country was the dominant business model of the nineteenth-century circus. Maintaining a permanent structure in one location with access to the same local audience proved to be its own challenging endeavor. Barnum's troubles also stemmed from the fact that the Hippodrome was just one part of a sprawling and unwieldy business empire. He decided to take his exotic show of elephants and acrobats back on the road, though aspects of the circus show would never leave the site entirely.

In the late 1800s, private entities financed and controlled stadiums and arenas. They had to generate revenue from gate receipts and cultivate other private sources to stay afloat. In an era before the welfare state took shape, government funding for stadium construction was inconceivable, though getting the blessing of local government officials was welcome and necessary.

In 1875, famed bandmaster Patrick Sarsfield Gilmore took over Barnum's lease on the Hippodrome and staged concerts and other shows at the barn. He spruced up the place, planting grasses and shrubs and installing fountains, to create a pleasant environment where spectators could enjoy a range of amusements. He also renamed the building "Gilmore's Garden," introducing the epithet that would become a permanent part of the building's identity.[17] The Westminster Kennel Club Dog Show was added to the venue's schedule and remained a regular event on the Garden's calendar for decades. In addition to the periodic return of Barnum's circus, a number of recurring acts unfolded in this period, including horse shows, bicycle races, and religious revival meetings. The most popular event Gilmore staged was prizefighting, which was then illegal in the state of New York. Only three-round "exhibitions" were allowed, and they generated interest among fans.

Yet the boxing exhibitions could not prevent Gilmore from encountering the same problems as Barnum. Boxing's fan base was growing, but the sport's dubious legal status prevented it from generating a large enough audience to provide a consistent revenue source. Dog shows, horse shows, and most of the bandmaster's events tended to cater to the elites who paraded around Madison Square Park. Despite efforts to offer a full schedule of activities, Gilmore could not make his Garden sustainable. Worse, the large tent that covered the building could not adequately protect spectators from inclement weather, especially during the winter months. Eventually, the site was taken over by the property owner, William Vanderbilt, Cornelius's son, who gave the building the name that would stick for more than a century: Madison Square Garden. Despite the new moniker, the building had a rather inglorious period of accidents because the hastily constructed structure was crumbling after almost two decades of use. In 1887, Vanderbilt sold the property to a syndicate of investors who called themselves the Madison Square Garden Group. The group decided to tear down the old structure and build a new one. A novel vision was required to keep the Garden afloat, and the group found the right man to implement it.[18]

The new Garden that arose at 26th and Madison was a perfect monument to the Gilded Age. Designer Stanford White, of the famous architectural firm McKim, Mead & White, refashioned the building from an "unsightly and rickety pile" into a "palace of pleasure." White's design made Barnum's Hippodrome seem like a run-down horse shed. The new Garden aspired to compete with the monumental structures of Paris, particularly the newly constructed Eiffel Tower. From the outside, the imposing building was decorated with yellow brick and white terra cotta, colonnades, balustrades, belvederes, and other flourishes that made it appear more like a European cathedral than a place of medium- and lowbrow entertainment.[19]

Once open, White's Garden was a hit, especially among the aristocratic set of the Gilded Age. It was a place to be seen in a neighborhood that already had its share of amenities for the affluent classes. The inside of the new Garden reinforced the fact that it was much more than a venue in which to watch the circus and horse shows. In addition to the 315-foot by 200-foot amphitheater that held six thousand seats, it contained a twelve-hundred-seat theater, a fifteen-hundred-seat concert hall, and a restaurant. The glass dome roof let in sunlight. Chandeliers hung from the ceiling. Not only did some of the same shows from the Barnum and Gilmore eras continue to play there, but also a new slate of theatrical and musical performances were put on. By the early 1900s, it housed speeches by local and national politicians. "Going to the Garden for whatever was showing was the essence of *bon vivantry* in the years surrounding the century's turn," the *Times* reported. "It was the place where sports, society, and politics met on common ground."[20]

But the most noteworthy aspect of the new Garden's design was its 320-foot-tall tower, which was similar to—some said a rip-off of—the Giralda bell tower at the Seville Cathedral in Spain. The tower was then the tallest structure in New York. When concerns about costs prompted the Garden's board to propose removing the tower from the design, White went ballistic. "For any sake, it needs a tower," he roared to the press. His public tantrum forced the board to keep the tower in the plans. The tower contained a new creation: the elevator, which allowed spectators to take in a panoramic view of the rapidly growing city. More importantly, the tower was the playhouse of the iconoclastic White, who had an apartment installed on the sixth floor that could only be accessed by a private elevator. It was there that he entertained many guests and acted upon his predilection for seducing girls and women. His disgraceful life came into view when he was shot and killed by Harry Thaw, who was purportedly furious with White for "deflowering" his wife, the well-known model and performer Evelyn Nesbit. In reality, White, Nesbit, and Thaw had more complicated relationships with each other than the press reported at the time. White's life and death in his beloved Garden added to the scandal-ridden quality of the "palace of pleasure."[21]

Atop the tower sat the most famous piece of the new building: a thirteen-foot-tall, eighteen-hundred-pound copper statue of Diana, the Roman goddess of the hunt, designed by sculptor Augustus Saint-Gaudens. She stood 322 feet above the street with her bow and arrow ready to shoot. The statue was installed on ball bearings that allowed her to twirl in the wind. The fact that Diana was nude contributed to the scandalous culture of the new Garden, but the statue turned out to be one of the features that was missed the most when the building was eventually demolished.

As beautiful as White's palace was, it was unable to overcome the same problem as its predecessor: it could not pay for itself. It cost $20,000 a month to operate the complex, and a $2 million mortgage hung over the facility. The horse shows, circus acts, dog races, and bicycle races brought in spectators, but ticket sales could not cover the building's debts, which had mounted ever since White insisted on decorating his palace without regard to cost. Audiences at the Garden only rarely extended beyond New York's elite. Before the 1920s, different social classes rarely intermixed at places like the Garden. The Garden's obsolescence hastened as the center of gravity of the city's social life moved uptown. The opening of Central Park in 1858 and the installation of subways drew the population of Manhattan northward.

Eventually, the property passed into the hands of New York Life Insurance Company, which was not interested in keeping Stanford White's money pit afloat. The company planned to build its headquarters on the site of the Garden. But forces were coming together that would allow the name of Madison Square Garden to carry on, even if this building would succumb to the wrecking ball. Catering to the people of *bon vivantry* was not the wave of the future. New forms of entertainment that would attract the masses enabled the Garden to maintain its status in the twentieth century. The key to that future was leaning in to the realm of athletics and, as it turned out, politics. Mass entertainment and politics would help salvage the Garden, and the man with that vision was Tex Rickard.

TEXANS HAVE HAD AN OUTSIZED IMPACT ON AMERICAN SPORTS, AND few exemplify that fact better than George Lewis "Tex" Rickard.[22] He was a huckster, a gambler, and an adventurer who hustled his way from a hardscrabble youth to fame and fortune as a boxing promoter. Born on January 2, 1870, he was the son of a Union Army officer who was raised as a cowboy in Henrietta, Texas. He eventually made his way to the goldfields of South Africa and the American West, where he sought to cash in on the gold rushes in Alaska, before he finally landed in Nevada. He opened a saloon and made some money before he found what would become his lifelong passion: boxing. He was not a pugilist, but he did have a gift for promotion and the gumption to muscle his way into compiling resources to promote the leading fighters of the early twentieth century. He was brash and flamboyant, and he was known for sporting his many hats and tailored suits and smoking his ubiquitous cigar. Like P. T. Barnum, James Bailey, and other impresarios, he traveled into towns with his performers to entertain. At each new location, he would build a temporary stadium to stage his own version of the "greatest show on Earth," and then move on to the next bout.

Rickard outbid other promoters to secure the right to promote arguably one of the most important events in American sports history: the "Fight of the Century" between African American champion Jack Johnson and the white former champion Jim Jeffries in Reno, Nevada. Pickard and sportswriters billed the fight as a racial contest between the "Negro" champion and the "Great White Hope." On July 4, 1910, thousands of people descended on Reno to see Johnson decisively beat Jeffries with a fifteenth-round knockout. The news of a black man defeating a white man in the ring set off riots across the country.[23]

After an unsuccessful sojourn as a rancher in South America, Rickard got back into the fight game in a big way. He set his sights on New York. His goal was to promote fights at the Garden, and circumstances broke his way to allow him to achieve this goal. The Garden had been a white elephant since its inception. Horse shows, dog shows, and circus acts had their constituencies, but they didn't generate enough revenue to keep the Garden solvent. At this time, stadiums and arenas were financed and controlled by private entities that relied on revenue to stay afloat. In an era before the welfare state would take shape after the Great Depression, government funding for stadium construction was inconceivable, though local government officials did have to sign off on new buildings.

Still, Tex Rickard, like the vast majority of the sports entrepreneurs who followed his path, did not need government funding to finance his vision of profitable entertainment. Rickard was one of the most important figures in American boxing history, and as such, he also became an important figure in the history of American stadium construction. He facilitated and capitalized on boxing's increasing popularity during the first two decades of the twentieth century. Following in the footsteps of Barnum and Bailey, who made the circus a recurring part of American popular culture, Rickard made the boxing "carnival" popular across the social spectrum.

Rickard had the good fortune of joining the Garden at the moment when the boxing lobby was gaining traction in the New York State Legislature. After many fits and starts, partly because of resistance from Progressive Era reformers who abhorred the violence of boxing, the sport and its supporters received a big boost when the Walker bill was signed into law on May 20, 1920. The law legalized and regulated the sport by instituting fifteen-round limits and requiring the licensing of boxers, managers, promoters, referees, and judges. It also set the groundwork for the creation of a state boxing commission whose role was to administer the licensing of those involved in the boxing profession. In actuality, boxing commissions became corrupt entities that tarnished the reputation of the sport, though this did not decrease its popularity. Over the next two decades, other states would adopt versions of the Walker Law, making boxing a fully legalized sport across the nation by 1934.[24]

Two months after passage of the law, Rickard signed an agreement with New York Life to run the Garden for $300,000 each year for ten years. Right away, the boxing impresario went to work. He developed a full slate of boxing matches during the fall and winter months and increased the amphitheater's seating capacity from ten thousand to thirteen thousand seats to pack in more spectators. During the first months of Rickard's management, boxing matches produced $1 million in earnings and drew a total attendance of 275,000 spectators. These were unprecedented figures for the Garden. One of those matches featured Jack Dempsey, the popular heavyweight champion, who defeated challenger Bill Brennan in December 1920 with a twelfth-round knockout. Stanford White's "palace of pleasure" was remade into Rickard's "Temple of Fistiana."

The boxing promoter also converted the building into a recreational space by installing a large swimming pool to attract the public during the summer months. The swimming pool put Rickard in touch with a number of patrons, including young New Yorkers looking for a place to play, relax, and unwind. However, the boxing impresario apparently was inappropriately close to some of them. In 1921, he was accused of sexually assaulting four girls. The accusations were eerily reminiscent of those about Stanford White's behavior. Rickard was indicted and spent time in the "Tombs," the city jail, while he awaited trial. Although the accuser's credibility was evidenced by the precise details of Rickard's apartment she provided, after an hour and a half of deliberation, the jury found him not guilty.[25]

As Rickard was emerging from his legal troubles, he decided to generate more revenue by making the Garden widely available for political events. Since the turn of the century, politicians had staged rallies at newly constructed convention halls in cities around the country. However, Republican and Democratic conventions outgrew smaller auditoriums and were increasingly held in stadiums and arenas. The Chicago Coliseum, for example, hosted five consecutive Republican National Conventions between 1904 and 1920. At the Garden, even before the infamous 1924 Democratic convention, national political figures, including Presidents William McKinley, Theodore Roosevelt, and Woodrow Wilson, gave speeches there. For the new Garden chief, civic events were a source of revenue. Rickard let the Democrats have the Garden rent free but then took all the profits from concessions. The 1924 convention would not be the last time the arena hosted events of mainstream political parties.[26]

Nationwide, stadiums and arenas continued to host major political events in subsequent years. In 1928, Herbert Hoover accepted the Republican Party nomination in front of more than seventy-five thousand spectators in Stanford Stadium. Four years later, both parties held their conventions in the then newly constructed Chicago Stadium on the city's West Side. For the rest of the century and beyond, arenas and stadiums served as the venues of choice for political parties.[27]

During his reign as head of the Garden, Rickard enhanced the building's stature on the national sporting landscape and turned it into a venue for mass politics. The building enjoyed perhaps its most successful period under Rickard's direction. It attracted more spectators and more events than it ever had during the fifty years since P. T. Barnum opened his Grand Roman Hippodrome.

However, New York Life was finished with the Garden as a real estate enterprise. The company announced that it had plans to tear down Diana's Garden. Despite Rickard's success in making the venue financially profitable, his landlord was no longer interested in the risky game of the sport and entertainment business. Boxing was proving to be the Garden's salvation, but it attracted a different social demographic than the aristocratic set that had been the building's primary constituency. Although New York Life's precise reasoning for abandoning the Garden operation may not be known, it is clear that the company determined that its interests were best served by joining the skyscraper-building craze and erecting a new forty-story structure. The company gave Rickard a year to vacate the premises.

Stanford White's "palace of pleasure" closed its doors after one last boxing match on May 5, 1925. The building was demolished soon after and eventually replaced by the forty-story New York Life Building that remains on the spot to the present. The iconic Diana was carefully taken down from her perch. A home was found for the statue at the Philadelphia Museum of Art. "I am sorry to say goodbye to the old place myself," Rickard told the press the night the building closed. "It has been good to me, and I have had a lot of fun in it, and I am rather proud of the fact that I am the only man who ever made it pay." Tex Rickard had taken the Garden from a playground for New York's aristocrats to a venue that welcomed the masses, the gangsters, and the hustlers. This would continue even after the Garden moved to yet another abandoned transit barn in Manhattan.[28]

Undaunted by New York Life's decision to raze the old Garden, Rickard, with his characteristic bravado, assembled a group of investors he called his "six hundred millionaires" to construct a new building uptown. Here again, the remnants of an old transit yard provided the real estate for a New York institution. He found an old trolley barn on Eighth Avenue between 49th and 50th Streets in the Hell's Kitchen neighborhood on the West Side of Manhattan, and there he built a new and improved Temple of Fistiana.

IT SEEMED LIKE ALL OF NEW YORK TURNED OUT FOR THE FIRST OFFI-cial event at the new Madison Square Garden on December 15, 1925. Surprisingly, it was not a boxing match. Rather, it was a hockey game between the New York Hockey Club and the Montreal Canadiens before a sellout crowd of seventeen thousand. "Park Avenue mingled with Broadway," the *New York Times* reported the next day. "And in the merry cheers which greeted the inaugural, the voices of the east and west sides harmonized for once in the applause of the city's representative citizenry."[29] It was the first time a professional hockey game was played in New York, and the crowd was a reprise of the assemblages that had gathered at the old building. Among the government officials present was mayor-elect Jimmy Walker, the Tammany Hall politician who pushed through the bill that legalized boxing and filled Tex Rickard's pockets. Though the Canadiens won the contest 3 to 1, the game was a hit with local fans, and the National Hockey League gained a following in New York. Later, Tex was inspired to create his own franchise, which was named the New York Rangers.

The arrival of professional hockey was a novel facet of the latest version of Madison Square Garden: Rickard also decided to keep the name of the old building, even though his new sports facility was located a mile and a half away from the old location. "Madison Square Garden" was a known entity in the sport and entertainment world, and Rickard wanted the "brand" of the building to travel with it. Architecturally, the new building was a far cry from Stanford White's Moorish castle. It looked like a factory, a barn, and a movie house all rolled into one. The most noteworthy aspect of the new building's design was the marquee, which gave it the look of the other movie theaters that architect Thomas Lamb had designed.[30] The marquee became the iconic image of the Garden during these years, announcing to the world the boxing matches, the performances, the circuses, the dog shows, the hockey games, the basketball games, and the political rallies and civic events that would take place during the forty-three years the building existed. Retail space for businesses was built along the arena's exterior on Eighth Avenue, making the Garden seem less like an arena and more like a movie house on a crowded Manhattan street. A plethora of businesses would use those spaces over the years, including cigar shops, hat stores, drugstores, and lunch counters. There was nothing majestic about the external appearance of Tex Rickard's new building. What was memorable about the Garden during those years was what took place after bodies walked under the marquee and entered the building.

Critics raved, not about the building's exterior but about all the modern engineering features: the ice rink that could be set up and disassembled by a sophisticated new freezing plant, the tiers of seating without pillars (though views were not as unobstructed as advertised), the escalators, and a ventilation system that promised to prevent the clouds of smoke and the reeking odors that had tainted the air in the old Garden. It was a fireproof steel and brick structure that did not contain a single piece of wood. It was the most modern arena at the time. Remarkably, this new building had taken only nine months to construct atop the remains of the old trolley barn. Various numbers were reported to the press, but it is likely that the arena cost around $5.5 million to build. It was financed by the Wall Street syndicate put together by the resourceful Rickard.[31]

The new Madison Square Garden might have been the most celebrated sport and entertainment arena in New York, but other facilities also became part of the city's growing sport scene. By the time Rickard opened the doors of his building on Eighth Avenue, New York had three professional baseball stadiums, including Ebbets Field, the home of the Brooklyn Dodgers, which opened in 1913; the Polo Grounds, the home of the New York Giants, which had relocated from its original location on 110th Street near Central Park to 155th Street in Coogan's Hollow; and the massive newly constructed

Madison Square Garden, Eighth Avenue and 49th Street.
Credit: George Rinhart/Corbis via Getty Images

ballyard in the Bronx called Yankee Stadium, which opened in 1923. Each of these teams developed a loyal following, and each stadium was raised in a wave of classic ballpark construction in the 1910s and 1920s. Other ballparks, including Shibe Park in Philadelphia, Forbes Field in Pittsburgh, League Park in Cleveland, Comiskey Park and Wrigley Field in Chicago, and Fenway Park and Braves Field in Boston, were manifestations of the growth of professional baseball in America's cities.[32]

But the twenties were not merely a time of the "classic" baseball stadium. It was also the period when various kinds of indoor and outdoor facilities were built in towns and cities throughout the country. Once again, Tex Rickard played a role. The mainstreaming of boxing and the growth of other indoor sports and entertainments such as hockey, ice skating, and, of course, the circus necessitated the construction of permanent indoor facilities. The days of promoters like

Rickard coming into town and building temporary wooden stadiums for boxing matches had passed. Buildings along the lines of the new Madison Square Garden became the prevailing trend. After the new Garden opened, Rickard sought to build a chain of "Madison Square Gardens" in various cities. The first such facility was the Boston Garden, which had an almost identical design as that of the Eighth Avenue Garden. Originally called "Boston Madison Square Garden," it was another arena built on top of a railroad station, and it opened its doors in 1928. Like the Eighth Avenue Garden, the Boston version had steep, low-hanging upper decks that allowed fans to feel like they were right on top of the performers. Also like the New York Garden, the building commonly called "Boston Garden" became known as a hockey and basketball arena, though it possessed its own history of civic and political events.[33]

Indoor arenas were opening in other parts of the United States and Canada—all of them impelled by the growth of boxing and the emergence of professional hockey, the latter of which took root in six cities during the 1920s. In addition to the Gardens in New York and Boston, new indoor arenas opened in Montreal, where the Forum housed the franchise that became the Montreal Canadiens; in Detroit, where the Olympia Stadium opened in 1927; in Chicago, where the Chicago Stadium opened in 1929; and in Toronto, where Maple Leaf Gardens opened in 1931. All these facilities formed key components in a broader network of indoor arenas that accommodated the circus, hockey, and the newly emerging ice shows such as the Ice Follies and the Ice Capades. And all became preferred locations for political rallies for mainstream politicians and insurgent political activists.[34]

At the same time, universities embarked on efforts to grow their institutions by making sports a vital part of the offerings. In the 1920s, college football stadiums were constructed on campuses across the country en masse. Earlier, in 1895, the University of Pennsylvania opened Franklin Field, and other Ivy League schools had followed suit, but it wasn't until the 1920s that universities devoted themselves to stadium construction. Many facilities were conceived of as memorials to those who served in World War I, but their construction was clearly compelled by the perceived revenue opportunity college football provided. The one-hundred-thousand-seat Los Angeles Memorial Coliseum, though built by the City and County of Los Angeles and the State of California, was the home field of the University of Southern California Trojans football team. Similar memorial stadiums were built in Berkeley, California; Urbana, Illinois; and many other college towns around the nation. In 1930, the famed Notre Dame college football program under legendary coach Knute Rockne opened its own stadium. Southern schools, too, embarked on a similar pattern of college football stadium construction. In 1926 in New Orleans, on the campus of Tulane University, for example, a stadium was built for the school's football program. Over time, it became a revenue generator as the host of the annual Sugar Bowl. The stadium-building craze was sweeping the country, and there seemed no reason for it not to continue.

Yet things changed as the decade drew to a close. On January 6, 1929, Tex Rickard came down with an acute case of appendicitis and died from complications after an appendectomy. A pioneer of stadium construction, Rickard was given a massive funeral in New York, and his body lay in state at the Garden. Months later, the stock market crashed on Wall Street. The Roaring Twenties was coming to an end, and the money generated by Rickard's extensive network of connections and promotional wizardry was drying up. The Great Depression would severely reduce the revenues that the Garden relied upon to be a moneymaker, though hockey and other acts enabled it to continue as a famous sport and entertainment venue. As the 1930s unfolded, however, political forces brewing thousands of miles away would have an even greater impact on the function of the arena. The reverberations of the rise of fascism in Europe traveled across the Atlantic, and America's stadiums and arenas transformed into battlegrounds where the era's political conflicts played out.[35]

It was at this moment when the function of the stadium as a meeting hall became central to the building's identity. The rising tide of fascism and the emergence of powerful labor, socialist, and communist movements had a profound impact on New York society and politics. The city's large European immigrant population made stadiums center stage in the global struggle against fascism and for labor rights. Indeed, as we shall see, Madison Square Garden and Yankee Stadium, the most modern facilities in the nation's culture capital, were where two key political and social events of the 1930s occurred.

Tex Rickard's barn on Eighth Avenue between 49th Street and 50th Street was much more than a place to see boxing matches, hockey games, and the circus. It became a battlefield for competing movements that aimed to convince Americans of the worthiness of their cause. The 1920s battles for and against nativism had intensified with the transatlantic fascist movement. The impending war in Europe had a particularly profound impact on New York. The metropolis utterly transfigured by massive European immigration during the nineteenth and early twentieth centuries essentially became another theater in the European conflict. The movements for and against fascism rose to prominence in New York politics and society, and the city's stadiums and arenas provided the space for those struggles to carry on. Politicians had long used the Garden as a stage for statecraft, but the political conflicts that unfolded in the 1930s assumed a more ominous tone. The intense social and political turmoil generated by the struggle against fascism, coupled with the suffering generated by the Great Depression, seemed to bring American society to the verge of collapse. Movements on the left and the right sought to present viable political alternatives to the dominant American political order that had emerged after the Civil War.

As would be the case throughout the rest of the twentieth century and into the twenty-first, the sport world and its venues were engulfed by political conflicts. The 1936 Olympics in Nazi Germany made the political implications of sport clear, even as Olympic leaders like the American sports administrator Avery Brundage tried to pretend that their endeavors could somehow remain politics free. A series of matches between an American boxer and a German boxer during the decade before the Second World War made sport an arena where the global conflicts over racism and fascism were fought. Sports were consumed by politics, and nowhere was that clearer than in the arenas and ballparks of New York City.[36]

SHOUTS OF "DOWN WITH MUSSOLINI!" AND "DOWN WITH FASCISM!" echoed throughout the Garden on November 28, 1934, during a rally celebrating the fifteenth anniversary of Local 89 of the International Ladies' Garment Workers' Union (ILGWU). The main speaker that evening was Giuseppe Modigliani, an Italian socialist leader who had arrived in the United States to inform American workers of the repressive nature of Benito Mussolini's regime in Italy. Modigliani implored American labor unions to see their struggle as part of a larger international movement against fascist authoritarianism. The crowd of twenty thousand people, many of them Italian Americans, offered rounds of applause to Modigliani and to New York City mayor Fiorello La Guardia. Speaking in Italian, the recently elected mayor praised the role of Italians in the city's labor movement. Other speakers that evening were David Dubinksy, president of the ILGWU, Representative-elect Vito Marcantonio, and socialist activists Norman Thomas and Arturo Giovannitti.[37]

Rallies such as these were commonplace at Madison Square Garden during the 1930s. Arena management had opened its doors to political groups of various kinds. The building had unofficially become an "arena of protest" where the city's varied labor, communist, and pro- and anti-fascist movements held numerous demonstrations. As the 1934 ILGWU celebration illustrates, these movements were dominated by New York's immigrant communities. Immigrants formed the backbone of the city's powerful labor movement, which gave New York a unique working-class organizing culture that was rooted in the struggles of local workers yet entangled in the international politics of interwar Europe. Although the labor movement was often plagued by internecine battles between socialist and communist organizations, these groups found common ground in taking a stand against the rise of Hitler and Mussolini in Europe. At the same time, Nazism and fascism polarized the city's immigrant communities. Some expressed pride in the rise of strongman leaders, while those on the left virulently rejected these antisemitic men and their repression of leftist movements.[38]

One group leading the movement against fascism was the Communist Party USA (CPUSA). Based in New York, the party staged regular demonstrations and rallies at the Garden even before Rickard moved his operation to the West Side. Many members were enticed by socialist and communist models in a period when the Depression shook confidence in capitalism. At first, the Communist Party centered its activities on promoting its cause in cultural events, such as Lenin Memorial Rallies and May Day Celebrations. Although Joseph Stalin's autocratic rule and communist sectarianism discredited the Communist International (Comintern) for many, the group still regularly drew support at rallies at the Garden, successfully mobilizing workers against racism and capitalist exploitation. CPUSA's influence grew during the "Popular Front" period (1936–1939), when the Comintern directed parties to form coalitions with noncommunist allies.[39]

Indeed, the main throughline in activism of this period was the struggle against fascism. A host of labor and religious organizations were active in combating the growing influence of Nazism. One of the first rallies to highlight Nazi persecution of German Jews occurred at the Garden on March 27, 1933. Every seat in the arena was filled, and thousands more people gathered outside to hear the event through loudspeakers. The American Jewish Congress and other religious leaders had organized the event and recruited politicians to speak out against Hitlerism two months after the Führer took power in January 1933. Speakers included Governor Al Smith and Senator Robert F. Wagner. Directing his remarks to those who had counseled him not to speak out against the repression of Jews in Germany, Smith, channeling the spirit of his 1924 campaign, argued that he had an obligation to "drag it out into the open sunlight and give it the same treatment that we gave the Ku Klux Klan."[40]

The ability of Jewish leaders to pack the Garden with supporters illustrates the impact of the movement against antisemitism during the 1930s. Yet, a countermovement of Nazi sympathizers also demonstrated its influence in New York politics. A year later, a group called Friends of the New Germany held a demonstration at the arena. Pushing back against the anti-fascist movement, the group organized the demonstration to denounce the campaign to boycott Hitler's regime and to instead defend its policies, turning the Garden into a Nazi meeting hall. Banners proclaiming JOIN THE DAWA, FIGHT THE BOYCOTT, and BOYCOTT THE BOYCOTTERS draped the stands. Ushers wore military uniforms and Nazi swastika armbands. The speakers' platform was draped in red with a large shield of the United States hanging over the center of the stage. On each side of the stage stood black columns decorated with the German eagle bearing a swastika. The rally organizers insisted they had no connection with the Hitler regime, though their sympathies were plain for all to see. Indeed, Nazism found a small but growing following among the German American population, especially in New York, a center of German immigration since the nineteenth century. George Sylvester Viereck, a German American poet, told the assemblage: "We Americans of German descent are Americans first before we are German sympathizers." The poet accused proponents of the Nazi boycott of fomenting racial dissension. "We resent the boycott not merely because it harms Germany," he argued. "We resent it primarily because it interferes with the revival of American prosperity and lays the basis for racial strife in the United States."[41]

The Friends of the New Germany demonstration caused a stir. It also prompted a response from local Communist organizers, who converged on the Garden to shut down the rally. "Down with Hitler!" they cried outside the arena. But their efforts were foiled by law enforcement. "LaGuardia's police took up the cudgels for the Nazi fascists," reported the *Daily Worker*, which accused the cops of brutalizing protesters. Fascists and anti-fascists continued to fight it out in the streets, in the press, and in the meeting halls of New York. A congressional investigation of the Friends of the New Germany concluded that the organization was an arm of the Third Reich, even though the Nazi regime distanced itself from the organization. By 1935, the organization had dissolved, but it was replaced by a new organization that sought to remake Nazism into an American patriotic endeavor.[42]

SITTING AMONG THE TWENTY THOUSAND SPECTATORS IN MADISON Square Garden on February 20, 1939, Dorothy Thompson was overcome by an overwhelming sense of déjà vu. Across the Atlantic eight years earlier, she had witnessed a Nazi rally of elaborate, codified rituals of hate. "I saw an exact duplicate of it in the Berlin Sports Palace in 1931," she wrote afterward in the *New York Herald Tribune*. "That meeting was also 'protected' by the police of the German Republic," meaning that, although the rally espoused racist and antisemitic ideas, it was allowed to occur by the government in power. That decision turned out to be a fatal mistake, Thompson surmised. "Three years later people who were in charge of that meeting were in charge of the government of Germany," she warned her readers. The rally at the Berlin Sports Palace had signaled to Thompson that a dangerous movement was on the verge of taking over Germany. She was an expert on such matters. She was a leading American journalist who had covered the Nazis in Germany and had experienced their power firsthand when she was kicked out of the country for writing critical assessments of the new regime.[43]

During Adolf Hitler's reign, the Nazis skillfully used sport facilities, such as the Sportpalast in Berlin, to legitimate their cause. The Führer had also orchestrated a powerful expression of his regime's power on a more dramatic scale during the 1936 Olympic Games, which were held in Nazi Germany's new Olympic Stadium. A few years later, Thompson found herself in the midst of another Nazi rally held not in Berlin but in New York City. On that ominous February evening in 1939 at the Garden, she was convinced she was seeing the same scene repeat itself. Thompson was there to cover a rally organized by the German American Bund, a small but visible pro-Hitler movement that was spreading Nazi propaganda in the United States. The event purported to be a patriotic celebration of George Washington's birthday and to stand for "true Americanism." However, the real aim of the event was to propagandize for Nazism. The Bund intentionally held the rally in one of the most famous arenas in the world in the "semitized metropolis of New York." By 1920, 50 percent of all Jews in the United States and 10 percent of all Jews in the world lived in New York City. Fritz Kuhn, the Bund's leader, announced his organization's purpose to the crowd. "We—the German American Bund—organized as American citizens, with American ideals, and determined to protect ourselves, our homes, our wives and children against the slimy conspirators who would change this glorious republic into the inferno of a bolshevist paradise."[44]

The night before, when a modest crowd of nine thousand watched the Montreal Canadiens defeat the New York Americans 5–4 in a National Hockey League game, there was little inkling of the furor Kuhn and his organization would generate. Soon after the game, arena workers prepared the Garden for its next event. As they had done many times before, they melted the ice, disassembled the rink, and stored it beneath the main floor. Then they arranged the arena for a meeting-hall-style affair, setting out rows of folding chairs and a stage on the arena floor.

But precisely who did the work of refashioning the Garden into a Nazi meeting hall is not altogether clear. It is likely that members of the Bund assisted the arena's staff. What is certain is that the decorations made the meeting's intent abundantly clear. As attendees entered the arena, they could not miss the gigantic portrait of George Washington hanging behind the stage. On each side of Washington were large flags of the United States, both the Betsy Ross thirteen-star flag and the modern version with forty-eight stars (Hawaii and Alaska had not yet been admitted into the Union). Interspersed with the American flags were the flags of the German American Bund, which included the ubiquitous swastika. Hanging from the balcony were two large signs: READ AMERICA'S FEARLESS PRESS: THE FREE AMERICAN!, which was a reference to a Bund publication, and another that read STOP JEWISH DOMINATION OF CHRISTIAN AMERICANS!

The event would turn out to be one of the more infamous in the venue's history. The German American Bund promoted the occasion as an "Americanization" rally in celebration of George Washington's birthday, but it was yet another meeting prompted by the intensifying conflict between pro- and anti-fascist movements in New York. The Bund promised to make this event the biggest one yet.

When the rally started, the Bund used the Garden to enact a fearsome, orderly manifestation of a Swastika Nation. A procession of brown-shirted *Ordnungsdiest*, commonly known as the "OD," a semi-militarily dressed band of bodyguards, marched up to the stage. Next, a group of youngsters formed a drum line and solemnly beat

The German American Bund George Washington Birthday Rally, February 20, 1939. *Credit: FPG/Archive Photos/Getty Images*

their instruments as they proceeded to the stage. Then a group of women dressed in the uniforms of the Red Cross marched into the arena. The crowd itself was impeccably dressed in suits and ties and dresses, as if they were attending a religious event. The leaders of the Bund could not have felt prouder of what they were able to stage that night. It was truly "a mosaic of pure Aryan humanity."[45]

For a little more than three hours, Bund leaders from around the country made their case for the indispensability of Nazism to "free America" from the damage done to it by Jews. J. Wheeler-Hill, the Bund's national secretary, recited a litany of problems facing the nation. His list reads like a timeless list of reactionary gripes that could be rehearsed in 1939 or 2023. Wheeler-Hill identified "the spread of radicalism with its inspired class hatred, racial sectionalism, political abuses"; the "moral erosion and subsequent disintegration of our national unity"; massive unemployment and the "stupendous total of our national public debt," among other calamities plaguing the United States. Meanwhile, Rudolf Markmann, the leader of the organization's Eastern Department, geared his remarks to debunking the idea that Nazis were a menace to American society. On the contrary, he insisted, the Bund was formed to counteract the anti-German "hate campaign" waged by Jews and their apologists.

The speakers were just getting warmed up, and as they came to the podium, they left little doubt about who they thought was responsible for America's afflictions. George Froboese lay the world's tribulations at the feet of Jewish exploiters of labor. The real problem, he insisted, was "Jewish moneyed interests" and "Jewish agitators, who are supposed to represent labor, but in reality never in their lives worked an honest day's hard manual work themselves." Indeed, "the Gentile American worker," he argued, "is being sold down the river by international Jewish interests." In Froboese's view, Jews were both capitalist exploiters *and* labor agitators who fomented class hatred. His speech revealed a particular antipathy for Jewish Communists whose goal was "Communist-infested and Moscow-directed domination." This is why the only solution was to work for a "Jew-free America."[46]

The crowd roared as the night's final speaker, Fritz Kuhn, the Bund's national leader, stepped to the podium. Kuhn, like so many members of the organization, was a German immigrant who was compelled by the antisemitic, nationalistic vision of Nazism. He was skilled at fusing Nazi propaganda with white American patriotism. In that sense, George Washington, the military man, the slave-owning Virginian, was the perfect Founding Father to emulate. Kuhn's ascendancy to leadership of the Bund was based on his charisma and his ability to exaggerate and embellish. In vintage demagogic fashion, Kuhn began his speech by telling the audience: "You will have heard of me through the Jewish-controlled press as a creature with horns, a cloven hoof and a long tail." The sarcastic statement elicited laughter from the crowd.

In his speech, Kuhn fused Nazism with what today would be called "white nationalism." He talked of the Civil War, and he lay blame for it at the hands of the North. As he told it, the Jews were responsible for giving formerly enslaved "negroes" the audacity to want equality. The Jewish figure, whom Kuhn derisively called "Moses," was among the "horde of adventurers, loafers, and sum of unscrupulous politicians which invaded the South." The Jewish agitator was a "good speaker who knew how to arouse the negroes, he preached a new outlook on life and freedom—freedom from labor and what to the colored people appeared freedom from moral and social restraint." Indeed, part of that freedom from "moral and social restraint" entailed encouraging the white supremacist nightmare of black men having intimate relations with white women. "'Would you like to sit at the table with your former masters?' Moses asked the Negroes. 'Would you like to go to the theater, dress like and sit next to the white ladies? *And would you like to have a white woman for a sweetheart?*'"[47]

Kuhn, and all the speakers that night, concluded that the task at hand was to eliminate Jewish domination and establish a "White-Gentile" republic. In short, a return "of our government to the policies of George Washington," which to Kuhn meant "aloofness from foreign entanglements, severances with the League of Nations."[48]

The Bund's staging of a White-Gentile nation almost came off without a hitch. However, there were two moments of disruption. Outside the Garden, thousands of protesters clashed with police, a force of 1,745 officers whose job was to maintain order and protect the Bund's First Amendment right to speak. The clashes and the dissidence expressed by protesters was given voice by two courageous individuals. As the parade of speakers spouted chapter and verse tenets of Nazi propaganda, Dorothy Thompson turned from observer of the proceedings to an active participant in them. She couldn't help but snicker and laugh *loudly*. Her defiance upset the Bund's admirers around her, prompting one to yell, "Get her out of here!" Though police and the OD tried to remove her from the premises, she flashed her press credentials and insisted that she stay. Eventually, she left of her own accord. Afterward, she was fiercely critical of arguments that hate groups like the German American Bund deserved the right of free speech. "I laughed because I wanted to demonstrate how perfectly absurd all this defense of 'free speech' is in connection with movements and organizations like this one."[49]

Another dissenter who channeled the anti-fascist energy from outside the building was Isadore Greenbaum, a Bronx plumber. Greenbaum appeared out of the crowd and charged the stage in order to stop Kuhn's sermon of hate, but members of the OD pummeled him mercilessly and removed him from the arena. The rally ended at 11:15 p.m., and the twenty thousand Nazi sympathizers left the Garden protected by city police. A week later, the Communist Party launched a counterdemonstration at the Garden. After the war broke out a few months later, New York City, and the Garden in particular, remained center stage for the struggle against Nazism and fascism. The building Tex Rickard built for his boxing business became one of America's battlegrounds for democracy. So, too, did other arenas and stadiums across the country. Indeed, at another stadium in New York, Nazism was delivered perhaps its most decisive symbolic blow.[50]

ON JUNE 22, 1938, A LITTLE LESS THAN A YEAR BEFORE THE GERMAN American Bund's demonstration, Nazism had already suffered a powerful defeat. The defeat didn't happen at the Garden or on the streets. Fittingly, it happened in a boxing ring in front of eighty thousand spectators at Yankee Stadium in the Bronx. To be sure, there was no way sports could be removed from the polarized politics of the 1930s, and there was no way for a contest between a black man and a white man to be removed from the racial rhetoric of the day. On that historic evening at Yankee Stadium, Joe Louis, aka the "Brown Bomber," faced off against the German champion, Max Schmeling. The bout was touted as a battle between democracy and fascism. Two years earlier, Schmeling had become the darling of the Hitler regime when he shockingly defeated the previously undefeated Louis in a twelfth-round knockout at Yankee Stadium. For two years, Louis waited for a chance at revenge. The Nazis touted Schmeling's victory, like the Olympic Games in Berlin, as irrefutable evidence of the superiority of the Aryan race. But those visions of Aryan supremacy were dashed by Louis's decisive first-round-knockout victory during the rematch. The overwhelmingly pro-Louis crowd cheered as the Brown Bomber knocked down Schmeling three times in the first round. After Louis was declared the winner, pandemonium ensued in the stadium and throughout the country and the world, thanks to a record-setting radio broadcast.[51]

Louis emerged from the ring a hero, especially among Jews and African Americans. By the 1930s, New York City, expanding beyond its original borders in lower and midtown Manhattan, stretched northward to the upper part of the island and out to the Bronx, Brooklyn, and Queens. The neighborhood of Harlem, just north of Central Park, had become the home of another group of newcomers to the city, thousands of black migrants who had arrived from the South and the Caribbean during the 1910s and 1920s. The black community of Harlem rejoiced as Louis, like Jesse Owens in the 1936 Berlin Olympics, dealt a decisive blow to racism and antisemitism. This was one reason why the *People's Voice*, a Harlemite newspaper, elevated the heavyweight champion to the pantheon of historically significant black liberation heroes by hailing him as "the most effective crusader since Frederick Douglass, John Brown, and Marcus Garvey in the battle for complete participation of Negroes in the life of our nation." As had been the case when Jack Johnson defeated Jim Jeffries in Reno in 1910, black achievement in a sporting event held in a packed stadium delivered a glimpse of what might be possible for black Americans in the twentieth century.[52]

Audiences at Madison Square Garden continued to glimpse this potential during the World War II years. Boxing and politics were the main events at the facility. On June 25, 1945, NEGRO FREEDOM RALLY was displayed on the arena marquee, along with an announcement of an upcoming boxing match between Rocky Graziano and Freddie "Red" Cochrane. Just below was a sign encouraging New Yorkers to BUY WAR BONDS. That June evening, African American activists and their white allies, especially those in the labor movement, staged the fourth annual Negro Freedom Rally at the Garden. In the summer of 1945, as the world war against fascism was winding down, the struggle against racism was just picking up. The rallies were part of the nationwide Double V campaign, spearheaded by the great activist A. Philip Randolph and a host of other organizers who argued that the defeat of fascism abroad was incomplete without a victory against racism at home in the United States. The campaign was much more than a movement for civil rights. It espoused an expansive vision of transformation that attacked racial discrimination in multiple realms, especially in the arena of employment opportunities. Jobs and freedom were uppermost in the minds of antidiscrimination activists during these years.

A host of big-name speakers, including black congressman Adam Clayton Powell and Benjamin Davis, the black Communist city council member, took the stage that night. "The Negro people may gain during the war, but we are not satisfied until we have attained full equality,"

Councilman Davis insisted in his speech. "We have destroyed Hitler, now we must destroy Hitlerism." Performing artists Paul Robeson, Josh White, and Pearl Primus gave their own artistic interpretations of Black Freedom. The rally showed how black Americans built upon the traditions of New York's European immigrant communities in making the Garden an arena of protest. During World War II and beyond, local Black Freedom organizations were fixtures on the Garden's calendar of events, part of a rotation of community groups that used the arena's stage to wage their battles for justice. This tradition of local activists using the Garden as a platform for claims-making would continue deep into the twentieth century.[53]

FROM THE GILDED AGE TO THE YEARS OF THE DEPRESSION AND THE war, the American stadium fulfilled a larger purpose than its commonly conceived function as a place of entertainment. Its early history is more expansive than baseball-centric narratives of stadium history suggest. Its origins can be traced to the emergence of nineteenth-century amusement culture such as the circus, which paralleled the rise of boxing and baseball. As stadiums and arenas evolved from temporary wood structures to more permanent buildings of concrete and steel with their own architectural qualities, they became much more than palaces of pleasure. Tex Rickard and subsequent managers of Madison Square Garden understood—and sometimes profited from—the staging of political events. Even though venues tended to be privately owned during these years, buildings like Madison Square Garden emerged as semipublic squares, where politics and protest, integral to American political culture, could play out. The stadium, therefore, was a place of politics from its inception. The struggles of European immigrant activists at the Garden showed how they pushed their way into the social world of the American stadium and American politics in general. Black Americans and other marginalized populations carried on and expanded upon these organizing traditions in subsequent decades.

Joe Louis's victory at Yankee Stadium and the Negro Freedom Rallies at the Garden signaled that a new day in the struggles of dispossessed Americans was on the horizon. At the end of the war, the movement against fascist-inspired white supremacy seemed to have emerged victorious. Fritz Kuhn's German American Bund entered the dustbin of history. In northern cities of the United States, the Black Freedom movement steadily chipped away at the structures of racial discrimination, including at baseball stadiums. In New York City, a cross-racial campaign against racial discrimination pressured the Brooklyn Dodgers National League franchise to break the color line in Big League baseball. In the South, however, the structural roots of Jim Crow were much deeper. Racial segregation not only persisted but also expanded at the same time its foundations were shaken in the North. One of the engines of that expansion was the sporting realm, and few places visibly manifested Jim Crow more dramatically than the college football stadium.

CHAPTER TWO

AMERICA'S
SUGAR BOWL

On January 1, 1941, more than seventy-three thousand spectators crowded into Tulane Stadium to witness the Sugar Bowl classic, the popular postseason college football game held every New Year's Day in New Orleans. It was a matchup of two undefeated teams: the Boston College Eagles and the Volunteers of the University of Tennessee. Among the thousands who made their way to the stadium was Lou Montgomery, Boston College's exciting running back, who ordinarily would have dressed in the locker room and taken the field with his teammates. On this particular day, however, Montgomery climbed the stadium's winding ramps to watch the game from the press box because southern custom, enforced by the bowl game's organizers, required that the Eagles bar him from playing in the game because he was black.

This was the seventh installment of the New Year's Day classic, and Sugar Bowl organizers anticipated it would be their best game yet. The pregame hype whipped the town into a frenzy as thousands of visitors, arriving from all over the country by special trains, buses, automobiles, and planes, converged on New Orleans to partake in the festivities. The Sugar Bowl classic had helped make New Orleans a holiday destination in the same way that the Tournament of Roses Parade and the Rose Bowl game turned Pasadena, California, into a popular place for the country's affluent classes to visit. When local boosters created the annual bowl classic, they envisaged the game as a vehicle to promote tourism and business in the Crescent City. Seven years later, the Sugar Bowl classic was turning out to be more than what they'd bargained for. The city's hotels were packed to such an extent that the local press begged New Orleanians to open their homes to visitors, who continued to stream into the city.[1]

After enjoying the merriment and revelry of the holidays in the French Quarter, visitors poured into Tulane Stadium on New Year's Day. The stadium was an immense bowl-like structure that loomed over Tulane University's campus and the surrounding neighborhood, two miles from the Mississippi River. Once dominated by sugar plantations in the early nineteenth century, the area was transformed after the decline of the plantations and the arrival of a new residential district and the university in the 1890s, followed by this large stadium three decades later. At the turn of the twentieth century, Tulane, which began as a medical college in 1834, was transitioning into a modern university.

Tulane Stadium made the university more than an institution of higher learning. The building turned it into a college football destination. Built by the university for its football program in 1926, it became the venue for the annual Sugar Bowl classic since the game's inaugural year of 1935. With the increasing popularity of the game, the stadium's seating capacity was raised from the original twenty-four thousand seats to seventy-three thousand seats in 1939. Yet another expansion increased capacity to eighty-two thousand seats in 1948, making Tulane the stadium with the largest seating capacity in the South. It also had a newly constructed press box atop the west end, built to accommodate 261 members of the media and hailed by boosters as the largest in the country.

On that humid New Year's Day in 1941, fans made their way to the Uptown district in New Orleans and filed into the stadium, climbing the ramps that snaked up the exterior to their bleacher seats. The game turned out to be a thrilling contest. The Eagles pulled out a 19–13 victory when Charlie O'Rourke, their lithe five-foot-eleven quarterback, scampered through the Tennessee defense for the go-ahead touchdown. After the game ended, excited Eagles fans stormed the field and tore down the goalposts. The win capped off a remarkable season for Boston College, arguably the best in the school's football history.

But all the excitement and glory for Boston College would happen without Lou Montgomery, the Eagles' talented running back. In this period, a "gentlemen's agreement" existed between northern and southern colleges and universities whereby northern schools would adhere to southern racial norms and laws by barring their black players from suiting up for play against white players. The 1941 Sugar Bowl was not the first time Boston College's only black player had been excluded from games against southern teams. Montgomery had been benched multiple times previously, including before the Eagles' regular-season game against Tulane in New Orleans earlier that season. The previous year, he had also been prevented from playing in the Cotton Bowl classic in Dallas.[2]

When the Mid-Winter Sports Association, the group that created the Sugar Bowl game, extended the invitation to Boston College, it was with the stipulation that Montgomery could not play. Boston College, as it had in the past, acquiesced to southern racism by accepting the invitation to the Sugar Bowl. In Boston, weeks after the bowl game, Montgomery received a characteristic guilt-driven tribute by his coaches, who lauded his "character" for silently accepting the humiliating situation while they disregarded their own complicity with racism. Years later, Montgomery admitted feeling bitter about having to sit out games against southern teams.[3]

Looking back at this routine occurrence of racial exclusion, it is astonishing to see how thoroughly the southern Jim Crow machinery erased Montgomery's presence from the team. Aside from one team photo in the published Sugar Bowl program, in which Montgomery appears unidentified, not one article mentions him or his contributions to the team. Not even the Boston sportswriters covered his exclusion from the game. Bowl organizers, the journalists, and the Boston College team itself all participated in the erasure of Montgomery's presence on the team. This disappearance might be jarring to the twenty-first-century reader, considering the preponderance of black players in college and professional football today.

Montgomery's erasure from the 1941 Sugar Bowl reveals how Jim Crow, the system of legalized and customary racial subordination in the South, sought to clear the presence of black people from the history of the South and from the district where the game itself was played. This everyday form of racial exclusion was embedded in the sporting culture of the South, in its rituals and performances, and in the very geography of southern college football. Such racial erasures were made both routine and spectacular in the South's college football stadiums, one of the region's most popular recreational spaces.

During the first decades of the twentieth century, alongside baseball ballparks and indoor arenas, college football stadiums grew in popularity across the country. Universities took advantage of the revolution in concrete and steel construction techniques, which enabled stadiums, like tunnels, bridges, and skyscrapers, to be built bigger and as more permanent parts of the American landscape.[4] These facilities were arguably more widespread than the ballparks that housed professional baseball clubs during this period. College football stadiums also tended to have larger seating capacities to accommodate audiences for a wider array of events.

Since their earliest incarnations, stadiums were racially segregated to varying degrees across the United States. In the North, the color line prevailed in baseball ballparks, where white professional baseball clubs sought to segregate black players and black fans. Racial boundaries were much more fluid in indoor arenas, especially during boxing matches, given the significant number of black boxers and the international nature of the sport. But in the apartheid-like system of the South, racial boundaries were strictly enforced. Although more stadiums for college football teams were built, racism limited full access to them. Black schools had to construct their own facilities or rent them from white institutions.[5]

A variety of cultural forms perpetuated racial hierarchies in the South: film, novels, radio, print journalism, and consumer culture. Jim Crow's public manifestations at the polls, in the public parks, at the schools, and at the lunch counters are well-known, but the stadium was also a prominent location in the geography of racism in the South. During the 1920s and 1930s, southern universities built football stadiums all across the region. In addition to Tulane, the core schools of the region's college football scene all built their stadiums during this period: the University of Kentucky, the University of Georgia, the University of Alabama, Auburn University, the University of South Carolina, the University of Florida, the University of Mississippi, Mississippi State, and Louisiana State. Of these, Tulane Stadium was arguably the most impactful structure because it hosted the region's major college football sporting event. The spectacle of the annual New Year's Day football game in a large venue filled with eighty thousand people and publicized on radio and television and in the print media presented a powerful mechanism to project the white South's self-image.

As a regional and national spectacle, the Sugar Bowl classic also played a key role in the growth of college football during the early decades of the twentieth century. The sport that had emerged out of rugby as a pastime of elite men at schools in the Northeast had rapidly developed into a national phenomenon, even as its violence continued to elicit criticism. It became particularly prevalent in the Jim Crow South, fueled by university students and alumni who saw football as a means to generate revenue and publicity for their cities and institutions. But it was more than that. It was a regional pastime that became central to southern masculine identity, especially as black activists steadily challenged segregation and white male supremacy as the century unfolded.[6]

The revenue-generating potential of college football was furthered by the advent of the postseason bowl games, which first began with the Rose Bowl in Pasadena in 1902. Civic boosters and businessmen joined with universities to turn football into a lucrative proposition. Legalized and customary racial segregation went hand in hand with commercialization. Four of the five major bowl-game classics were hosted by cities in the Jim Crow South: Dallas, El Paso, New Orleans, and Miami, which heightened southern influence on the business of college football. If immigrant working-class politics shaped the culture of northern arenas like Madison Square Garden, in the Jim Crow South, the stadium became a major theater for staging the South's commitment to white supremacy.

The spectacle of racial segregation can be clearly seen in the history of the Sugar Bowl New Year's Day game at its original site on the campus of Tulane University. Although the game today is associated with the Louisiana Superdome, its home since 1975, it originated in the area that was once the heart of the region's plantation economy. The campus and the stadium were constructed on lands that were once sugar plantations, which meant that the legacy of slavery and the practice of Jim Crow were reenacted year after year during the Sugar Bowl. Sugar Bowl organizers and their business partners went to great lengths to market New Orleans as a tourist destination while trading in romanticized images of the plantation past and the Confederacy. While other southern postseason bowl games grudgingly desegregated in the late 1940s and early 1950s, the Louisiana state government forced the Sugar Bowl to postpone racial integration well into the 1960s. Tulane Stadium was a monument to white supremacy until the civil rights movement of the 1950s and 1960s finally forced the desegregation of a New Orleanian, and southern, institution.[7]

FOR MORE THAN A CENTURY, CROWDS HAVE GATHERED IN THE UPTOWN district of New Orleans to relax and play at Audubon Park, attend school at Loyola or Tulane University, or cheer for their favorite athletes on university athletic fields. But one evening in 1795, a crowd came together to witness an event that would dramatically transform the region. The occasion has become part of New Orleanian lore, thanks to the apocryphal history written by nineteenth-century historian Charles Gayarré, a child of the local planter class who chronicled the moment when New Orleanians figured out how to manufacture sugar. Sugar and slavery had keyed the development of European colonies in the tropical climates of Brazil and the Caribbean, but the subtropical environment of Louisiana seemed to conspire against planters' efforts to turn the juices from the tall cane stalks into granulated sugar. The crowd gathered at a boiler house not too far from where the campus of Tulane would eventually be built.[8]

> Would the syrup granulate? Would it be converted into sugar? The crowd waited with eager impatience for the moment when the man who watches the coction of the juice of the cane determines whether it is ready to granulate. When that moment arrived, the stillness of death came among them, each one holding his breath, and feeling that it was a matter of ruin or prosperity for them all. Suddenly, the sugar-maker cried out with exultation, "It granulates!"[9]

Gayarré's highly dramatized account remains a foundational story in the rise of the sugar industry in New Orleans. He was the grandson of Jean Étienne de Boré, the man credited as the first to granulate sugar in Louisiana on that day in 1795. De Boré, a Francophone North American planter, was also the first mayor of New Orleans when it was under French colonial rule. Previously, his wealth had been based on the cultivation of indigo by slave labor. By the 1790s, with his indigo properties teetering on collapse, he took a risk by investing in sugar. This was a dicey proposition, given the lack of success planters had in producing sugar in the subtropical climate of Louisiana. Indigo had been the export commodity of choice up to that point. However, with the assistance of two experienced sugar men from Cuba and Saint-Domingue, de Boré set up a *trapiche*, the eighteenth-century mule-driven sugar mill modeled after those built on Caribbean plantations. On that historic day in 1795, the men and women who worked for him granulated his first batch of cane, turning a $4,000 investment into a $12,000 profit. De Boré's "discovery" would go down in Louisiana lore, and the story would be retold over and over again by local elites and the local government, including those who desired to craft romanticized portraits of plantation life and planter resourcefulness to market their city to a national audience.[10]

The de Boré plantation story illuminates New Orleans's deep connections to the broader history of slavery and sugar production in the Western Hemisphere. Although New Orleans is within the borders of the United States, it is also a Caribbean city. Along with the migrants and the commodities that have flowed into the Gulf Coast from the Caribbean are the hurricanes that have caused so much destruction for centuries. An equally lethal arrival from the Caribbean was the sugar plantation of the eighteenth century, which dramatically transformed the Louisiana Gulf Coast, setting it on the same course of wealth, enslavement, and death that had marked Caribbean societies of Barbados, Jamaica, Haiti, and so many other islands overcome by sugar and slavery.[11]

We do not know the identities of the enslaved Africans who made sugar granulation possible that day in New Orleans. We cannot precisely name who planted the cane, who cultivated the cane, who cut it with a machete, who loaded the heavy stalks onto a cart, who hauled it to the boiler house, who carried out the specialized labor of feeding the cane into the *trapiche*, who extracted the cane juice, who put it in kettles over the fire and turned it into molasses, who decanted the molasses and turned it into crystallized sugar. We do not know who built and maintained the plantation itself, who tended its gardens, who fed the master and his family, and who was sold away when plantations in the area went defunct in the 1820s. We do know, however, that what became the Uptown district, which eventually became the site of Tulane University and its stadium, was where the wealth and misery of sugar and slavery in lower Louisiana were born.[12]

The plantation complex that, like a hurricane, had torn across the Atlantic to Brazil and the Caribbean and that had generated enormous profits for planters and misery for the enslaved people arrived in Louisiana, bringing the same cycle of wealth and destruction to the region. In subsequent years, sugar plantations, worked by enslaved laborers,

rapidly sprung up along the banks of the Mississippi, radically transforming the region. What became known as America's "sugar bowl"
arose from the violence and backbreaking labor of enslaved individuals and their descendants in subsequent centuries. None of this history
would be acknowledged when the Louisiana "sugar bowl" experienced
a revival in the twentieth century.[13]

The deep history of sugar and slavery illuminates how that legacy
became entangled in the growth of college football in the South. In the
decades after the Civil War and emancipation, sugar remained a main-
stay of the Louisiana economy, but by the 1930s, the region, like the
rest of the country, was experiencing the hardships generated by the
Great Depression. The time was ripe for New Orleans to look to other
sources of development and prosperity, and Fred Digby and James
Thomson, two local sports enthusiasts, knew it. Digby and Thomson
were newspapermen eager to promote the Crescent City. In 1926, they
attended the Rose Bowl game in Pasadena, which convinced them that
New Orleans could host a similar bowl-game extravaganza. "What the
little city of Pasadena has done with the Tournament of Roses, New
Orleans can do a hundred times better with a Carnival of Sports,"
Digby insisted.[14]

Thomson, the publisher of the local daily the *New Orleans Item*,
and Digby, the paper's sports editor, went to work. They lobbied the
public and the Southern Conference, the leading college football
league in the region, to support their plan for a winter sports carnival
and a postseason college football game, but without success. It took
five years for them to finally make some headway with local elites and
college athletic officials. Digby eventually became the driving force
behind the creation of the Mid-Winter Sports Association, a group
of leaders of local civic, professional, and athletic clubs who shared a
passion for sports. The association was founded in 1934 as a nonprofit
organization for the purpose of creating a winter carnival of competitions in the sports of track, tennis, yachting, golf, and basketball and a
New Year's college football postseason game. The association modeled
its efforts on those of the Pasadena Tournament of Roses Association,

which pioneered the concept when it created the annual Rose Parade and New Year's Day college football game known as the Rose Bowl.[15] Marketing Pasadena as the "Mediterranean of the West," the city's boosters made the Tournament of Roses a nationally recognized event. Digby held a vision of a sports carnival that would both promote New Orleans as a tourist destination and foster "understanding" of southern culture for a national audience.

A contest was held to pick a name for the New Year's Day classic. Fittingly, the name that was chosen was "Sugar Bowl," which followed the pattern of other cities naming their postseason game after commodities produced in their respective region.[16] The name seemed to fit perfectly because New Orleans was "near the heart of Louisiana's mammoth sugar cane industry and Tulane Stadium was situated on the site of Étienne de Boré's sugar plantation."[17] Indeed, the Mid-Winter Sports Association convinced Tulane University to let it use the stadium for the event. By marketing the New Year's Day classic as the "Sugar Bowl," members of the association self-consciously chose to market the event as a southern cultural phenomenon steeped in the region's plantation legacy and its twentieth-century manifestation of Jim Crow segregation.

THE THIRTY-NINE MEN OF THE MID-WINTER SPORTS ASSOCIATION fashioned themselves as selfless civic leaders. The "Sugar Bowlers," as they liked to call themselves, were the driving force behind the creation of what would become one of the more popular tourist attractions in New Orleans, and it remains so to this day. They were a group of professionals and businessmen who shared a passion for sports and a desire to promote their city. Digby, a charter member, served as the group's secretary for many years. He left his newspaper job at the *Item* to be the group's general manager, a position he held until his death in 1958. He also filled the role of historian, and his vision of the winter sports festival and the Sugar Bowl's relationship to southern identity was profoundly influential.

Other influential members of the association were Irwin Poche, a charter member who directed the association's Pageantry Committee for many years. Poche's work on the committee helped ensure that the pregame and halftime entertainment was almost as noteworthy as the football game itself. Paul DeBlanc was another charter member whose work in real estate made him a valuable asset to the association. He served in many capacities, including as president during the tumultuous period of desegregation. These men, like all members of the association, were sportsmen with memberships to many of the city's elite clubs and who served on the boards of various organizations, which gave them access to invaluable contacts who could facilitate their work with the association.[18]

The Mid-Winter Sports Association emerged at the precise moment when local leaders and businesses were turning toward tourism to stimulate the economy. Myths of a harmonious antebellum plantation society and the "lost cause" of the Confederacy became central motifs in the refashioning of twentieth-century New Orleanian identity. The city's booster elite were not shy about promoting the region's plantation past and Confederate legacy, but they were committed to forward-thinking economic development first and foremost— economic development in the midst of the Great Depression was their top priority. The transformation of New Orleans into a service economy was underway, and the Sugar Bowl helped to expedite this process. The prospect of new business coming to town excited chamber of commerce folks, restauranteurs, and hotel owners. Indeed, groups like the Sugar Bowlers figured out a way to harmonize the plantation past with a vision of a modern New Orleans.[19]

The Sugar Bowlers, like other New Orleanian boosters, tended to be moderate segregationists who understood that promoting their city on the national stage meant acting as southern ambassadors to the North. Creating a winter calendar of sports competitions was an ideal way to promote the culture—and the athletic talent—of the South. Though their bylaws obligated them to be "free of political entanglement," such a position proved to be untenable because carrying out their mission entailed pushing for public resources to support their efforts. Organizing the Sugar Bowl carnival of sports also meant necessarily perpetuating the system of racial subordination and creating an outlet whereby they could imagine themselves reenacting the Civil War.

Indeed, football's militarized culture made it the ideal sport to symbolically restage the conflict between the North and the South. This was clear right from the very first instantiation of the classic in 1935, a game between the Temple University Owls and the Tulane Green Wave. In the words of historian Stephen Norwood, "The football player could be seen as a stand-in for the vanished Confederate Soldier." During the pregame ceremonies, the Temple marching band unveiled a giant papier-mâché sugar bowl on the field. The Temple band played "Yankee Doodle," and the Tulane marching band played "Dixie." Local promoters portrayed the ceremonies as a friendly restaging of the Civil War. "Twenty-eight thousand fans, uncovered, stood while the band played 'Dixie' before the classic struggle. Let it play 'Dixie' today and tomorrow for all next week," wrote journalist Charles Dufour. "Yes suh!" Dufour continued. "Every one of those lads was fighting the Civil War over again in New Orleans' first Sugar Bowl classic." Still, by all accounts, the inaugural Sugar Bowl was a success, and the Mid-Winter Sports Association capitalized on the moment by advocating for the expansion of Tulane Stadium.[20]

Branding the college football classic in the image of the region's plantation legacy meant that the business and philanthropic motives behind the association's efforts were inextricably linked to the legacy of slavery and the ongoing practice of racism. Promoting the Vieux Carré went hand in hand with celebrating the region's plantation past. "So numerous and varied are the phases of interest here," the 1935 Sugar Bowl program informed readers, including, "the Mississippi River, the great plantations with massive moss-draped oaks and antebellum negroes," among other delights, in a kaleidoscopic portrait of the many tourist activities for travelers. In effect, the program promised visitors would meet nineteenth-century "Negroes," not real black people who were alive in the twentieth.[21]

The Sugar Bowlers' business partners went all out to promote local industries. And in the context of the Great Depression, generating economic activity was of the utmost importance. Front and center in the Sugar Bowlers' promotional efforts was the sugar industry, which remained important to the regional economy. It still relied on the exploitation of black workers, as it had during the era of slavery. Game programs and local newspapers advertised various sugars and the plantations that produced them. The American Sugar Refining Company regularly advertised its Domino brand. Playing on the football metaphor of the "All-American," one advertisement displayed its line of sugars on top of a rendering of the Sugar Bowl Stadium.[22]

Another company prominently displayed in game programs was the Godchaux Sugar Company, which owned some of the larger plantations in the region. Articles touting the prospects of sugar, in its most sanitized version, carried the ubiquitous theme in the promotion of the game while obscuring the exploitative dynamics that were always embedded in the making of the commodity. A 1937 *New York Times* article entitled "Sugar Bowl Prospers" put it plainly: "For mill owners, agriculturists and Negroes cutting the cane, prosperity is not around the corner but right in the middle of the block."[23]

STADIUMS MAKE POSSIBLE THE SPECTACULAR STAGING OF A SOCIETY'S ideologies and self-perceptions. In the 1920s, the college football stadium became an increasingly popular venue to display such aspirations. In this period, college football and Major League Baseball were surging in popularity. College football's rise to prominence convinced universities across the country to invest in building stadiums. Fans and alumni of these schools partnered with athletic departments to defeat faculty and administrators who believed that football's crass commercialism had no place at institutions of higher learning. Schools were enchanted with the idea of building permanent concrete and steel structures as symbols of identity and progress.[24]

Beginning with the University of Pennsylvania opening Franklin Field in 1895, university stadiums were built throughout the country: Harvard Stadium in 1903, the Yale Bowl in 1914, Stanford Stadium in 1921, the massive Los Angeles Memorial Coliseum in 1923, and of course, the legendary Notre Dame Stadium in 1930. The iconic stadiums of the Midwest, including Michigan Stadium and many of the facilities on the campuses of major universities, were also built in the 1920s. In the 1930s, stadium construction became state policy when federal funds from Franklin Roosevelt's Public Works Administration (PWA) were used to construct a wide variety of facilities across the United States. Southern schools such as Louisiana State University, the University of Mississippi, and the University of Arkansas were beneficiaries of these funds. Burdine Stadium in Miami, the facility that eventually was renamed the Orange Bowl, was also financed, in part, by PWA funds.[25]

In 1926, Tulane University, its football team succeeding on the field, joined this wave of stadium construction. Like other universities, it saw the possibilities that sporting events could bring for alumni engagement and fundraising. But after fielding winning football teams in the 1920s and 1930s, the program fell behind other nearby competitors during the 1940s. Although the sport remained popular with students and alums, over time, the costs and hassles of running a football program made administrators less enthusiastic about it.[26]

The university's ambivalent attitude toward football did not stop the men of the Mid-Winter Sports Association from seeing Tulane Stadium's potential as an attractive venue for the Sugar Bowl. Their fervent commitment to stage the annual bowl game on Tulane's campus breathed life into a facility that might have remained on the periphery of the local sporting landscape. Though the facility was university property, over time it became a de facto civic institution that was arguably the city's most important gathering place from the 1920s until the opening of the Louisiana Superdome in 1975. Over the next four decades, the Sugar Bowlers would turn the stadium into an iconic venue that symbolized the South's rise to prominence in the college football landscape. Even though the building was officially known as Tulane Stadium, it eventually became better known as the "Sugar Bowl Stadium."

From the 1930s to the late 1950s, the Sugar Bowlers cajoled and lobbied Tulane's reluctant administration—and a more willing public—to invest in the facility's expansion. The Sugar Bowlers needed more seats available to sell enough tickets to finance their operation. They certainly kept an eye on the competition: the organizers of the Orange Bowl classic in Miami and the Cotton Bowl classic in Dallas, and football boosters in other parts of the South who were also promoting their own postseason bowl games. Warren Miller, the head of the association, warned his colleagues in 1937: "Miami is building a bowl; Dallas is building one; Memphis will this year be able to hold a football game. If we sit still, we are actually sliding back down hill and our chances are gone. We have got to keep up with the other cities that are competing against us."[27]

The Sugar Bowlers successfully made the stadium the model college football venue in the South. They assiduously engineered deals with Tulane's administration and the city to fund the stadium's rapid expansion from a single-decked facility of twenty-four thousand seats in 1926 to a gigantic concrete and steel double-decked stadium that could hold more than eighty-two thousand spectators, the largest in the South by the late 1940s, and, as the Sugar Bowlers liked to point out, the largest steel double-decked stadium in the world. Lights were installed in the late 1950s, making the venue available for night games. By the late 1960s, the existence of the stadium made it possible for the Saints to be established as a National Football League (NFL) expansion franchise. The stadium even hosted three of the first nine Super Bowls during the 1970s.

Though it was a massive stadium, it had the feel of an intimate space, partly because it was erected in the middle of a campus and a residential neighborhood. The west side of the stadium literally brushed

Tulane Stadium, 1972 Super Bowl. *Credit: The Historic New Orleans Collection*

up against the backyards of homes on Audubon Boulevard. Over the years, Tulane was flooded with letters from neighbors who complained about all the nuisances that stadiums bring: noise, rowdiness, traffic, etcetera. Like all football stadiums at the time, the Sugar Bowl Stadium contained wooden bleacher seats with little leg room, which created the sensation that fans were literally sitting on top of each other. In footage of bowl games and Super Bowls at the stadium, fans seem to spill out of every single corner of the facility. The intimacy of the venue undoubtedly heightened anxieties when racial segregation appeared vulnerable in the 1950s. Like many stadiums that last as long as Tulane Stadium did, the venue became a beloved institution, especially among white New Orleanians. Since much of its history occurred during the Jim Crow era, it became a monument to racial exclusion.

Maintaining a white supremacist order during the Jim Crow era took work, especially at a stadium, which by definition is an institution that draws people together—a "site of convergence," in the words of geographer Chris Gaffney.[28] It entailed creating an elaborate system of ticket allocation that sought to ensure the separation of fans by race. Right from the very first bowl game, the Mid-Winter Sports Association ensured that racial segregation would be strictly enforced. Black spectators were confined to a couple hundred seats in a section in the remotest corner of the north end of the stadium, far away from the action. Meanwhile, the vast majority of the tens of thousands of seats were designated for whites only. By the late 1940s, the association was printing tickets explicitly designated for persons of the "Caucasian Race."[29] These stipulations were bitter pills for black fans to swallow, which inevitably led them to look askance at the annual Sugar Bowl festivities and to focus on developing their own sporting competitions.

Front and back of a ticket to the 1954 Sugar Bowl. *Credit: Author's personal collection*

Segregating tickets by race was but one facet of establishing a Jim Crow order at the Sugar Bowl. It also involved the creation of rituals that made white supremacy seem normal and desirable. The exaltation of white supremacist ideologies through pageantry was not unlike the techniques Nazi Germany employed during the 1936 Olympic Games, which used the technology of the stadium to make white supremacy into a powerful spectacle. Although pageantry had always been central to the Sugar Bowl's activities, the pomp and the festivities became more elaborate when cracks in the Jim Crow edifice appeared in the 1950s, especially after the historic *Brown v. Board of Education* Supreme Court ruling that outlawed segregation in May 1954. It is not by accident that white women, cast in the white southern feminine ideal, became more visible participants in the pregame, halftime, and off-the-field festivities during these years. "In response to African American demands for equality, white southerners turned to their beauty queens," historian Blair Roberts astutely writes. Beauty queens were increasingly put into the foreground as the prospect of racial equality seemed like a distinct possibility.[30]

The expansion of the Sugar Bowl's pageantry program during the 1950s can be seen in this light. In 1951, Irwin Poche, the longtime Sugar Bowler and head of the association's Pageantry Committee for many years, created the Sugarettes, a group of high school–age women, to perform precision routines at the game. The committee visited the local Sugar Festival in the nearby cane fields of New Iberia, Louisiana, to identify young women who could participate in the Sugar Bowl festivities.[31] Next on the committee's agenda was the creation of a Sugar Bowl queen and her court. Though queens appeared at the game a few times during the 1930s, they became permanent fixtures in Sugar Bowl ceremonies during the 1950s.

Beginning with the 1955 Sugar Bowl game between the University of Mississippi and the United States Naval Academy, the Sugar Bowl queen became a significant part of the festivities. During the pregame ceremonies, the head of the association gave the queen a gigantic crown and a kiss. The queen also participated in postgame banquets with the two teams. Poche and the Pageantry Committee hired cheerleading and drill teams from all across the South, especially from Texas, a state with renowned marching band and precision drill team traditions, including the nationally famous Kilgore Rangerettes from Kilgore Junior College, the Apache Belles from Tyler Junior College, and the Tournettes from Ball High School in Galveston, Texas, showing how Sugar Bowl pageantry was intended to be a southern-wide celebration.

The pregame and halftime festivities of the 1955 game vividly reveal how an amplified southern white supremacist celebration became an unmistakable part of the game's ceremonial culture. After Janet Kerne, the first Sugar Bowl queen, was crowned on the field and the Naval and Mississippi marching bands performed, a group of local high school students in traditional Acadian dress performed folk dancing to commemorate the bicentennial of the Acadia migration to Louisiana. Before the head knocking on the gridiron was slated to begin, the crowd of eighty-two thousand stood with their heads bowed as the Reverend H. F. J. Rest led a prayer for peace, another pregame ritual, followed by a performance of "The Star-Spangled Banner" while the American flag was raised.

The performance of sectional reconciliation—the reunification of the North and the South—became more evident during the half-time ceremonies. Soon after the Ole Miss marching band paid tribute to the Naval Academy, students unfolded a gigantic Confederate flag and pulled it across the field over the heads of the band. Once the flag had made its way across the field, the band formed the word *Dixie* and played their alma mater. Next, the Sugarettes, clad in red-and-white ballerina skirts and white waistcoats, performed a number of dance routines. This was followed by the Navy marching band playing a couple of numbers before forming a massive letter *M* as a tribute to Mississippi as they played their own rendition of "Dixie." Ole Miss would make multiple visits to the Sugar Bowl classic in the late 1950s and early 1960s, and each time the band would prominently display the "Rebel flag" in performances. No wonder black sportswriter Sam

Lacy described the scene as "the most nauseating spectacle that could have been visited upon the unsuspecting millions of New Year's Day televiewers." Lacy was one of many black Americans who found the Sugar Bowl scene to be distasteful.[32]

LONG BEFORE THE CIVIL RIGHTS MOVEMENT IN THE SOUTH TOOK shape in the mid-1950s, black activists and sportswriters criticized the Sugar Bowlers for their adherence to segregation. Paralleling the trajectory of the broader Black Freedom movement in the South, much of this criticism initially took the form of pleas for humane treatment within the context of segregation. In 1941, for example, Clarence Laws, leader of the local branch of the National Urban League, tepidly asked Tulane president Rufus Harris to clarify the availability of tickets for black spectators for the upcoming Sugar Bowl game after he noticed that they were not yet available. He hoped that Harris could "pass the information on to those colored persons who wish to attend the game, many of whom have witness[ed] this classic since it was inaugurated seven years ago," Laws wrote. "I believe that the cost of placing tickets on sale would be a sound investment in racial good will and understanding."[33]

However, by the mid-1950s, almost a decade after Jackie Robinson broke the color barrier in Major League Baseball, black activists were less likely to see racial segregation as compatible with racial goodwill and understanding. After the *Brown v. Board of Education* decision, black activists were eager to test the new legal landscape. In December 1954, after the Naval Academy accepted the Sugar Bowl committee's invitation to play Ole Miss in the 1955 Sugar Bowl, leaders of the National Association for the Advancement of Colored People (NAACP) pressured Navy to repudiate the Sugar Bowl's segregated seating policy. "Such a condition would cause gross violation of the Navy policy of racial integration," argued NAACP leader Clarence Mitchell.[34] Navy did not have any black football players on its roster, but it did have some black midshipmen who were planning to attend the game as spectators. The academy, which had desegregated only six years earlier, had to decide whether it would comply with the Sugar Bowlers' stipulation that its allotment of thirteen thousand tickets was for "Caucasian persons only." Though Navy had the reputation of being the most "southern" of the military academies, and though it had only a small number of black enlistees among those who would travel to New Orleans, the academy obtained permission to seat its black and white students together in its allocated section on the east side of the stadium. When asked about the academy's decision, Bernie Grenrood, the association's president, tersely told the press: "I believe that Navy's statement speaks for itself. I have nothing to add." The game came off without incident. Eleven black midshipmen sat with the far more numerous white enlistees in the designated stadium section and watched their team rout Ole Miss 21–0.[35]

The following year, the Sugar Bowlers once again sent a signal that they were willing to go along with the new federally mandated desegregation when they decided to invite the Panthers of the University of Pittsburgh to compete against the Georgia Tech Yellow Jackets in the 1956 Sugar Bowl. They did so with full knowledge that Pitt's roster included an African American fullback and defensive back named Bobby Grier. Whereas the previous year the Sugar Bowlers had allowed desegregated seating for Navy personnel only, this time they allowed spectators from any racial background to sit in the section of the stadium designated for Pitt ticketholders. The association also allowed black journalists to enter the stadium's press box.[36]

But 1956 was not 1941, and Grier, unlike Lou Montgomery fifteen years earlier, was going to play in the Sugar Bowl. A new day was at hand. The momentum toward racially integrated rosters had slowly developed in professional sports in the years after Jackie Robinson broke the color line in baseball in 1947. In the world of college sports, northern universities were now reluctant to comply with the odious "gentlemen's agreement," and the Sugar Bowlers knew it. In 1946, the football players of Pennsylvania State University (Penn State) refused to play the University of Miami after the latter insisted that the school

Bobby Grier. *Credit: The Historic New Orleans Collection*

bench its black players. In 1948, the Sun Bowl committee in El Paso, Texas, created a headache for itself when Lafayette College in Pennsylvania refused their invitation after they requested that the school keep its black players off the field. Students at Lafayette launched a major protest in response to the Sun Bowl's refusal to allow the full roster and the committee had to invite another team instead.[37]

And the Sugar Bowl's competitors were beginning to extend invitations to teams with black players. The same year as the Lafayette College debacle, the Cotton Bowl in Dallas invited Penn State, including its two black players, Wallace Triplett and Dennie Hoggard, to play Southern Methodist University. The Orange Bowl in Miami eventually followed suit in 1955, though both bowl committees tried to duck desegregation as long as they could by prioritizing all-white southern teams whenever possible in subsequent years. The gentlemen's agreement that had structured intersectional college football contests no longer held sway over northern universities. Jim Crow's days in college football seemed to be numbered.[38]

Still, arch-segregationists refused to go along with the winds of change. Resistance to Grier's presence came not only from segregationists in Louisiana but also from Marvin Griffin, the governor of Georgia, who fiercely protested Grier's participation in a game against the team that represented his state. "The South stands at Armageddon," Griffin declared. "The battle is joined. We cannot make the slightest concession to the enemy in this dark and lamentable hour of struggle." Yet despite Griffin's strident objections, students at the University of Pittsburgh and Georgia Tech stood firmly by the notion that Grier should play in the game. Grier did play: "the first Negro ever to play in the Sugar Bowl," reported the New Orleans *Times-Picayune*, though the Panthers suffered a tough 7–0 defeat in front of a packed house of 82,985 spectators. The Yellow Jackets benefited from a questionable pass-interference penalty called against Grier, which enabled Georgia Tech to score the only touchdown of the contest. By all accounts, the game came off without a hitch, though Grier was forced to be housed and entertained separately from his white teammates.[39]

Arch-segregationists in Louisiana and elsewhere in the South had seen enough. The flames of a "massive resistance" movement against *Brown* and any effort toward dismantling segregation, a phenomenon that has eerie parallels to today's white grievance politics, were fanned throughout the South by a group of dedicated pro-segregation politicians. In the immediate aftermath of the *Brown* decision, an athletic contest with merely one black player drew panic-stricken segregationist politicians to stamp out any flicker of desegregation. Up to this point, custom had been an effective means of maintaining segregation in Louisiana sports. However, now that the walls of segregation were starting to crack, the added force of the law was required to buttress white domination.

In Louisiana, segregationist politicians zeroed in on the sports world and the Sugar Bowl in particular. In July 1956, six months after Grier's debut in the Sugar Bowl, the state legislature banned interracial mixing at sporting events and at virtually all social functions. In the legislative session that summer, the state government passed a slew of laws mandating segregation for waiting rooms, toilets, eating facilities, and water fountains. The bill that seemed to target the Sugar Bowlers particularly was House Bill 1419, which prohibited "dancing, social functions, entertainments, athletic training, games, sports or contests and other such activities involving personal and social contacts in which the participants or contestants are members of the white and Negro races."[40]

Democrat Willie Rainach, a leader of the ultrasegregationists and advocate for segregation laws who fashioned himself as an objective party in the matter, insisted that he was merely responding to "public pressure" against integration. "There is a lot of public pressure being built up against such measures," he claimed, "particularly there is growing resentment against integration in sports programs." A few weeks later, Rainach told the press that the Sugar Bowl group seemed "to be placing the dollar sign above the color line." Meanwhile, House Bill 1419 sent shock waves among the Sugar Bowlers, who tried to tactfully push back against it. They started with behind-the-scenes lobbying of Governor Earl K. Long, a moderate segregationist who was ambivalent about signing such a bill, cognizant of the impact that it could have on tourism in New Orleans. At a meeting on the evening of July 12, the Mid-Winter Sports Association voted to authorize the group to "ask someone for an audience with the Governor . . . to explain why the bill should be vetoed."[41]

But these closed-door efforts were unsuccessful. Getting more desperate, the Sugar Bowlers took their concerns directly to the public. In a full-page message published in the New Orleans *Times-Picayune*, the association pleaded with readers to call for Governor Long to veto HB 1419. In "Don't Let Hysteria Replace Reason," the Sugar Bowlers reminded New Orleanians that they had "played host to intercollegiate champions in every sports activity from every section of this country." The passage of the law would limit "competition only between local or near local universities, and would, in the main, almost eliminate contests which would include the great universities of the East, North, and West." The law would not only prevent scheduling games with Army, Navy, and other northern schools but also seriously curtail the ability of the group to invite college basketball powers like Dayton and Notre

Dame to play in the Sugar Bowl sports carnival. The basketball tournament was gaining popularity. This is why the Sugar Bowlers sent out an appeal "to the other sports governing bodies and to the Sports Fans of the State of Louisiana to join with them in requesting Governor Long to veto this bill."[42]

Unfortunately for the Sugar Bowlers, reason would not triumph over hysteria on the question of integration in the South during the 1950s. Seeing the strong support for maintaining segregation, Governor Long reluctantly signed the bill into law. For the previous two decades, the "reasonable" men of the Mid-Winter Sports Association had made their bed with Louisiana's arch-segregationists. Now, in the rapidly changing context of the post-*Brown* era, they suddenly discovered that their vision for New Orleans ran afoul of those who wanted to put the color line before the bottom line. Later that summer, a bill they supported to exempt the Sugar Bowl from HB 1419 did not make it through the state legislature. Soon after the law's passage, northern schools, including Wisconsin and Pittsburgh, pulled out of competitions with Louisiana schools. Television networks also indicated that they were reluctant to televise Sugar Bowl events for fear of boycott by civil rights activists. The Sugar Bowlers had little choice but to schedule only schools from the segregated South for the winter sports carnival, as they would do for the next nine years.

THE TEPID GESTURES OF THE MODERATE SEGREGATIONISTS WERE NOT going to tear down the great wall of Jim Crow racism. It was the revitalized Black Freedom movement of the 1950s and 1960s—known to most Americans as the civil rights movement—plus historic court decisions and the federal government's enforcement of those rulings that led to the demise of the Jim Crow order in the South. In the aftermath of the *Brown* decision, a host of new Black Freedom organizations did the work of taking down the great wall of Jim Crow segregation, including Martin Luther King's Southern Christian Leadership Conference (SCLC), a revitalized National Association for the Advancement of

Colored People (NAACP), and the Student Nonviolent Coordinating Committee (SNCC). These organizations, which spearheaded protests, from the Montgomery Bus Boycott of 1955 to the powerful Freedom Rides and sit-ins, dramatically altered the landscape of racial power in the South. The movement resulted in monumental federal legislation, including the Civil Rights Act of 1964 and the Voting Rights Act of 1965, even as resistance to racial equality persisted in the years and decades that followed.[43]

The Black Freedom movement had an enormous impact on Jim Crow sports and the stadiums and arenas that housed them. In Texas, professional sports entrepreneurs signaled to the nation that they were willing to exchange segregation for the chance to own franchises in professional baseball and football. In the 1950s and 1960s, owning a professional sports franchise was increasingly seen as a potentially lucrative endeavor. Lamar Hunt, K. S. "Bud" Adams, and Clint Murchinson, from prominent white oil-baron families, each founded new pro football franchises and signed black players in 1960. In order to have a sports franchise in the city of Houston, Roy Hofheinz, the charismatic politician who spearheaded bringing National League baseball to the city, promised desegregated rosters and a new desegregated domed stadium. Similar calculations were made in college sports in Texas and the Upper South states of Maryland, Virginia, and North Carolina. Even in Deep South New Orleans, a group of boosters and sports enthusiasts indicated a willingness to address the segregation issue so they could field a professional football franchise in the city.[44]

After their failed attempt to stop the arch-segregationist forces in 1956, the Sugar Bowlers watched the arc of history unfold in Louisiana from the sidelines. Black activists and friendly judges in federal courts created the conditions for a post–Jim Crow athletic order to finally emerge in the state. Joe Dorsey, an African American boxer from New Orleans, filed a lawsuit against the Louisiana Boxing Commission claiming that the law limited his ability to earn a living in the boxing ring. In 1958, Dorsey won his case, though the victory did not apply to the segregated-seating aspects of the law. Meanwhile, the NAACP filed two lawsuits against Louisiana's interracial-mixing laws. In 1963, in the cases *Barthe v. New Orleans*, which outlawed segregation in parks and recreational spaces, and *Bynum v. Schiro*, which banned segregated seating, the NAACP finally managed to have the last of the segregated-seating laws struck down with wins at the district court of Louisiana. These rulings were eventually upheld by the US Supreme Court. In his July 1963 decision, Judge John Minor Wisdom opined: "Time has run out. There is no defense left. There is no excuse left, no excuse which a court, bound by respect for the rule of law, could now legitimize as a legal justification for a city's continued segregation of government facilities. There is left not even that last-ditch token desegregation."[45]

The Sugar Bowlers and Tulane's administration took note of the court decisions, but they could afford to stand pat as the walls that shored up the Jim Crow order collapsed all around them. Although the passage of the segregation laws in 1956 forced them to select all-white teams, their bowl game continued to attract interest from fans and the sporting press. Indeed, in the late fifties and early sixties, crowds in excess of eighty thousand packed the Sugar Bowl Stadium to see games featuring teams from the all-white Southeast and Southwest Conferences, such as Ole Miss, LSU, Alabama, Baylor, Rice, Texas, and Arkansas. In 1961, Paul DeBlanc wondered in amazement how they had "been exceedingly fortunate in the last five years since intergration [*sic*]—that we have come up with games with larger national interest."[46]

After the court rulings in the summer of 1963, the group had the chance to once again invite northern teams to play in the Sugar Bowl. Though the association had been opposed to the arch-segregationists, some members were still ambivalent about integrated seating. In a September 12, 1963, meeting, during a discussion of pageantry planning for the upcoming Sugar Bowl game, Irwin Poche told his colleagues that he was accustomed to "colored men on the field but he does not want to say Okay about the seating." Indeed, the question of integration remained a touchy subject within the group. At the same gathering, the group agreed to schedule another meeting "to have a wide open discussion on the future plans of the Sugar Bowl with regard to integration," but the purpose of the meeting would be kept secret. Perhaps tellingly, no minutes of that meeting were kept.[47] The Sugar Bowlers eventually invited Syracuse University, a team with prominent black stars, to play in the 1965 Sugar Bowl. The attendance for the game was sixty-five thousand fans, leading some to speculate that the subpar figure reflected resistance to the presence of black players in the game. Some scattered protesters made the point clear when they showed up outside the stadium with banners that read INTEGRATION HAS RUINED THE SUGAR BOWL.[48]

Meanwhile, Tulane University was also a laggard on desegregation. Lawsuits, protests from some students and faculty, and the threat of losing essential foundation support finally compelled the school to admit black students in 1963. Admitting black students into the classroom was one thing. Having them represent your school on athletic teams in a stadium full of spectators was another matter entirely. It wasn't until 1966 that the university allowed a black student athlete to perform when Stephen Martin suited up for Tulane's varsity baseball team. Black football players wouldn't take the field until 1971, when Charles Hall, John Washington, Robert Johnson, and Charles Inniss suited up for Tulane, eight years after the school began to desegregate. As was the case with many southern schools, the last bastion of Jim Crow was the football stadium because of its centrality to white male identity.[49]

Even in this new context of desegregation, the Sugar Bowl classic remained associated with southern white racial norms and traditions throughout the remainder of the sixties and into the early seventies. The 1970 matchup between the Ole Miss Rebels and the University of Arkansas Razorbacks resembled the games of the fifties, when the Rebels were regular participants in the bowl game during the days of "massive resistance." No black player suited up for either team, and there were few black fans in the stands. The overwhelmingly white crowd of 82,500 watched Archie Manning, the Ole Miss All-American quarterback and eventual patriarch of the Manning family of star quarterbacks, lead the Rebels to a 27–22 victory. The pageantry remained virtually unchanged, even if the neo-Confederate rituals had toned down a bit by 1970. All-white marching bands and cheerleading squads performed during the pregame and halftime festivities. As in the past, the white Sugar Bowl queen was crowned and kissed by the chair of the Mid-Winter Sports Association. Though a large Confederate flag was not unfurled by the marching band, plenty of them were waved by Ole Miss fans in the stands. Watching the game on video decades later, one would never guess that racial segregation had been outlawed by the federal government sixteen years earlier and that southern schools were supposed to be desegregated by that point.[50]

The media did its part in showcasing a pristine image of the white South staged at Tulane Stadium to millions of viewers across the country. By 1970, the Sugar Bowl was televised by the ABC television network, which projected a vision of a Dixie that was alive and well and seemingly unaffected by the convulsions produced by the Black Freedom movement and the mobilization against the war in Vietnam. Scenes like these delighted Richard Nixon, the recently elected president of the United States, who specifically cultivated a following among southern white football fans aggrieved by the prospect of racial integration. The descendants of these fans would be a reliable base of support for the right-leaning Republican Party for decades to come.[51]

Still, in the early seventies, the days of all-white teams in southern college football performing in the Jim Crow college football stadium were coming to an end, prompted in part by embarrassing defeats at the hands of schools with integrated rosters. Two years after Archie Manning thrilled the Rebel faithful, the Oklahoma Sooners football team showed up at Tulane Stadium and the 1972 Sugar Bowl with an integrated squad and trounced the all-white Auburn University Tigers 40–22, with millions watching the telecast on ABC Sports. Defeats like these led integration holdouts in the Southeastern Conference to the unmistakable conclusion that the time had come to recruit black athletes.[52]

WATCHING FOOTAGE OF SUGAR BOWL AND NFL GAMES AT TULANE Stadium from the mid-1970s can make one wonder what all the fuss was about. For the last Sugar Bowl game at the aging stadium on New Year's Eve 1974, the Florida Gators featured an all-black backfield, including a black quarterback. They faced off against the racially integrated Nebraska Cornhuskers. Just a few weeks earlier, and after being denied access to Tulane Stadium for decades, Louisiana's black college football powers, the Grambling State University Tigers and the Southern University Jaguars, took the field in front of 76,753 spectators, the largest crowd ever to see a football game between two black schools. It was an event that made black sports fans and sportswriters proud: "Black college football's finest hour," in the words of noted black sportswriter Brad Pye Jr. Watching the Jaguar and Tiger marching bands wage their "battle of the bands" on the field, one could not help but wonder how far the facility and New Orleans sports had come in just a few short years. A few weeks later, the Jaguar band performed once again at the 1975 Super Bowl, the last game ever to be played at Tulane Stadium. The era of racially integrated sports in the South had finally arrived.[53]

However, the next chapter of sports in New Orleans would not take place at the stadium that the Sugar Bowlers made famous. Much to the relief of residents in the surrounding neighborhood, Tulane Stadium would no longer host any major events. In 1975, the center of gravity of New Orleans sports shifted downtown to the $163 million Louisiana Superdome, and that is where it has remained since. In the decades that followed, the Sugar Bowl classic's identity as a tradition rooted in black erasure and a glorified plantation past was somewhat supplanted by a new image of a modern, racially integrated city, marked by a futuristic domed stadium that resembled a massive spaceship. The reality of two generations of white fans sitting in the bleachers of the out-door stadium in the old plantation district faded into the background, replaced by racially integrated crowds spectating in upholstered seats in air-conditioned comfort.

Tulane Stadium was condemned right after the 1975 Super Bowl, and the university, which had always been ambivalent about the facil-ity and the game that made it famous, demolished the large bowl-like structure in 1980. Tulane University gave the old building a ceremo-nial send-off and presented fans with the opportunity to purchase commemorative souvenir versions of the splintering wooden seats that fans had sat on for half a century.[54]

Though the monument to racial exclusion had been demolished and the university had slowly admitted black and other nonwhite stu-dents, the area of the former de Boré plantation remained an affluent and predominantly white section in an otherwise predominantly black city. In fits, just as New Orleans and major college football had in the South, Uptown moved into a new era. Even as America struggled to deliver on the promise of racial equality enshrined in law, the Jim Crow stadium had finally passed into history.

CHAPTER THREE

NATION TIME AT THE COLISEUM

The preseason National Football League game between the Los Angeles Rams and the Oakland Raiders at the Los Angeles Memorial Coliseum ended around nine o'clock in the evening on Saturday, August 19, 1972. The Raiders soundly beat the Rams 34–9, but the game score was irrelevant to the army of men whose job began when the game ended. Their task was to prepare the Coliseum for the next day's event, and they had to do it expeditiously. The stadium hosted many kinds of affairs over the years, and the work of preparing the Coliseum for another event was hardly unusual. After all, the cavernous one-hundred-thousand-seat structure in south-central Los Angeles was never simply a sports facility.

As thousands of fans headed for the exits, the group of workmen with large cloth bags scoured the aisles, picking up hot dog wrappers, beer cups, bottles, and peanut shells, among other kinds of debris left behind by the spectators. While the cleanup staff worked in the stands, another crew of workers took to the field at three in the morning to install a gigantic seven-foot-high stage for the event that was to take place the very next day. In the middle of the field, they put together an intricate assemblage of metal poles, fixing them vertically and horizontally, before they laid a stage of hundreds of long wooden planks across the metal skeleton underneath.

Hours later, more workers converged on the Coliseum field that bright and sunny morning, a day miraculously less smoggy than a typical one in Los Angeles. A team of technicians installed temporary light towers over the stage and erected gigantic black speakers around the makeshift performance space to ensure that spectators sitting throughout the immense stadium would hear the events of the day. Audio and video recording equipment was also set up to document the historic occasion. "It's going to be the best sound that's ever been," one technician insisted, as others stood nervously smoking their cigarettes and observing the work at hand. Per the agreement between event organizers and Coliseum management, chain-link fences were set up around the field and stage to ensure that spectators could not come onto the grass field. Hundreds of red, black, and green balloons were blown up and tied down by gigantic nets. The lights, the stage, and the cameras made the scene into an Angeleno-style Hollywood studio set.[1]

The preparations continued as Melvin Van Peebles, the black director of the hit film *Sweet Sweetback's Baadasssss Song*, found himself with another job that day. Instead of standing behind a camera, he was convening a group of men to discuss the security protocol for the event. The atypical head of security gave instructions to an unusual crew of security guards, which included only black officers from the Los Angeles Police Department; members of the Sons of Watts, a radicalized street gang; and other young men. A few hours later, the spectators began to arrive resplendent in a dazzling array of colorful outfits. The event's low ticket price ($1) helped ensure a large turnout.

More than a hundred thousand Angelenos showed up that day to attend what turned out to be an extraordinarily memorable event in the city's history. They did not come to cheer on the Rams or the University of Southern California (USC) Trojans, the famous local college football team. Nor were they there to hear a presidential candidate (Richard Nixon or George McGovern) campaign for the upcoming national election that fall, as had happened in the past in the immense stadium. Instead, they'd come—the overwhelming majority of them people of African descent—to hear, dance, and groove to the sounds of leading musicians of Stax Records, the pioneering record company that promoted the "Memphis Sound" of soul music in the 1960s. Hailed by promoters as the "Black Woodstock," the concert, called Wattstax '72, was the climactic event of the Watts Summer Festival, an annual event established by black community leaders in the aftermath of the 1965 Watts uprising. The spectacle of tens of thousands of black people in one of the nation's most iconic venues added to the immensity of the event itself. The scene was a marked contrast to the fury of black Angelenos that was unleashed on the streets of Watts seven years earlier. Indeed, Wattstax '72 was a high point for the national and local Black Power movement, signaling a moment of political possibility and unbridled cultural expression.

The fact that this dramatic event happened at the Los Angeles Coliseum was not by accident. Since the time in the 1920s when significant numbers of African Americans had arrived in Southern California from the South, they had agitated for access to public spaces like the Coliseum. By the sixties and seventies, a vibrant black radical and nationalist movement was having an impact on the city's recreational life and politics. This cultural influence was felt in mainstream institutions, such as Hollywood, and its political impact was evident in local electoral politics.[2] Even in the face of ongoing racism and police violence, black Angelenos, like African Americans throughout the country, emerged from the struggles of the 1960s ready to make their hard-won freedoms more concrete. The era of segregation and subordination seemed to be at its end, and a new day was on the horizon.

One place where the new day seemed to be dawning for black Americans during the sixties and seventies was the American stadium. The stadium became an indicator of the dramatic social changes that were occurring because the sport and entertainment industries grew by leaps and bounds at the precise moment when the civil rights movement was transforming American society and politics. America was undergoing a sports revolution that turned professional sports from a regional dynamic into a national obsession. Professional sports expanded beyond the East and Midwest into the Sunbelt and to the West Coast. The dominant sports leagues—Major League Baseball, the National Football League, the National Basketball Association, and the National Hockey League—used their de jure or de facto monopoly power to beat back competitors and eventually supplant preexisting regional leagues. New sporting configurations emerged, more sports franchises were formed, and desegregation opened up new employment opportunities for talented athletes. Television joined radio and print media to widen the audience of spectator sports. The growing visibility of sports turned stadiums into major platforms for black aspirations for equality.[3]

At the same time, the rise of pop and rock music also created a new cultural environment for black cultural expression and representation. Though the Beatles' famous Shea Stadium concert in 1965 helped usher in the era of "stadium rock," black musical acts were also performing in stadiums and arenas across the United States. Motown artists such as the Jackson 5 and Marvin Gaye sang the national anthem at sporting events while they, and many others, packed stadiums and arenas for their own performances. It was in this period that stadiums and arenas became the venues of choice for an industry looking to maximize audiences. Black Americans, like all Americans, were heading to the ballpark and the arena to see their favorite players and their favorite musicians. During the sixties and seventies, the music industry, like the sports world, was realizing visions of a post–Jim Crow United States of America at stadiums and arenas.

The Jim Crow stadium wasn't just passing into history. African Americans were actively pushing it into the American past. They populated the fields and stands during these years, and they helped make the stadium into a semipublic square where they could voice their aspirations for justice and equality. In a sense, what had transpired at the Negro Freedom Rallies in Madison Square Garden during the

1940s spread to other stadiums during the fifties, sixties, and seventies. Civil rights organizations, especially Martin Luther King's Southern Christian Leadership Conference, partnered with local groups to stage rallies at stadiums and arenas in Detroit, Chicago, and Los Angeles. When they were unable to rent stadiums and arenas, they descended upon them to protest outside the building's walls.

The Black Freedom movement gained greater access to ballparks and arenas because more of these venues were public institutions. Though several facilities, such as Cleveland's Municipal Stadium, had been publicly owned before World War II, the vast majority were in private hands. This dynamic changed dramatically after the war, when the baby boom and economic prosperity created new markets for professional sports and entertainment. The expansion of professional sports, which began in the late forties and continued almost without end afterward, led to more stadiums being built across the nation. Suddenly, sports franchises wielded enormous political influence. State and local governments competed against each other for the opportunity to have a major-league sports franchise in their city. For the first time, building sports stadiums generated enormous political capital for politicians. With some exceptions, public financing and management became the norm. The financial downsides of public investment in stadiums would become well-known, but the upside was that public management made stadiums more likely to be subject to community input.[4]

Though it was built in the 1920s, the Los Angeles Memorial Coliseum in many ways pioneered public stadium management. Even in the decades when the sports industry was rapidly expanding, public management led to stadiums that, in design and in practice, subordinated private sports interests to the stadium's public mandate. In Los Angeles, public management created an environment of accountability, especially in the sixties and seventies, when the Black Freedom movement gained significant political influence. Some of this influence translated into electoral politics, as black Angeleno voters began to elect black candidates to office. Moreover, black officials became part of the Coliseum management operation. In this sense, the history of the Coliseum reflects a larger dynamic that unfolded in cities across the United States.

IN THEIR CLASSIC BOOK *BLACK METROPOLIS*, DECADES BEFORE ORGA- nizers staged the Wattstax '72 concert, the pioneering black sociolo- gists St. Clair Drake and Horace Cayton saw something noteworthy about black fans' conduct at ballparks and other sporting venues. Their pathbreaking sociological study of African Americans in Chi- cago revealed the experience of black people in the era of the first Great Migration, from the 1910s through the 1930s, when millions of African Americans left the rural South for northern cities. Meticulously doc- umenting the varied struggles that marked black people's transition from rural to urban life, Drake and Cayton noted a peculiar dynamic when black Chicagoans entered an increasingly important American institution. "At ball-parks, wrestling, and boxing arenas, tracks, and basketball courts, and other spots where crowds congregate as spec- tators," they wrote, "Negroes will be found sitting where they please, booing and applauding, cheering and 'razzing,' with as little restraint as their white fellows."[5] Even as black people encountered job discrim- ination, housing segregation, police harassment, and white vigilante violence, they could, and did, create freedom spaces for themselves at stadiums and arenas. This freedom practice occurred even when black fans entered white stadium spaces, partly because of the absence of segregation laws in the North.

What Drake and Cayton observed in 1930s Chicago had devel- oped in black sporting spaces even in the more restrictive environ- ment of the Jim Crow South. During the first half of the twentieth century, when legalized and customary racial segregation governed the sports world at all levels, black athletes, sportswriters, and spec- tators created what the historian Derrick White has called "sporting congregations" that were organized by black institutions.[6] Games and events organized by historically black schools were community happenings, even when they had to be held in shabby, second-rate facilities. More often than not, black institutions were forced to rent stadium spaces from white landlords. The separate and unequal structure of Jim Crow prevented black schools from having the resources to build and control their own courts and arenas.[7]

A similar dynamic unfolded at the professional level. Negro League baseball also was a community event, even though the vast majority of Negro League clubs were forced to rent field space from white stadium owners. Pittsburgh's Greenlee Field, built by black entrepreneur Gus Greenlee, was one of the very few stadiums built and controlled by a black baseball club owner.[8] Still, black leagues took advantage of what little opportunities they could. It is perhaps not surprising that Drake and Cayton's observations of black spectators took place in Chicago, the city that hosted the annual East-West All-Star Game, arguably the most famous event in the history of the Negro Leagues. Created by Gus Greenlee in 1933, the game was the showcase event of the black baseball season for more than two decades. During those years, the best of the Negro League players displayed their talents in what was a national event for African Americans, who descended on Chicago to watch their heroes every summer.[9]

As the era of integration took shape after the color barrier in professional sports broke in the late 1940s, African American spectators, just like black athletes and performers, became more visible in stadiums and arenas. The story of integration of black athletes is well-known, but the experiences of black fans at stadiums after integration is not. As black male players filled up rosters of major sports teams in baseball, basketball, and football, black fans showed up at the ballpark with and without tickets. Jackie Robinson's signing with the Brooklyn Dodgers brought black fans to Ebbets Field and other baseball stadiums in record numbers, though that meant fewer black fans attended Negro League baseball games.[10] Black patrons could afford to purchase tickets in an era when admittance was still reasonably priced and seats were available. When they could not buy a ticket, they found other ways to become part of the scene in or around the stadium. Even if white fans might have found them an unwelcome presence, black fans went out to the ballpark and enjoyed the game undeterred.

African Americans also became more visible at stadiums because many venues were in close proximity to their inner-city communities. Sometimes African Americans became fixtures among the workers who labored and recreated inside and outside the ballpark. They sold programs, they parked cars, and they worked as concessionaires. At Cincinnati's Crosley Field, the home stadium of the Reds National League Baseball franchise located in the city's predominantly black West End neighborhood, Jim Shelton was a local legend. Nicknamed "Peanut Jim," Shelton was a striking figure. For years, he stood outside the stadium wearing a long tuxedo coat and top hat selling hand-roasted peanuts. "I know they hot, they smoking," he would yell to arriving fans as he stoked the fire under his cart, where he roasted the peanuts.[11] After the West End suffered the effects of having Interstate 75 blast through the neighborhood, Shelton moved with the Reds to Riverfront Stadium when it opened in 1970. Black entrepreneurs like Shelton were—and sometimes still are—integral parts of the stadium scene.

Future baseball All-Star Dave Parker grew up in the sixties less than a block from Crosley Field. When he was a kid, he snuck into games and hung out with friends in the stadium parking lot. As a teenager, he got a job at the ballpark. "I started working at Crosley Field as a vendor when I was fifteen, slinging hot dogs and popcorn in the right field stands," Parker recalled. During games, he broke up the monotony of selling concessions by fantasizing about becoming a Major League ballplayer and playing for his hometown team. "I lost myself in the sounds of the crowd, imagining the PA announcer calling my name as I stepped to the plate," Parker remembered years later.[12]

Parker's experience was not uncommon. From the 1960s onward, young black men congregated, recreated, and hustled in stadiums across the country, especially in cities that had been transformed by the migration of African Americans. In cities like Oakland, Baltimore, Cleveland, Detroit, and Los Angeles, black people predominated among the concessionaires and young fans who congregated in and around the stadium. Basketball Hall of Famer Kareem Abdul-Jabbar fondly recalled his experiences playing at the Cobo Arena in downtown Detroit during the seventies. "At Cobo there'd be this fabulous organist who had to be out of some great black church," Abdul-Jabbar wrote in his 1983 autobiography *Giant Steps*. The fans would really get involved in the game, even cheering the exploits of players from visiting teams, like Abdul-Jabbar, and they would turn out in their finest threads. "People would come dressed to kill, men with the big hats, women in the best coats with their big fur collars. The whole atmosphere was like a black social event," he wistfully recalled.[13] As the era of Jim Crow was collapsing in the South, a similar dynamic unfolded in Atlanta, New Orleans, and Houston.[14]

As many white families fled the cities for the suburbs in the decades after World War II, the ballpark became a place where urban black youth could, and did, congregate. The visibility of black fans at stadiums and arenas in the decades after the war is striking, especially because many of the midcentury facilities were constructed in suburban environments that were supposedly out of reach for African Americans.[15] Even as stadium builders imagined catering to the suburban demographic, stadiums attracted people from across the social spectrum. Indeed, the prominence of young black men in and around stadiums sometimes caused anxiety among white fans who perceived the local stadium or arena as the turf of young black men. As stadiums and arenas were built in more suburbanized areas in the sixties and seventies, young black men drove or took mass transit to the happening spot in town.

Stanley Burrell, who eventually became known as the rap star MC Hammer, is an exemplary case of a young African American whose formative experiences happened at the ballpark. The oft-told story goes that the East Oakland native was dancing and doing imitation James Brown splits in the Oakland Coliseum parking lot when he caught the eye of Charlie Finley, the owner of the Oakland A's baseball franchise. The cantankerous Finley took a liking to Burrell and invited him and his friends to the owner's private box to watch a game. Soon thereafter,

Finley hired him to be a bat boy and eventually a gofer who carried out various duties in Finley's skeletal front office. "I impressed him, and he put me to work in the office running errands," Burrell remembered years later. A notoriously cheap owner, Finley paid the teenage Burrell $7.50 per game, gave him the title "executive vice president," and made him the eyes and ears of management when the team owner was not at the ballpark. On one occasion, Finley even insisted that Burrell announce a game on the A's radio broadcast, much to the dismay of the network, which demanded the youngster get off the air after a half inning. It was during these years that Burrell acquired his "Hammer" nickname because of his resemblance to Henry Aaron, the legendary slugger nicknamed "Hammer." Burrell had the good fortune of meeting his namesake in the clubhouse in 1975.[16]

Then there's the story of Marvin Cooper, otherwise known as "Dancing Harry," an African American man who danced on the

MC Hammer and Henry Aaron, the original "Hammer," 1975.
Credit: Ron Riesterer/Photoshelter

sidelines at Baltimore Bullets NBA games in the late sixties and early seventies. His appearances were inspired by Bullets star Earl "The Pearl" Monroe, whose playground style of basketball made him a cult figure among East Coast fans. Monroe, who first spotted Cooper dancing at a local nightclub, soon saw him dancing on the sidelines at Bullets home games at the Civic Center in downtown Baltimore, and he became a fan. When Monroe was traded to the New York Knicks in 1971, Cooper followed him to New York, transferring his act to Madison Square Garden. In New York, Cooper's act became more choreographed; he donned a hat and a cape and danced and cast spells on opposing teams. Emerging from the shadows of segregation, black spectators, like white fans, expressed themselves freely by dancing, yelling, cheering, and developing new forms of spectatorship.[17]

The black presence at stadiums and arenas across the United States was more than a consequence of black ingenuity. It was also a result of the great freedom struggles of the sixties. The civil rights movement demonstrated its strength by holding rallies in previously inaccessible stadiums and arenas. The freedom rallies at Madison Square Garden in the forties and fifties became bigger and more frequent in the sixties. The most famous demonstration of the movement's power was the 1963 March on Washington, when 250,000 people showed up at the Washington Mall. Throughout the decade, the movement also turned out large crowds to stadiums and arenas across the country. The SCLC joined with local groups to hold rallies in different parts of the country. In 1961, the group partnered with local civil rights activists and religious leaders to organize a rally in Los Angeles's Sports Arena, next door to the Coliseum. More than fifteen thousand spectators crammed into the arena, and ten thousand more stood outside to hear King discuss the Freedom Riders' efforts to withstand the violent reactions of white southerners to their dogged efforts to desegregate interstate transit.[18]

In June 1963, in front of twenty-five thousand people at the Cobo Arena in downtown Detroit, Martin Luther King delivered an earlier version of his famous "I Have a Dream" speech. The SCLC also helped organize rallies at Chicago's Soldier Field in 1964 and again in 1966 to combat housing discrimination. Coretta Scott King joined with protesters against the Vietnam War in a large demonstration in San Francisco's Kezar Stadium in 1967. African American activists dissented and protested at ballparks across the country.[19]

The influence of the civil rights movement at the stadium was also apparent in the organization of sporting events specifically designed to support Black Freedom organizations. The stunning assassination of Martin Luther King in April 1968 compelled sports leagues and corporate sponsors to do something for the cause of racial equality. In 1968, the New York Yankees partnered with the National Urban League, the civil rights and urban advocacy organization, and Ballantine Beer to sponsor a black college football game between Grambling and Morgan State University at Yankee Stadium. Competitions between black college football rivals were always popular in southern black communities. Up to that point, the most well-known was the Orange Blossom Classic, the annual football game organized by Florida A&M and other black colleges beginning in the 1930s. The game was originally held in Jacksonville, Florida, but the heyday of the classic took shape when it was held in Miami. The game was a segregated affair, but like the Negro League East-West All-Star Game in Chicago, it was a big hit in black communities, drawing large crowds to the Orange Bowl stadium in Miami for many years.[20]

Since the mid-fifties, Grambling had attempted to convince white stadium owners to allow its team to play other black teams on their fields. On multiple occasions, for example, Grambling asked Tulane University for permission to play in the stadium. The school was rebuffed each time.[21] Yet the Grambling program became one of the strongest in the black college football circuit during the sixties. Led by their legendary coach Eddie Robinson, who went on to win more football games than any other coach in college football history, Grambling became a black college football power, winning nine conference championships and eventually producing two hundred professional football players. Thanks to its coach, players, and Collie J. Nicholson, the tireless promoter of the football program, the little school in rural northern Louisiana became the "Notre Dame of Black College football." Its reputation gained a big boost after Jerry Izenberg, a prominent journalist for the Newark *Star-Ledger*, and Howard Cosell, television broadcaster for ABC Sports, collaborated on a television documentary: *Grambling: 100 Yards to Glory!* The show aired in January 1968, and it helped make Grambling into an iconic black college football program.[22]

The 1968 contest between Grambling and Morgan State at Yankee Stadium was the first time a black college football contest was held at a major stadium in the North. Robinson and Morgan State coach Earl Banks were convinced that playing a game to benefit the National Urban League would be an appropriate way to honor Dr. King. The proceeds from ticket sales were used for the Urban League's street academy program, which sought to help adult school dropouts obtain their general equivalency diploma. More than sixty thousand fans, most of them African Americans, came through the turnstiles to see Morgan defeat Grambling 9–7.[23] The contest generated $200,000 for the Urban League. The game was hailed as a major step toward racial integration in big-time college athletics, but it was also remembered by players and spectators as a dramatic staging of black pride in a historically white space. George Nock, Morgan State running back, recalled years later that he had "never seen that many black people going into a stadium in my life." Doug Porter, Grambling's assistant coach, also recalled the "wall of noise that hit us . . . we had never heard this kind of roar from a crowd and I looked up into the stands and there were all of these people of color." William C. Rhoden, the future *New York Times* columnist who was then a Morgan State freshman football player, recalled leaving the field "thankful to be part of something this big, this black, and this beautiful."[24]

The Grambling–Morgan State game kicked off a period of holding black college football classics at major stadiums across the country.

In 1969, the Los Angeles Urban League partnered with sponsors to host what it called the Freedom Classic at the Los Angeles Coliseum. Proceeds from the game funded the Urban League's job-training programs. Building upon its notoriety, and its need for revenue, Grambling became a repeat contestant in the Freedom Classics in Los Angeles during the early seventies. Los Angeles was a logical city to host a Grambling game, given the city's large numbers of black Louisianan migrants, who comprised a substantial portion of the mass migration to California that occurred from World War II to 1970.[25]

A key promoter of the game was Brad Pye Jr., the local sportswriter and Coliseum Commission official. Pye, himself a product of the black Louisiana diaspora in Los Angeles, rallied support for the Freedom Classics in his columns for the *Los Angeles Sentinel*. More than sixty thousand fans turned out to see Grambling face off against Alcorn State in 1969. The game returned for the next four seasons, though attendance steadily declined each year.[26] Still, the 1973 Freedom Classic was popular enough to attract black and white Hollywood celebrities to participate as well as boxing legend Muhammad Ali, singers Marvin Gaye and Marilyn McCoo, and Tom Bradley, the newly elected first black mayor of Los Angeles.[27]

Increasingly, sporting events served as fundraisers for black organizations. Even the more conservative Major League Baseball did its part, and a Los Angeles stadium was once again the venue for a historic occasion. As with the 1968 Grambling–Morgan State game, the King assassination was the catalyst. In March 1970, the Los Angeles Dodgers partnered with the commissioner's office and baseball players from across the country to host an exhibition game to support the SCLC's effort to build the King Center in honor of the slain civil rights leader. The game, billed as an "East vs. West Classic," featured two teams with an impressive cross-racial group of past and present All Stars and Hall of Famers, including Willie Mays, Henry Aaron, Frank Robinson, Roberto Clemente, and many others. Joe DiMaggio, the retired New York Yankee legend, managed the East team, while Roy Campanella, the Dodger legend, led the West squad. More than thirty thousand came to Dodger Stadium to see the East team win 5–1, but the result of the game was irrelevant. The benefit raised $30,000 for the SCLC. The event illustrates not only the impact of the civil rights movement on American sporting culture but also how a concern for social good shaped sports during the 1960s freedom movements. Professional teams were willing to adjust their schedules and allow their players to participate in an important social cause.

Black spectators came out to the ballpark for sports events and to demand their rights, but they also came out for other forms of entertainment as another industry sought to capitalize on this new market. The sixties and seventies were a boom period for the music industry, made evident by the rise of stadium rock concerts. Starting with the Beatles' historic concert tour when they performed at stadiums across the country—most memorably at New York's Shea Stadium in 1965—rock-band promoters began booking musical acts in large arenas and outdoor stadiums to maximize profit. San Francisco–based Bill Graham, the concert promoter, pioneered the concept when he organized concerts at San Francisco's Kezar Stadium in the mid-seventies.[28] Other music events, such as the Monterey Pop Festival and Woodstock, lent momentum to the rising number of music performances in front of larger audiences.

But the sixties and seventies were not merely the heyday of stadium rock, a phenomenon that tended to cater to white audiences. A number of black and Latin musical events occurred in mainstream stadium spaces and parks during this period. In 1969, black organizers put together the Harlem Cultural Festival in which a staggering number of big-name soul, gospel, pop, and Latin acts performed, including Mahalia Jackson, Nina Simone, and Sly and the Family Stone. More than three hundred thousand people turned out for free concerts at Mount Morris Park over the course of six days.[29] In 1970, Tulane University departed from its segregationist legacy when it organized the "Soul Bowl" concert in its massive football stadium, featuring Isaac Hayes, Ike and Tina Turner, and James Brown, among other black artists, to raise money for scholarships for black students. In 1973, Fania

Records held a concert at Yankee Stadium, where forty thousand fans witnessed the emerging salsa revolution on the legendary baseball field.[30] In 1974, the Fania musicians held another famous concert in the Roberto Clemente Coliseum in Puerto Rico with virtually the same lineup that performed in Yankee Stadium plus the legendary vocalist Celia Cruz. That same year, the All Stars performed in the Zaire '74 concert that preceded the Muhammad Ali–George Foreman fight at the 20th of May Stadium in Kinshasa, Zaire, a performance documented by Leon Gast in the documentary film *When We Were Kings*. Soon after, other corporate-sponsored festivals, such as the Kool Jazz Festival, emerged across the country. Latin and soul musical acts were hot, and they found a growing audience at concerts held in publicly owned stadiums and arenas. Even though they were driven in part by the interests of the music business, these music festivals created opportunities for spectators and performers to create their own sense of belonging in urban public spaces. Black and nonwhite audiences were part of the new market for stadium entertainment.

Black and Latin musical acts were hot in the early seventies, but the Wattstax '72 concert was the most spectacular and perhaps the most politically impactful. By the time it was organized in the summer of 1972, profound changes in American society were occurring in stadiums and arenas all over the country. Continuing a process that began in the 1920s, stadiums were being refashioned into sites of powerful protest and community building, especially as their numbers proliferated during the post–World War II era. For the first time in the country's history, fans from across the social spectrum came to the ballpark and the arena to spectate, to play, and to protest. They forged a new recreational culture in older stadiums and arenas as well as in the new concrete, modernist structures built during the sixties and seventies. They saw their favorite athletes smack home runs and score touchdowns. They marched to stadiums singing "We Shall Overcome." They hollered and screamed in response to Marvin Gaye's sultry voice bellowing out "Distant Lover." The national Black Freedom movement helped to spearhead this extraordinary transformation. Yet, the patterns that emerged on the national stage in this period had, in many ways, begun long before in Los Angeles.

FROM AUGUST 11 TO 17, 1965, FIRES BURNED SEEMINGLY UNABATED IN Watts. A traffic stop sparked a massive rebellion against all the injustices that afflicted the South Los Angeles community. The passage of the Voting Rights Act in Washington just nine days earlier signified a major triumph for the Black Freedom movement, but this legislative change, however impactful, did not address the grinding poverty and oppressive conditions many African Americans continued to experience in communities across the country. After six days of rioting and police repression, thirty-four people had died and hundreds were injured, many at the hands of the police. Fourteen thousand National Guardsmen were called in, four thousand black people were arrested, and $45 million worth of property was damaged.[31] However, even before the fires were finally extinguished, the communities of South Los Angeles were

The Ike and Tina Turner Revue with Ikettes, Soul Bowl, Tulane Stadium, 1970.
Credit: The Historic New Orleans Collection

already emerging from the rubble. Not long after South Los Angeles was besieged by fires, smoke, and police bayonets and bullets, black Angeleno community organizers decided that what had transpired during those horrible and violent days would never be forgotten. Black activists and some white liberal allies were determined to show that Watts was evidence of a black community on the move, not one defeated by violence.

In the years that followed, an impressive number of community organizations formed to respond to the needs of South Angelenos. The Watts Writers Workshop, the Watts Labor Action Committee, the Mafundi Institute, and *Soul Magazine*, among many other groups, emerged. These groups had divergent and sometimes conflicting visions of community improvement, but they all shared the goal of addressing the multiple crises affecting black Angelenos. These institutions sought to respond to the needs of a community devastated by unemployment, housing discrimination, and police harassment while also seeking to create a new identity that discarded "Negro" for "Black." A strong undercurrent in this community-empowerment effort was Black Nationalism, a long-standing black political and intellectual tradition that was taking a new form during the late 1960s. Black Nationalism certainly had its limits. As black feminists have long pointed out, Black Nationalism was based on a strong current of masculinism that tended to marginalize black women. Still, in the years after the Watts uprising, a Black cultural renaissance was taking shape among black Angelenos. Older concepts of Black self-help and autonomous institution building were infused with a new identification with African cultural roots and the decolonizing world in Africa and Asia.[32]

One organization that surfaced from the ruin was the Watts Summer Festival. Led by Tommy Jacquette and Maulana Karenga, among others, black cultural workers sought to commemorate the uprising while signaling to the world that Watts was on the rebound. Black Nationalists like Jacquette and Karenga argued that a revolutionary culture rooted in African heritage would help African Americans liberate themselves from racist oppression. The Watts Summer Festival was born in this, the heyday of "Black is beautiful."[33] Over the years, even as it was plagued by financial troubles, the Watts Summer Festival became a genuine community event, buoyed by the plethora of black community organizations that were created after the Watts uprising. The festival featured musical acts, films, workshops, concessionaires selling food and other items, beauty pageants, and parades. The festival made Black Nationalism mainstream as black celebrities, including many athletes such as Muhammad Ali, Jim Brown, and Rosey Grier, served as the grand marshal in the parades. The annual festival was an expression of blackness even as different organizations struggled to define what that meant. This local movement for black pride would receive an unexpected boost during the summer of 1972.

That boost came in the form of the visionary work of Al Bell, a record producer with a unique vision of business, community, and consciousness. It was a vision he learned from Jesse Jackson, the civil rights activist who was then running the SCLC's Operation Breadbasket program in the late 1960s. The program used boycotts and other direct-action campaigns to push for white-owned businesses to hire African Americans. After hearing Jackson speak, Bell was taken by his conception of black self-help. "It was like going to a church service, but the emphasis was on economic development and civil rights," Bell recalled afterward.[34] As a leader of an up-and-coming record label, Bell wanted his music to be a "mirror of the black community," not just in Memphis but also around the country.

Bell's label was the legendary Stax Records in Memphis, Tennessee. Founded by Jim Stewart and Estelle Axton in 1957, Stax Records recorded many African American singers who would become legendary figures, including Rufus Thomas, Otis Redding, the Staple Singers, and Isaac Hayes. By the late sixties, the racially integrated company had refashioned itself into a paragon of black enterprise under Bell's leadership. When he first started at Stax, the former deejay turned into a jack-of-all-trades, writing songs, recruiting new musicians, and promoting acts. He eventually became head of the label in 1972, the same year he and Jesse Jackson helped Stax achieve its greatest heights.

Eager to expand its audience on the West Coast and motivated to do something for the black community in Los Angeles, Forrest Hamilton, the head of Stax's West Coast office, approached Tommy Jacquette about getting involved in the Watts Summer Festival. At first, the idea was to have a few Stax musicians perform at the festival in Will Rogers Park in South Los Angeles. However, with visions of a "Black Woodstock" floating around in his head, Hamilton and the festival eventually decided to have nearly all Stax's stars among the thirty-two acts in the lineup. In July 1972, Stax Records announced that it would partner with Watts Summer Festival organizers to hold a concert in Los Angeles.[35] The concert was moved to the Los Angeles Coliseum once it became clear that Stax could finance the show and provide nearly all its stars for the performances. Although the Coliseum was far from an ideal acoustic environment for a musical event, the stadium was big enough to accommodate the expected large audience.

Stax was not the only company eager to participate in this historic event. Joining Bell's label to underwrite the concert was the Schlitz Brewing Company, which was represented by Willie Davis, the black former All-Pro defensive end who had starred on the Green Bay Packers championship teams in the sixties. In 1970, Davis bought a beer distributorship in the Watts district, and his revenue soared, in part a result of the business he generated among black consumers. By the time of the concert, Davis's face was plastered on Schlitz billboards around the city, and he eventually became the first black executive in the company's history. Given Davis's connections to South Los Angeles, his presence at the festival was not coincidental, revealing the interplay of business and politics in the heyday of Black Power and the importance of sports figures to the development of that relationship.[36]

Yet, the Wattstax endeavor was not designed to cash in on the popularity of black musical acts. The community spirit of the event was clear in the low ticket price ($1) and the pledge to donate revenues to the Sickle Cell Anemia Foundation, the Watts Summer Festival, and the recently opened Martin Luther King Hospital in South Los Angeles. The show ultimately raised $73,363 for the three entities. The concert was organized to replicate the model developed by the black college football Freedom Classics: a partnership between a corporate sponsor and a black organization in the interest of black community service and empowerment.

Bell grasped the historic importance of the concert, and he was eager to document it, not only by creating an audio recording that would result in a double album but also by producing a documentary. To this end, he secured the David Wolper Picture Company to produce a film of the event, which was eventually contracted with Columbia Pictures for financing and distribution. Stax's new film division, Stax Films, coproduced the film with Wolper's company. Directed by Wolper's frequent collaborator, the award-winning Mel Stuart, the film was released the following year to much fanfare throughout the country. During his illustrious career, Wolper produced a number of black-themed films, including the *Rafer Johnson Story*, a documentary on the black Olympic gold medalist, and most famously *Roots*, the hit television miniseries. At Stuart's insistence, the film crew for *Wattstax* were all black, a decision that undoubtedly gave the film an unusual authentic quality for a Hollywood production. This commitment to black participation led one celebratory observer to call the concert and the film "the first all-Black entertainment event of its size and scope ever to be completely Black controlled!"[37] Though the claim was not necessarily true because the endeavor was a cross-racial collaboration, nevertheless, Wattstax exemplified the apparent promises of black capitalism in which profit motives could be harmonized with community service. It also illustrated mainstream Hollywood's interest in black Los Angeles in the years following the Watts uprising after years of exclusion, marginalization, and racist caricature.[38] Wolper's company not only created a visual record of the concert but also facilitated connecting the concert to the historic venue where it took place.

Wolper's stature helped the concert organizers secure a meeting with the Los Angeles Memorial Coliseum Commission. When representatives of Stax Records, Wolper's Picture Company, and the Watts Summer Festival attended the monthly meeting of the Coliseum

Commission to pitch their idea of having a concert at the stadium on July 5, 1972, they were only the latest in a host of nonsport entities that had requested use of the historic facility. Architecturally, the Coliseum appeared to be a gigantic football arena, but throughout its history, it served as a venue for many different kinds of events. The stadium's management operation showed that it allotted space and time to local community gatherings, even though it was the city's main professional and collegiate athletic facility. This is likely why the Wattstax organizers believed they had a good chance of securing the venue for their event.[39]

Originally built to attract the Olympics to Los Angeles, which it did in 1932, the facility eventually became one of the most important venues in the United States. It hosted two Super Bowls, Major League Baseball's World Series, and the 1960 Democratic National Convention, along with countless other cultural and civic events. In a metropolitan area defined by suburban sprawl, the Coliseum was one of the few places where Angelenos of all classes, races, and genders congregated.

The Coliseum's stature was also defined by its unique architecture. Designed by John Parkinson, the architect of many important buildings in Los Angeles in this period, the stadium was anchored into a preexisting gravel pit in Exposition Park, located just south of the city's downtown district.[40] The elliptical-shaped, single-tiered structure was modeled on the Yale Bowl, the bowl-shaped facility in New Haven, Connecticut, that influenced stadium designers of this period. The fact that the playing field was set in a gaping hole at the base of a gravel pit concealed the mammoth size of the stadium, an immensity that was evident once spectators walked through the stadium's tunnels and beheld the sight of the stands and the field. Over the years, countless fans and players have underscored the powerful experience of traversing the Coliseum's dark tunnels, particularly the one that leads from the locker rooms to the field. Woody Strode, the pioneering African American football player for the University of California, Los Angeles (UCLA) Bruins, vividly recalled the pulsating energy that he felt in the building as he prepared to play the historic 1939 game against crosstown rival USC: "When I ran out of the tunnel onto the field the sight nearly took my breath away; I nearly hyperventilated. There were 103,500 paid admissions and there must have been another 5,000 when you counted all the press people, the vendors, the officials, and the gate crashers. It was a splashy, colorful ocean of people."[41]

If players and spectators were often taken by the Coliseum's vast size, they also noted another distinguishing feature: the four-hundred-foot-wide concrete peristyle on the east end of the stadium. Like many stadiums built in the 1920s, this one was designed to be a memorial for World War I veterans. However, the columns and arches with the torch that were added for the 1932 Olympics separated this stadium from other bowl-shaped structures of the period. Over the years, the peristyle became a Memorial Court of Honor that commemorated not only military veterans but also significant figures in the city's sporting and civic history.

Another reason the Coliseum was an appealing venue for the Wattstax concert is because it was a known entity to black Angelenos. The building at 3911 South Figueroa Street was located in south-central Los Angeles, the historic heart of the city's black community, though the area changed considerably with the influx of migrants from Mexico and Central America during the 1980s and 1990s. Although African Americans encountered periodic white resistance to their presence at the stadium, over time the facility became an expression of what liberal civic leaders envisioned as a "playground of the people," a publicly accessible facility open to all Angelenos. This was certainly the vision of Kenneth Hahn, the longtime county supervisor and steadfast proponent of publicly controlled sports facilities who advocated for black Angelenos throughout his long political career. Hahn claimed in 1987: "The essence of a great community is providing great facilities so that people have the right to assemble and the right to free speech. These basic constitutional rights are put into effect in the Coliseum and Sports Arena."[42] This was consistent with the Coliseum Commission's mandate to make the arena available for "political conventions, religious gatherings, civic meetings, trade shows, conventions, and youth rallies."[43]

As early as the 1920s, people of African descent were a visible part of the sporting and broader cultural scene at the Coliseum, on the field and in the stands. Although the "invisible walls of steel" of restrictive covenants and job discrimination limited the opportunities available to black Angelenos, they did not prevent people from entering the playing fields and contributing to the region's rich sporting culture.[44] African Americans played on sports teams at all levels, though racial quotas often circumscribed their numbers. By the late sixties and early seventies, nevertheless, nearly all local professional and collegiate sports teams featured black athletes. Moreover, musical acts featuring black performers, including Mahalia Jackson, the legendary gospel singer, held concerts at the Coliseum. Local and national black activists organized rallies at the stadium and the neighboring Sports Arena multiple times, including the 1961 Freedom Rally, Martin Luther King's speech in 1964, and the memorial service in April 1968 commemorating the death of Dr. King. Even radical Black Power groups held events at the Coliseum and Sports Arena, as was the case when the Black Panthers, Maulana Karenga's US organization, and other groups organized a "Free Huey" rally to call for the release of Panther leader Huey Newton in February 1968.[45]

Black Angelenos' participation in Coliseum events was facilitated by the fact that the stadium and the neighboring Sports Arena were publicly controlled facilities. Both venues were managed by the Coliseum Commission, a body comprising city, county, and state officials. Formed in 1945, the commission—though plagued by endless power struggles and corruption—successfully operated the Coliseum for much of its history. Some of the commissioners were elected officials who were deeply influenced by New Deal liberalism, the idea that the government should play an active role in equalizing access to goods and services. The Coliseum, as far as they were concerned, was a public good. By the early 1960s, nearly all the city's professional sports and college teams played at the Coliseum. Even though the sports teams

were top-priority tenants, and the commission set the schedules of the
USC Trojans, the UCLA Bruins, and the Rams, the commission also
reserved space on the calendar for local community organizations,
such as the Mexican American Community Foundation. Public officials had a larger say in the usage of the Coliseum than college football
programs and sports team owners did.[46]

The commissioners were also cognizant of the growing power of
black voters in the city. Prominent liberal politicians, including John
Anson Ford and Kenneth Hahn, both dominant forces on the Coliseum Commission for several decades, were generally sympathetic to
black concerns. By the late 1960s, the commission began to include
black members, including city councilman Gilbert Lindsay and Brad
Pye, the longtime local black sportswriter. Pye himself had advocated
for the desegregation of the Coliseum's press box. By 1968, both Lindsay and Pye were appointed to the Coliseum Commission, a fact that
was celebrated in 1971 by the Los Angeles *Sentinel*, the local black
newspaper, which praised the commission for bringing more events to
the stadium and the arena, including contests featuring black college
football teams.[47]

The influence of black activists and black public officials at the Coliseum illustrates the political leverage they possessed to stage the Wattstax concert. Al Bell and his fellow Stax executives arrived in a city
where African Americans were making inroads into the city's politics.
In July 1972, the Coliseum management agreed to rent the Coliseum
to the concert organizers on the condition that spectators remain in
the stands throughout the entirety of the event, allowing only a mini-
mum number of people on the field. At last, everything was set to stage
the concert. The venue was picked, tickets were sold, the performers
were booked, and the stage and the lights were readied for a historic
day at the Coliseum.[48]

WHEN JESSE JACKSON, SPORTING AN AFRO, MUTTON-CHOP SIDEBURNS,
a necklace, and a PUSH button affixed to a dashiki, stepped to the

microphone to give the opening address at the Coliseum shortly after three in the afternoon, he must have been taken by what he saw before him. The stadium was packed. The audience of a hundred thousand was the largest crowd of black people at a public event in the United States since the March on Washington in 1963. The crowd was resplendent in an extraordinary assemblage of outsized hats, zebra-print suits, dashikis, hot pants, and boots, among other elaborate clothing configurations. Black people wore naturals, braids, and every other conceivable black hairstyle that existed in 1972. Wattstax was indeed a fashion show of sorts, where audience members crafted their own way of spectating and participating by dressing as outlandishly as the performers on the bandstand. Jackson looked out at the audience and proclaimed: "This is a beautiful day. It is a new day. It is a day of black awareness. It is a day of black people taking care of black people's business." As far as he was concerned, Jackson was looking out at a Black Nation. "Something has happened in America, the government has not changed, politics has not changed, but something has happened to the Black Man in America. 'Nation Time' has come," he proclaimed. To Jackson, the transformation of Black America was evident right there in Los Angeles. "In Watts we have shifted from burn baby burn, to learn baby learn. We have shifted from having a seizure about what the man got, to seizing what we need. We have shifted from bed bugs and dog ticks to community control and politics."

The new forms of black politics were exemplified by the partnerships with corporate America forged by People United to Save Humanity (PUSH). The man who fashioned himself as the "Country Preacher" couldn't help but take a moment to call attention to the good work his organization was doing by divulging a series of commitments it had secured from the Schlitz Brewing Company. Flanked by Al Bell and Willie Davis, he announced Schlitz's promise to hire more black workers, work with black companies, and invest in black institutions. It was the black capitalist vision of black empowerment again, and Jackson, somewhat accurately, saw the entertainment industry producing unique opportunities for Black America. "This is the one

industry where because of our gifts as singers and actors, we can produce and distribute and consume," he told the audience. To the Country Preacher, the commitments made by Stax and Schlitz demonstrated
the kind of work that was necessary to carry black people forward.[49]

Indeed, 1972 was "nation time" for African American activists. Liberation seemed to be at hand. Though she was largely shut
out by the overwhelming masculinism of Black Nationalist politics,
Shirley Chisholm's candidacy for the presidency was a sign of new
political possibilities. More directly relevant to the gathering at the Coliseum was the inaugural Black National Political Convention that had
been held five months earlier in Gary, Indiana. At the convention, Jackson had drawn upon Amiri Baraka's poem "It's Nation Time," leading the audience in call-and-response in the confines of a local high
school.[50] Now, during his opening address at Wattstax, Jackson signaled the call again, this time in front of one hundred thousand spectators in an Olympic-sized arena. With Bell and Davis standing with
him, Jackson led the audience in the familiar "I Am Somebody" litany:

> That is why I challenge you now to stand together. Raise your
> fists together. And engage in our national black litany. Do it with
> courage and determination: I am Somebody! I am Somebody! I
> may be poor, but I am somebody. I may be on welfare, but I am
> somebody. I may be unskilled, but I am somebody. I am Black,
> Beautiful, and Proud! I must be respected. I must be protected. I
> am God's Child!

As he was revving up the crowd, he quickly invoked the spirit
of the Gary convention by moving into a call-and-response with the
audience:

> **Jackson:** When we stand together, what time is it?
> **Audience:** It's Nation Time!
> **Jackson:** When we say no more yes abouts, what time is it?
> **Audience:** It's Nation Time!

Jackson: What time is it?
Audience: It's Nation Time!

Jackson then introduced singer Kim Weston, who offered a stirring rendition of "Lift Every Voice and Sing," the song known as the "Black National Anthem." The crowd continued to stand with their fists raised and joined Weston in the chorus. Jackson's powerful invocation, Weston's performance, and the audience's response set the template for how performers onstage and spectators in the stands would interact for the remainder of the day. Guest emcees Melvin Van Peebles, Richard Roundtree, Fred Williamson, William Bell, and Billy Eckstine introduced the talented acts all afternoon. Lesser-known performers sang one song each, and better-known acts played for twenty minutes each. During their set, the Staple Singers sang their hits "Express Yourself" and "I'll Take You There," among other songs, and Pops Staples rapped

Jesse Jackson and Al Bell.
Credit: Michael Ochs Archives/Getty Images

to the audience about the importance of Black pride. The Rance Allen Group, David Porter, Tommy Tate, and Albert King each stirred the crowd during their twenty-minute sets of blues, gospel, and R & B hits. As the sun started to set over the west end of the stadium around 5:30 p.m., the Bar-Kays took the stage in their stunning white outfits with decorative gold chains draped down their chests. Like Isaac Hayes's famous gold-chain suit, which he donned later in the concert, the Bar-Kays' display of the gold chains revealed the attitude of black performers and black cultural nationalists toward slavery: Black people no longer felt the need to be imprisoned by the legacies of slavery. They could flaunt it in the form of decorative chains while affirming a longer history rooted in the pre-plantation African past.[51]

Saxophonist Harvey Henderson stepped to the microphone wearing a giant white afro wig, a gold collar, a midriff-exposing white vest, and silver bracelets on his biceps and told the crowd: "It's been said many times, in many places, that freedom is a road seldom traveled by the multitude. But we would like to invite each of you to go with us and perhaps you will see a side of life you've never seen before." As they broke into their popular tunes "Son of Shaft" and "Feel It," in their sparkling outfits, the Bar-Kays created an Afrofuturist aesthetic that invited the audience to enact a future of freedom not yet seen before.

As dusk settled on the Coliseum, the audience began to get restless. Then, Rufus Thomas, the "Prince of Dance" known for his hit dance tunes, took the stage in a hot-pink suit, shorts, cape, and white go-go boots and opened his set with "Breakdown." Members of the audience began to climb over the fences that had been erected to prevent them from entering the field, causing concern for the concert organizers. After finishing the tune, Thomas addressed the excited audience:

RT: "Hey, can you hear me out there?"
Audience: "Yes!"
RT: "Alright, I want everybody . . . don't want no one on the field . . . not yet!"

Crowd: (*laughing*)
RT: "Now, when I tell you to get on the field, *then* you get on the
      field! Then I might just get out on the field with ya!"
Audience: (*more laughing*)

The crowd was barely off the field when Thomas began his hit
song "The Funky Chicken." "Y'all come on in now," he called out to
the audience. "Come right on down front." Directly invited, audience
members did what they were commanded and rushed on the field as
the all-black security force looked on in bewilderment. Remarkably,
the crowd did not tear up the field. Thousands of women, men, and
children flapped their arms and did their version of the Funky Chicken
or whatever else they wanted to dance. Everyone at the Coliseum, it
seemed, disregarded normal stadium-spectating decorum and became
a Dancing Harry. By the time the song ended, the field was completely
filled with people.

In what could have been a tension-riddled moment, Thomas brilliantly asserted control over the crowd. He clearly understood that the
crowd needed to release its energy, and he managed to let them do so,
undoubtedly against the wishes of the concert organizers. Suddenly,
the field was transformed into a mega-sized *Soul Train*–like dance
floor. Indeed, some of the *Soul Train* dancers who popularized "lock-
ing," the early-seventies dance craze, including Don "Campbellock"
and Damita Jo Freeman, were flashing their moves in the stands while
Thomas performed.[52]

After the crowd got down to the Funky Chicken for just over four
minutes, Thomas again skillfully managed the audience: "Now wait a
minute! Wait a minute," he yelled. "We all together out here! We all
gonna have some fun, but you ain't supposed to have your fun on the
grounds. You supposed to be in the stands." After he asked the crowd
to return to their seats, he revised "Power to the People," a familiar
Black Power slogan, to ask not for rebellion but for conformity: "More
power to the folks, let's go to the stands," he repeated over and over.

"That's right. It might be a little slow, but you just got to go. How about it, brother? Power to the people, let's go to the stands! Power to the folks, let's go to the stands." As the majority of the crowd miraculously returned to their seats, Thomas then addressed a recalcitrant spectator who wasn't quite ready to depart the dance floor. After shame and embarrassment failed to get him off the field, Thomas then instructed spectators—not security—to get him off the field: "Just take him right on off and everything will be alright," Thomas insisted. Audience members then rushed on the field and ushered the man off, just as Thomas commanded. Although some members of the audience continued to stay on the field during the rest of Thomas's performance, eventually concert organizers contained them and the concert resumed. Wattstax concluded with a performance from the show's headliner Isaac Hayes just before the scheduled ten o'clock end time. The extraordinary day was a marked contrast from a number of other moments of crowd unruliness at concerts and sporting events during the 1970s.[53]

Perhaps more than any other moment during the concert, the interaction between Thomas and Wattstax spectators reveals the spirit of fun and pleasure that animated the entire event. At the Coliseum on that day, black Angelenos sent a message that they did not need the rough hands of law enforcement; they could organize their own affairs, including something as big as a gathering of tens of thousands to commemorate an important time in the community's history.

Wattstax was a memorial, a concert, and a political rally all at the same time. Black musicians and audience members remade the stadium into something more than a place to sit and spectate. The crowd at Wattstax created a sense of freedom by dressing to the nines and bringing their own slogans, their own cheers, and their own dances into the American stadium. Perhaps this is why Melvin Van Peebles, one of the emcees, characterized the concert as "the black way of commemorating" an uprising that had nearly destroyed the heart of the black Angeleno community seven years earlier.

IN THE WEEKS THAT FOLLOWED, THE VAST MAJORITY OF COMMENTA-
tors and reviewers who covered the event deemed the Wattstax concert a smashing success. Judy Spiegelman, writing for *Soul Magazine*,
the black LA publication, commended Stax artists and executives
"not just for a beautiful show, but for putting their concern and ded-
ication to the people on the line—and carrying through with it."[54]
Al Bell and the Watts Summer Festival organizers were thrilled with
the event and the positive publicity it produced. Stax Records even
received a commendation on the floor of the US Senate. California
senator Alan Cranston applauded "the Stax Organization and those
associated with them in this project. They are, indeed, inspirational
examples of good citizenship to all Americans of every race, creed,
and national origin." Months later, the Wolper–Stax film was also
widely acclaimed, though it was less of a hit at the box office.[55]

There were a few discordant notes in the chorus of praise in the
days after the concert. Lance Williams's review in the *Los Angeles
Times* described the concert as a "treasure trove of highs and lows—as
many of the latter, unfortunately, as the former." Williams praised the
Rufus Thomas band, but he criticized the lengthy delays between acts
and had few good things to note about Hayes's performance, which he
dismissed as having "all the elements of a colossal déjà vu." Another
more forceful criticism came from a spectator who lamented what she
saw as the misbehavior of the crowd at the concert: "I've just returned
from the Wattstax '72 Concert at the Los Angeles Coliseum and I must
say that I left sort of disappointed," she wrote in *Soul Magazine*, "not
because of the entertainers but because of the Black people. It's really
a shame that most Black people don't know how to act." The writer
hated to see the crowd dance on the field during the Rufus Thomas
performance. With a tinge of respectability politics infused into her
complaints, she wrote: "It's about time for us Black people to get ourselves together. The police had to take a Black sister away in handcuffs
because she wouldn't give up the seat she was sitting in to the people
who had really paid their dollar," the writer fumed. "A gang jumped

on a brother and they had to close down a snack stand. All of this ain't necessary," the writer continued. "Is this any way to act? No." These criticisms pale in comparison to the positive reactions and to the film release a few months later.[56]

Meanwhile, the Wattstax concert was one of several events cementing the fact that stadium concerts were here to stay. Stax was by no means the only record company to discover the publicity and profit potential of staging musical acts in stadiums and arenas. Black musical acts packed stadiums and arenas all over the United States. The Jacksons; Marvin Gaye; Earth, Wind, & Fire; B. B. King; and Aretha Franklin—in short, all big-name black artists—could be seen by fans from all backgrounds at these venues. Corporate sponsors also got in on the emerging stadium concert business. The impresario George Wein started the Kool Jazz Festival, which toured many celebrated jazz and R & B artists in stadiums and arenas into the 1980s. At the same time, white rock bands such as the Rolling Stones, The Who, Journey, and countless others made stadium rock a recurring feature of the music business. Stadium concerts enabled millions of fans to see their favorite performers live and in person, and they invariably played a key role in American community formation, even if the notoriously exploitative music industry designed such huge concerts to extract as much profit from musicians as possible. Although benefit concerts continued to be put on regularly, they seldom, if ever, achieved the explicit political messaging that Wattstax produced.[57]

THE WATTSTAX CONCERT WAS MUCH MORE THAN A GREAT SHOW. IT was a dramatic demonstration of the inroads African Americans made into American culture and society during the civil rights and Black Power era. The concert indicated not only that the era of formal and informal segregation was passing into history but also that stadiums were important theaters of placemaking, where marginalized people could transform spaces that had been built for other purposes. As for other concerts in this period, African Americans and marginalized groups were converting public spaces of exclusion into spaces of affirmation. Even in the face of economic dislocation and ongoing police repression, at Wattstax African American performers, workers, and spectators staked claims to urban space by asserting their presence on the field and in the stands of the Coliseum. In this, the heyday of Black is beautiful, what the performers, the organizers, and the spectators did at that memorable event was create a celebration of Black Nationhood.[58]

But the Black Nation that the concert organizers had envisioned never quite came to fruition. The Stax–Watts Summer Festival partnership turned out to be the high point of Black Nationalism and black entrepreneurship in Los Angeles—and perhaps in the country as a whole. Though Stax pledged continuing support for the festival, and it followed through the very next year, Al Bell and the company became embroiled in legal and financial troubles that eventually led to a declaration of bankruptcy in 1977. Still, the label's reputation and its impact on the history of American music had been secured. Meanwhile, the Watts Summer Festival chugged along, although it, too, saw a decline through the decade. One year after Wattstax, the festival drew an impressive seventy-five thousand spectators to its concert at the Coliseum, but only thirty-five hundred attended the concert in 1974.[59]

On the political front, however, Wattstax '72 was part of an upward trend for black Angelenos in the early 1970s. One year after the concert, Tom Bradley became the first African American mayor in the city's history. One of the crowning achievements of his twenty-year reign, as his administration saw it, was the 1984 Olympic Games, which were held at the Coliseum, an event hailed as the last financially successful Olympics. The Bradley era came to an ignominious end as the city was torn apart by the war on drugs and crime and the sledge-hammering effects of police violence that culminated in the infamous Rodney King beating in 1991 and the riots that exploded in South Los Angeles one year later.[60]

Nevertheless, in the moment of 1972, the magic the Wattstax concert created at the Los Angeles Coliseum seemed to indicate the battles of the Black Freedom struggle were being won. The freedom and enthusiasm that St. Clair Drake and Horace Cayton noted at ballparks in 1930s Chicago were evident at the Coliseum and at stadiums across the country throughout the 1970s and for years thereafter. In retrospect, Wattstax stands out as an almost unthinkable event: an unapologetic expression of black politics and black pleasure underwritten by corporate sponsors in a gigantic stadium and documented by a Hollywood film company. Dramatic as the concert was, it was but one of a number of unprecedented forms of politics and pleasure that occurred in American stadiums during these years, many of them in the interest of the Black Freedom struggle. Black America continued to challenge the forces of deindustrialization, discrimination, and police violence, but concerts like Wattstax and the placemaking activities of black fans in stadiums across the country signaled the changes that had occurred in American society since the collapse of Jim Crow. Even as these battles for Black Freedom were won, however, another longer legacy of racism persisted unabated.

CHAPTER FOUR

SETTLER STADIUM

On a bright Sunday afternoon, September 20, 1962, nearly forty thousand people descended on the new national monument in Washington, DC. They weren't converging on the Lincoln Memorial or the US Capitol. They were making their way to DC Stadium, later renamed Robert F. Kennedy Memorial Stadium, to watch the Washington Redskins, the city's pro football team, face off against the St. Louis Cardinals. The stadium, built the year before, was a government-controlled fifty-thousand-seat public facility that was the first of its kind: a circular, double-decked multipurpose structure specifically designed to stage both baseball and football games. The previous year, their first in the new facility, the Redskins finished with a pitiful record of one win, twelve losses, and one tie, the latest in a long string of losing seasons. However, early in the '62 season, the team's new star, flanker Bobby Mitchell, led the franchise to two surprising performances on the road, and fans turned out this Sunday to see whether the usually woeful team could continue its good fortune during its first home game in Washington. Fans walked, took the bus, or drove to the new facility at the foot of East Capitol Street on the banks of the Anacostia River.

Washington fans were not disappointed. Early in the game, quarterback Norm Snead dropped back to pass at the St. Louis forty-one-yard line. In football parlance, the play was a "play action pass," in which the quarterback pretends to hand the ball off to a running back to make the opposing defense react to a running play. He then pulls the ball back to give himself extra time to set up a passing play. The play action pass worked perfectly. As a Cardinal defender charged toward him, Snead lofted a pass toward the speedy Bobby Mitchell, who raced past Cardinal cornerback Pat Fischer, the defender fruitlessly trying to prevent him from catching the ball. Snead's pass looked overthrown, but Mitchell put on a final burst of speed at the five-yard line, caught the ball over his shoulder, and raced into the end zone for a touchdown. Fans rejoiced. The cheerleaders cheered, and the team's marching band blared its fight song as the home team took a 7–0 lead. Later in the first half, Mitchell caught another touchdown pass, and Washington eventually defeated St. Louis, 24 to 14.[1]

This 1962 home opener in DC Stadium was not only a rare Redskins win but also a sign of a new era in the nation's capital. Bobby Mitchell was the first African American star on the pro football team that had resisted desegregation the longest, the team owned by staunch segregationist George Preston Marshall. The franchise that had suffered through many losing seasons with an all-white roster now suddenly had a black player who was making exciting plays and leading the team to victories. Mitchell joined the team because Stewart Udall, the US secretary of the interior, stipulated that the Redskins could not play home games in a federally controlled stadium unless Marshall desegregated the roster. Soon more black players would don the team's burgundy and gold colors, and black fans would become more numerous at the team's new stadium. The team was seemingly overcoming its segregationist past, and the United States government played a decisive role in that process.

The Redskins were remaking their image in a new and modern facility. Yet the process was marred by another very old pattern of racism. As the team took the field, they were greeted by a detachment of white men in headdresses and burgundy and gold uniforms who played "Hail to the Redskins," the team's fight song. Alongside the band were the Redskinettes, a cadre of women in burgundy, white, and gold uniforms shaking pom-poms and sporting wigs of black braids with yellow feathers. The newly desegregated Redskins were cheered on by a group of white people engaging in the centuries-old practice of "playing Indian."[2] Even as the team was embarking on a new era of desegregation in a new facility, it remained steeped in the traditions of racist caricaturing of Native Americans. The franchise had been playing Indian since its inception in 1932, and it would continue to do so for sixty more years.

The history of the stadium in Washington, DC, is a story of a nation and a city wrestling with the legacies of both settler colonialism and slavery. After many losing seasons as an all-white outfit, the city's pro football franchise became an exemplar of racial integration from the 1960s until the mid-1990s. The team was enormously successful on the field, winning three Super Bowl championships while performing before a fiercely loyal and racially integrated fan base in one of the loudest stadiums in the country. The home field, affectionately dubbed "RFK," became one of the most beloved football venues in the country. And yet it was more than that. It was a federally managed venue that was renamed after Robert F. Kennedy, a slain national hero who exemplified midcentury liberalism. The stadium was a national monument.

RFK's heyday coincided with an unprecedented period of "home rule" in Washington, DC, when the federal district with no direct representation in the US Congress—the result of a peculiar governmental arrangement—was granted municipal control of local affairs. During the 1960s, African Americans became a demographic majority in DC, and as in other cities across the country, they gained representation in local government and politics. In subsequent years, as black political and cultural influence grew, the district became known as "Chocolate City."[3] At the same time, the city's favorite team perpetuated—and profited from—the odious traditions of Indian mascotry. The civil rights movement forced the government to address anti-black racism, and it convincingly advocated for a more expansive vision of democracy. It did not, however, provoke a concomitant interrogation of the deeper history of anti-Indian racism and its remnants in popular culture, such as Indian mascotry.

From the time the city's pro football franchise moved from Boston to Washington in 1937, the team's home stadiums—Griffith, Kennedy, and later FedEx Field—were places where Washingtonians created community. In Washington, as in other places where Americans have gathered to cheer on teams with Native names and mascots, this commonality was forged on the premise of settler colonialism and Native disappearance. Municipal unity, like national unity, was predicated on "settler memory," the caricaturing of Native Americans as a noble conquered people of the American past rather than a people who deserve rights and recognition in the American present.[4] The story of Washington's NFL franchise and the city's pro sports stadiums reveal the importance of settler memory to American sporting culture.

The franchise's unprecedented popularity during the three decades after desegregation was facilitated by the democratization of the American stadium. Even as the stadiums built in this period were envisioned as venues for the suburban automobile age, they turned out to be among the most democratically constituted congregation spaces in US history. More stadiums and arenas were built across the country to accommodate the growing popularity of the sport and entertainment industries. Fans of the Atlanta Braves, the Cleveland Indians, the Kansas City Chiefs, the Chicago Blackhawks, and the numerous college teams with Native names cheered on more diverse playing rosters among more diverse crowds in new stadiums. Americans from a wider variety of backgrounds could participate and spectate in unprecedented numbers in what was becoming an increasingly important community institution. Sometimes this meant that a wider array of people could perpetuate the forms of exclusion that persisted through this period.

Settler colonialism at the stadium in the nation's capital began long before the football franchise's home stadium became part of the city's monumental landscape, before its multiracial fan base assembled to tailgate in the parking lot. It originated during the reign of the team's founder and longtime owner, George Preston Marshall, when the franchise began play in another city over four hundred miles away.

THE LAND BENEATH RFK STADIUM, LIKE THE ENTIRE CITY NOW known as Washington, DC, was not originally owned by the US government. It was first inhabited by the Nacostine people and smaller groups of Algonquian-speaking peoples who lived along the banks of the Potomac and Anacostia Rivers. Nacotchtank, a trading center, was the largest of the indigenous settlements in the area. Within forty years of the arrival of English colonists in 1608, the Native population had rapidly declined, and within a century, the world of the local indigenous peoples of the region was gone, replaced by European settlements and tobacco plantations worked by enslaved Africans. Eventually, those plantations were overtaken by an urban society centered on the institutions of the federal government. The region that became known as Washington, DC, resulted from a compromise among Alexander Hamilton, James Madison, and Thomas Jefferson: the federal government would acquire centralized power over the nation's financial institutions in exchange for locating the nation's capital in the slaveholding South. President George Washington picked the location along the banks of the Potomac River.[5]

In the twentieth century, the nation's capital became a city of monuments to the establishment of the US federal government. The most well-known of these are located in the National Mall: memorials to Abraham Lincoln, George Washington, and, most recently, Martin Luther King Jr., among others. On the far eastern edge of the city, in line with the Mall, is RFK Stadium. Although the Mall is the most recognizable area of the city to visitors, few monuments had as much local significance as RFK Stadium. If the National Mall was constructed for visitors, RFK was a monument built for Washingtonians.

Before the construction of RFK Stadium, Washington's main sporting and entertainment venue was Griffith Stadium. The ballpark was named after Clark Griffith, the former Major League Baseball player, manager, and longtime owner of the Washington Senators baseball franchise. The "Old Fox," as he was affectionately called, was the most influential figure in the team's history from the time of his arrival in 1912 until his death in 1955. Griffith Stadium opened in 1911, during the era that baseball historians like to describe as the "golden age" of concrete and steel ballparks. Stadiums of this era, such as the Polo Grounds, Ebbets Field, Wrigley Field, Fenway Park, Comiskey Park, and Forbes Field, are often the subject of much romanticized commentary. While others were praised for their unique designs, Griffith Stadium was, in the words of historian Brad Snyder, "an architectural blight."[6] No ornate rotundas, no fancy facades were evident at Washington's version of the classic ballpark. Over time, the stadium evolved from a single-decked roofless facility to a stadium that resembled an Erector Set. As the years went by, the club added unevenly constructed doubled-decked grandstands and a single-deck concrete bleacher section beyond the left-field fence. The ballpark also had the smallest seating capacity in the American League (ranging from 27,000 to 32,000 seats), though organizers often found ways to accommodate more spectators for events when necessary. The stadium's small capacity was usually not a concern because the team's poor performance on the field meant that few fans turned out for Senators games. The 1904 quip of sportswriter and humorist Charles Dryden, "Washington—First in War. First in Peace. Last in the American League," stuck with the team for decades.[7]

Though aesthetically unremarkable, the ballpark had its unique features and charms. Like all the classic ballparks, the stadium was embedded in a densely populated neighborhood, LeDroit Park, a predominantly black middle-class district where the famous black U Street corridor was located. Because homeowners had refused to sell their land when the stadium was constructed, the center-field fence jutted in toward the infield at a sharp right angle so as to avoid the homes that stood beyond the fence. Just up the street was Howard University, known as the "capstone of Negro education" in that era.

A ballpark in a southern city meant that the facility was forced to adhere to the norms of Jim Crow. Nevertheless, Griffith Stadium was not as rigidly segregated as Tulane Stadium or other venues in the Deep South. Its location in the midst of a black neighborhood meant that black Washingtonians were very much a part of the ballpark's scene. Although discrimination characterized much of DC life, at the ballpark black and white Washingtonians congregated in separate and sometimes overlapping spheres. During Senators games, black fans tended to be relegated to the right-field stands, but they could sit anywhere they wanted during black sporting events. Moreover, Clark Griffith cultivated relationships with black leaders and black institutions, including Negro League baseball teams.[8] Indeed, Jim Crow professional baseball brought additional revenues to the Old Fox, and Griffith was willing to bend the color line by signing players from Cuba, who appeared racially ambiguous in US terms. For this reason, black fans of the team expected Griffith to eventually sign a black American player. Yet the owner refused to desegregate his playing roster until eight years after Jackie Robinson broke the color line. In 1955, the team drew upon its connections to Cuba when it made Carlos Paula, an Afro-Cuban ballplayer, the first black Washington Senator.

The little ballpark gained a national profile because it was a favorite stop for politicians. Griffith reserved seats for presidents, vice presidents, and other public officials at Senators games. His ballpark was the site of the annual ritual of the president throwing out the first pitch on Opening Day. Beginning with William Howard Taft in 1910 until Richard Nixon in 1969, every US president threw out the ceremonial first ball at the beginning of the Major League season. The regular appearance of the president of the United States at Washington's ballpark cemented baseball's reputation as America's national pastime. It also ensured that DC stadiums would become theaters of presidential statecraft—a way for each administration to use sport to reinforce its legitimacy in the eyes of the American public. This tradition would continue when the focus of sports in the district shifted to RFK Stadium on the east side of town.

In the beginning, Griffith Stadium was the center of the Washington sports scene, not only because it was a venue for DC's baseball teams, but also because it became the home field for the team that turned out to be the city's most popular and longest-running sports franchise: the Redskins. Although Griffith Stadium was designed for baseball, it was as much a football stadium as it was a baseball facility. Indeed, all the so-called classic baseball stadiums hosted many other kinds of events, including boxing matches and religious gatherings, to ensure a constant flow of spectators. Baseball fans were only one of a number of constituencies showing up at the old ballpark on Georgia and Florida Avenues.

Griffith struck gold when George Preston Marshall's football team arrived in Washington in 1937. Born in Mason County, West Virginia, in 1896, Marshall grew up in the capital and became a prominent Washingtonian after he took over Palace Laundries, his family's laundry business. Palace became the largest chain of cleaners in the region. After years of managing the business, Marshall decided to get into sports and founded an NFL franchise in Boston in 1932. The team, originally known as the Boston Braves, changed its name to the Redskins one year later to create a separate identity from the local National League baseball team, the Boston Braves. The team's names were squarely within an established tradition of sports teams adopting and caricaturing Native American names and culture.

Marshall's anti-black racism is well-documented, but his propagation of Native American mascotry is his most enduring legacy. The practice predated the creation of the team. Native nicknames and mascots have been part of American sporting culture since the 1880s. Numerous high schools, colleges, universities, and professional teams named their teams "Warriors," "Braves" "Indians," "Chiefs," and other names attributed to Native Americans. Many of these teams showcased white mascots costumed in Indian dress. These nicknames carried stereotypes of Indian warrior cultures that were easily transposed onto the culture of competitive sports. Over time, they were justified as honorific gestures toward the dignity and resistance of indigenous peoples to conquest and colonization. In fact, these nicknames perpetuated shallow racist renderings of Native culture. By the time Marshall started his franchise, Indian nicknames and mascots were widespread and seen as acceptable.[9]

Marshall's franchise became one of the most notorious teams engaging in Native mascotry. Like countless other Americans, he figured out a way to make money from playing Indian. In Boston, he had stiff competition from the city's two pro baseball outfits, the National League Braves and the American League Red Sox, as well as a host of college teams. After a season of paltry attendance figures, Marshall went all in on promoting his franchise as an "Indian" team. During the early twentieth century, on the national stage Native Americans had the reputation of being skilled football players. The extraordinary achievements of Jim Thorpe, a legendary athlete, and the football programs at boarding schools, such as the Carlisle Indian School in Pennsylvania, brought national attention to Native American athletes. Marshall sought to refashion his team into one that played "Indian football." He changed the team's name to "Redskins" after moving it to Fenway Park, the home field of the Boston Red Sox. It seems likely that "Redskins" was partly inspired by the name "Red Sox," the team that rented Fenway Park to Marshall's team.[10]

Marshall also hired well-known football coach William "Lone Star" Dietz, a man who spent his life posing as an Indian football player and coach for Carlisle and other teams. Decades later, team owner Daniel Snyder claimed that Marshall adopted "Redskins" as the team name to "honor" Dietz, his "Indian" coach. However, the claim does not stand up to historical investigation because there is no evidence that Dietz's employ inspired the owner to change the team's name. It is more likely that the decision to adopt the name was a marketing ploy. Marshall encouraged Dietz to recruit Native American players and have them apply war paint to their faces. Still, five years of playing

Indian in Boston failed to attract fans to Redskins games. After the 1936 season, the owner moved his team to his hometown.[11]

Marshall's franchise called tiny Griffith Stadium home for twenty-three seasons, and it retrofitted the ballpark to serve its own interests. The football gridiron was laid out across the baseball field, from the grandstand on the first-base side of the diamond to the left-field stands. Marshall then set up temporary bleachers in right field so that the seats could face the sideline. He also used the stadium as a prop for his Indian show. He installed tipis on the box atop the bleachers. Much to the delight of Marshall—and Griffith—the largest crowds at the old ballpark came to see football games, not the woebegone Senators.

Marshall was a showman who loved publicity. He saw a football contest as a spectacle, not merely a game. "The only reason Marshall wants the team is to be on a stage," former associate Harry Wismer told *Sports Illustrated* in 1961. "He used to tell me 'Don't worry if you don't win.'"[12] His flair for the dramatic was enhanced by his marriage to actress and silent film star Corinne Griffith, who also helped cultivate a show-business culture in the franchise during the years she was married to Marshall. "She—who is Mrs. George Preston Marshall—has brought subtle stagecraft to the forbidding reaches of the football stadia," writer Bob Considine claimed. "A Redskins game is something resembling a fast-moving revue, with cues, settings, music, pace, tableaux, and hold your hats boys—a ballet. But the amazing part of it all is that there's room left on the program for a football game."[13] The team's elaborate halftime shows showcased a variety of performances. Stages would be installed on the field where showgirls could perform. Every holiday season, Santa Claus would make an appearance in a sleigh or sometimes in a helicopter. The shows were often the main event, especially as the team's fortunes on the field declined during the 1950s.

Yet, Corinne Griffith's biggest, and most infamous, contribution to the team's performance culture was her writing of the lyrics to the team's fight song, "Hail to the Redskins." Soon after the franchise

Halftime show at Griffith Stadium, with faux tipis in the background, 1954.
Credit: National Archives

arrived in DC, bandleader Barnee Breeskin suggested that the team have a fight song. He supplied the music and the song's title. All that was needed was the lyrics, and Griffith obliged.

> *Hail to the Redskins.*
> *Hail Victory!*
> *Braves on the warpath*
> *Fight for old DC*
>
> *Scalp 'um, swamp 'um, we will*
> *Take 'um big score*
>
> *Read 'um, Weep 'um, touchdown,*
> *We want heap more.*
> *Fight on, fight on, till you have won,*

Sons of Wash-ing-ton
Rah! Rah! Rah!

Hail to the Redskins.
Hail Victory!
Braves on the warpath
Fight for old DC

The fight song quickly became a hit with the new team's fans. Breeskin and Griffith's song would be played and sung countless times at games and at many functions for the next eighty-five years. Yet the popularity of the song obscures its anti-Indian roots and its Hollywood-infused stereotypical depictions of Native peoples. Griffith's lyrics reveal the making of the "white man's Indian," portraying Indianness through the usage of broken English ("Take 'um big score / Read 'um, Weep 'um, touchdown / We want heap more") and the romanticized portrait of Native people as warriors ("Braves on the warpath").

The song's celebration of Native masculinity through warfare reduced indigenous people's life-and-death struggle against genocidal policies to the fate of a football team on the gridiron. It is reminiscent of the ways Sugar Bowlers in New Orleans reenacted Civil War battles. Performances of "Hail to the Redskins," like Native mascotry, appeared to bestow praise on the positive attributes of a conquered people who no longer existed; in fact, these attributes are conferred on dead Indians. In subsequent years, the team would try to sanitize the song by abandoning the broken English, but the lyrics' colonial roots and meanings would remain intact.

The fight song was in place, but who would perform it? "We had a team; we had a song; so we had to have a band," Corinne Griffith recalled years later.[14] A year after the franchise arrived in Washington, volunteers formed a 150-piece marching band, and Griffith designed their burgundy and gold uniforms. Marshall took a personal interest in the band, observing rehearsals and inserting himself into the planning of the playlist. Week after week for decades, "Hail to the Redskins" was played and sung after touchdowns and other positive developments on the field for the home team. The band entertained fans during pregame and halftime shows. It also accompanied the team on road trips, performing at the opposing teams' stadiums in distant cities. The Washington Redskins Band became the longest-running marching band in professional football. As the years went by, the band and the fight song became as recognizable as the gridiron players who donned the burgundy and gold.

This penchant for the spectacle put Marshall in line with southern football promoters who relished staging the rituals of the Lost Cause of the Confederacy on the gridiron. Redskins games resembled the pageantry of the Sugar Bowl, where white femininity and Southern identity were central to the show. Some of the same junior college drill teams that performed at the New Year's bowl game, such as the Apache Belles and the Dixie Darlings, performed at halftime shows in Washington. Marshall was a well-known segregationist, an unrepentant bigot who held onto his racist beliefs until the day he died. He was an opinionated, volatile, and arrogant man who didn't care what people thought. "We'll start signing Negroes when the Harlem Globetrotters start signing whites," he once crowed.[15] Still, he was not a racist who put the color line before the bottom line. His racism was infused with his desire to make money on Southern whiteness. How else can one explain his ability to turn an Upper South team from a moderately segregationist region into a segregationist team of the Deep South?

Though his wealth was based on his family's laundry business, he made more money with his football franchise. From a business standpoint, he was an innovator. He took full advantage of the fact that the Redskins were the southernmost NFL franchise until the league expanded into Dallas, Atlanta, and New Orleans in the 1960s. He was among the first to market his team on radio and television through a vast media network that extended throughout the South. He once (unsuccessfully) reached out to the Sugar Bowlers to stage a game for

his team in New Orleans.[16] The Redskins became Dixie's pro football team. "Dixie" was regularly performed at home games and was
included in the team's highlight films. By the 1950s, the franchise was
hosting "Days of Dixie" when the team would dedicate home games to
each southern state. As pressure increased for Marshall to integrate his
roster, he defiantly altered the lyrics to his team's fight song. The line
"Fight for Old DC" was changed to "Fight for Old Dixie."

Marshall's embrace of Native mascotry and Southern racism did
not detract from the team's budding popularity with the district's
sports fans. His decision to relocate his franchise to Washington
turned out to be a stroke of good fortune. From the team's very first
season, fans packed Griffith Stadium to see the team, its star quarterback Sammy Baugh, and Marshall's vaudeville-style halftime shows.
"Out there at Griffith Stadium yesterday there were 30,000 arguments
that professional football has caught the fancy of Washington," legendary sports columnist Shirley Povich noted toward the end of the
team's first season in DC.[17] The Redskins Band became a local institution, performing at games and at venues around town. Marshall's
team was overshadowing Griffith's Senators, who routinely finished
near the bottom of the American League on the field and in attendance after the team's last pennant-winning season in 1933. Meanwhile, Marshall's team was successful on the field, winning the NFL
championship in its very first season in Washington, and it remained a
championship contender through the World War II years. Even as the
Redskins slumped in the standings in subsequent seasons, the team
continued to be profitable. Marshall lined his pockets—not only with
revenues generated by ticket sales and corporate sponsorships, but also
with dollars produced by his vast radio and television network. The
franchise's popularity in DC gave the team leverage to advocate for a
new stadium as the old ballpark began to show its age in the 1950s.

EFFORTS TO BUILD A STADIUM IN THE NATION'S CAPITAL BEGAN IN THE
early twentieth century. Initially, the impetus came from those who

sought to join the international Olympic Movement. City boosters and federal politicians saw European capitals building national stadiums to house Olympic events, and they argued that DC should build its own national stadium. In the midst of the stadium-building boom of the 1920s, a campaign to build an Olympic-sized arena as a memorial to soldiers who died in World War I ensued. Plans were drawn up for a one-hundred-thousand-seat stadium in honor of the political legacy of Theodore Roosevelt that would house the Olympics, Army–Navy football games, presidential inaugurations, and other events. Various sites around the city were considered, but efforts were thwarted by a variety of factors, especially the fact that DC was governed by the federal government and had no elected representatives in Congress, as outlined in the US Constitution. Local policies were subject to the whims of federal legislators, who came from all over the country and had little incentive to care about district affairs. This unusual governmental structure made it difficult to raise funds and carry out a sustained campaign for a stadium. Efforts were also stalled by the fact that Griffith Stadium already existed, though most agreed that it was too small to accommodate national events.[18]

The factor that finally led to the construction of a stadium in the District of Columbia was the changing sports business in the post–World War II years. In the 1950s, as many in the United States emerged from the war with newfound prosperity and time for leisure, attendance figures for nearly all sports teams shot up. Professional sports franchises, especially Major League Baseball teams, prompted by the expansion of the country's population to the west, sought new markets for their teams. Team owners looked to capitalize on pro baseball's boost in popularity, and postwar economic growth propelled some teams to look for fans in other cities. The search for new markets fueled a desire for new stadiums, and the cultural capital accorded to "America's national pastime" enabled baseball team owners to command the stadium deals they desired. What they found in many parts of the country were politicians looking to attract professional teams to their city. Enticing a baseball team to your city carried an increasing amount of prestige during a decade when professional sports broadened in appeal. More often than not, politicians could summon the political capital and taxpayer money to publicly finance a new stadium. This set the modern stadium scene in motion. The age of the publicly financed midcentury stadium had arrived.[19]

Although teams in the fledgling world of pro football were accustomed to moving around the country, no Major League Baseball franchise had relocated since 1903. The Braves' move from Boston to Milwaukee in 1953, the Browns' move from St. Louis to Baltimore in 1954, the Athletics' move from Philadelphia to Kansas City one year later, and, of course, the move of the Dodgers to Los Angeles and the Giants to San Francisco in 1957 were seismic shifts in the sport industry. With the exception of the Dodgers, who built their own stadium (with a major assist from the local government), the Braves, Orioles, and Giants moved into new (or refurbished) publicly financed and managed stadiums. Indeed, the Braves were arguably the first team to perfect the stadium scenario when they moved to Milwaukee in 1953 and then moved again to Atlanta thirteen years later. Each move enabled the team to enjoy a new stadium built by taxpayers as well as lucrative radio and television broadcast contracts that yielded additional revenue. Marshall's Redskins and Griffith's Senators were testing the same waters when the idea of a new stadium in the district arose in the 1950s. Anxieties increased among Washington sports fans and officials when politicians in Los Angeles began to court the Senators.[20]

The threat of franchise relocation finally compelled Congress to build a new stadium in DC. In 1957, Congress passed the District of Columbia Stadium Act, which authorized the DC Armory Board to float $6 million in bonds to construct, maintain, and manage a stadium.[21] As would happen countless times over the next half century, stadium proponents underestimated the cost of stadium construction. What was initially promised as a $6 million structure in 1957 ballooned into a $24 million facility by the time it opened in 1962. Ironically, the new stadium did not keep the Senators in town. Calvin Griffith, Clark's informally adopted son who took over the franchise after the Old Fox's death, moved the team to Minneapolis. Faced with the wrath of Congress and the local baseball fan base, the American League quickly replaced Griffith's team with a new franchise in the nation's capital. The team began play at the old Griffith Stadium in 1961 and would move into the new stadium in 1962.

Yet, the football franchise that was set to move into brand-new DC Stadium was turning out to be a political problem for the team's new landlords. Newly inaugurated president John F. Kennedy could not overlook Marshall's well-known refusal to employ black players. In March 1961, President Kennedy signed Executive Order 10925, which established a Committee on Equal Opportunity, which, among other things, ensured nondiscrimination in government employment practices. The policy authorized his secretary of the interior Stewart Udall to target Marshall's franchise, which he described as "the last citadel of segregation of professional sports."[22]

Udall was confident that this policy would be "met with wide applause." He was right. In the fall of 1961, the NAACP and the Congress of Racial Equality (CORE) staged a campaign against Marshall's hiring practices at stadiums in Los Angeles, San Francisco, Cleveland, and Houston and at the team's first home game in the new stadium. Holding signs with messages such as REDSKINS ONLY HIRE WHITE SKINS and PEOPLE WHO CAN'T PLAY TOGETHER, CAN'T LIVE TOGETHER, antidiscrimination activists attacked Marshall's intransigent attitude toward integration. Meanwhile, the American Nazi Party staged a counterprotest outside DC Stadium at the same game, imploring Marshall to "Keep the Redskins White."[23] Although Marshall was initially recalcitrant in the face of Udall's pressure, he eventually relented by signing Ernie Davis, the Heisman Trophy–winning running back out of Syracuse. When Davis remained noncommittal about playing for Marshall, the team traded him to the Cleveland Browns for Bobby

Mitchell, the talented flanker back who became the team's first black star. Mitchell would have a long Hall of Fame career with the team as a player and an executive. He symbolized the franchise's new identity. So did the team's new home.[24]

WHEN WASHINGTONIANS FIRST ENCOUNTERED THEIR NEW STADIUM on East Capitol Street, they marveled at what they saw. Edwin Shrake, the *Sports Illustrated* writer, put it well when, in a 1965 feature story, he described the new stadium: "When you come down East Capitol Street from town early on a Sunday afternoon, passing through the eyeball gauntlet of kids on row-house porches, suddenly there is D.C. Stadium—gray marble and white steel and concrete in sweeping Bowditch curves, a thing that looks ready for flight, as if it is pausing briefly in a pasture before taking off again." Shrake's reference to flight highlighted the stadium's futuristic design. Other stadiums built during the 1960s adopted a similar aesthetic. The new facility made Griffith Stadium look like a junk pile. It was a bigger building with clean lines, a symmetrical design rather than the jagged edges and mismatched contours of the old stadium. Bob Considine, local sportswriter, described DC Stadium as a "graceful steel and concrete doughnut."[25]

The "concrete doughnut" label would stick. Envisioned as a facility that would accommodate both baseball and football, DC Stadium was one of the first "multipurpose stadiums" in the United States. The term has proved to be somewhat misleading because stadiums and arenas were multipurpose since the earliest days of American stadium construction. But it was true that architects were asked to design facilities that would appeal to baseball team owners and the increasingly powerful coterie of men who ruled professional football. Previously, pro football franchises had little choice but to play in facilities built for baseball. By the 1960s, as the popularity of football grew, team owners like Marshall had more influence on stadium design. The key design element that enabled the modern stadium to accommodate both sports was the orange slice–shaped tier of 6,400 movable seats on the field level, which made it possible to configure the field for football or base-ball. Movable stands became a standard feature of many stadiums built in the 1960s.

At the time, the new DC Stadium seemed worthy of high praise. It was a two-tiered circular structure with an undulating roof that provided cover and shade for 60 percent of the seats in the stadium. The sweeping curves of the roof produced a visual roller-coaster effect. Previously, multiple seating decks were held in place by pillars, an engineering necessity that unfortunately obstructed the view of many spectators. DC Stadium featured a cantilevered design that enabled two tiers of seating to be installed without the pillars that had annoyed fans for decades. Fans climbed to their seats in the upper deck without too much trouble using the gently inclined ramps that curved around the stadium. At Marshall's insistence, the stadium had twenty-one-inch-wide seats, wider than the then customary sixteen-inch seats. The stadium also provided state-of-the-art accommodations for players, the press, and the VIP crowd. At the mezzanine level, private boxes were installed for the Washington elite, including the president of the United States. Like its immediate predecessors—County Stadium in Milwaukee, Metropolitan Stadium in Minnesota, Candlestick Park in San Francisco—and many venues afterward, this stadium was built for the automobile age, surrounded by parking lots that accommodated almost twelve thousand cars.[26]

The architectural and engineering firms that worked on the stadium reflected the changing of the guard in stadium architecture. The DC Armory Board hired George L. Dahl as the stadium's architect while Ewin Engineering Associates and Osborn Engineering were the project's engineers. Coming into the 1960s, Osborn Engineering had been the leading stadium builder in the country, designing many stadiums, including Yankee Stadium, Notre Dame Stadium, and Cleveland's Municipal Stadium, among others. While Osborn's grandest structures were Yankee and Municipal Stadiums, the firm's style tended to be less opulent and more functional. Stadiums such as County Stadium in Milwaukee, Metropolitan Stadium in Minnesota, and Municipal Stadium in Kansas City exemplify the Osborn style of baseball ballpark: simple constructions marked by multiple tiers held up by pillars. Meanwhile, other firms such as Praeger, Kavanagh, and Waterbury began to make their mark by designing the futuristic structures of the sixties and seventies, most famously Dodger Stadium and Shea Stadium, and the renovated Yankee Stadium. Other firms would follow their lead in modernist design for the new stadiums and arenas built over the next two decades.[27]

President Kennedy cast a part for the new stadium in his national program of physical fitness. "It is my hope that this stadium will become an enduring symbol of the American belief in the importance of physical fitness and of the contributions which athletic competition can make to our way of life," the president wrote. Promoting athletics was the federal government's responsibility. "It is particularly fitting that the Stadium has been built on Federal land which is held by your Government in trust for the recreation and enjoyment of the people," Kennedy elaborated. "In the years ahead, it is incumbent on all of us to help assure that the major athletic, and other events which we shall witness here will bring pride and honor not only to our Nation's capital, but to all the people of our country."[28] From the White House's perspective, the new stadium was much more than a venue for Washington sports fans. It was a structure, like the city's other monuments, that would honor the nation as a whole.

Of course, Marshall was eager to make the new stadium a prop for his re-creation of Native American caricatures. Although declining health during the 1960s forced him to relinquish management of the team, the anti-Indian performance culture he created remained very much alive. One game program from 1962 features a gigantic tipi on top of DC Stadium, showing how the old stereotype of Native American dwellings was modernized to conform to the new stadium. Though Marshall was unable to set up an elaborate village of tipis as he had at Griffith Stadium, the team did install a fake totem pole behind one of the end zones. The longtime Indian-head logo was painted on the grass field. Eventually, "Redskins" in bold burgundy letters was painted into the end zones. The Redskin Marching Band was prominently placed in field-level seats behind the visiting team's bench. Eventually, the band would have its own section behind the end zone on the east side of the stadium. The band, the annual arrival of Santa Claus, and other forms of entertainment from the Griffith Stadium days were transferred to the new stadium. Moreover, "Dixie" was still performed at team functions, and it remained in team highlight films as late as 1965.

WITH THE NEW STADIUM CAME A NEW ELEMENT TO THE TEAM'S PER-formance culture. In 1961, the team introduced the "Redskinettes," cheerleaders who would become a prominent part of the team's sideline entertainment. "They are high-stepping, foot-stomping look-alikes who, each home game, appear on the field to strut its length even before the band emerges," reported the *Washington Post* in September 1969. Approximately forty women in their twenties and thirties dressed as "Indian maidens" in burgundy, gold, and white short dresses and ankle-high white go-go boots with burgundy fringe shook pom-poms and twirled batons on the sideline. They were Pocahontas impersonators, with feathers attached to their braided wigs. This all-volunteer group—uncompensated cheerleading labor has a long history—became a key part of the entertainment at the stadium. Like other cheerleading squads, they were forbidden to fraternize with players, and their behavior was carefully scrutinized. When touchdowns were scored, they waited for the band to play "Hail to the Redskins" before embarking on their arm-waving, high-kicking "touchdown routine." They were also all white until local black organizations began to agitate for the inclusion of black women on the squad. Laverne Johnson became the first black cheerleader in 1968.[29]

By the time of Marshall's death in 1969, his reputation as a staunch segregationist was fading in favor of a narrative that emphasized his contributions to pro football. Edward Bennett Williams, the new majority owner of the team, nonsensically told *Sports Illustrated* in 1965 that he didn't think "Marshall was actually racially prejudiced." Rather, "he had become obdurate because people kept pushing him on the question. It wasn't his Southern TV network either. He simply had a block on the subject, a suicidal block."[30] Two years before Marshall's death, the team's alumni and friends erected a monument to him in front of the stadium. One side of the burgundy rectangular granite memorial proclaimed Marshall as "Founder of the Washington Redskins, Pioneer of the National Football League." On the other side was, of course, the Indian-head logo, with the inscription "Washington Redskins Organized in the Nation's Capitol [*sic*] 1937." DC's stadium had been envisaged as a monument, and the Marshall memorial etched the team's racist legacy in stone.

It is easy to tell the beginning and the end of the story of the Washington pro football team's racism with George Preston Marshall at its helm. It is much harder to explain the persistence of racism when it is perpetuated by historical actors who disavowed racism or by those who were themselves victimized by racial oppression. Indeed, the Washington team's popularity grew in the decades after the original owner's death. Marshall fading from the scene reflected the changing environment at Redskins games at RFK Stadium. Though the stadium was designed for baseball and football, it ultimately became a football stadium, especially after the sorry Senators once again left town and unceremoniously moved to Arlington, Texas, in 1972, after ten years of losing baseball.[31] Beginning in the 1960s, pro football games at the new ballpark were even more of a happening than when the team played at Griffith Stadium. Journalists liked to highlight sightings of presidents, members of Congress, and Supreme Court justices in Edward Bennett Williams's box; careful observers noticed how crowds were drawn from a cross section of the city. "They may come by limousine from Maryland or Virginia or Spring Valley, by taxis from the hotels, by foot or bus from the poorer sections, but they come," Edwin Shrake wrote in *Sports Illustrated* in 1965. "They come partly to see the Washington Redskins and partly to be seen seeing them."[32] While the team was developing a cross-class, cross-racial constituency, football became an especially favored pastime of the Washington political elite: "The result is that up in the owners' boxes—each of which has 23 seats priced at $7.50 and sold only to owners and their friends—the view is a good one: an excellent stadium with every chair being sat on, and the Redskinettes in their black wigs with yellow feathers and braided pigtails and the bandleader perched atop a huge tom-tom while the musicians blast away at *Hail to the Redskins!* for the delight of gentlemen in neckties and ladies in mink. A Redskin game is a social event, and that is a lucky thing."

What transpired at RFK Stadium happened at stadiums and arenas across the country. Starting with the Los Angeles Sports Arena in 1959 and continuing to the end of the decade with the opening of the new Madison Square Garden in 1968, futuristic buildings designed to cater to the public's growing interest in basketball, hockey, and rock concerts appeared in various cities and suburbs. The vast majority of arenas and stadiums built in the 1960s were publicly controlled structures that were compelled to cater to a wider constituency than followers of baseball, the fan base of which was declining as other sports and forms of entertainment grew increasingly popular. These buildings were also governed by public entities, such as the DC Armory Board, which, however corrupt, were compelled to fill seats for a wide variety of events. Baseball purists criticized the "concrete doughnuts" of the 1960s on aesthetic grounds, but the buildings that popped up in Washington, New York, Philadelphia, Pittsburgh, San Diego, Atlanta, and Houston drew crowds from across society, even as they were meant to draw customers from the car-driving suburban populations. As Daniel Rosensweig perceptively noted, the so-called multipurpose suburban ballpark of the sixties and seventies was more inclusive than the stadiums that were built in downtown areas after the nineties: "Cheap tickets, wide public concourses, and a lack of segregated seating enabled an unprecedented degree of fan diversity and mixing."[33]

From the mid-1960s until the team left the stadium in 1996, Redskins tickets were among the hottest items in town. The franchise that underachieved on the field throughout much of the Marshall era transformed into one of the best teams in the league. During the 1970s, under mercurial head coach George Allen, the team was a playoff contender with a fully integrated roster of popular white and black players. In the 1980s, the team's glorious period under Coach Joe Gibbs, the franchise enjoyed its most successful run by fielding multiple playoff teams and winning three Super Bowl championships. One of those championship teams was led by Doug Williams, the first black quarterback to win a Super Bowl in 1988. By the late 1980s, the team that was once a bastion of segregationist anti-black and anti-Indian racism was now seen as a paragon of racial progress.[34]

Over time, the new stadium took on the reputation of a gritty, functional building that was home to the league's most rabid fan base. Starting in 1967, Redskins games were sellouts and would be for fifty years, until 2018. Every fall and winter weekend, fifty-five thousand fans, many dressed in "Indian" costumes, packed the stadium and implored their team to "scalp" their opponents, especially their hated rival, the Dallas Cowboys, one of the league's most successful franchises that marketed itself as "America's Team." Cowboys games were occasions when myths of the American West were deployed to describe the battles on the field. Games were pseudo-reenactments of the Indian Wars of the nineteenth century, except that the team from the US capital was dressed up as the Native Americans.

A Redskins "super fan" debuted at one of those Cowboys games during the integration era. On October 2, 1978, Zema Williams attended a Cowboys–Redskins contest at RFK dressed in his interpretation of Indian attire. He saw the possibilities of being a crowd entertainer. A phenomenon began once the television cameras discovered him in the stands. Williams would attend virtually every home game—and many away games—for the next thirty-eight seasons before his death in 2016. With a fake headdress and a toy tomahawk, he developed the persona of "Chief Zee" and dressed in burgundy and gold from head to toe. He became a local legend and the unofficial mascot of the team. He also befriended Wilford "Crazy Ray" Jones, a black fan of the rival Cowboys who fashioned himself as the unofficial mascot of his team. The ironies of black men as mascots of teams that restaged the colonial battles of the Old West at football games was lost on the vast majority of fans during these years. It was only toward the end of Williams's life, as criticisms of the Washington team's nickname became more pronounced, that more commentators and critics pointed out the cruel ironies of his persona. As Native studies scholar Richard King has astutely observed: "In effect, one of the entitlements of citizenship granted to African Americans by the civil rights movement was the capacity to take and remake Indianness, to reimagine themselves

A cross-racial crowd at RFK Stadium, 1978.
Credit: DC Public Library, The People's Archive

as part of something bigger by owning Indians." By participating in the long-standing tradition of playing Indian, black fans assumed the right to caricature Native Americans, as white people had done for centuries.[35] This practice of anti-Indian racism, however, would not go uncontested.

A SMALL BUT VOCAL GROUP OF APPROXIMATELY FIVE HUNDRED Native Americans from different nations across the country converged on Washington, DC, one week before Election Day in 1972. The gathering was months in the making. They came to present their case before the US Congress and the president of the United States. The demonstration, which became known as the Trail of Broken Treaties, was a protest against the ongoing abuses and mistreatment of the United States' indigenous people. Protesters arrived with a list of twenty demands that ranged from redress for treaty violations to the abolition of the Bureau of Indian Affairs and creation of a more effective administration, the restoration of stolen lands, and petitions for religious freedom and cultural integrity. Staging this dramatic protest in the nation's capital would help galvanize the emerging American Indian Movement (AIM). The protesters occupied the Bureau of Indian Affairs building for five days before winning some concessions from the US government. The Trail of Broken Treaties did not achieve all its goals, but it did revitalize the American Indian Movement.[36]

The movement aimed to attack the many cultural manifestations of anti-Indian racism, including the practice of using Native nicknames and mascots. Earlier that year, Russell Means, one of the movement's leaders, had filed a lawsuit against the Cleveland Indians baseball team. He sued the franchise for its continual use of its racist symbol Chief Wahoo, a caricatured smiling red-faced Indian. Means charged that the symbol was "libelous, slanderous, and clear defamation of the American Indian." Speaking directly to those who ignored the harm of Indian mascotry, he equated the Indian stereotypes with the forms of racism that were seen as unacceptable by the public. He articulated an argument that would be made over and over again for the next several decades: "What if the Atlanta Braves were called the Atlanta Germans and after every home run a German dressed in military uniform began hitting a Jew over the head with a baseball bat? What would German Americans and Jewish people have to say about that?"[37]

The movement against team mascots and logos achieved some successes. In the early seventies, several college, high school, and other amateur teams abandoned Indian names and logos. Activists then targeted intransigent professional teams, including the professional football team in the nation's capital. Weeks after Russell Means filed his lawsuit, Native American activists paid a visit to the office of Edward Bennett Williams, Redskins' majority owner, to convince him to change the team's name. Among those visitors was LaDonna Harris, Native American advocate, and her husband, Fred Harris, the Democratic US senator from Oklahoma, both active in the US government's programs to address Native concerns. The group requested that the team revise its rituals, including the Redskinettes' practice of wearing "Indian" wigs. They also forcefully argued for the revision of the lyrics of "Hail to the Redskins," especially the phrases: "Hail to the Redskins, Hail victory! / Braves on the warpath / Fight for Old DC / Scalp 'um, swamp 'um. We will take 'um big score / Read 'um / Weep 'um / touchdown / We want heap more." Harold Gross, an attendee at the meeting, said in disgust: "I don't know any Indians who talk that way."[38] Afterward, Williams said little, claiming that the meeting was a "listening session," but he did promise to take these concerns to the team's board.

A few months later, Williams issued the team's response. He promised to alter the lyrics of "Hail to the Redskins." The offending words were eventually changed to "Run or pass and score—We want a lot more! / Beat 'em, swamp 'em, touchdown!—Let the points soar!" The Redskinettes discarded their Indian Maiden look and instead adopted the emerging sexualized fashions of NFL cheerleaders popularized by the Dallas Cowboys Cheerleaders. The wigs were tossed and the short dresses were replaced with tight-fitting burgundy and gold bodysuits with higher-heeled white go-go boots. Williams, resting on his liberal credentials, believed these changes were satisfactory. "I have spent my life believing in the absolute, total equality of people," he told the press. "I don't close my mind when somebody tells me I'm doing something offensive." He then went on to make yet another oft-articulated defense of Native nicknames: "If there was anything involved but the glorification of the American Indian, we would change our nickname," the team owner contended. Native activist Laura Wittstock vehemently disagreed. "Any commercial use of a race of people can't be glorification," she insisted.[39] Wittstock and her fellow Native activists lost the battle against Edward Bennett Williams in the early 1970s, but they continued to press on the issue of Indian nicknames and mascots for decades to come.

Not all Native Americans felt that team logos and mascots were damaging. One year before activists visited Williams, Walter "Blackie" Wetzel, a Native American leader and member of the Blackfeet Nation, approached the team to redesign the team's helmet. He successfully convinced them to adopt a logo with an image of what he saw as a dignified Native American warrior. The logo resembled the image of an Indian warrior the team had used in other marketing materials for years, which had been modeled on the Indian head on the Buffalo nickel in wide circulation earlier in the century. Wetzel was one of a number of Native Americans who felt that the logos and mascots were not offensive. Another was Levi Walker Jr., a Chippewa/Ottawa Native who played the role of Chief Noc-A-Homa, the mascot of the Atlanta Braves. Walker answered critics of his mascotry by identifying himself as "a serious citizen interested in civic affairs and bettering the plight of my own race. I never wanted to be a paleface. Call me a redskin. I like it. It is a compliment."[40] Such arguments were music to the ears of team officials, who used Native acceptance as justification for their degrading cultural practices.

In subsequent years, the Washington franchise remained obstinate in the face of growing criticism of Native mascotry, but eventually some Washington supporters began to question the allegiance to the team's odious tradition. At a pep rally for the Washington pro football team at Union Station in January 2000, journalist Courtland Milloy was unnerved by the scene he witnessed: "One of the things I've always liked about having a winning football team is how it brings our community together," he wrote. "We could all root—black, white, whatever—for our side. Nothing like a common enemy—say, the Dallas Cowboys—to make us forget our differences. But even this relatively harmless bit of fantasy is no longer possible for me, not after seeing how hurtful the pep rally at Union Station was for [Suzan] Harjo." Milloy's reflection came as he watched Zema "Chief Zee" Williams obliviously asking Harjo if she was having a good time at the rally as the Redskins Band blared a "Hollywood version of Indians-on-the-warpath music." Harjo, a Native American activist, grimaced and later characterized Williams as a "black man [who] gets paid to put on an Indian outfit and tap-dance for the white man."[41] Milloy's article reveals the ways even longtime football fans began to see the cruelty of a community coming together around a phenomenon that celebrated the degradation of Native peoples. Native activism was finally moving the needle on the question of Indian mascots and logos.

Suzan Harjo was one of many Native activists who worked to change public opinion on the question of Native mascots in the 1990s and beyond. Activists used the occasion of the Christopher Columbus Quincentennial in 1992 to bring greater attention to the legacies of the conquest and colonization of the Americas and the continuing struggles of indigenous peoples. Native Americans were not noble "braves" of the American past, they forcefully contended. They were "still here," still part of contemporary US American society. Harjo, the Cheyenne/Muscogee writer and activist and longtime resident of Washington, DC, was one of the key persons in that struggle. She made the nickname and mascot issue a priority after she was traumatized while attending a Washington game at RFK in 1974. However, it wasn't until the early 1990s that the movement gained traction. In 1992, Harjo was part of a group that attacked the team name through US trademark law. Activists filed a lawsuit to cancel the federal trademarks for the Washington Redskins on the grounds that they are "disparaging" to

Native Americans. She initially won her case, but an appeal overruled the decision on a technicality. Years later, she helped inspire another lawsuit, *Blackhorse v. Pro Football, Inc.*, which turned out to be successful. As she noted in an interview in 2012: "In 1970, there were more than three thousand of these Native references in American Sports. Today there are only nine hundred. We've eliminated two-thirds of these offenses and that's a societal sea change."[42]

Another pivotal moment in the movement's history was the protest staged at the 1992 Super Bowl in Minneapolis. Native American activists used the occasion of the Redskins' appearance in the Super Bowl to heighten awareness of the ongoing nickname issue. The game's location in Minneapolis, a historically significant city for Native activism, gave the protest added importance. Protesters gathered outside the Metrodome and occasionally confronted fans who wore team regalia. Tellingly, the American Indian Movement activists were joined by the NAACP, the Urban Coalition, and the National Organization for Women, showing how Native American issues were being taken up by other activist organizations in the 1990s. The protest took advantage of the media coverage of Super Bowl week to make their voices heard. "We say to [Redskins team owner] Jack Kent Cooke," AIM leader Vernon Bellecourt declared, "this is 1992. The name of your football team has got to be changed." One of the placards held by demonstrators read: SHOOK OUR HANDS/TOOK OUR LANDS. FOR THE GAMES/TOOK OUR NAMES. WHAT'S NEXT?[43] The demonstration did not faze the franchise but was a testament to the movement's effectiveness in highlighting the issue's ongoing importance to indigenous communities. Though more small victories were forthcoming, it would be another three decades before the odious logo and nickname practice would come to an end.

ON DECEMBER 22, 1996, 56,454 FANS GATHERED TO SEE THEIR FOOT-ball team play at RFK Stadium for the last time. The stadium, state-of-the-art in 1961, was now too small and basic for the new age of mega football stadiums. A new stadium in suburban Maryland was ready to house DC's beloved football outfit the following season. The team sent RFK off with a 37 to 10 victory over the archrival Cowboys. Fans cried, cheered, stomped, and shook the building as they had done for thirty-five years. The colonial legacy was ever present. One fan hawked commemorative doormats that read: REDSKINS LAST STAND. After the game ended, fans streamed on the field and grabbed pieces of turf as souvenirs while the Redskins Band played the fight song and "Auld Lang Syne." Television broadcasters Pat Summerall and John Madden waxed poetic about the stadium. Summerall, who visited RFK countless times as a player and as a broadcaster, articulated the feelings of many in the television audience: "When you walked in here, you just got sort of a damp feeling, when you walked through the dugout out on the field, when you walked up in our booth, you had that feeling of intimacy, you were close to the fans. . . . There's no place like it. All of the new stadiums they can build are going to be a thing that is necessary, but you're never going to get the feeling that you had here."[44]

RFK's swan song as a pro football stadium illustrated the coming end of the midcentury multipurpose stadium. Going forward, pro football and baseball franchises would command their own increasingly costly facilities. The deep attachments to the midcentury stadium exemplified how these facilities, often derided for their supposed unappealing aesthetics, fostered connection and community formation. In Washington, DC, too often the community and connection were based on the disappearance of the nation's original inhabitants.

The story of the Washington, DC, stadium is about much more than the persistence of the franchise's racist rituals created by George Preston Marshall. It reveals how social exclusion can occur in a community that imagines itself as inclusive. Communities perpetuated settler colonialism and other exclusionary ideologies even as they engaged in a seemingly innocuous activity, such as spectating at a football game. Stadiums like RFK functioned like other sacred spaces, such as churches, synagogues, temples, and mosques, where communities have been forged. At the stadium, crowds congregated and engaged in collective rituals week after week, year after year. The routines of commuting to games, tailgating in parking lots, sitting in the stands with fellow fans, donning the home team's colors, and cheering them on were powerful experiences of commonality. At RFK Stadium, these rituals were particularly impactful not only because of the intimacy of the venue and the cross-racial character of the Washington fan base but also because they were sanctioned by the federal government.

This history of exclusionary inclusion continued after the team moved to a new stadium in suburban Landover, Maryland, in 1997. In the decades since, the franchise has gotten a lot of mileage out of its past glory years of the 1970s and 1980s. The team floundered on the field and in the public eye during the tenure of the infamous owner Daniel Snyder (1999–2023). Meanwhile, the stadium in Landover turned out to be a generic football facility that boasted more seats and luxury suites for Washington's VIP crowd but not much else.

In Washington and in many other parts of the country, the colonial legacy of Indian mascotry continued unabated as would other forms of exclusion—and the struggles against them. In the civil rights era, African Americans and other non-Native racially marginalized groups were incorporated into sports fan communities. Nevertheless, at stadiums and arenas, racial inclusion did not lead to an interrogation of other hierarchies that were equally pernicious. As the struggles for equal access to stadiums unfolded during the 1970s, other groups, particularly women, would break barriers in their confrontation of equally rigid patterns of subordination.

CHAPTER FIVE

THE INNER SANCTUMS

On the night of October 18, 1977, the home team's locker room at Yankee Stadium was mobbed with reporters and well-wishers celebrating the New York Yankees' twenty-first championship. The legendary franchise that had won far and away the most World Series titles in baseball history had been slumbering in mediocrity for the previous thirteen seasons. A championship was long overdue, and the man who helped bring the title home was Reggie Jackson, the team's controversial star outfielder. Reporters from the local and national media came with their tape recorders, notepads, microphones, and cameras, eager to interview Jackson after he hit three dramatic home runs that led the Yankees to this championship-clinching win over the Los Angeles Dodgers, 8–4.

ABC Sports, which broadcasted the game on national television, sent Bill White into the locker room to interview the champions. White, a former All-Star player himself, had become the first black broadcaster for a Major League team when he was hired by the Yankees in 1971. On that memorable night in the locker room, an unacknowledged moment of racial progress occurred as the country watched White interview Jackson: two black men occupied center stage of America's national pastime while a throng of athletes and journalists surrounded them. In the crowded clubhouse, Jackson told the world how he did it and how grateful he was to all his supporters. The locker room, like the rest of Yankee Stadium, had just undergone a $100 million renovation, all of which was paid for by the City of New York. But such unpleasant thoughts were long forgotten as the team and the city celebrated their long-awaited championship.

As the hooting and hollering and the champagne pouring and guzzling transpired in the Yankees' dressing room, a young journalist waited outside the locker room, hoping to obtain quotes from Jackson and other star players. Melissa Ludtke, unlike the men sportswriters and broadcasters who'd covered the game that night, could not enter the locker room because Bowie Kuhn, the commissioner of Major League Baseball, had barred her and all women journalists from entering team clubhouses during the World Series. Ludtke never did get a chance to interview Jackson or any other Yankees that night because, when the hero finally emerged from the clubhouse, on his way to the next round of celebrations, he was too tired to be interviewed. She left the stadium with no real chance to cover the game thoroughly as her many male peers with access to the Yankee clubhouse were able to do.[1]

Melissa Ludtke was one of a growing number of women working at stadiums and arenas in a newfound role as sports journalists in the 1970s. A few of them were beat writers covering teams; others, like Ludtke, were stuck in secondary roles as fact-checkers for seasoned male colleagues. Still, the twenty-six-year-old researcher-writer for *Sports Illustrated* was thrilled at the opportunity to cover the New York Yankees and other Major League Baseball clubs. At that time, covering a Major League Baseball franchise was a prized gig in the world of sports journalism. "The times that I spent up at the ballpark when I first got the baseball beat," she recalled years later, "and I would just literally be on that D train up to Yankee Stadium and I would just be so excited that I could be there."[2]

THE EXPERIENCE THAT NIGHT OUTSIDE THE YANKEES' LOCKER ROOM epitomized the frustrations she endured as a young woman trying to make it in the male-dominated world of sports journalism. Though she considered herself lucky to have the position, she often was the only woman at the ballpark, subject to cold shoulders and insults from players and fellow sportswriters. When the World Series had begun a week earlier, she had been excited to have the chance to cover the sport's showcase event. Before the first game of the series, she received a press pass that granted her access to the locker room. However, as she sat and watched the first game, she was summoned to the press box and abruptly told by representatives of the commissioner's office that she could not enter the locker room after all. For the remainder of the series, she watched as her male colleagues disappeared into the locker rooms and emerged with stories she was not privy to. Months later, she and her bosses at Time Life filed a historic lawsuit that would change the course of sports journalism history.

Since its earliest incarnations, the social world of the stadium has always been predicated on varying forms of gender exclusion and segregation. Though these venues were envisaged as places of leisure for elite and eventually working-class men, the constant need to expand the customer base ensured that women would find a place in stadiums and arenas across the country. As the century unfolded, women joined the crowds of spectators. Still, women's places at the stadium remained circumscribed. In outdoor facilities, if they weren't spectating, they were usually relegated to the role of sideline performers, such as cheerleaders or musicians, while men competed on the field. Indeed, the Jim Crow stadium made the projection of white femininity at pregame and halftime shows central to the perpetuation of Southern white male domination. Indoor arenas were a less stringent environment given that they housed events such as the circus, ice skating, and other forms of entertainment with significant numbers of women performers.[3]

But, in the 1970s, the gendered world of the American stadium was upended. Spurred by the second-wave feminist movement, women fought fiercely to create new places for themselves in the sports world after decades of subordination. Once again, the stadium became a place of social and political protest as it emerged as a key battleground for gender equity. The passage of Title IX of the Education Amendments Act (1972) profoundly changed the gender composition of American sports. The law outlawed sex discrimination in any educational institution that received federal funding, but it had the unintended effect of creating the legal framework on which women's participation in high school and college sports could grow. The arrival of the first women's professional tennis tour, spearheaded by a cadre of athlete activists, including Billie Jean King and Rosie Casals, bolstered the argument that there was a market for women's professional sports. Various women's pro sports leagues came and went in subsequent years, but the growth of women's sports at the college level, even with persistent male resistance, revolutionized American sporting culture. Women were entering stadiums and arenas as athletes in unprecedented numbers.[4]

But there were two areas of the sports world where male resistance remained particularly pronounced: the press box and the locker room, which were seen as exclusively male dominions. During the Jim Crow era, a racial system of separate but equal was intertwined with an equally pernicious system of gendered geography in the American stadium. After integration began in the late 1940s, black men and other nonwhite men were allowed to compete with white men on the field, and some were eventually allowed to consort and work with white men in the press box and the locker room. Yet women, irrespective of their racial background, remained confined to the roles of sideline entertainer and spectator while only grudgingly being granted space on the field of play. A gendered geography of the stadium persisted even as racial barriers collapsed under the weight of the civil rights movement. Racial and ethnic inclusion was predicated on the continuation of gender exclusion. In the 1970s, the terrain of struggle shifted from outside the walls of the stadium to its inner sanctums. As Melissa Ludtke remarked on the stubborn resistance of men to the rise of women sportswriters: "It was about our invasion into the whole world of sports. And the locker room, I guess, this is where they decided to take their final stand." Indeed, the press box and the locker room turned out to be the nerve centers of the sexist world of the stadium.⁵

THE RELATIONSHIP BETWEEN THE PRESS AND THE STADIUM HAS always been complicated, marked by both interdependence and divergent interests. Most early baseball stadium builders did little to take the press into account when they designed their stadiums. Seats for fans were the primary concern of stadium designers. Originally, members of the press were seated in open-air sections among the fans. When radio arrived on the scene in the 1930s—and later television in the postwar era—most team owners were leery of the press because they feared it would subtract from the profits generated by gate receipts: If fans could listen or watch the game at home, why should they come out to the ballpark? Team owners such as George Preston Marshall were among the first to understand the revenue potential of selling broadcast rights to radio and television networks. Once his fellow laggard team executives saw that radio and television did not have a negative effect on attendance, stadium builders accommodated the press accordingly. Indeed, they found that radio and television only enhanced the anticipation for spectacle and excitement at the stadium.

During the 1920s era of stadium construction, it was the college football stadium that first gave the press box a prominent place in stadium design. Universities sought to capitalize on the popularity of the game by creating spaces for the press to do what it did best: provide the public with tales of the outstanding exploits of athletes on the field. Bowl-game committees were quick to see the light on the power of the newspapermen and broadcast journalists. Following in the footsteps of their counterparts on the Tournament of Roses Committee in Pasadena, the Sugar Bowlers in New Orleans made sure the media could publicize their bowl game. Tulane Stadium's single-tiered press box grew larger and larger with each renovation.

Bowl-game committees weren't the only constituencies in the college football world that saw the benefits of sport media coverage.

Universities themselves became enchanted with the idea of building permanent concrete and steel structures to promote their institutions on the national stage. What better way to do that than by creating spaces for the newspapermen and broadcast journalists to promote schools to national and international audiences? The university stadium craze was particularly impactful in the Midwest as universities in Ohio, Minnesota, Illinois, Michigan, and Indiana all plunged ahead to build stadiums on their campuses.[6]

Michigan Stadium, the facility that became known as the "Big House" decades later, was particularly influential. The University of Michigan built the massive seventy-thousand-seat facility in 1927. Soon after, in 1930, the University of Notre Dame, home of the most popular college program in the country, built its facility modeled on Michigan's. Notre Dame Stadium was among the first to clearly set aside structures to accommodate the press. The entrepreneurial Knute Rockne, the team's legendary football coach, spearheaded the drive for a stadium that could properly showcase his team. The extraordinary popularity of the team and its legendary "Four Horsemen" backfield gave Rockne and the football program enormous leverage to push for a campus stadium. Notre Dame hired Osborn Engineering, the same architectural firm that designed the stadium in Ann Arbor and other stadiums throughout the country. Both facilities would have brick exteriors, and both would have prominently placed press boxes that accommodated the increasingly important media industry.[7]

Press boxes were enlarged and became more elaborate after World War II. In 1956, the *Michigan Daily* boasted of the stadium's new press box, what the university aptly dubbed a "communication center," which contained multiple levels that served many purposes. The layout of the new press box revealed how sophisticated its function had become in the decades since the war. On the first level was the dining room for the university president. On the second tier was space for the press and university public relations personnel. On the third tier was an open-air deck for photographers and TV cameras. The top level contained seventeen soundproof and wired broadcast booths, darkrooms for photographers, and a special box for the university president. Ann Arbor's communication center foreshadowed the emergence of the luxury suite that would dominate stadium design years later.[8]

At the Los Angeles Memorial Coliseum, creating adequate space for the press was a paramount concern as the facility prepared to host the international throng of journalists who would cover the 1932 Olympics. After the Olympics, the demands for media space increased as the number of journalists and technicians attending events grew dramatically. The Coliseum Commission boasted of its bigger press box installed in 1948 that was "convenient for the great communications industry to satisfy a waiting world's appetite for news." Of course, local sportswriters were thrilled with their new digs: "Absolutely tops anything I've ever seen or any place I've ever worked," crowed Brandon Dyer, *Los Angeles Times* sports columnist.[9]

Baseball stadiums were a bit slower to accommodate the press, mostly because teams relied on gate receipts to generate profits. Eventually, as team owners understood that radio and television coverage would increase—not decrease—ticket sales, they began to construct covered press areas for sportswriters. Early "classic ballparks" such as the Polo Grounds, Ebbets Field, Comiskey Park, and Tiger Stadium squeezed press boxes into mezzanine sections or onto the upper decks. Still, even larger Osborn-designed structures such as Yankee Stadium and Cleveland Municipal Stadium had rather makeshift press-box sections. At the original Yankee Stadium, the press box was installed as an open-air space in the loge section right in front of the fans.

Press boxes were upgraded in the decades after World War II. Older facilities expanded their press facilities, and new stadiums were built to accommodate new television technologies during the 1960s and after. Most inserted press boxes in covered areas protected from the elements that had enviable views of the action on the field. These upgrades were impelled by the expansion of radio and television booths, which required better microphones and sound technologies so that viewers and listeners could hear announcers during the games.

Arrangements for the press at indoor arenas varied depending on the event and the facility. Ringside seats at boxing matches enabled journalists to experience the violence of the sport up close and personal. Meanwhile, basketball and hockey writers and announcers often found themselves crowded into small areas in the stands. At the Boston Garden, the building that was modeled on Tex Rickard's Madison Square Garden on Eighth Avenue, journalists and announcers were situated "high above courtside," in the words of the famous announcer Johnny Most. Even in the modern Madison Square Garden that opened in 1968, reporters had to climb into the press area that was crammed into the stands.[10]

Whereas press boxes initially were unglamorous areas set up for the press, locker rooms were envisioned for use by athletes and performers, not journalists. Most dressing rooms were rudimentary. Players put their possessions in metal lockers. Sometimes only hooks were provided. They sat on long benches, stalls, seats, or stools. Some stadiums, such as the Yale Bowl, didn't even have a dressing room, much to the dismay of the athletes who performed there over the years. Many facilities had only a small number of showers. After the arrival of the midcentury stadium, dressing rooms became a bit more comfortable, with carpeted floors, wider stalls, and bigger spaces for trainers to operate. Even then, large football players were forced to jam themselves into locker rooms that tended not to be made for the sport's large playing rosters. It wasn't until the 1990s, when stadiums were packed with amenities, that one could classify locker rooms as comfortable.

As radio and television encroached on print journalists' turf, writers flocked to the locker rooms to interview players. Increased competition compelled journalists to create unique storylines surrounding the action on the field, and getting players' and coaches' immediate reactions after a game became critically important, especially for the inside scoop on team dynamics. Journalists forced their way into the tiny quarters with their microphones, tape recorders, and cameras, making the work environment in the locker room all the more unpleasant.

Still, the locker room joined the press box as an essential workplace for reporters.

Working conditions for the press during much of the twentieth century were less than glamorous, but the press box and locker room functioned as newsrooms of sorts, where knowledge of the events at the stadium was created and disseminated to the public. A place in the press box and the dressing room carried the privilege of authorship— the power to narrate what transpired on the field of play and to interpret its larger meaning for readers and the whole nation. White men assumed that role from the earliest days of the journalist guild, and many loathed to give it up.

The privilege of authorship enabled sportswriters to develop regional and national reputations. The legendary Grantland Rice became a national figure through his epic tales of the remarkable exploits of athletes on the field. He played a key role in the mythmaking around Knute Rockne's Notre Dame football program. As was his wont, he waxed poetic about the team's incredible running game, which he dubbed the "Four Horsemen," inspired by the movie *The Four Horsemen of the Apocalypse* with Rudolph Valentino. After watching the Fighting Irish defeat Army 13–7 in October 1924, Rice penned:

> Outlined against a blue, gray October sky, the Four Horsemen rode again. In dramatic lore, they are known as Famine, Pestilence, Destruction, and Death. These are only aliases. Their real names are Stuhldreher, Miller, Crowley, and Layden. They formed the crest of the South Bend cyclone before which another fighting Army team was swept over the precipice at the Polo Grounds this afternoon as 55,000 spectators peered down upon the bewildering panorama spread out upon the green plain below.[11]

Reporters' overheated prose was shaped by the cozy relationships sportswriters had with the sport teams they covered during that era. Rice and other writers relied on coaches like Rockne for inside information and also for favors, such as gigs as official scorers and speaking engagements. Baseball franchises provided sportswriters with expense accounts, free food and drinks before and after games, and even free trips for wives and children. No wonder Roger Kahn, the famed baseball writer, memorably described baseball writers as "hairy-legged cheerleaders sans pompoms."[12]

Teams and their sportswriters bonded in the inner sanctums of the stadium: the press box, the press room, and the locker room. These bonds were created out of necessity. To do their job, journalists needed cooperation from teams, and teams wanted writers to provide positive publicity. These male-only relationships forged a homosocial world in these areas of the stadium. Connections were also made in bars and restaurants outside the ballpark. For many years, New York–based writers sidled up to star athletes, coaches, and owners at Toots Shor's restaurant in Manhattan, but the stadium remained the key point of contact. Even though the life of the sportswriter could be taxing, laden with endless travel, pressure-packed deadline writing, and low salaries, it could also be a ticket to stardom. Maybe that's why men held—and still hold—onto these jobs for *decades*. Aside from the smaller number of black writers who wrote for the black press and Latino writers who wrote for Spanish-language newspapers, the job of the sportswriter was locked down by white men.

The press box was male turf. Period. Virtually all members of the media who came to the ballpark or arena—radio announcers, television announcers, technical workers, cameramen, photographers, public relations people—were men, and virtually all of them were white. The words NO WOMEN OR CHILDREN were printed on press credentials and etched into signs outside press boxes and locker rooms in stadiums throughout the country. The men who covered sports prided themselves on their imagined ability to be objective, insisting that they knew the games they covered better than those who played them. "There's no cheering in the press box" was the mantra of the midcentury sportswriter. Though they often acted as the voice of team management, journalists fashioned themselves a role akin to that of the theater critic. They built their stature on their exclusive access to the inner sanctums of the stadium environment. Before games, men gathered in the press room, enjoyed free food and booze supplied by teams, then interviewed players and coaches down on the field, jotting down information or recording it. After locker-room interviews, sportswriters returned to their typewriters to punch out pieces and then rush them to their editors by wire service before the deadline for the next edition. In the press box and at the press tables, they opined about what they saw on the field while puffing on cigars and cigarettes.

Such a scene was not very attractive to the few women who had access to it before the 1970s. Doris O'Donnell, a Cleveland-based writer, wasn't impressed with the press's accommodations during her brief visits in the 1940s. "A press box is nothing more than make-shift, weather-worn tables for typewriters and Western Union equipment and folding chairs. There is nothing plush about it. Usually it is crowded and untidy," she wrote. Locker rooms were even less appealing. *Steamy, smelly, dirty,* and *overcrowded* are the words that characterized stadium dressing rooms. [13]

Press boxes and locker rooms were sealed off through an alliance of sportswriters, stadium managers, teams, and leagues. The Baseball Writers' Association of America (BBWAA), founded in 1908, and the Pro Football Writers of America (PFWA), founded much later in 1963, were granted the power to control access to the stadium press areas. These groups are advocacy groups for journalists, but they also kept a tight grip on who could access the sportswriting guilds. These organizations were, of course, dominated by white men.

A quick look at the careers of some prominent writers of this era makes the white male privilege abundantly clear. Grantland Rice spun his florid tales for fifty years. Red Smith covered sports for five decades. Dick Young started as a messenger boy before becoming a sportswriter at the New York *Daily News*, a position he held for forty-five years. Jerome Holtzman punched out stories on his typewriter for Chicago newspapers for fifty years. Radio and television announcers enjoyed similar job security. The beloved and gifted longtime announcer of

the Los Angeles Dodgers, Vin Scully, painted vivid pictures of baseball games using his microphone for almost seven decades. Even
today, the overabundance of white men in sports journalism remains
staggering.[14]

The era of ornate sportswriting waned in the 1960s as a younger
generation of scribes began to write more critically of teams and management. Though the hairy-legged cheerleaders remained, younger
writers, derisively called the "Chipmunks" by their senior colleagues,
were concerned with matters other than documenting and celebrating athletes' exploits on the field. They rejected the embellished style
of Grantland Rice and his contemporaries, and they shunned the
reporting of the Red Smith era. Such writers as Larry Merchant, Stan
Isaacs, and Phil Pepe adopted an irreverent critical eye toward sports
figures. Rather than tell tales of athletic heroism, they snooped around
the stadium, the clubhouses, the bars, and the restaurants looking for
behind-the-scenes stories, including less-heroic stories on womaniz-
ing, drinking, and off-the-field antics.[15] A classic text crafted in this
mode is Jim Bouton's *Ball Four*, which was coauthored by erstwhile
Chipmunk Leonard Shecter. Yet for all their revolutionary impact on
sports journalism, the younger white male sports scribes of the 1960s
helped keep their profession exclusively white and male. When women
arrived in press boxes and locker rooms in the 1970s, many seethed
with resentment. In 1979, Maury Allen, one of the Chipmunks, bluntly
told fellow baseball writer Roger Angell: "The idea of a girl romping
through a clubhouse filled with naked athletes is not going to be good
for the game."[16]

EVEN BEFORE THE FEMINIST REVOLUTION OF THE 1970S HIT THE
world of sports, women had always done much more than romp
around ballparks looking for men. Though men remained the primary
customers attending games at ballparks, the ever-present need to generate revenues compelled ballclubs to expand their fan bases. Baseball
clubs developed "Ladies Days" promotions to attract women to the

ballpark. Meanwhile, stadium designers like the Osborn Engineering Company began to design stadiums to make women "as comfortable as possible" at the ballpark. Indoor arenas scheduled events to attract women patrons, such as the circus and ice-skating shows. Starting in the 1920s, the Ice Follies and Ice Capades attracted women spectators to see Sonja Henie and other figure skating stars. These shows, like the circus, were key events that made the circuit of arenas all over the country for decades.[17]

Women could be in the stands or on the stage as performers, but they were strictly prohibited from the press box and the dressing room. In the post–World War II era, these contradictions were thrown into stark relief. In the 1960s, modernist stadiums such as the Houston Astrodome employed smartly dressed "usherettes" to show customers to their seats. As the sexual revolution came to the sports world, women were prominently stationed on the sidelines as dancers and cheerleaders.[18]

One way women could get close to the press box was by serving as an organist. Today most stadium music is prerecorded or produced by deejays, but at midcentury, music was played by skillful musicians who entertained fans. To be sure, the organist was a key part of the sideline action. In the 1930s, organists began to perform at arenas and appeared a little later at outdoor stadiums. Though most were men, women found their way into this key role, too. Gladys Gooding was a pioneering organist who performed at Madison Square Garden and Ebbets Field for many years before her death in 1963. Gooding was the first in a line of women who played the organ for the Dodgers franchise.[19]

The sixties and seventies turned out to be the heyday of the stadium organist. Two of the most revolutionary were Jane Jarvis and Nancy Faust. Jarvis, a pianist, had a long tenure playing the organ for the Braves at Milwaukee County Stadium and for the Mets at Shea Stadium from 1954 to 1979. Faust played a Hammond-3 organ for the White Sox at Comiskey Park in Chicago for forty-one years. She also played the famous Chicago Stadium organ at Bulls basketball and

Blackhawks hockey games during the seventies and eighties. Though Faust initially faced resistance from fans and was sometimes trivialized as "pert" and "pretty," she completely revolutionized the role of stadium musician during the 1970s. First positioned in the center-field bleachers and eventually moved to the upper deck behind home plate, Faust became a fixture at Comiskey Park. Rather than only striking up tunes to entertain fans between innings when there was a break in the action, Faust inserted her music into the game itself. A master improviser who used her instrument to comment on the action, she played what became known as "walk up" music and riled fans at the rambunctious Comiskey Park. She played for the team at its new ballpark until her retirement in 2010.[20]

Women were part of the fan base and sideline entertainment, but, before the 1970s, only a few ventured into the realm of sports journalism. Ella Black wrote pieces from a "woman's perspective" in *Sporting Life* for a brief period in 1890–1891. Jeane Hofmann wrote about Pacific Coast League baseball games in the 1930s and 1940s. In 1942, she was the first woman to sit in the press box in Wrigley Field in Los Angeles. Doris O'Donnell tried to gain access to press boxes at baseball stadiums along the East Coast. She reported being 2–2, having been admitted to the press areas in Baltimore and Washington but denied at Yankee Stadium and Fenway Park. "I didn't really care because my seat alongside the Indians dugout was far superior to the upper deck and I could see and hear much better," she wrote.[21]

The sportswriter with the most sustained career was Mary Garber. She reported on the Atlantic Coast Conference and historically black college or university (HBCU) sports for decades and was one of the very few women who attained a regular beat covering local sports. Working in North Carolina, she managed to secure quotes from players and coaches, even though she didn't have access to locker rooms for most of her career. In the late seventies, when younger writers were challenging these conventions, Garber was discovered by the national press. She retired in 1985 after a forty-year career.[22]

Another pioneer was Elinor Kaine, who loved football and had the audacity to believe that she could write about it. The Smith College graduate was stuck in an advertising job, but her passion lay elsewhere. In the early 1960s, she aspired to write about professional football. But there was no place for her to do so. No matter. She created her own space. She started *Lineback*, her own football newsletter, and peddled it to avid readers. She wrote the newsletter, photocopied it, and hired friends to stuff it into envelopes in her Upper East Side Manhattan apartment so that it could be mailed out to readers or dropped off at nearby restaurants. Readers loved her unconventional approach to sports journalism. Rather than provide scores and highlights and describe players as superheroes, she instead humanized them, offering information on their lives. She wrote about rumors of their off-field activities, and she pleased gamblers by offering lines from Vegas. Soon her newsletter had a circulation of twelve thousand readers, and Kaine became a national sensation.

The popularity of Kaine's writings made her a sought-after syndicated columnist. Her angle was football "from a woman's perspective," a domesticating marketing device that obscured the fact that she knew football better than most men. Indeed, Kaine was routinely dismissed as a "pert" "Tokyo Rose" who was not a serious journalist. "Men pro football fans have certainly made it hard for a girl to enjoy the game," she admitted. "They pretend football is too complicated for a female to understand, hoping to keep the gridiron a no woman's land. Beat them at their own game!" She did all her reporting while having very little access to players and certainly with no access to the press box or locker room.

By the late 1960s, Kaine secured a membership in the Pro Football Writers of America association, which gave her the status of an accredited reporter. Such a membership should have allowed her to apply for press-box privileges, yet she was consistently rebuffed at stadiums. Once, she applied for a press credential for a New York Giants football game. She was told: "Listen, girl: the turf at Yankee Stadium is sacred. No female is ever going to put her foot on it—at least as long as I'm here."[23]

In the summer of 1969, the "girl" applied for a press pass so she could cover the first-ever game between the New York Jets and the New York Giants at the Yale Bowl in New Haven, Connecticut. Bill Guthrie, a New Haven sportswriter who was in charge of the press box, ignored her requests. This time, she sued the Jets, the Giants, Yale, and the City of New Haven, charging that there was no legal justification for preventing her access to the press box. She was right. Her opponents eventually relented and agreed to grant her a seat in the press area. When she arrived at the stadium, she was disappointed to find that their notion of the "press area" was a seat where old newsreel photographers used to sit under the press box. "We've saved this for you," the press-box staff told her gleefully. Unlike other writers, she did not have a desk or any space to take notes. Meanwhile, plenty of seats were available in the press box. At that moment, she realized who her real enemies were. "It was the writers who were against me, the teams didn't give a shit. They didn't want me in there," she wrote. "They wanted it for themselves."[24]

Although she was granted access to the press box in the Orange Bowl stadium in Miami the next season, it seems like the slights and the disrespect eventually got to her. After the Yale Bowl episode, she told the press: "I'm just tired of getting treated like garbage. I hate to get kicked around by such little people. I really don't know what I'm going to do—I don't want to be made a fool of anymore." A year later, she got married and moved to France. Her sportswriting career abruptly ended.[25]

Kaine's encounters with sexism in football journalism reflected the obstacles all women sportswriters encountered, even though she was able to break through farther than most. Still, she saw her counterparts in the baseball world as less fortunate. "I'm lucky I'm not a baseball writer," she wrote. "It sounds like football is conservative, provincial and full of old fogeys, baseball has a mind that's strictly centuries B.C."

Kaine's colleagues who sought to break into the baseball beat during those years would wholeheartedly agree.

THE WOMEN JOURNALISTS WHO WERE BRAVE ENOUGH TO TRY TO cover pro baseball in the early 1970s encountered the stiffest resistance from the male guardians of the stadium's inner sanctums. At beloved "classic" ballparks such as Comiskey Park in Chicago, women sports journalists met with hostility if they dared to veer into the press box or the Bard's Room, the private bar where writers and other celebrities gathered. Lynda Morstadt, a twenty-five-year-old sportswriter for the *Waukegan News-Sun*, a local suburban publication, found this out when she walked into the press box on April 19, 1972. Morstadt, whom male writers had described as "pert and vivacious" and a "curvesome chick," was given a frigid reception. Soon after, she was forcibly escorted out of the press box by Stu Holcomb, the White Sox general manager. According to Morstadt, Holcomb "grabbed me by the collar and threw me out," supposedly because her newspaper was not entitled to a press credential. "I can't believe it's because I'm from a small paper," she said to the press. "I think it must have something to do with my sex." Holcomb vehemently disagreed. "Sex has nothing to do with it," the Sox general manager insisted. "The press box is for regular metropolitan writers from Chicago and the visiting press, not for suburban writers." Holcomb did not apologize for his actions. "Sure, I took her by the arm," he snapped. "How else was I going to get her out of there? If she wants to be one of the men, she has to act like one and not burst into tears. I'm running this press box." Holcomb's huffing and puffing notwithstanding, Morstadt was eventually given access to the press box.[26]

The Morstadt episode at Comiskey Park was a sign of things to come. It was an indication that increasing numbers of women journalists were testing the boundaries of the ballpark's gendered geography. As second-wave feminism reshaped America, a new generation of women stormed the gates of professions previously locked down by white men. These were young, college-educated women. Most were white and inspired by the civil rights movement and the larger freedom struggles of the sixties to go where no woman had gone before. Some used long-standing survival techniques such as persistence and diplomacy to work their way through the sexist system, which allowed only a few women to advance while men continued to dominate the profession. Others resorted to lawsuits, directly challenging the archaic sexist cultural beliefs that determined the career prospects of men and women. In this period, civil rights laws and court rulings seemed to indicate that the law was on their side.[27]

One domain women took by storm was the world of journalism. In the early 1970s, women sued news publications across the country to allow them to move beyond ancillary jobs such as secretarial work and fact-checking to the status of writers and editors. Up to that point, nearly all reporters and writers were men. Prompted by the successful 1970 class-action lawsuit against *Newsweek*, when women staff members charged the magazine with discriminating against them on the basis of their sex, news outlets scrambled to find women journalists.[28]

Whereas Elinor Kaine opted for marriage and a life abroad over the experience of banging her head against the wall erected by the football writers clique, Jeannie Morris made inroads into the world of sports journalism. Morris, the wife of Chicago Bears football player Johnny Morris, got her first job writing columns for the *Chicago American*. When the newspaper offered Johnny a job writing columns, he suggested that they hire Jeannie instead. As was Kaine's, Jeannie Morris's column was touted as football writing for women, and hers was entitled "Football Is a Woman's Game." Morris quickly moved beyond this gig into the world of television, where she partnered with her husband to be an Emmy Award–winning tandem for thirty years. She wrote and produced many of her own stories, a rarity for women in the profession at the time. Morris eventually left the world of sports journalism for documentary filmmaking on topics beyond sports. Years later, when asked about the sexism she faced in sports journalism, she

claimed, "It didn't bother me," even as she tersely recalled the moment
when baseball legend Ted Williams tried to kick her out of his team's
dugout. Instead, she persisted doing her work. "I wasn't crashing locker
rooms," she insisted. Still, Morris acknowledged that her marriage to
a prominent NFL star facilitated her less-confrontational approach to
negotiating sexism.[29]

Just persisting and doing her work was also the strategy of Diane
Shah, an Indiana University graduate who began her career as a journalist writing for the *National Observer*, the weekly publication owned
by Dow Jones. In September 1972, only a few months after Morstadt
was thrown out of the press box at Comiskey Park, Shah arrived at
another hallowed baseball cathedral, Boston's Fenway Park, with a
press credential to cover the Boston Red Sox. So did Madeline Blais,
a recently hired reporter for the *Boston Herald*. Both encountered
frosty receptions from the Red Sox public relations staff and players.
Team officials tried to dissuade them from interviewing players on the
field and in the dugout. When Shah met with Bill Crowley, the team's
public relations person and gatekeeper of the press box, he informed
the young sportswriter: "I'm not sure what your legal status is, but
around here we don't let women into the press box. Or onto the field.
Or into the dugout." Shah pressed on, yet Crowley refused. "I had
become increasingly annoyed with Major League Baseball's attitude
toward women," she recalled years later. "Back then we were lured to
the ballpark with pantyhose giveaways and half-price tickets." Teams
had treated women as sideshows. "In Philadelphia, they could roam
the stands in cute little miniskirts as ushers. In Baltimore, they could
rush onto the field between innings to sweep off the bases . . . those
were baseball's concessions to women." After she threatened to sue, the
team and the local baseball writers had a change of heart and grudgingly granted her permission to enter the press areas of the ballpark.[30]

But Blais's and Shah's problems were just beginning. They had to
contend with the seething resentment of the press-box gatekeepers.
Now that Blais and Shah were allowed in the press box, a horde of
women disguised as sportswriters was sure to follow, Crowley insisted.

Worse, the specter of women in the press box and locker room created the possibility for something more calamitous to transpire. "Because of you, the American family will be destroyed," Crowley growled at Shah. Meanwhile, Blais received similar treatment, as she reported in her article published the next day:

> If any one group has to be educated about female sportswriters it's the male reporters themselves. They sit in the press gallery with their cigars invariably poking out of their mouths, wearing hats and saying: You're ruining our racket.[31]

This hit the nail on the head. The women who began to arrive in larger numbers discovered that the white men who controlled these corners of the ballpark—and, therefore, sports journalism—had been running a racket for years. Men weren't occupying these positions because they were smarter or because sports were too complicated for women to comprehend. They controlled the sportswriter domain because they had decided that this was a realm of society that they were entitled to dominate. As the number of women sportswriters gradually increased, the truth about sportswriting was exposed.

To be sure, Shah's and Blais's "invasion" of Fenway Park in 1972 did not destroy the American family. Neither did it abolish sexism in sports journalism. By the end of her six-day stint covering the Red Sox, Shah reported that the team's PR staff had finally come around and eased off their restrictions. However, the women's presence in the press box did not change the larger circumstances facing women sportswriters. "Another male stronghold has fallen," *Los Angeles Times* sports columnist Charles Maher wrote prematurely in a 1975 article profiling women sportswriters who had gained access to the press box. The women in Maher's piece hardly conveyed the idea that the battle for legitimacy and the right to fully access stadiums to do their jobs had been won, though. One writer featured in Maher's story, Betty Cuniberti, recalled male colleagues telling her, "It sure is nice to have some decoration around here." She said, "Sometimes I just laugh it off, but sometimes—it depends on my mood—I'll say 'Hey, buddy. I'm not a decoration. I'm a writer.'"[32]

Women writers might have gained limited access to the press box, but the locker room was still off-limits in the early seventies. As press outlets hired more young women to cover teams, women continued to struggle against obstacles thrown up by team and league officials. These gatekeepers handled the matter of women sportswriters on an ad hoc basis. While Betty Cuniberti was covering the Oakland Raiders football team, she was forced to arrange for players to talk to her in the tunnel outside the clubhouse. When Lesley Visser was assigned the New England Patriots beat by the *Boston Globe* in 1975, she was forced to wait outside the locker room, not infrequently in freezing temperatures, to interview players and rely solely on their goodwill. The vast majority of women reporters had to accommodate themselves to some sort of separate but equal principle that forced them to interview players in separate rooms or in hallways, not in the locker room. Shah, Visser, and others took pride in the fact that they could persist, occasionally outsmart their colleagues and the recalcitrant men who ran the teams, and do their jobs anyway. Yet the structure of exclusion remained, especially in baseball and football stadiums. Indeed, women sportswriters made the deepest inroads in the indoor arenas where hockey and basketball were played.

THE MONTREAL FORUM—A HOCKEY SHRINE—WAS BUILT DURING THE stadium boom of the 1920s, as was Madison Square Garden. The Forum was home to the legendary Montreal Canadiens pro hockey franchise until its doors were closed in 1996. The team won an astonishing twenty-five Stanley Cup championships during the seventy seasons it played at the Forum. On January 21, 1975, the building made the news, not because of a Canadiens victory but because of a significant moment in the history of sports journalism: this was the first time women sportswriters were allowed in a professional team's locker room. The setting was the National Hockey League (NHL)

All-Star Game, the annual event when the league's best players face off against each other in an exhibition game. Despite the presence of all the league's stars, All-Star Games are usually boring affairs. However, this particular occasion turned out to be more exciting than most.

It all started at the press conference, when reporters gathered to ask coaches, players, and league officials questions during the typical pregame ritual. Suddenly, a reporter asked whether women journalists were going to be permitted to interview players in the locker room. Much to the surprise of everyone, the answer was yes. Robin Herman was among the group of reporters stunned by the league's unexpected decision. "That was how it all began. It was treated as a joke. . . . I had no plans to make it happen, or anything. I couldn't believe it." Herman was one of the first women hired by the *New York Times* to cover sports, and she was assigned the hockey beat. She found the players largely receptive of her presence, but she still had to contend with the gate-keepers keeping her out of team clubhouses. Like all women reporters, she was forced to wait outside dressing rooms and rely on the good-will of players and public relations staff to secure interviews. Now, she and Marcelle St-Cyr, a Canadian sports reporter for a Montreal radio station, were suddenly given access to the previously off-limits locker room.[33]

However, when they walked into the dressing room, St-Cyr and Herman soon discovered that they would not be able to do their normal job. "For one brief ridiculous moment, I thought perhaps for a while that we would go unnoticed amidst the crush of about 60 reporters," Herman wrote. But when they entered the crowded Forum dressing room, a player shouted, "They are here!" A ruckus ensued. Players scrambled for towels, and cameras and microphones were pointed at Herman and St-Cyr rather than the players. "The eyes of our colleagues immediately turned to us," St-Cyr recalled years later. "They machine-gun[ed] us with their cameras." The women journalists, not the game, became the story of the evening. Jokes, pranks, and laughter made it almost impossible for Herman and St-Cyr to do their job that night. St-Cyr managed to interview Montreal Canadiens superstar

Guy Lafleur, who stood naked in front of his locker. "When I'm interviewing you, why would I talk to you looking down?" St-Cyr recalled
telling players. "My microphone is there [at the height of your mouth]!"
Notwithstanding the brouhaha, St-Cyr completed her interviews—
while Herman wrote—and filed her game story before deadline.[34]

The reaction to the "girls in the locker room" was immediate, and
much of it was negative. While some colleagues and fans supported
the reporters, others vehemently opposed them. The notion of women
writers in the locker room was anathema to critics, even if civil rights
law gave them legal access to the space. Years later, St-Cyr recalled fellow newsmen blaming her and Herman for disrupting their work. To
her men colleagues, the specter of women reporters signaled that they
were there to take their jobs and direct the attention of athletes away
from the men with the tape recorders, pads, and pencils. Meanwhile,
Herman received hate mail from fans. "It's hard to address a harlot disguised as a reporter," wrote one letter writer, "but I just want to warn
you that you cannot do such a thing with impunity. It's wrong, no
matter how many women libers might dumbly applaud it." How dare
women presume the right to have access to the sacred space of the stadium dressing room? To critics, Herman, St-Cyr, and their peers were
little more than "harlots" who were only looking to sneak a peek at
finely sculpted athletic Adonises.[35]

Despite the criticism and despite the spectacle the players and the
media produced, what transpired at the Montreal Forum that night
was indeed a turning point. "Mini sports history was made when Marcelle and I crossed the threshold of that room," Herman wrote a few
weeks later. "It was an important moment, for it loudly heralded the
fact that female sports writers are a reality and that they must be dealt
with." The 1975 All-Star Game at the Montreal Forum announced
the arrival of women sportswriters in the locker room, and the furious reaction to them revealed that there was much more at stake than
player privacy or journalistic integrity.[36]

The entrance of Herman and St-Cyr into the Montreal Forum
locker room intensified the arguments over the presence of women

journalists at stadiums and arenas that would ensue for many more years to come. Prompted by the presence of women in what had been all-male preserves, the so-called locker-room debate that raged in the sports world revealed deep sexual anxieties. The American stadium was exposed as much more than a neutral place of recreation and spectatorship. It was an arena where sexual boundaries had been firmly established and policed. But in the 1970s, those boundaries were being interrogated, and the answers to the question of why women could not access locker rooms seemed increasingly nonsensical. Press boxes were not simply places where sportswriters churned out their stories. They were places where white men reinforced their position as *the* authors of the American story. The locker room was not simply a room where men showered, changed, and bantered. It embodied the core logic of sexism and patriarchy that produced the misogyny that often fueled "locker room" talk.

Male sportswriters continued to make excuses for gender exclusion. The stadium dressing room, like the press box and the dugout, they said, was a space that was too vulgar for "ladies" to inhabit. The locker room could not be open to women for that would introduce the more volatile element of sex into the equation. They claimed that players' wives would object to women reporters' presence or that their presence was an invasion of players' privacy. Women's libbers, as real and imagined feminists were derisively called, were simply going too far.

Behind these claims was an inadvertent admission that the presence of women in the locker room exposed the fantasies that some men writers quietly inhabited. Maury Allen, the longtime New York sportswriter who was opposed to women in the locker room, said as much to baseball writer Roger Angell in a revealing 1979 *New Yorker* article: "Sex is a very significant aspect of athletes' lives," Allen opined. "If you think about it, you realize right away that athletic performance and sexual performances always go hand in hand." Allen used as his example the New York Jets superstar quarterback and sex symbol Joe Namath. "Why did Joe Namath become such a national hero? Because he was macho. Because deep down in our hearts *we* wanted all those broads." The right to access the locker room and the press box was the right of male sportswriters to live vicariously through athletes, to share in their triumphs and conquests on and off the field.[37]

Stephanie Salter, another in the first wave of women sportswriters in the 1970s, touched on this curious combination of admiration and contempt her peers held for athletes. "I'm always amazed at the amount of hostility among the male writers that is directed at the players," she told Angell in the same article. "You hear them asking these smart-aleck questions that are meant to show up the players and prove that the writers know as much about the sport as the players do. It's as if they're fighting over who will be the leader of the pack: which of us is more virile—me with my pen or you with your bat?" Salter also perceptively noted how the arrival of women in the press box and the locker room disrupted the adolescent mentality men held toward women. "There are good girls—the ones they marry—and there are the other ones, the kind they shack up with on the road. We women writers are a challenge to that simple filing system. They just don't know what to make of us."[38]

The women who came to the ballpark and the arena with their pens, pads, and typewriters seemed to drop out of the sky. They were smart, and they were educated. Many of them were as knowledgeable about sports as their male peers. They had been introduced to sports by their mothers, not just their fathers. As youths, they'd played sports until sexism pushed them into conventional roles. Now they were daring to be sportswriters who were authoring another kind of story about sports in America. They were able to put their finger on the pulse of contradiction that shaped the relationship between men sportswriters and athletes. They saw the contempt and admiration that fueled many of the men who worked in the world of sports journalism.

After the civil rights era, racism, sexism, and patriarchy vexed the relationships between white male writers and the multiracial athletic labor force. Jane Gross, the daughter of the longtime sportswriter Milton Gross, might have detected one of the issues at stake in the locker-room wars of the seventies when she bluntly told Roger Angell:

"I wonder if a lot of the suggestions that men make about women reporters may not have something to do with sexual envy of blacks." As Gross told it, racism and sexual insecurity lay at the root of white men's reactionary posture toward women in the locker room. Her observation was based on a lifetime of intimate knowledge of the stadium environment. As a child, she had often accompanied her father to his place of work, whether it was the ringside press tables in Madison Square Garden or the stands of spring-training baseball games. She also drew from her own experience of being among the first women writers to cover professional basketball in the mid-1970s.

Gross's first beat was the New York Nets pro basketball team for *Newsday*, where she encountered the sport's predominantly black athletic labor force. Basketball, like hockey, was looking for more publicity as it competed for the attention of the American sports fan. She couldn't help but notice the relatively open atmosphere that existed in pro basketball locker rooms. "I'm sure black players treat me differently from the way they treat male writers. They don't think I'm a honky—I'm another oppressed minority," Gross divulged to Roger Angell. Gross's comments touched on the existing racial dynamic as the first wave of women sportswriters arrived in locker rooms. The vast majority of these pioneering women were white, young, college-educated women. They entered racially integrated locker rooms where many of the stars were black. Women sports reporters of color, such as the groundbreaking baseball writer Claire Smith, did not come on the scene until a few years later. Gross's was an era when black stars like Reggie Jackson would stroll buck naked through the locker room in front of women writers. It was one thing for white male writers to be in proximity of undressed black men in intimate spaces, but it was quite another for young white women to be so "dangerously" close to black male sexuality. White women seemed to be trampling over the deep-seated fears of the white supremacist imagination.[39]

This was inadvertently revealed in a 1982 encounter Diane Shah had with Gene Mauch, then the manager of the California Angels franchise. A decade removed from her time as an early-career reporter for the *National Observer*, Shah was writing for the *Los Angeles Herald Examiner*, which had hired her as the first woman sports columnist at a daily newspaper. On one occasion in the midst of the pennant race, Shah walked into Mauch's office after a game as he was speaking to reporters. As soon as Shah joined the group, Mauch abruptly stopped speaking and walked out of his office. A little while later, she asked Mauch why he walked out, to which he confessed: "I know you can be in here, but it makes me sick to my stomach to see you walking around in front of all these naked [he used the N word to finish the sentence]. You remind me of my daughter. I think about my daughter, and it makes me sick." According to Shah, the Angels manager began to cry.[40]

The fact that Mauch, a white manager who was not known as a racist, revealed this vulnerability to a younger white woman is telling. The presence of Shah and other women reporters in the locker room disrupted the historical role of the white patriarchal figure protecting white femininity from untamed black men. The scenario was straight out of the same white supremacist imagination on display at halftime and pregame shows at the Sugar Bowl during the Jim Crow era. The presence of white women in the dressing room years later made the threat of black male sexuality seemingly a reality, especially now that women were able to roam freely in locker rooms across the country.

Samantha Stevenson further stoked those fears in the late 1970s. She was one of the few women sportswriters who rejected the less-confrontational path of working around sexism through persistence and tact and directly challenged the myths that kept women out of the press boxes and the locker rooms while foregrounding her own sexual agency. Stevenson was a freelance writer who began her career in Dallas in the early seventies before moving to Philadelphia, where she challenged the same stonewalling tactics teams deployed to keep women out of dressing rooms. Still, Stevenson stood out among her peers. "We'd never seen the likes of Samantha Stevenson," a basketball executive recalled years later. "She'd come in the locker room dressed provocatively." "Provocative dress" is often in the eye of the beholder, but basketball star Julius Erving recalled a similar impression when he said that Stevenson was "comfortable playing the flirt in pursuit of an exclusive story."[41]

Like many women sports journalists, Stevenson's writing took the human interest angle, highlighting players' and coaches' experiences off the field. However, her stories had an edgier tone because she discussed the drug use and sexual activities of players and ballpark workers for daily newspapers such as the *New York Times* and *Philadelphia Inquirer*, as well as men's magazines such as *Playboy* and *Oui*. Unlike her peers, Stevenson did not shy away from the sexual tensions that emerged while covering athletes. In "Confessions of a Female Sportswriter," published in *Oui* in August 1978, she put all the sexual tensions that terrified men and women journalists out there on the proverbial table for everyone to see. She did so by first debunking the myth that the locker room was too vulgar a place for women.

> Let's get something straight, OK? The locker room isn't a turn-on. It's all a giant myth. It's not like watching your lover undress and feeling hot flashes. You're asking questions and they're answering and it's all cold-blooded business. They all say "fuck" a lot, in various grammatical forms, and talk about pussy. So? We worldly women say "fuck" a lot and talk about length and size.[42]

Stevenson detailed the predictable sophomoric harassment she was subjected to in the dressing room, but she also offered her own perspective in a way that would please *Oui* readers: "When you are doing your job, you don't have time to worry about things smelling— besides most male athletes have more after-shave and perfumes spraying around than women," Stevenson wrote. "Occasionally, a beautiful body will pass by and your thoughts leave your notebook for a second to playfully think of a perfect fantasy. I could easily see myself with all my clothes off in the steamy showers, with my choice of men offering me soaps and suds. That small insight doesn't make me a bad reporter: it just makes me honest."[43]

The piece also described the physical attractiveness of JoJo White, the African American star point guard of the Boston Celtics, whom she described as "the premier body man in the NBA." Stevenson pulled no punches: "You see his legs and his wonderful ass loping down the court with incredible quickness. The burst to the hoop is slow motion grace," she continued. "But when you head to the showers with these guys, there are few surprises. They all have a penis." In other words, a woman seeing a penis in the course of doing her job was no big deal. Here, Stevenson assumed the role of gazer at the male body instead of being the one subject to the male gaze. Why not bluntly address the question of sex? After all, sex was all her male peers could see when she and her colleagues walked into the locker room. "If reporters and athletes had their way," Stevenson wrote, "you'd be fucking your brains out with all of them. That's mostly what they think you're doing anyway."[44]

Even if one dismisses Stevenson's reporting as salacious gossip, it is clear that her unapologetic writing about sex and drug use exposed the ballpark's inner sanctum as a zone of transgression. Decades later, the revelation of her relationship with Julius Erving revived arguments against women in the locker room.[45] Still, the uproar about women in the locker room and the sexualized and sexist characterization of them obscured the core issue facing women sportswriters. What was at stake was not the fate of the American family or the prospect of women reporters having sex with players or even players' privacy. What was at stake was the question of equal access and job discrimination: Would the newly enshrined civil rights laws extend to the stadium's inner sanctums? A historic court ruling would provide the answer.

LIKE DIANE SHAH, ROBIN HERMAN, JANE GROSS, AND ALL THE OTHER women sports reporters of the 1970s, Melissa Ludtke had to figure out how to navigate the perilous terrain of the stadium environment.

After *Sports Illustrated* magazine hired her, she learned how to be a sportswriter on the fly, watching her male colleagues do their jobs and apprenticing with senior writers such as William Leggett and Roger Kahn. As importantly, she learned how to find allies among the multitude of men who controlled access to the ballpark. During the 1977 baseball season, much of her time was spent at Yankee Stadium. That was a tumultuous season for the Yankees, marked by conflict between Reggie Jackson, the team's newly acquired star, and its manager and owner, the volatile Billy Martin and George Steinbrenner. Yet the war between Jackson and Martin did not prevent success on the field: the Yankees won the American League pennant that season. Thus, the team that eventually came to be known as the Bronx Zoo was a dream for journalists eager to cover on-the-field excellence and off-the-field drama.

Ludtke relied on persistence and diplomacy to gradually gain access to the Yankee locker room. "The issue of locker room access was never raised by me within the confines of the magazine or anyone else I know who was covering that sport [baseball] at the time," she remembered years later.[46] Like other women sports journalists, she had to hope players would extend goodwill and give her interviews and that the media relations staff would allow her to do her job. Through her developing relationship with Yankees staff member Micky Morabito, she was eventually able to gain a press pass that gave her access to the locker room. With the Yankees heading to the World Series that year, she seemed to be in line to gain more valuable work experience. As the 1977 World Series approached, she took the unnecessary step of requesting permission from the Dodgers, the Yankees' opponents, to enter their locker room, even though she already possessed her press credentials.[47]

For a researcher-reporter whose job was to fact-check and help her senior colleagues write stories, these arrangements seemed satisfactory. However, as she sat in the auxiliary press area in Yankee Stadium during the first game of the series, she found out that it was totally *un*satisfactory to Major League Baseball commissioner Bowie Kuhn. She was summoned out of the press box and told that she and all women reporters could not enter team clubhouses during the World Series after all. To Ludtke, Kuhn's decree was just another of the hassles she had to put up with during her short time working the baseball beat. One week later, on the night the Yankees won the series, she was forced to endure the humiliating experience of waiting outside the team's locker room as players celebrated and talked with her male colleagues about their triumph. After the series ended, however, and after weeks of attempting to negotiate a solution with Commissioner Kuhn's office, her bosses at *Sports Illustrated* decided that they had no choice but to pursue legal action. Once again, the courts would decide on gender equality in the world of journalism. Ludtke agreed to be the plaintiff in a lawsuit against Major League Baseball, the City of New York, and the New York Yankees. The case would be heard by Judge Constance Baker Motley, a pioneering civil rights attorney who'd become the first black woman to serve as a federal judge when she was appointed to the US District Court in Manhattan in 1966.[48]

The lawsuit generated endless debate and commentary. Though some male reporters were sympathetic to Ludtke's cause, most trivialized it as an insignificant issue. Red Smith, the longtime sportswriter, quibbled with Ludtke's account of her exclusion and questioned her competence as a journalist. Deriding her as "*Sports Illustrated's* Joan of Arc," Smith argued that the point of locker-room access was overblown. "Had she been thus occupied, she would have missed the gathering in another room down the hall where managers of both teams and key players on both sides were present to answer all her questions." Like other male critics, he reasoned that if women were granted full access to dressing rooms, male reporters should also have access to women's locker rooms.[49]

Readers and other journalists sounded their own alarms by focusing on player privacy and dismissing Ludtke as a publicity-starved woman who simply wanted to see naked athletes. Ludtke reminded her critics, however, that it was not a question of sex or privacy but rather whether the persistence of sexism would prevent her and her peers from doing their jobs. "Ever since the question of equal access to locker rooms was raised in October 1977, baseball has succeeded brilliantly in making equal access appear as a moral and not a political problem, as sexy, but not the sexist issue that it is," she wrote. "All I and other female sportswriters want is a chance to compete on an equal level with the men. Without access to the locker room, that is not often possible."[50]

Major League Baseball countered by arguing that giving women access to the locker room constituted an invasion of players' privacy. "It is our view that it is not a fair thing for our players and they are entitled to some reasonable privacy," the commissioner explained to sportscaster Howard Cosell in January 1978. "We don't think it is fair to the rest of the press and we also don't think to a lot of our fans who would have great reservations about this." However, Ludtke's lawyers insisted that policies that excluded women reporters from the locker room violated the Equal Protection clause of the Fourteenth Amendment of the Constitution. They argued that the Yankees, Major League Baseball, and the American League should be considered "state actors" that were "entwined" with the City of New York because Yankee Stadium was public property. Thus, the discrimination Ludtke experienced was unlawful because state entities were required to comply with civil rights laws. The stadiums of the 1970s might have been aesthetically unpleasing to architectural critics, but one of their attributes was that they were governed by a legal structure that made stadium managers accountable to the public. This was the legal argument that helped bring down racial discrimination at stadiums in the early 1960s, and now it was going to help ensure gender equality almost two decades later.[51]

On September 27, 1978, Judge Motley ruled in favor of Ludtke. All reporters, irrespective of gender, should have equal access to athletes, even in the locker room. A subsequent appeal by Major League

Baseball was denied. While Judge Motley's ruling set an important legal precedent, it only applied to stadiums in New York. It could not compel teams and leagues in other states to abide by the decision. This enabled Commissioner Kuhn to pass the buck and turn over responsibility of locker-room policies to each team. The ad hoc nature of locker-room access ensured that the struggle would continue in the years to come.[52]

The *Ludtke v. Kuhn* decision had an impact, but it did not end the discrimination and harassment women sports reporters faced in covering Major League Baseball. During the 1984 National League playoffs, Claire Smith was rudely forced out of the San Diego Padres locker room when she tried to interview players. Padres star first baseman Steve Garvey came out of the dressing room and gave a shaken Smith the quotes she needed to file her story.[53] The incident compelled new commissioner Peter Ueberroth to rule that all locker rooms would be open to all journalists. Still, harassment and lewd comments continued. Susan Fornoff, a sports reporter for the *Sacramento Bee*, received a live rat in a small, gift-wrapped box from Oakland A's player Dave Kingman. By the late 1980s, however, the accumulated effect of lawsuits and increasing criticism of the blatant sexism eventually improved work conditions for women covering baseball.[54]

The final battles for access to the locker room were waged against the National Football League, the league with perhaps the most reactionary gender politics. As in baseball, clubs had differing policies regarding locker-room access, which created an environment of confusion and continuing discrimination. The situation came to a head in 1990 when Lisa Olson, a sports reporter for the *Boston Herald*, was victimized by New England Patriots players' horrific harassment in the team's home locker room at Foxboro Stadium. Olson successfully sued the Patriots—and the incident produced bad press for the franchise—but the sexist backlash from players and fans was so severe that she was forced to leave the country for a period of time. However, the Olson case was egregious enough to compel franchises to alter their policies, and the conditions facing women football journalists improved, even though their role remained circumscribed.[55]

DURING THE 1970S, THE STADIUM ONCE AGAIN EMERGED AS A PLACE of politics and social change. Women sportswriters showed how stadiums were not merely places of play, even if the world of sportswriting had been men's exclusive playpen for decades. Before the 1970s, the system of separate but equal determined women's experience in stadiums and arenas: women were allowed to be spectators and sideline entertainers, and sometimes they could be performers, but they were totally excluded from the press box and the locker room. The gendered geography of the stadium was exposed when women challenged long-standing sexist assumptions and practices of discrimination. Merely by showing up to work in the press box or the locker room, they unmasked the enduring system of women's subordination. They successfully argued that stadiums were places of employment and that gender discrimination denied them the right to work like anyone else. Because of their persistence, activism, and legal action, the stadium became a place where citizenship rights were expanded and redefined.

The transformation of the press box and the locker room during the seventies and eighties, like the transformation of the stadium itself, was influenced by the feminist movement. Pioneering women dedicated to careers in sports journalism catalyzed this massive social change, even if some of them did not self-identify as feminists. The fact that stadiums and arenas were publicly managed facilities made them subject to the newly crafted civil rights laws. The gendered geography that kept women out of the inner sanctum of the stadium was eventually altered. By the 1990s, women sports reporters had successfully built upon the incremental gains of the previous decades. Finally, the ballpark and the arena appeared to be open to all, but only future struggles would further democratize stadiums and arenas across the country.

CHAPTER SIX

OUT AT
THE BALLPARK

I n the summer of 1982, Marsha Veale and her colleagues on the Gay
Games Organizing Committee had a herculean task in front of them
preparing Kezar Stadium, an aging facility on the southeast corner
of Golden Gate Park near the Haight-Ashbury district in San Francisco, for a first-of-its-kind sporting event: the inaugural Gay Games.
The city's Recreation and Parks Department, which oversaw the
fifty-seven-year-old concrete stadium, had largely neglected it. After
the San Francisco 49ers, the local NFL franchise, had left Kezar years
earlier, the stadium was less of a priority for the city as the gravity of
the city's sports scene shifted to Candlestick Park, the team's new home
stadium. Still, Gay Games organizers were determined to whip the
old building into shape. For weeks, Veale and her team arrived with
hammers, wheelbarrows, and saws to fix the decaying stadium. They
repaired damaged seats, ripped out those that could not be fixed, filled
in holes, and made the old facility safe for their special event.[1]

Kezar had hosted countless events over the years, but it had
never staged anything quite like this. On August 28, 1982, a modest
but very vocal crowd of ten thousand people made their way into the
sixty-thousand-seat stadium to witness the opening ceremonies of the

Gay Games. The organizing committee, led by former Olympian Tom Waddell, sought to create an international sports competition that was an antidote to the hypercompetitive Olympic Games. Waddell's vision was realized beyond his expectations.

Despite the small crowd, the Gay Games was a major success. For the opening ceremonies, more than thirteen hundred gay and lesbian athletes from across the United States and countries as far as Australia and Peru triumphantly paraded around the field. The spectacle of athletes openly and unapologetically carrying flags representing their country and signs signaling their sexual orientation was extraordinarily powerful and emotionally overwhelming for many who witnessed it. In the face of rising homophobia and opposition from the US Olympic Committee (USOC), which refused to let the organizers use the word "Olympic," the opening ceremonies and the Games were a major victory for LGBTQ communities. As one observer noted: "I have been Gay for 25 years, and out of the closet for the past ten years, but never have I been as proud to be a Gay man as I was Saturday while watching those beautiful athletes file onto the field."[2]

The freedom movements of the 1960s had achieved significant political, social, and cultural gains for America's marginalized communities. During the 1970s, black people and other populations of color built on the advancements made possible by the civil rights movement. The second-wave feminist movement gave women entrée to arenas of American life they had been excluded from previously. LGBTQ communities were more forcibly claiming their rights and achieving an unprecedented degree of political representation. The election of Harvey Milk to the San Francisco Board of Supervisors in 1977 signaled the potential of gay political power. Moreover, communities of color and LGBTQ communities were revolutionizing popular music and culture by ushering in the disco revolution.

However, these advances ran into strong reactionary countercurrents. White resistance to the Black Freedom movement zeroed in on busing and affirmative action. This was the era of violent white protests against the court-ordered desegregation of schools in Boston, and the

Regents of the University of California v. Bakke Supreme Court decision, which banned institutions from using quotas to achieve racial
equity in college admissions, began the decades-long rollback of affirmative action programs. Conservative activist Phyllis Schlafly attacked
feminism by building a powerful campaign against the Equal Rights
Amendment. Meanwhile, homophobia intensified during the late
1970s. The "Save Our Children" movement led by Anita Bryant, the
famous singer and anti-gay crusader, launched a fearmongering campaign to portray the extension of civil rights laws to gays and lesbians
as the sanctioning of pedophilia. At the same time, the fervent cultural
backlash against gay influences in American popular culture, such as
the anti-disco movement, were reactionary responses to the inroads
LGBTQ people were making into US politics and society. These movements, among others, helped to create the conditions for a conservative
counterrevolution that resulted in the election of Ronald Reagan to the
presidency in 1980.

It was fitting that the American stadium became a major site of
struggle for the gay rights movement. What had transpired in the
1930s, when the stadium was an arena for the struggle against fascism,
or in the 1960s, when the Black Freedom movement used the stadium
to rally support for civil rights, unfolded again in the late 1970s and
1980s when the question of gay rights intensified in the United States.
Chicago's Comiskey Park became the site of a sudden anti-disco riot,
while in San Francisco and New York, two epicenters of the gay liberation movement, the stadium became an important locus of activism. In the face of a powerful homophobic backlash and the onset of
the HIV/AIDS crisis, LGBTQ activists pushed back and created their
own institutions, like the Gay Games, while they crafted a radical conception of health care. As in previous decades, the stadium functioned
as the arena where what it meant to be an American was defined and
fought over.

It is perhaps not by accident that LGBTQ incursions into the stadium space occurred when there was a relative lull in stadium construction. After the stadium-building boom of the sixties and seventies,

when forty-eight stadiums and arenas were built for Major League teams across the country, the pace of construction slowed considerably. Only four outdoor stadiums were built for major professional sports franchises during the 1980s as opposed to seventeen that would be built for baseball and football teams a decade later. By no means was this a complete stoppage in stadium building. Indeed, eleven indoor arenas were built for NHL and NBA teams during the eighties. Yet, it was a period when most sport franchises were content to share stadiums and arenas with other teams and other entertainment industries. Before long, sports teams would renew their efforts to make municipalities build new stadiums. In the 1980s, however, most of the existing arenas and stadiums remained teams' primary homes. The municipally controlled stadium, where public entities exerted influence over usage, was still largely intact during the decade. This arrangement gave the public greater access to these facilities, a situation that activists took full advantage of. Though stadium use largely followed the desires of the sports industry, the stadium continued to operate as America's public square.

THE STADIUM, LIKE THE SCHOOL BOARD, THE GOVERNMENT, AND THE radio airwaves, was a battleground of the gay liberation and reactionary forces that were gaining strength in US society. In fact, it was the baseball stadium, the setting of "America's national pastime," where a segment of the anti-gay movement decided to take a most dramatic stand. In the minds of anti-gay activists, the United States was becoming too gay, and the ballpark seemed to be an ideal location to attempt to restore a white heterosexual order. On the night of July 12, 1979, in Comiskey Park in Chicago, the White Sox, the city's American League baseball franchise, partnered with local rock radio station WLUP to host a promotion called "Disco Demolition Night" during a twi-night doubleheader against the Detroit Tigers. The promotion, which was organized by twenty-eight-year-old team executive Mike Veeck and the station's popular twenty-four-year-old disc jockey Steve Dahl, granted discounted admission to anyone who came to the game with a disco record. The records were placed in a box and would be blown up during a ceremony between the two games.

Music fans converging on stadiums was hardly unusual in the 1970s. Since the historic Beatles concert at Shea Stadium in 1965, music promoters had increasingly used stadiums and arenas as venues for their acts because they accommodated larger crowds that resulted in bigger paydays for musicians, record companies, and other ancillary components of the music business. Moreover, stadiums seemed to be better environments for crowd control in comparison to the unwieldy pigpen-like atmosphere of the Woodstock festival in 1969. After the Beatles' demise, groups like Led Zeppelin, the Rolling Stones, The Who, and Pink Floyd performed in stadiums and arenas across the country. The 1972 Wattstax concert at the Los Angeles Memorial Coliseum and the 1973 Fania All-Stars concert at Yankee Stadium showed how black and Latin music acts were also part of the entertainment circuit. Other R & B and pop acts performed at stadiums and arenas, including Earth, Wind, & Fire, Gladys Knight and the Pips, and the Ohio Players. What was unusual about this particular occasion on July 12, 1979, was the purpose of the gathering. Fans did not come to see the Rolling Stones or The Who. Rather, most of them came to deliver a public rebuke of another musical genre that was threatening to depose rock from its top status in American popular music. A cultural war was raging, and Steve Dahl, the WLUP disc jockey, was ready to lead the charge.

During the mid- to late 1970s, disco was sweeping the nation. A dance music that was first popular in urban queer communities and communities of color was suddenly becoming mainstream, especially after *Saturday Night Fever* hit theaters in 1977. The movie and its record-setting soundtrack, which featured the Bee Gees, took disco into white suburban America. A year after the movie was released, approximately fifteen to twenty thousand disco clubs existed across the country. The Bee Gees became a hot musical act on the stadium circuit. In 1979, they capitalized on their fame by embarking on a multicity tour, playing at major stadiums and arenas all over the country. Radio stations, long the arbiters of musical taste in the United States, were suddenly playing more and more disco. And stations that had previously played classic rock music dumped their rock formats in favor of disco, and their ratings soared.[3]

The latter development was particularly galling to Steve Dahl, who had been fired from his job as deejay for WDAI in Chicago after the station abruptly shifted to a disco format in December 1978. Though he landed on his feet with another job only a few months later, Dahl decided to wage a war against disco, calling on rock-and-roll fans and others to be "dedicated to eliminating Disco Dystrophy in our lifetime."[4] Dahl interpreted his firing as evidence of his disfranchisement rather than as an everyday occurrence in the cutthroat world of the entertainment business. Indeed, he saw the radio station's decision as a manifestation of a troubling trend in American culture. Disco was not only taking over the airwaves but also turning white men into a nation of Tony Maneros, the lead character played by John Travolta in *Saturday Night Fever*. "It's an affliction in which you're forced to wear white three-piece suits, blow dry your hair for two hours, do dances in a sexually-extroverted manner, and wear a cocaine spoon around your neck," Dahl claimed with derision to anyone who would listen. Evoking the image of the three-piece-suit-and-gold-chain-wearing man who dances and drinks piña coladas was a trope he repeated again and again in numerous interviews. His caustic humor both trivialized disco while making it seem threatening. Humor became the coded language to rage against his imagined displacement of the straight white man from centrality in American society. It was a formula that successfully incited his radio audience.[5]

During his radio segments, he would play a few minutes of a disco song and then simulate blowing up the record. On other occasions, he'd elicit many laughs by pulling out Donna Summer records and cracking them over his head. He had a particular disdain for rock musicians who recorded disco tunes, such as Rod Stewart. Stewart's "Do Ya Think I'm Sexy" formed the basis of Dahl's musical parody, "Do

You Think I'm Disco," which told a tale of a presumably straight man unable to secure a date with a woman who preferred to party at a disco club. By the end of the tune, the man discovers the error of his ways. Rather than continuing to chase women who won't give him the time of day, he melts down his gold jewelry into a Led Zeppelin belt buckle, ditches the three-piece suit, and listens to rock-and-roll music. What the misogynistic, homophobic anthem, along with a host of other stories reported in the press, revealed was that the most threatening thing about disco was that gay men seemed to be displacing straight men in attracting women's affections.[6]

Notwithstanding claims to the contrary, the anti-disco movement was much more than a funny disc jockey poking fun at a musical genre. Over the course of the spring and summer in 1979, Dahl's one-man campaign escalated into a massive crusade against disco. Years later, he reflected on his ability to "tap into some disenfranchisement on the part of the young rock and roller." Disco was one of many targets attacked by a broader reactionary movement against civil rights, women's rights, and gay rights during the mid- to late 1970s. The backlash against the expansion of rights was a war raged along racial, gendered, and sexual lines. Although in subsequent years Dahl went out of his way to dispute claims that he was racist and homophobic, the rhetoric and the violent tenor of his movement illustrate that the stakes were much higher than he acknowledged. Like others in the reactionary backlash, Dahl used coded language rather than explicitly hateful rhetoric. The movement against the Equal Rights Amendment (ERA) and the anti-busing movement learned how to use the terms *values* and *save our children* rather than overt racist or homophobic rhetoric to justify their causes. Others co-opted the language of "rights" and "freedom" to restrict the rights of others. These tactics have been tried-and-true rhetorical strategies used by conservative movements ever since.[7]

Indeed, the anti-disco crusade turned out to be much more than Dahl deriding disco on his radio broadcasts. It also involved the formation of groups, like his Insane Coho Lips Anti-Disco Army, which claimed to have seven thousand members, whose purpose was the "eradication and elimination of the dreaded musical disease known as disco." In June 1979, the group began to directly confront disco fans at clubs and at disco events in the Chicagoland area. Only direct confrontation could stop the threat of disco, Dahl insisted. Similar anti-disco campaigns were waged throughout the country. As far as he and his fans were concerned, the fate of heterosexual manhood was at stake. Men were blow-drying their hair, dousing themselves with cologne, heading out to disco clubs, and, worse, dancing and acting like gay men. Given the increasingly confrontational nature of the anti-disco movement, it made sense for its leaders to pick a baseball stadium, itself imagined as a traditional bastion of conservative American values, for Dahl's movement to make its most dramatic stand.[8]

And yet Comiskey Park in the late 1970s was a somewhat odd place for an anti-disco event. As one of the oldest stadiums in the United States that was built during the golden age of stadium construction in the 1910s, Comiskey Park was often portrayed as one of the most traditional ballparks in the country. Nevertheless, in the late 1970s, the stadium's atmosphere was anything but traditional. This is because the team that played its home games at the ballpark, the Chicago White Sox, was run by Bill Veeck, the renegade nonconformist team president who fashioned himself as the everyman team owner. He was the son of Bill Veeck Sr., who had been the president of the Chicago Cubs National League team during the 1920s. The younger Veeck grew up in ballparks working for his father in virtually every aspect of stadium operations. Experiencing his formative years at Wrigley Field, the Cubs' home stadium, instilled an abiding love for the ballpark atmosphere. Indeed, Veeck played a decisive role in making Wrigley the beloved ballpark that it eventually became. He designed its bleacher section, installed its famous hand-operated scoreboard, and planted ivy against the stadium's outfield walls, giving the ballpark its distinctive look. Veeck was a genuine baseball enthusiast rather than a team owner simply looking to make a buck. His unconventional attitude made him a beloved Chicago figure and a reviled person among his fellow team owners.

During his career as owner of the Cleveland Indians, the St. Louis Browns, and the Chicago White Sox, he did everything in his power to attract fans of all types to the ballpark. To the renegade Veeck, the ballpark was a place for everyone. His calling card was the baseball promotion, using P. T. Barnumesque gimmicks designed to bring fans out to have a good time. "The most beautiful thing in the world is a ballpark filled with people," Veeck was fond of saying. When he owned the St. Louis Browns in the early fifties, he hired Eddie Gaedel, a little person, to hit in a Major League game. On another occasion, he held a manager-for-a-day promotion that allowed fans to coach his team from the stands using placards. During his tenure as president of the White Sox, he held ethnic nights, such as "Polish Night," "Irish Night," "Mexican Fiesta Day," as well as long-standing promotions like Bat Day. His team even held a "Disco Night" featuring a dance competition only a few weeks before the infamous Disco Demolition promotion.[9]

Veeck's promotional flair enlivened the Comiskey Park experience during his two stints as owner of the White Sox (1959–1961 and 1976–1980). He revamped the standard scoreboard into something more spectacular, what he called an "exploding scoreboard," which set off a theatrical display of lights, fireworks, and explosions after White Sox home runs. The center-field bleachers were a quintessential Veeckian scene. He installed a shower so that fans could cool off on hot days. He set up a barber so that spectators could get a haircut or a shave while watching the game. Veeck made Comiskey Park a happening place, and the team's fan base loved him for it.

In 1979, however, the White Sox team president unwittingly allowed his ballpark to become a theater for the reactionary anti-disco crusade that was sweeping the nation. Indeed, the sixty-five-year-old White Sox president likely had little inkling of the depths of the anti-disco movement. As far as he was concerned, Disco Demolition was just another promotion designed to boost attendance. The White

Sox were performing poorly on the field, so Veeck leaned more heavily on his gimmicks to bring fans to the ballpark. It was his son, Mike,
who was largely behind the Disco Demolition idea. Mike enjoyed
Dahl's radio shtick and shared the deejay's disdain for disco. Bringing Dahl and his army of disco haters to Comiskey seemed to be a
great idea. However, even Mike Veeck could not fathom the forces
that would be unleashed at the ballpark on that hot night in July.

Bill and Mike expected thirty-five thousand fans that evening.
Even before the six o'clock start time of the first game in the doubleheader, it was clear that they had drastically underestimated the
number of people who would converge on the old stadium. The crowd
quickly overwhelmed ushers and security guards and pushed into the
ballpark. Comiskey's seating capacity, which was 44,494 in 1979, was
easily exceeded. Estimates of the crowd that night, which included
the thousands of fans who could not be accommodated inside the stadium, vary from 50,000 to 90,000. Even more fans were stuck in traffic on the nearby Dan Ryan Expressway. Undaunted, some fans who
were unable to secure a ticket took matters into their own hands and
climbed into the park through the outfield portals. Once inside, many
hung variations of DISCO SUCKS banners all over the stadium. By the
middle of the first game, the aisles were overflowing with spectators.
There was no place for fans to go except onto the field.[10]

Riled up by Dahl's radio rants and primed in a culture of confrontation, the supporters of the anti-disco crusade were not there to
cheer on the White Sox. Indeed, many of them had little interest in
the ballgame and were more interested in wreaking havoc. A telling
moment occurred before the game as singer-actor Alan Cassman sang
"The Star-Spangled Banner." Cassman, dressed in a black three-piece
leisure suit with a white butterfly collar and sporting a feathered haircut, seemed to be doing his best to resemble Tony Manero. As Cassman sang: "What so proudly we hailed," someone in the crowd yelled
"faggot," an epithet that revealed the undercurrent of homophobia that
permeated the anti-disco movement. Given all Dahl's rantings against

the Tony Maneros of the world, it was no wonder that Cassman elicited such a response from a member of the audience. It was a clue to what lay in store later that evening.

The crowd's unruliness unfolded soon after the first game of the doubleheader began. Recurrent chants of "Disco sucks!" echoed through the ballpark as spectators flung fireworks, bottles, and other projectiles onto the field. Stadium crowds in the seventies were often unruly, but the scene at Comiskey that evening was extreme even by the standards of the day. The projectile of choice was records, which were transformed into dangerous frisbees as they sliced onto the diamond, some nearly hitting players. The beer was flowing, and the smell of marijuana wafted through the stadium all night long. Crowds at Comiskey were always rambunctious, but the mood that night was more menacing than normal.

After the first game ended, a 4–1 win for the Tigers, the main event of the evening—the Disco Demolition program—ensued. Steve Dahl, dressed in military fatigues and a World War II–style army helmet, rolled onto the field in a jeep as the self-styled commander of the Insane Coho Lips Anti-Disco Army. At his side was Lorelei Shark, a model that WLUP used to promote the radio station. Her appearance as Dahl's sidekick was meant to reinforce an aggressively straight masculinity. "This is now officially the world's largest anti-disco rally!" Dahl yelled into the microphone. "We rock and rollers will resist, and we will triumph," he insisted. After he led the crowd with "Disco sucks!" chants, he alerted them to the presence of a large crate that was filled with disco records. In actuality, the box contained only a fraction of the thousands of records fans had brought to the park that night. As promised, the crate was detonated, and the crowd joined Dahl in roaring its approval. Comiskey Park suddenly resembled a war zone. Smoke filled the air and broken records were strewn all over the outfield grass. Revisiting the telecast decades later, one can't help but associate the event with ritual book burnings employed by reactionary movements at other moments in history.

The grounds crew undertook the unenviable task of cleaning up the mess. After the record-demolition ritual, Dahl and his crew departed in his jeep and disappeared into the night. But the festivities were far from over. As the grounds crew tried to ready the field for the second game of the doubleheader, and as players warmed up, thousands of people suddenly swarmed the field. The promotion was over, and the riot commenced. Fans slid down both foul poles, tore up the field, stole bases, lit bonfires, and destroyed the White Sox batting cage. Bill Veeck, Mitch Michaels from WLUP, and popular White Sox announcer Harry Caray fruitlessly pleaded with the rioters to get off the field. Caray begged the revelers to go back to the stands so that the White Sox could win the second game of the doubleheader. The rioters could not have cared less about a White Sox win. They came to take a stand against disco, not cheer for the Sox. Nancy Faust, the popular organist for the team, played various tunes to coax the fans off the field to no avail. After a while, Chicago Police Department's tactical force was called to disperse the crowd. Thirty-nine arrests were made and, miraculously, only a few people were injured. The fact that the crowd was almost exclusively white undoubtedly influenced the police officers' relatively casual approach toward the rioters. It is hard to fathom the police using the same methods to disperse a crowd of black revelers from the nearby district of Bronzeville.

The relatively mild use of force by the police has contributed to the notion that what transpired that evening was simply an episode of overmuch revelry rather than a dangerous reactionary event designed to make a statement against a perceived threat to American society. Though the police quickly restored order, the field was severely damaged and determined to be unplayable, causing the White Sox to cancel the second game of the doubleheader. The next day, the American League ruled that the White Sox failed to fulfill their responsibility for ensuring a playable environment, and the game was forfeited to the Tigers.

Debates about the meaning of that infamous night at Comiskey Park continue to rage decades later. In the years since, Dahl has vehemently denied that his movement was racist and homophobic. "I'm worn out from defending myself as a racist homophobe," he wrote in a 2016 retrospective. "I like to think of it as illustrative of the power that radio has to create community and share similarities and frustrations," he insisted. However, placing him and his anti-disco army in the larger context of the resurgent movement against civil rights and gay rights reveals that he and his campaign were engaging in classic reactionary behavior. Dahl turned out to be a prototype of the angry white shock-jock radio personality that would come to prominence in subsequent years. Moreover, the only nonwhite people at Comiskey that night were playing on the field or working in the stands. The racial dimensions of the episode were clear to Vince Lawrence, a black usher who recalled white fans yelling "Disco sucks!" while breaking a Marvin Gaye record in front of his face. For many in the crowd, the fact that Gaye was not a disco performer was irrelevant. Disco was coded as gay and black.[11]

The history of disco portrays Disco Demolition Night as a catalyzing event in the rapid decline of the musical genre. In subsequent months, disco tunes dropped off the *Billboard* charts, and disco performers saw gigs disappear almost overnight. What was in one moment a popular craze that swept up seemingly everyone abruptly became a widely ridiculed and disparaged culture. Although the musical genre lost popularity among the straight white suburban set, and it elicited disdain from fans of the newly emerging cultural phenomenon of hip-hop, disco and its variants did not die after the Dahl debacle at Comiskey Park. In Chicago, disco influenced the emergence of a new dance musical genre called house music, which became popular in black and Latino urban communities in the 1980s. Many pop-music artists, from Madonna to Beyoncé, would dip into the disco repertoire in the years to come. Indeed, the music of America's marginalized communities continued to influence popular culture and politics, as became evident in yet another old stadium on the West Coast a few years later.[12]

KEZAR STADIUM WAS YET ANOTHER FACILITY THAT WAS BUILT DURING the stadium construction boom of the 1920s. In 1922, the estate of Mary Kezar left the city of San Francisco $100,000 to build a memorial for her family. The city augmented the gift with $200,000 and built a stadium on the site of horse stables, wedged into the southeast corner of Golden Gate Park. Unlike most facilities, Kezar was not constructed for a particular professional or college team. Rather, it was conceived as a municipal stadium for local high school and college athletic competitions, including soccer, football, and track and field. Though, like all stadiums, it was hailed as "second to no other municipal field in the United States" at the time of opening, it was, in fact, a no-frills, Spartan structure. It was a poor man's Los Angeles Coliseum: a less-extravagant oval-shaped single-tiered structure. However, it fulfilled the function as the city's main athletic field for decades. Since the day Kezar opened its doors in 1925, the stadium has hosted all sorts of events: track-and-field competitions, boxing matches, World War II reenactments, high school and college sports, and pro football. It became a beloved and reviled San Francisco institution. Uncomfortable splintering bleachers, unsightly restrooms, aggressive seagulls, and rowdy crowds characterized the world of Kezar.

The stadium was home to the San Francisco 49ers from 1946 to 1971. It also hosted the East-West Shrine Bowl college football classic for many years. These events put the stadium on the national sporting landscape even as it maintained the intimate feel of a high school sports facility. It was analogous to the classic baseball stadiums, such as Wrigley Field, so often celebrated by baseball ballpark enthusiasts, a neighborhood stadium built in a densely populated urban area. When the automobile age arrived after World War II, Kezar's lack of parking forced fans to try their luck in the surrounding neighborhood. It was a facility open to spectators of all backgrounds, including Italian immigrants as well as African Americans. The stadium held a special place in the hearts of generations of San Franciscans.[13]

After the departure of the 49ers, the stadium seemed more and more to be the home of the city's budding countercultural and radical movements. It was a stone's throw from the Haight-Ashbury district, the epicenter of the Summer of Love of 1967. Kezar hosted large political demonstrations, including two rallies against the war in Vietnam in 1967 and 1972. Though the stadium remained the home field for many high school football teams, the rowdy, masculine working-class crowds at 49er games in the fifties and sixties were replaced by fans of rock music and the counterculture during the seventies. Kezar became part of the stadium rock phenomenon, hosting a number of rock concerts organized by Bill Graham. Thus, by the early eighties, it made sense for this community stadium to house an event organized by the city's burgeoning gay and lesbian community.

San Francisco in the 1970s was a hub of the gay liberation movement. More and more gays and lesbians made their way to the city, and an extraordinary explosion in the number of grassroots LGBTQ organizations took place. As the city's reputation as a gay mecca grew, so did the queer population, rapidly expanding from approximately 90,000 in 1972 to approximately 150,000 by 1978, out of a total population of around 700,000 people in the county. The Castro district rose as a gay neighborhood in the few years after the 1969 Stonewall uprising in New York City, when an increasing number of queer folks were "coming out."[14]

As they had in the pre-Stonewall era, bars and bathhouses played a central role in gay social life. In San Francisco, these institutions were supplemented by new grassroots collectives, such as the Gay Community Softball League, founded in 1973. The league was a welcome environment for gay men of all types, including Glenn Burke, the super-talented black baseball player who was the first openly gay Major League Baseball player in the late 1970s. Though he was hounded out of the Major Leagues, he managed to find a home in San Francisco's gay softball scene. Sports also served as a refuge for lesbian women, who created their own softball and bowling leagues. The annual Freedom Day parade also took shape and became one of the largest events in the nation. Publishing houses, newspapers such as the *Bay Area Reporter,* coffeehouses, bookstores, theaters, and gyms were pillars in the city's social life. The powerful gay liberation movement also produced results at the ballot box. Queer access to city government expanded with the election of George Moscone in 1975 and, of course, the historic election of Harvey Milk to the San Francisco Board of Supervisors in 1977.[15]

The city's status as a gay center did not prevent it from being affected by the nationwide anti-gay reactionary movement. Inspired by Anita Bryant's "Save Our Children" anti-gay campaign in Miami, California state senator John Briggs spearheaded a campaign for Proposition 6, a voter referendum that proposed forbidding gays and lesbians from teaching in California schools. A resourceful grassroots movement led by Milk and other gay and lesbian activists built a powerful coalition to defeat the bill. Just a few weeks later, however, Dan White, an aggrieved white former member of the San Francisco County Board of Supervisors, walked into City Hall and proceeded to assassinate both Moscone and Milk. White had resigned his position, then became incensed when Moscone refused to support his desire to be reinstated. The shocking murder was devastating to many in the city. The situation worsened when, a few months later, unbelievably, White was convicted of manslaughter instead of murder and given a light sentence. The verdict spurred the massive White Night riots as the gay community reacted to the White verdict with outrage. It was in this cauldron of community upheaval that the project of the Gay Games took shape.[16]

"I WILL TELL YOU UNABASHEDLY THAT THE FIRST GAMES WERE MY idea," Tom Waddell wrote in his diary in 1983, "a very idealistic notion that had been growing in my head for many years. I simply had to wait for the proper time for it to happen." The idea might have been percolating in his head for years, but it emerged because of his exposure to the gay sports scene in San Francisco. Accounts of the origins of the Gay Games contain slight discrepancies. Waddell claims they came about after he watched a gay men's bowling tournament with Mark Brown, a fixture in the city's gay softball and bowling leagues. Brown insists that Waddell joined the bowling league in 1978, but Waddell makes no mention of his participation in the bowling league years before. In any case, it is clear that the existing gay sports scene influenced Waddell's vision of a large gay sports competition. Indeed, the experience of competing in an openly gay sporting event, as opposed to competing in a mainstream competition and keeping his sexual identity hidden, likely helped Waddell realize that the time was right for a bigger gay and lesbian sporting event.[17]

Tom Waddell, like many gay men during these years, migrated to California and arrived in 1970. He became a prominent athlete and physician, but he was not born with class privilege. Born Thomas Flubacher in 1937, he had a rough childhood growing up in Paterson, New Jersey. As a young man, he found his way under the guidance of Gene and Hazel Waddell, who essentially adopted him and encouraged him to pursue his passions. The Waddells exposed him to the pleasures of kinesthetic activity. Gene was an acrobat and Hazel was a dancer, and both had a profound influence on Tom as a youth. Though he developed a passion for dance, he opted for sports because he was worried about homophobia. "I really wanted to be a dancer," he recalled years later, "but who were the dancers in the late fifties? They were 'faggots.'" Dancing carried the suspicion of being gay. "There was a stigma. I didn't want to be 'a homosexual.' I wanted to be a person." Waddell's recollections reveal his larger perspective on sport and sexuality. The scourge of homophobia led him to fear that others would see him as a "homosexual" and, therefore, not a person. Sport could provide the acceptance and the normativity that he desired. It also provided the physicality that he craved. Track and field was his calling, and he became a topflight decathlete during the fifties and sixties.[18]

Waddell's peripatetic life eventually took him from medical school to a stint working in the civil rights struggle in Selma, Alabama, to the

US Army, where he was a medical officer and paratrooper until he indicated that he would claim conscientious objector status instead of serving in Vietnam. He expected to be court-martialed, but instead he was sent to train with the US Olympic team. At the age of thirty-one, he made the team as a decathlete and competed at the 1968 Olympics in Mexico City, where he finished sixth among thirty-three competitors. He also publicly supported Tommie Smith's and John Carlos's Black Power protest during the Games, an act that drew the ire of the US Olympic Committee. After more stops on his career track, including serving as a physician for a Saudi prince, he eventually settled in the Mission district in San Francisco. In 1976, he became one of the first athletes to come out as gay in an article published in *People* magazine.[19]

Waddell's association with Mark Brown led to the creation of the Gay Games. Brown was a well-known figure who was active in the city's softball and bowling leagues while also covering sports for the *Bay Area Reporter.* Waddell, Brown, and Paul Mart formed the United States Gay Olympic Committee on June 15, 1980. Brown's contacts helped spread the word, and Waddell traveled across the country promoting the concept and finding enthusiastic support. Soon after their group was formed, however, they got word from the US Olympic Committee that they could not use the word *Olympic* without USOC's permission. They'd presumed that the term *Olympic* was generic. Why should they not? After all, all sorts of organizations and businesses used the word. As Waddell noted, there were thirty-three listings in the San Francisco phone book that used the term *Olympic.* But what they learned was that a piece of legislation, called the Amateur Sports Act of 1978, prohibited use of the term "for the purpose of trade, to induce the sale of any goods or services, or to promote any theatrical exhibition, athletic performance or competition." Thus, they were forced to change the name of their organization to San Francisco Arts & Athletics, Inc. (SFAA). This would not be the last time they would hear from the US Olympic Committee.[20]

Nevertheless, SFAA's organizational efforts continued apace. They set up shop in an office in the Castro district and went to work. An indication of the LGBTQ community's political strength was SFAA's ability to obtain the support of local leaders, including Mayor (and future Senator) Dianne Feinstein. Their political clout helped them secure the necessary venues for the event, including facilities at San Francisco State University, San Francisco City College, and Kezar Stadium, the old stadium in Golden Gate Park that was managed by the city's Recreation and Parks Department. The Gay Games were set to take place from August 28 to September 5, 1982.[21]

The idea of the Gay Games included artistic exhibitions and concerts in addition to athletic competitions. Waddell and the organizing committee were committed to a vision of participatory sports, one where athletes would be encouraged to do their best. Although Waddell claimed to be inspired by the "true" Olympics vision of community and understanding forged through international sports, what was planned for the Gay Games deviated substantially from the model of the International Olympic Committee (IOC). This event was about neither the triumph nor the struggle. It was about the participant. SFAA rejected the hypercompetitive, hypercommercialized, and nationalistic character of the Olympic Games and most mainstream sports competitions. The Gay Games would offer a more inclusive alternative, inviting athletes from all backgrounds and abilities, young and old, heterosexual, bisexual, gay, lesbian, and so on. "The goal is self-fulfillment, participation," Waddell told the *San Francisco Examiner*. "No ageism, sexism or nationalism." Some competitions, such as relay races, would have men and women competing together, and athletes represented cities, not nations.[22]

Gay Games organizers were also committed to women's participation. Women athletes were still fighting for equal treatment in the global Olympics, but women's participation in the Gay Games was an outgrowth of the long-standing role sports played in lesbian communities. For that reason, the committee sought out athletes and leaders in local lesbian communities. Rikki Streicher, a pioneering community leader who owned Maud's, one of the longest-existing lesbian bars in the country, was among the committee's earliest supporters.[23]

Another important figure was Sara Lewinstein, who was active in the local lesbian bowling and softball leagues—she had the contacts to ensure substantial lesbian participation in the event. Lewinstein became much more to Waddell than a key collaborator. Their deepening relationship led them to marry and have a child together. In a sense, the Waddell–Lewinstein union exemplified the aspirations of the leaders of the Gay Games movement. The idea was for the Games to bring the gay and lesbian communities together and implement an administrative structure that reflected gender parity rather than the normal male-dominated structure of most sports institutions at the time.[24]

But, for all the radical participatory ethos of SFAA, the effort was also marked by Waddell's homonormative vision, which alienated many members of the gay community. Whenever Waddell could, he emphasized that the Gay Games aimed to destroy negative stereotypes of gay people, especially gay men. He envisioned the event providing the perfect occasion to debunk stereotypes "of men with lisps who cross their legs like women, mince down the street, and have wrist drop." In *Gay Olympian*, Dick Schaap, Waddell's biographer, wrote: "Tom felt the gay community was represented in public only by its most outrageous elements, by drag queens and leather boys, who were, in his view, only a small percentage of the community." According to Schaap: "The majority of gay men, Tom knew, were, like himself, professionals, doctors, lawyers, advertising men, salesmen, men who went to the theater and the cinema, who voted and ate out, bowled and played softball and rooted for the 49ers. They were not flamboyant lusting for attention."[25]

Waddell had assimilationist impulses, even though he never deviated from his commitment to defend gay life. He wanted gays and lesbians to celebrate their identities, but he also wanted them to be seen as men and women and not to be overdetermined by their sexual orientation. This is why critics of the Gay Games movement highlight the problems with the movement's desire for acceptance from the imagined heterosexual mainstream. The Gay Games movement was, as Judy Davidson has written, "from its inception, an assimilationist project." And yet, a closer look at the Gay Games festivities at Kezar Stadium reveals how the organizers were unable to keep the limp-wristed, campy, and effeminate men at bay. They, too, wanted to publicly celebrate their way of life at the Gay Games.

Yet, before the Games could begin, Waddell and SFAA had to contend with the aggressive hostility of the United States Olympic Committee. The USOC denied Waddell's requests to use the term *Olympic* in the event's title. Then, on August 9, 1982, only a few weeks before the Games were scheduled to begin, USOC tried to lay the hammer down on Waddell and his committee by filing papers to prevent the group from using any *Olympic* terminology, claiming SFAA was not "suitable" to use the term. The USOC tried to dissuade some athletes from participating by threatening to exclude them from the opportunity to compete in the 1984 Olympic Games. With the backing of the dubious Amateur Sports Act, the USOC was able to force SFAA to undertake the costly endeavor of erasing the word *Olympic* from all its publicity and posters and ephemera. The USOC refused to budge even as it faced widespread condemnation of its capricious actions.

Tom Waddell illustrating the hypocrisy of the USOC.
Credit: Federation of Gay Games

As it turned out, the Gay Games didn't need the blessing of the lords of the USOC after all. The morning of August 28, 1982, was gray and damp. Marsha Veale and the stadium renovation team had gotten Kezar ready enough to seat up to thirty thousand spectators, though a much smaller crowd of ten thousand ultimately showed up that day. Still, the enthusiasm in the air was palpable. The athletes gathered outside the stadium, and spectators filed inside to sit on Kezar's uncomfortable bleachers as rain sprinkled the crowd. But the dreary weather and the dilapidated stadium did not dampen their spirits. Right before the start of the ceremony, the rain stopped and the fog lifted. Rita Mae Brown, the well-known writer and activist, took the stage as the event's emcee and told the crowd: "We're here today not to celebrate homosexuality but to celebrate and affirm individual freedom."

Despite the USOC's threats, the ceremony had the unmistakable influence of Olympics-style rituals. The Gay Games put together its own transcontinental torch run, which had begun weeks before at the historic Stonewall Inn and concluded at Kezar. USOC officials must have groaned when they learned about the opening ceremony's conclusion, when a torch was lit to mark the beginning of the Gay Games. The torch run and lighting were totally modeled on the Olympic torch ritual. After the torch was lit and the national anthem was sung, the Freedom Day Marching Band performed with baton twirlers, who proved that gay men "too have strong wrists."[26]

The highlight of the ceremony was the procession of athletes. They entered through the tunnel on the west side of the stadium and paraded around the field. The crowd stood and roared continuously as athletes held signs indicating the city or country they represented. Some wore uniforms, some were dressed in civilian clothes. They came from Belgium, Canada, Germany, Ireland, New Zealand, Australia, France, Peru, and Scotland and from cities and towns all over the United States. The San Francisco team came dressed in cobalt-blue jackets and pants, Canadian players wore white shirts and red pants, and Belgians sported green and yellow. Meanwhile, the New York delegation wore shirts and ties. It was an impressive sight: athletes of all shapes and sizes representing so many distinct communities.[27]

After the procession, a celebratory yet defiant air was palpable during the speeches of Waddell and local officials. Congressman Philip Burton condemned the USOC's mean-spirited treatment of the Gay Games. Doris Ward, a member of the County Board of Supervisors, elicited a thunderous ovation when she unapologetically declared: "It is my prerogative to make proclamations, and I do proclaim this, the Gay *Olympic* Games." The continuous roar of the crowd revealed the outpouring of emotion by many who witnessed this historic festival at rickety old Kezar Stadium. "When the Gay Games are remembered," wrote Scott Treimel in the *Bay Area Reporter*, "the crux of that memory will be what happened next: the parade of athletes. This had been the center of the dream and this is what coaxed the tears." A sixty-seven-year-old named Bill Vocke wept as he watched the parade of athletes: "I've waited my whole life for this kind of demonstration," Vocke told Stephanie Salter, the pioneering sportswriter who was among the first women to cover sports for a major newspaper. "I was born in a closet and got blown out of the closet. You have no idea what it means to have gone through what we did and then see this at the end."[28]

Narratives of coming out of the closet were repeated during the week of the Gay Games. Jill Ramsey, one of the hundreds of volunteers who helped organize the event, told the *Bay Area Reporter*: "The Games offer another place to 'come out' besides a dark bar."[29] The bar had always been a central institution in gay and lesbian social life. The Gay Games made it possible for them to come out in an outdoor space, the stadium, the building that had heretofore been identified with heterosexual men. These accounts of the opening ceremony are akin to the accounts of the impact of Wattstax ten years earlier. Though the attendance at the Gay Games was much smaller, the impact was also powerful. The crowd was moved by the spectacle of seeing so many of "their" people celebrated in a space usually denied to them.

After the parade of athletes and the speeches, it was time for rock star and queer icon Tina Turner to take the stage. Twelve years before, she had performed with Ike and the Ikettes at the Soul Bowl concert at Tulane Stadium to raise money for scholarships for black students. Now, in 1982, she showed up in an animal-print dress sans her abusive ex-husband Ike, celebrating another part of her fan base. In the midst of her rebirth as a rock-and-roll solo artist, Turner performed the Rolling Stones' hit song "Jumpin' Jack Flash." Just a few years later, she would sing many more rock songs all over the world in front of some of the largest crowds in stadium rock history. The festivities continued after Turner left the stage.

For the next week, competitions took place throughout the city. Thirteen hundred athletes from twelve countries and twenty-eight states competed in sixteen events, including basketball, billiards, bowling, cycling, diving, golf, marathon, physique, powerlifting, soccer, softball, swimming, tennis, track and field, volleyball, and wrestling. The events that drew the biggest crowds were the track-and-field, wrestling, and physique competitions. Tom Waddell informed the press that the Gay Games were projected to break even financially, which was a major success considering that SFAA had put together the expansive event on a shoestring with their small operation running out of the Castro Street office.[30]

The closing ceremony took place on September 5, 1982. A small but exuberant crowd took over Kezar Stadium to celebrate what turned out to be an undeniably successful event. Among the highlights were another procession of athletes and a performance by Stephanie Mills, the star from the black Broadway musical *The Wiz*. One of the true ironies of the event unfolded during the performance of the Gay Games Flag Corps. As their routine drew to a close, they broke into Antonia Rodriguez's disco version of Ritchie Valens's famous song "La Bamba." The crowd clapped and danced as the corps danced off the field. In the summer of 1979, Steve Dahl had proclaimed the end of disco at Comiskey Park. Three years later at Kezar Stadium, gay and lesbian athletes and their fans showed that disco and dance music were alive and well, and they did so by enjoying a disco-ized version of a famous rock-and-roll tune composed not by a white man but by Valens, a Mexican American. The seemingly innocuous performance sent a message that was loud and clear, even if it was not noticed by the press: disco was not dead, gays and lesbians were still dancing, and the roots of rock and roll were not white but black and brown.

A revisiting of the closing ceremony also shows how the event was transformed into something much more than Tom Waddell's homonormative vision. Indeed, during the week, many of the gay organizations that Waddell perceived to be perpetuating "negative" stereotypes made their presence felt. At the finals of the basketball competition, the Hayward Rah Rahs, the "outrageous cheerleaders from Oakland," and the Sisters of Perpetual Indulgence, the popular street performance and gay advocacy group, led cheers and performed on the sidelines. Waddell and SFAA tried to keep the men in drag away from the scene, but they could not keep them from showcasing their centrality to gay performance culture.

The point was emphatically made by novelist Armistead Maupin, the emcee at the closing ceremony. "As one who had a deep and abiding fear of recess," Maupin applauded "the fags of all nations, sissies, and bull dykes and plain old garden variety queers" who had participated in the Gay Games. He urged the crowd to "stop apologizing to our oppressors and get to the business of living our lives." In what must have sounded like a direct rebuke of Waddell's assimilationism, the novelist declared: "I know that there are people out there who say that these Games are meant to dispel stereotypes, to show that we are no different from the rest of the world around us, but I'm sorry, I don't buy that. We *are* different! And it's time that we said so."[31] Indeed, the limp-wristed queers would not be shunted aside, and even if they were put off by some of the assimilationist tendencies of the Gay Games organizers, they still understood the event's historic importance for LGBTQ communities. Though the rituals of the opening and closing ceremonies were modeled on those of the Olympic Games, what was staged on the field and in the stands of Kezar was an unmistakable manifestation of queer pageantry that was evident to all who attended.

The Gay Games of 1982 became Gay Games I when SFAA decided to host another Gay Games event in San Francisco four years later. But, in the intervening years, the lives of many participants, including Tom Waddell, would be turned upside down by a deadly plague that wreaked havoc, especially among gays and lesbians.

READERS WHO PICKED UP THE AUGUST 7, 1986, EDITION OF THE BAY *Area Reporter* would have read all about the festivities planned for Gay Games II—the parties, the athletic competitions, and the various cultural activities. They also would have seen a large advertisement by the SF AIDS Foundation on page 13 of the newspaper: "A Message About AIDS to Male Athletes & Visitors" welcomed visitors to the Games and reminded them that they were arriving amid "a deadly sexually-transmitted epidemic." The ad pleaded with visitors to "please don't have unsafe sex while you're here." The list of unsafe sex practices included "anal intercourse without condom, rimming, fisting, blood contact, share sex toys or needles, semen or urine in mouth, vaginal intercourse without a condom." The foundation hoped that everyone would "take home wonderful memories of exciting events" and "warm new friendships." Finally, using a sport metaphor, the foundation called upon everyone to "play to win, and play to live."[32]

The AIDS crisis formed the backdrop of Gay Games II, which was held August 9–17, 1986. The disease that was just becoming known by the broader public during the 1982 Gay Games was an epidemic four years later. The excitement and anticipation were tempered by the recurring ritual of grieving those who'd lost their lives to the virus. San Francisco's LGBTQ communities were in mourning. However, the volunteerism that organized the Games was representative of the grassroots activism and social life that had characterized the gay and lesbian communities in San Francisco for decades. Community organizations pivoted toward the work of advocacy and care as an increasing number of people died of AIDS. To be sure, the politics of health and safe sex was established by the communities afflicted with AIDS in places like San Francisco. As Tom Waddell put it: "We may have one of the highest incidents of AIDS cases in the nation, but we are by far the 'AIDS Awareness Capital' of the world." Waddell spoke from personal experience. By the time of Gay Games II, he had become infected by the virus.[33]

While SFAA continued full speed ahead to organize the Games, the planners had to operate within the context of continual harassment from the USOC and intensifying homophobia catalyzed by the emerging Christian Right. In 1984, the USOC filed a suit against SFAA demanding that the group pay for the USOC's $96,000 legal fees. A lien was placed against Waddell's home to coerce compliance with the legal ruling. Meanwhile, SFAA's struggle to use *Olympic* in its event's title reached its end when the Supreme Court narrowly affirmed the USOC's right to monopolize the use of the term *Olympic*. At the same time, the AIDS epidemic fueled anti-gay activism, with many arguing that the government had no reason to address a disease that afflicted supposedly "immoral" gay men. These beliefs shaped the Reagan administration's attitude toward AIDS, which did not acknowledge the existence of the disease until 1985.[34]

Once again, Kezar Stadium would be the venue for the opening and closing ceremonies of Gay Games II. As they had before, the committee spruced up the stadium to make it look as attractive as possible. The bleachers were peeling, and weeds had sprung up through the cement. Yet, even as dilapidated as it was, the stadium still fulfilled its purpose. Roy Coe, who chronicled the 1986 Gay Games II, visited the stadium with Bud Coffey, the director of the opening ceremony. Coe recalled the emotional impact the ceremonies four years before had had and was imagining a similar scene at Gay Games II. "As Bud spread out the blueprints, I looked up suddenly and felt a spine-tingling chill run up my back. Tears came to my eyes as I imagined the climax of our years of preparation. The stadium was a beautiful sight. It was hard to leave that afternoon and head back to the office." Kezar was acquiring a new reputation as it entered its later years. It had transformed from the scene of raucous football fans to one where the city's queer

communities were affirmed in a public manner. As in 1982, the stadium hosted the most memorable moments of the Games.[35]

Gay Games II was a much bigger affair than the first festival. Any
doubts about the popularity of the Games were laid to rest in 1986. The
event was well on its way to becoming a mega sporting event. The number of participants was 3,842, nearly three times the number who participated in 1982. Athletes came from thirty-seven states and sixteen
foreign countries and two US territories. SFAA made a concerted effort
to further internationalize the event, reaching out especially to "Third
World countries." A roster of participants came from Brazil, Mexico,
Nicaragua, the Virgin Islands, Samoa, Australia, Canada, England,
France, Greece, Ireland, Italy, Japan, the Netherlands, New Zealand,
and West Germany. Efforts to include US athletes of color were largely
successful. As in 1982, even if most participants were people defined as
"white" in the United States, the event was a transracial, international,
and transcultural affair.

The Games also had a more robust arts component. Even those
who had no interest in sports attended. Indeed, it was as much a cultural festival as a sporting event. SFAA's Cultural Events Committee
staged twenty-two events, including readings, plays, concerts, parades,
films, and dances. Among the programs for the week were "Kindred
Spirits & New Works: An Art Exhibit Featuring Black Artists," a staging of Jean Genet's play *The Maids*, "the Zuni Man-Woman," a program on alternative roles that was held at the Woman's Building in the
Mission district, and of course a cabaret event.[36]

The stated goal of Gay Games II, as for Gay Games I, was to
"demonstrate that homosexuals are not different." Yet, for all its
assimilationist rhetoric, the programming surrounding Gay Games
II shows that its primary purpose was not to convince straight America of the legitimacy of gay and lesbian life. The primary constituents were the gays and lesbians who had created this community
event in an effort to survive the rising tide of homophobia—and, as
it turned out, a deadly disease that was largely ignored by the federal
government.[37]

Medal winners,
Gay Games II, 1986.
Credit: Robert Pruzan collection
(1998–36), Gay, Lesbian, Bisexual,
Transgender Historical Society

As was the case in 1982, the highlights of the 1986 gathering were the opening and closing ceremonies at Kezar. The festivities followed a similar script as 1982's: the parade of athletes followed by politicians' speeches, including one from Mayor Dianne Feinstein. Tom Waddell was honored, as was the entire SFAA board of directors. There was an array of performances by precision dancers, marching bands, and black women singers, including Broadway sensation Jennifer Holliday and native San Franciscan Cindy Herron, later of En Vogue fame. At the closing ceremony, Waddell announced that the next Gay Games were to be staged in Vancouver. San Francisco's LGBTQ communities had done their work. A new sporting event was now part of the international sporting landscape, whether the lords of the IOC and the USOC liked it or not.

Gay Games II was hailed as a major success, though the event still had its critics. Don Hiemforth expressed the sentiments of many who found Waddell's assimilationism off-putting: "I've nothing against those who enjoy sports of any kind," he wrote in a letter to the *Bay Area Reporter*, "but I most strenuously object to the Waddells of this world denigrating the sissy/faggots of this world." Indeed, Hiemforth insisted that the "sissy/faggots of gay life and gay culture paved the way for the Waddells and his ilk many, many years ago and made such things as even the Gay Games possible." Though many like Hiemforth were understandably annoyed by Waddell's insistent disregard for non-normative gay men, Stephan Pardi, a Gay Games volunteer, found the event rejuvenating, especially in a period of gloom caused by the AIDS crisis. "As a native San Franciscan, I have seen many changes in the City and in our community; most recently, a definite and understandable downtrend. However, during that week, a special, warm, wonderful and rare quality descended upon us, and lifted our burdened hearts and saddened spirits. It was as catching and spreading as the virus, but this time, everyone affected welcomed it."[38]

Less than a year after Gay Games II, Tom Waddell, like so many others, died from AIDS-related complications. His historical role in the gay rights movement was secure. His career as an athlete and activist created a space for gay and lesbian athleticism and showcased the broader community's sporting cultures, even if his vision was augmented in ways he might have disagreed with.

San Francisco's gay and lesbian communities showed what it was like to come out at the ballpark and celebrate their undeniable imprint on American society. More than three thousand miles to the east, another group of gay and lesbian activists insisted on making their presence felt in the American public sphere. LGBTQ activists continued to pioneer the freedom struggles of the 1980s, and like their fellow activists in San Francisco, they took their cause to a stadium.

ON MAY 4, 1988, AN UNUSUAL MESSAGE FLASHED ACROSS THE AUXILiary scoreboard at New York's Shea Stadium during a regular-season National League game between the New York Mets and the Houston

Astros. A crowd of 29,936 fans watched the Mets easily defeat the Astros 8–0, but they saw a lot more than a one-sided win for the home team that evening. Typically, the Diamond Vision scoreboard flashed messages to welcome groups in attendance or wish "happy birthday" to fans. This night, a large and exuberant group of spectators seated in three different sections of the stadium was at the game to make another point. "Welcome the National Women and AIDS Day Committee" flashed across the Diamond Vision as the group roared its approval. Organized by the Women's Caucus of the AIDS Coalition to Unleash Power (ACT UP), they had come to deliver a public service announcement: AIDS was a disease that did not just afflict gay men as was commonly thought in the late 1980s. It also afflicted women. The solution, they tried to tell fans that night, was safe sex, and the responsibility fell on heterosexual men as much as it did on women.

The scoreboard message was one of the highlights of ACT UP's incredibly successful demonstration at Shea Stadium. The organization, formed in March 1987 in New York City, was a political action group that had come together with an extreme sense of urgency to end the ongoing AIDS crisis. The 1988 Shea Stadium demonstration was a vivid example of the group's growing visibility. ACT UP's decision to use the stadium to deliver its message was effective: thousands of people at the ballpark as well as many others watching on television witnessed the scoreboard notice. The activists left the ballpark that evening with a sense of accomplishment. They had co-opted the presumed heterosexual space of Shea Stadium to deliver an urgent public service announcement that was not being delivered by the government or anyone else.

Shea Stadium was a highly unlikely venue for an AIDS awareness demonstration. It was, like so many public works in twentieth-century New York City, a creation of Robert Moses, the so-called master builder. It was constructed in the aftermath of the Brooklyn Dodgers and New York Giants departing for California in 1958. Moses wanted to build a stadium in Flushing Meadows Corona Park in Queens, the site of the 1939 and 1964 World's Fairs, a place that the Dodgers had rejected but that the new franchise that came to be known as the New York Mets accepted. Ground was broken in 1961, and the stadium opened for business in April 1964. Named after William Shea, one of the driving forces behind a National League franchise to replace the Dodgers and Giants, the stadium was a modernist, multipurpose structure.

Like many midcentury stadiums, Shea was imagined as an entertainment venue for white suburbanites. Erected in Flushing Meadows Corona Park in the middle of a freeway interchange that connected Robert Moses's Grand Central Parkway with the Van Wyck Expressway, the ballpark seemed to be the perfect setting for suburbanites who were fleeing New York City for Queens and Long Island in the post–World War II years. Like RFK Stadium, Shea turned out to be less of a pretty picture of white suburbia and more of an unremarkable, functional structure that was very much a part of the city. It was accessible via the nearby freeways that the great Robert Moses had built and well connected to Manhattan and other boroughs via public transportation. The stadium was reachable not merely by the suburban commuter Long Island Railroad but also via the elevated subway train, which made it possible for urbanites to trek out to Queens. This is precisely the route the ragtag group of AIDS activists traveled to Shea Stadium on that memorable night in 1988.

In the months leading up to the Shea Stadium demonstration, ACT UP was making a name for itself, joining a larger national movement demanding that the indifferent federal government address the AIDS crisis. Though the group was initially dominated by gay men, by the spring of 1988, the organization encompassed other constituencies affected by AIDS. It was in this context that Maxine Wolfe and other women activists began to address the concerns of lesbian and straight women. What became known as the Women's Caucus of ACT UP launched the series of nonviolent direct-action protests that the group became known for. In January 1988, the caucus organized five hundred people to storm the offices of *Cosmopolitan* magazine after it published an article that claimed heterosexual women could not get AIDS. Other actions followed in subsequent weeks before the group decided to coordinate with other branches across the country and launch a "Nine Days of Rage" campaign in late April and early May to promote awareness of the various ways communities were affected by AIDS. It was within this campaign that the Women's Caucus concocted the plan to invade Shea Stadium.

One day of the Nine Days of Rage campaign would focus on women's experiences of the epidemic. Up to that point, 4,769 women had been diagnosed with AIDS, and the number of women who had contracted HIV through sexual contact was rising rapidly. Maxine Wolfe saw the hypocrisy of public service advertisements telling women to carry condoms while straight men were not held accountable for their sexual behaviors. The real question was clear: How do we address the role of heterosexual men in spreading HIV? So, the group put their heads together. "What is a place that is considered quintessentially heterosexual male?" they asked. It was Debra Levine, a new member of the group, who replied, "A baseball game!" They chose Shea Stadium as the site of their demonstration when they found out that the Mets had a home game scheduled in the middle of the Nine Days of Rage. Demonstrating at the stadium would give them the platform and the audience they desired to convey their message that AIDS was not merely the concern of gay men. The women's group ran with the idea and decided, following the organization's protocols, that they would propose it to the larger ACT UP group at their weekly meeting.

Suddenly, the Women's Caucus of ACT UP was tasked with presenting the proposal for a demonstration at a baseball game to a room of gay men. Not surprisingly, the membership did not like the idea, arguing that staging a protest in the unfriendly confines of a baseball stadium was doomed to fail. Indeed, sporting events were hardly hospitable environments for gays and lesbians. However, Maxine Wolfe encouraged them not to presume that the ballpark environment was more homophobic than other parts of society. Wolfe's group offered a clearer picture of who actually attended games at Shea. "Do you know who goes to Shea Stadium?" they asked. "*We* go to Shea Stadium. Kids go to Shea Stadium on Friday nights to pick each other up. Queers go to Shea Stadium." Then, almost as if on cue, all "the closet ballgame queers," as Wolfe jokingly recalled years later, admitted to their peers that they, in fact, also liked to attend baseball games. The idea gained legitimacy, and the plan for the Women and AIDS Day action was on.[39]

Yet staging such an event at Shea Stadium was risky business, and it required careful planning. ACT UP had to figure out how to get into the stadium, how to disseminate their message, and how to handle the ubiquitous presence of the police, who were becoming increasingly hostile toward ACT UP. The organizers came up with a masterful plan. They engaged in a massive effort of repurposing ballpark rituals for their own purposes. First, they took advantage of the special group sales packages the Mets made available to the public. Their source was Debra Levine, who was familiar with the Mets through her work on a public art event in the stadium parking lot at the same time. The team offered two free tickets to groups that purchased forty seats. Moreover, buying a certain number of tickets entitled a group to post a message on the team's fancy full-color Diamond Vision scoreboard.

Weeks before game night, Wolfe and Levine trekked out to the ballpark to investigate the protest site and to purchase tickets. They hoped to get into the stadium to ascertain the width and length of the sections to calculate the size of the banners they would unfurl. However, they were told by the ticket office that they could not enter the stadium because it was undergoing preseason renovations. Undaunted, they saw an open corridor and walked in, only to be stopped by a security guard. They played the role of clueless "femmy" women who were unaccustomed to the protocols of attending a baseball game. "Oh, you know, this is our very first baseball game and we're coming here with a whole bunch of friends," Wolfe recalled telling the security guard. "We wanted to see the seats and we're worried because we don't know anything about it and don't you think we can just go inside and just look?" Their act convinced the guard to relent, and Wolfe and Levine checked out their seats and measured the dimensions of the sections.[40]

They'd bought tickets in three sections in the upper deck of the U-shaped stadium; a total of 252 seats were either purchased or donated.

In a coordinated call-and-response pattern, each section would unfurl banners displaying different messages: AIDS KILLS WOMEN; MEN, USE CONDOMS; NO GLOVE, NO LOVE; DON'T BALK AT SAFER SEX; STRIKE OUT AIDS; and of course, SILENCE = DEATH, the group's well-known slogan. The ingenious plan gained momentum, especially after it was publicized in the *Village Voice* newspaper. Soon, Wolfe was receiving phone calls from other activist friends who wanted to participate in the novel demonstration.

The Women's Caucus realized they had one more factor in their favor. In addition to flashing placards and large banners in the stands, they hoped to reach fans by leafletting before the game. They printed thousands of flyers with playful appropriations of baseball terminology, but they had to figure out how they would disseminate them without running afoul of the police. The City of New York owned the stadium and the surrounding parking lot. However, the stadium was leased to the Mets, and the parking areas were leased to Kinney

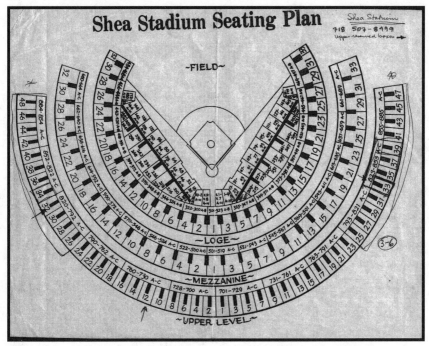

ACT UP's Seating Plan at Shea Stadium. *Credit: Lesbian Herstory Archives*

Parking Company. The group discovered that a street between the stadium and parking lot was a legal no-man's-land where they could set up shop freely without harassment from the police or stadium employees. It turned out to be the ideal location to disseminate flyers and condoms. As was the case with activists in the black and women's freedom movements, gay and lesbian activists took advantage of the public nature of stadium management to repurpose the space for their own benefit.

The Shea Stadium action took place without incident. The Mets might have been nervous about selling tickets to a queer activist group, but they ultimately concluded that ACT UP was just another organization that wanted to attend a ballgame. The team also agreed to disseminate the information packets that ACT UP prepared for the press. Activists coordinated their banner unfurling. They chanted their slogans, and some even managed to enjoy a lopsided Mets victory. The demonstration caught the attention of the local press. Moreover, there is no evidence that they were harassed by fans. Perhaps most remarkably, the stadium cameras flashed an image of two women kissing on the scoreboard, much to the group's delight. This was very likely an unprecedented occurrence in the history of ballpark entertainment. Decades before sports teams adopted LGBTQ+-friendly gimmicks, including the now ubiquitous "kissing camera," the fact that the camera displayed two women kissing in 1988 in a baseball stadium is extraordinary.[41]

The Shea Stadium action, like the Gay Games competitions earlier in the decade, illustrates how LGBTQ communities used stadiums as venues to build community, protest homophobia, and make their presence known to the broader public. It also shows how the stadium continued to serve the function of public square. Even amid rising ticket prices in the 1980s, they remained accessible to a public that was wider than the American sports fan. As leaders in the struggle against AIDS, gay and lesbian activists delivered their message loudly and often. The Shea Stadium action showed how the struggle against AIDS became part of a broader campaign for accessible quality health care. The case for immediate health care was made all over the country, at the Centers for Disease Control and Prevention, the National Institutes of Health, the White House, the headquarters of *Cosmopolitan* magazine, and the great American cultural institution: the baseball stadium.

The Shea Stadium demonstration has gone down in the annals of ACT UP history as one of the more important actions that helped propel the organization to national prominence. "We not only got to twenty thousand people who were in the ballpark, but it was televised around the country and we gave out leaflets," Wolfe recalled. "We reached an incredible number of people in an audience we'd otherwise never have been able to get to."[42]

WRITER AND HISTORIAN SARAH SCHULMAN HAS CHARACTERIZED the history of LGBTQ communities in this period as "a story of a despised group of people, with no rights, facing a terminal disease for which there were no treatments." From the late 1970s until the late 1980s, LGBTQ communities faced intensifying hostility in US politics and society. The "Save Our Children" campaign of Anita Bryant, the assassination of Harvey Milk, the reactionary anti-disco movement, the rise of the Christian Right, the election of Ronald Reagan, and, of course, the mass death caused by HIV/AIDS threatened the survival of gay and lesbian communities. And yet, this was also the period when gay and lesbian activists had a profound influence on American society by insisting on widening the conceptions of American citizenship and transforming American popular culture. They fought these battles in the statehouses, in city halls, in the streets, and in the stands and on the fields of America's stadiums.[43]

The gay and lesbian movement in this period marked the beginning of the end of the accessible municipal stadium. In 1989, the San Francisco Recreation and Parks Department finally razed ancient Kezar Stadium. Unlike many other stadium demolitions, the building's demise did not result from a sports franchise pressuring local officials for a new facility. The city simply reached the point when a sixty-thousand-seat venue was no longer needed in Golden Gate Park. Still, many mourned the demise of the sixty-four-year-old building. M. J. Murphy, a writer for the *Bay Area Reporter*, couldn't help but remember the glorious moments of the Gay Games that occurred there only a few years earlier. "Walking past there the other day I could almost hear the yells and cheers of the crowds in the rubble that used to be Kezar," he wistfully recalled. "It's a shame that the old place had to come down."[44] Fortunately for the city, Kezar was tastefully renovated into a smaller stadium that catered to the surrounding community.

Kezar's conversion into a community facility was not the typical outcome for the twentieth-century stadium. Venues with much shorter shelf lives than Kezar, many of which had housed events of the freedom struggles in the 1960s through the 1980s, were soon abandoned and demolished. In the years to come, the increasingly powerful sports industry and a new cadre of architects and ballpark enthusiasts were eager to say goodbye to the midcentury so-called cookie-cutter facilities, such as Shea Stadium. These once-touted state-of-the-art stadiums were suddenly perceived by ballpark enthusiasts and sports franchises as eyesores that needed to be replaced with fancier, amenity-filled stadiums and arenas that prioritized the needs of pro sports more than the broader American public's. The movements that sought to bring the stadium in line with the country's professed democratic principles would find it much harder to insist upon their presence in the years to come. An institution that largely accommodated America's marginalized peoples between the 1960s and the 1980s would soon be turned into a tool of domination in America's newly gentrifying cities in the 1990s and beyond.

CHAPTER SEVEN

CORPORATE TEMPLES OF EXCLUSION

I n the 1980s, at the same time that Northern California became the site of the gay liberation movement in sports, it was also the incubator of a sports revolution of another kind entirely. A slipshod operation of a pro basketball team was floundering and failing miserably in Kansas City, Missouri. An NBA team known as the Kings announced that it was moving to Sacramento, California, after only twelve seasons in Kansas City. The announcement was in some ways unsurprising. Two years earlier, a real estate businessman named Gregg Lukenbill was part of a Sacramento-based ownership group that purchased the Kings for $10.5 million with an eye toward moving the team to his hometown, even though at the time of purchase the new owners claimed they had no interest in moving. To Lukenbill, the fact that Sacramento was the twentieth-largest media market and the sixth-fastest-growing city in the country qualified it for a pro sports franchise.[1] The new Kings' owner got his wish when the league approved the proposal to move the team in April 1985. On the other hand, the relocation was somewhat surprising because pro sports teams typically did not move to small "cow towns" like Sacramento, whose only claim to fame was that it was California's state capital. However, Lukenbill worked hard to ensure that the city was ready for its new team. The Kings' arrival created the impetus for a new arena, and it was at that moment when a seemingly routine franchise relocation became the precursor of a major revolution in stadium construction and the business of sports in general.

In previous decades, pro sports franchises often used the threat of relocation to attain better stadium deals, and this was a major driver of stadium construction nationwide. As the four major professional sports leagues in the United States (NFL, MLB, NBA, and NHL) gradually gained monopoly power in the sports industry, either through the courts or through effective lobbying of Congress, they commanded more leverage vis-à-vis public officials. The monopoly power of sports leagues kick-started the midcentury stadium construction wave when Milwaukee, Baltimore, Kansas City, Los Angeles, and San Francisco built new facilities for the Braves, Orioles, A's, Dodgers, and Giants baseball clubs, respectively. These franchise moves also created the expectation that governments would do whatever they could to provide the infrastructure and financing for stadium construction. This was how DC Stadium for George Preston Marshall's Redskins and the short-lived Washington Senators was built in the nation's capital.

By the 1980s, franchise moves in professional sports were more commonplace as teams followed the template established in previous decades. In 1982, Oakland Raiders owner Al Davis moved down the coast to Los Angeles against the wishes of NFL commissioner Pete Rozelle, triggering a nasty attenuated legal battle between Davis and the league. Two years later, Baltimore Colts owner Robert Irsay broke the hearts of his loyal fan base when he infamously moved the team to Indianapolis by sneaking out of town in Mayflower trucks in the middle of the night. These franchise relocations triggered enormous controversy as fans and critics argued that owners were clearly putting greed ahead of any sense of loyalty to the cities and fans who supported their teams. However, the criticism did not stop other owners from using the threat of relocation to get advantageous stadium deals.

Franchise moves in the NBA were also common, but they tended to be signs of weakness, not strength. Professional basketball teams would eventually get their chance to play the stadium game, but that moment had not yet arrived in the 1980s. Pro basketball was still struggling to expand its audience in the United States, and the league was littered with vagabond franchises that were searching for fans. With some exceptions, NBA teams had only begun play in the late 1960s, and thus, they did not have the deep connections to communities that baseball teams and football teams possessed.

Franchise instability in the NBA continued in the 1980s, even as the league rose in popularity. In 1984, a real estate businessman named Donald Sterling moved the Clippers franchise from San Diego to Los Angeles. Eight years earlier, the team had moved to San Diego from Buffalo, where it had been known as the Buffalo Braves. The Kings, like the Clippers, was one of a number of franchises that moved multiple times throughout its history. The Kings was a fairly mediocre team that never really gained a foothold in Kansas City. It began as a semipro team in Rochester in 1923 before it joined what became the NBA in 1948 and moved to Cincinnati in 1957. The team gave it a go in the Queen City for fifteen seasons until it packed up and moved once again. The next stop was actually *two* cities, Kansas City and Omaha, where the Kings split home games for six years before finally settling in Kansas City for just seven seasons. Then it headed to Sacramento, a city with no history of major professional sports franchises. In comparison to the contentious moves of the Raiders and Colts, the Kings' departure for Sacramento was almost a nonevent.

In retrospect, the move acquires a larger historical importance. Lukenbill successfully cajoled the Sacramento Board of Supervisors into rezoning an area on the outskirts of town to allow him to erect a new arena for his team. He quickly constructed a temporary facility while the board figured out how to finance and build a permanent arena. The most noteworthy aspect of the Kings' arrival in Sacramento was not the move itself but the name of the team's new arena. The new building was not named after the team or in honor of local veterans.

Instead, it was named after a corporation. Lukenbill had hatched an agreement with the Atlantic Richfield Corporation (ARCO), one of the biggest oil companies on the West Coast. On August 26, 1985, the company signed a ten-year $7 million contract for the naming rights to the new arena. It would be known as ARCO Arena. "We didn't want a name that sounded like a commercial. Arco Arena has a pretty good ring to it," Kings vice president Bob Whitsitt told the press. Whitsitt continued: "We're not hanging a banner that says 'Arco.' It's not a commercial anymore, it's the name of our building. It just so happens that the name of our facility happens to be the name of a commercial sponsor," he said. Simple as that. Sacramento mayor Anne Rudin praised the ARCO name as a "creative way" to finance the Kings operation. "Advertising is used in so many ways. It's appropriate to use it to benefit Sacramento and the team," she insisted.[2]

By getting Atlantic Richfield to put its name on the arena for a large fee, Gregg Lukenbill jump-started a revolution in the sports industry and, by extension, in the history of American stadium construction. A few years later, Great Western Bank came to an agreement

ARCO Arena, Sacramento, 1985. *Credit: Rocky Widner/NBAE via Getty Images*

with Jerry Buss, the owner of the Los Angeles Lakers, to put its name on the Forum, the team's home arena. The Forum, which team owner Jack Kent Cooke had informally dubbed the "Fabulous Forum" when he built the arena, was now officially called the Great Western Forum. The next year, an arena built for the Timberwolves, the NBA's new expansion franchise in Minnesota, was named the Target Center, after the emerging department store corporation. Within a few years, stadiums built for baseball and football joined the trend of corporate naming rights. Team owners and municipalities could not resist the advertising dollars lavished upon them by corporations eager to jump into the lucrative game of sports advertising. Over the course of the next thirty years, virtually every stadium and arena in the country would be named after a corporate sponsor. The days of memorial stadiums and arenas were coming to an end. Stadiums, once attached to places and local histories, were now becoming a new kind of corporate billboard.

Stadiums had always been entangled in the commercialization of sports, even as they served as public commemorative and civic spaces. Company sponsorships were pivotal to making sports franchises viable, and the stadium space was the logical venue to display these partnerships. One only needed to look at scoreboards to see the impact of company sponsorships on sports teams and the places where their games were played. When stadiums and arenas became publicly owned and managed during the mid-twentieth century, advertisements of corporate sponsorships were less prominent, relegated almost exclusively to scoreboards. In some cases, stadiums were named after team owners' companies. But the Kings–Atlantic Richfield deal ushered in a new era of franchises and corporate sponsorships. Stadium naming-rights deals were suddenly seen as viable mechanisms of stadium financing and construction.

The rise of the corporate naming-rights agreement dovetailed with the explosion of stadium construction after Lukenbill's sojourn to Sacramento. During the next three decades, the United States embarked on another stadium construction boom, one that was much larger than the previous upsurges of the 1920s and 1960s. Hundreds of arenas and stadiums were built for professional sports franchises all over the country. Stadiums became more numerous, cost more money, and occupied more real estate even as facilities' seating capacity decreased. What is more, they were products of a new type of urbanism. Stadium architects abandoned concrete designs for buildings decorated with brick, glass, and steel. Once admired for their modernist aesthetics, midcentury stadiums were derided as "concrete doughnuts" by sports franchises and like-minded journalists and architectural critics, who claimed that these earlier designs were ugly and failed to satisfy fan bases. Yet the praising of new stadium design obscured the astronomical construction costs. Facilities that had cost tens of millions of dollars in the 1980s cost more than a billion dollars in the early 2020s. Moreover, stadiums and arenas proliferated because most sports franchises were no longer willing to share their facility with other teams. Whereas sports teams once did not have the power to demand their own stadiums from public officials, during the final decades of the twentieth century the balance of power decisively shifted toward sports franchises.

Lukenbill's ARCO Arena was a tiny, intimate, fan-friendly facility because it was designed to be a temporary home while a larger permanent structure was built. The new stadiums and arenas that were built in subsequent years took up larger footprints in the urban and suburban landscape. They symbolized the outsized impact of the sports industry in late-twentieth- and early-twenty-first-century America. In a sense, the United States embarked on a second Gilded Age. The new palaces were not adorned with towers and statues of Roman goddesses built on private property, like Stanford White's Madison Square Garden. Rather, they were adorned with tiers of luxury suites and premium seating built on public property that catered to affluent corporate fans and were plastered with billboard advertisements as far as the eye could see. Commerce and consumption displaced the stadium's historic role as a venue of public recreation and civic engagement.

Stadiums and arenas might have been providing more entertainment options for Americans, but after the 1980s, they looked more like monuments to the widening income gap and racial inequities of a new age of gentrification. Unlike the Gilded Age of a century before, few if any sections of these new mega structures were reserved for working-class spectators, who were priced out of the stadium altogether unless they were present as workers in the stands or on the field of play. Though team owners and politicians touted stadiums as engines of economic development and revitalization, they were, in fact, more often resource-sucking money pits that provided poor returns on investments.[3] They were also increasingly segregated and heavily secured. The freedom movements of the 1960s enabled athletes and performers to knock down the racial barriers that had kept them off the courts and fields of play. By the 1990s, they were performing for whiter and more affluent spectators, who at once admired and resented the fact that they were watching players and entertainers who made salaries more than what they perceived to be deserved.

COMMERCIALISM HAD ALWAYS BEEN AN INEXTRICABLE PART OF American stadium design. Companies had advertised their products in stadiums since the facilities' earliest incarnations. Baseball stadiums were among the first to showcase billboards around the park. Local companies played a key role in popularizing baseball, for example, in the game's earliest days. Chief among the businesses that emerged as team sponsors were breweries. Beer barons sometimes owned teams and venues outright. In the 1880s in St. Louis, Chris Von der Ahe, the German beer magnate, pioneered the practice of investing in baseball to sell his beer. His team, the St. Louis Brown Stockings of the American Association—derided by the established National League as the "Beer and Whiskey League"—made the early ballpark into a carnivalesque atmosphere akin to Coney Island. At Von der Ahe's ballpark, tickets were cheap, and plenty of alcohol flowed in the beer garden installed in the outfield. The flamboyant beer baron died broke and the American Association went belly up, but alcohol advertising and consumption became alluring parts of the stadium scene, much to the dismay of the rival clubs in the National League.[4]

Company advertisements and consumer culture continued to be part of the stadium environment. The baseball stadiums that were built during the 1910s and 1920s regularly featured advertisements on scoreboards and outfield walls. Shaving, cigarette, and oil companies were prominent advertisers during this era. Still, the connection between breweries and baseball clubs fostered the more lucrative relationships. The banning of alcoholic beverages by Prohibition in 1919 was a setback for sports entrepreneurs like New York Yankees owner Jacob Ruppert, but it did not prevent him from pouring some of his beer wealth into his Yankees franchise. Beer and baseball were a business combination that outlasted the temperance campaigns against alcohol. Whether it was legal or not, alcohol and baseball helped make the sport and the stadium popular among spectators across social classes.[5]

Only a few stadiums were named after companies during these years. The historic Wrigley Field in Chicago was named after the team's owner, William Wrigley, the chewing gum magnate whose name certainly advertised his company. However, the naming of Wrigley was more reflective of the tendency to name ballparks after individual team owners rather than after companies. Many of the baseball stadiums of the era were named after team owners, including Comiskey Park, Navin Field, and Ebbets Field. Meanwhile, college football stadiums possessed generic names (Tulane Stadium, Michigan Stadium, Notre Dame Stadium), or they were christened as memorial stadiums to honor those who had served in World War I.

The advent of radio and, eventually, television broadcasting in the decades after the repeal of Prohibition in 1933 deepened the connection between company sponsors and baseball stadiums. Sanctioned by organized baseball's antitrust exemption, baseball clubs were able to sell the right to broadcast their games to radio networks. These rights were paid for by advertising dollars and, most often, those dollars were supplied by local breweries. The opportunity to advertise their beers to a large radio listenership was too good to pass up. The union between baseball and beer solidified.

Evidence of this marriage was plastered on scoreboards in professional baseball stadiums across the country. The scoreboard was the place where advertisers proudly showcased their team sponsorship. By the 1950s, fifteen of the sixteen teams in the American and National Leagues had beer companies for sponsors.[6] With the notable exception of Forbes Field, the home stadium of the Pittsburgh Pirates franchise, Big League ballparks featured prominent billboard advertisements of breweries. In Milwaukee, the Miller Brewing Company financed the construction of the scoreboard at the new County Stadium.[7] At Brooklyn's Ebbets Field, the Schaefer Brewing Company had a large display on the Dodgers' scoreboard, as did Ballantine & Sons at Yankee Stadium, and Ruppert's brewing company with the Knickerbocker billboard at the Polo Grounds. Rheingold Beer, which sponsored radio broadcasts for the Mets, the new National League franchise that formed in 1962 after the Dodgers and Giants left for the West Coast, placed a large billboard on the main scoreboard in center field.

The Anheuser-Busch brewing company of St. Louis knew a good thing when it saw it. In 1953, the company purchased the St. Louis Cardinals baseball team. August "Augie" Busch was following in the footsteps of Von de Ahe and Ruppert, using a baseball team to advertise his beer business. He also purchased Sportsman's Park, which he renovated and renamed Budweiser Stadium. However, MLB commissioner Ford Frick vetoed the idea, arguing that it was inappropriate for a stadium to be named after an alcoholic beverage. Undaunted, Busch renamed the stadium "Busch Stadium," supposedly in honor of his family, but he also made sure to install a gigantic Budweiser advertisement on the scoreboard.[8] That same year, St. Louis's other baseball team, the Browns, was sold to a Baltimore-based ownership group led by two of the city's beer barons, Zanvyl Krieger of Gunther Brewing Company and Jerold Hoffberger of the National Brewing Company.

Both companies sponsored the broadcast rights of the team, now named the Baltimore Orioles, and had their company names plastered on the stadium scoreboard for years. The partnerships between breweries and baseball were prominent parts of the advertising and design of stadiums through the post–World War II era.[9]

While baseball stadiums were commercializing, football stadiums started off virtually devoid of advertisements. Professional football was still in its embryonic stage in the years after the National Football League formed in 1920, and all pro football teams were tenants in stadiums built for other purposes, usually baseball or college football. Before the 1970s, the vast majority of large facilities that could accommodate football were built by universities for their own football programs. Even though college football was very much a commercial enterprise, the ethos of amateurism prevented the placement of corporate advertisements in stadiums. Despite their large seating capacities, most football stadiums were no-frills structures with few amenities. Fans sat in uncomfortable bleacher seats and read the score on small scoreboards. A similar sensibility prevailed at indoor arenas, even though broadcasts of boxing matches were sponsored by companies who paid for broadcast rights to air those contests. Throughout the century, at the vast majority of stadiums and arenas, minimalism was the rule when it came to billboard advertising, even when accounting for the more numerous companies advertising at baseball stadiums. Most Americans did not object to this balance between civic life and commercialism. Indeed, they relished it, as a revisiting of the history of midcentury stadium construction undoubtedly reveals.

ON APRIL 17, 1964, A GORGEOUS SPRING DAY, A RADIO ANNOUNCER SAT down behind his microphone on a historic occasion in New York City. Bob Murphy, an announcer for the New York Mets, prepared to call the first game ever at the team's brand-new stadium. "Well, this is the big one, no doubt about it," he enthused to his radio audience. "This is the one we've been talking about, dreaming about, waiting for—

opening day at Shea Stadium!" During the broadcast, he marveled at
the "5-tiered $25 million ballpark." He informed listeners of the sta-
dium's numerous innovations, including the field-level seats installed
on tracks so they could roll into a different configuration to accommodate a football game, the "beautiful" scoreboard, the light towers that
would provide superior lighting for night games, and the symmetrical
field dimensions.[10]

During a break in the action a short while later, he raved about the
ballpark's accessibility by public transit. "It couldn't be more accessible," he asserted, even though the many fans who were driving to the
game would have vehemently disagreed as they sat stuck in massive
gridlock outside the stadium. When he marveled at the view beyond
the outfield fence, he probably overlooked the pollution billowing from
the thousands of cars streaming off the nearby Van Wyck Expressway.
However, he could not overlook the almost constant ear-splitting roar
of airplanes that soared over the stadium as they took off and landed
at nearby LaGuardia Airport, though he surmised that the jets were
"taking a purposeful trip over the stadium today to give the people a
chance to see it."

Still, these nuisances did not detract from the exciting atmosphere
of the new facility. Fans loved the brand-new ballpark, which, from an
amenity standpoint, was an upgrade from the Polo Grounds, the old
ballyard that had been the home field of the Giants for decades and
the Mets for their first two years. Shea's giant scoreboard beyond the
right-field fence flashed a message that encapsulated the mood of the
day: "Isn't this the most beautiful stadium of the world," leading *New
York Times* columnist Bob Lipsyte to wonder if the omission of the
question mark was intentional or a scoreboard glitch.[11]

Beautiful was the operative word to describe Shea and all the new
stadiums that opened during the sixties and seventies. Indeed, "beautiful stadium" has undoubtedly been one of the most overused phrases
in the English language for quite some time. It is a characterization that
has been invoked every time a new stadium is built, including those
that opened during the era of modernist stadiums, which baseball

historians and architectural critics now deride. "Beautiful stadium" is the catchphrase of the stadium booster, who does the work of promoting a franchise's new home. However, usage of the phrase also reveals how architectural aesthetics change over time. Beauty is in the eye of the beholder, but notions of the beautiful are historically contingent. There is no such thing as timeless beauty, as an examination of stadium history makes clear. Even though the stadiums of the mid-twentieth century have many critics, the majority of contemporary fans enjoyed their modern conveniences and simple designs. These facilities also provided relatively affordable recreational options for many Americans. Affordability and the impact of the freedom movements gave Americans unprecedented access to the nation's iconic stadiums in the midcentury years.

More often than not, the newer stadiums of the sixties and seventies were praised by boosters, journalists, and fans for their modern conveniences. Wider seats, spaciousness, better concessions, and accessibility were all attributes. They were also concrete manifestations of modern technology that delivered a pleasanter experience for spectators. In 1965, the Astrodome in Houston, the country's first indoor stadium, was loved by fans, who no longer had to suffer the oppressive Texas heat. Baseball purists were miffed by the Dome's indoor environment, the artificial turf, and the large and noisy scoreboard, but a generation of Houstonians adored the facility.

The characterization of midcentury stadiums as "beautiful" might make twenty-first-century readers scratch their heads. The Oakland Coliseum, a building that has been widely ridiculed over the past few decades, was once considered aesthetically pleasing. "A spectacular ornament to the community," gushed *San Francisco Examiner* columnist Prescott Sullivan when the Coliseum opened in 1966. "Huge and circular, it looked so nice we couldn't take our eyes off of it." *Oakland Tribune* columnist Ed Levitt was almost orgasmic when he praised the Coliseum as a "concrete Goddess" that was the "Miss America of all sports palaces. Each inch of her vast body was excitingly fresh and wholesome and suddenly we were overcome with a tingling sensation of pride."[12] Even the circular "cookie-cutter" stadiums that opened in Cincinnati, Pittsburgh, and Philadelphia were praised initially. The *New York Times* sports columnist Leonard Koppett characterized Three Rivers Stadium in Pittsburgh as "one of finest of the 13 new parks occupied by major league baseball in the last 10 years." Roy Blount Jr. wrote in *Sports Illustrated* that Philadelphia's Veterans Stadium was "much more hospitable than its run-down predecessor. In fact, it is a beautiful place."[13]

As these reviews of the midcentury stadium and arena suggest, the era prioritized utility and convenience over architectural flourishes. Indeed, the stadiums and arenas of the sixties and seventies, including baseball stadiums, displayed minimal corporate advertising. Because the vast majority of facilities were publicly managed, stadium and arena managers were reluctant to allow an excessive number of corporate billboards inside. Advertisements were relegated to scoreboards. The ad-free walls then served as blank canvases for fans to adorn with homemade signs and banners, at the encouragement of team management. Indeed, the 1970s were the heyday of banners and signs made by fans. Years later, they would be replaced by ubiquitous corporate signage.

An exemplary design of the sixties was RFK Stadium in Washington, DC. During its first eighteen seasons as a baseball and football facility, RFK Stadium displayed two advertisements on its large scoreboard: one for the *Washington Post*, the other for Peoples Drug. All the facilities built during the sixties and seventies allowed only minimal advertising. Even Dodger Stadium, Walter O'Malley's privately constructed baseball palace in Los Angeles, which opened in 1962, featured only small signs advertising the Union 76 Oil Company, which paid for exclusive rights to scoreboard advertising.

Fans often grew irritated at excessive commercialism at the stadium. In 1971, the Los Angeles Memorial Coliseum Commission, the group of public officials who managed the facility, decided it was time for a new scoreboard for the fifty-year-old building. The commission was presented with a deal it could not pass up. Atlantic Richfield

Minimal advertising at Riverfront Stadium, 1978. *Credit: Blake Bolinger, Flickr*

Oil Company and American Airlines agreed to finance the new electric scoreboard.[14] The agreement allowed both companies to place
bright and colorful, but relatively small, billboards underneath the
scoreboard. The billboards and the accompanying announcements
annoyed some fans and sportswriters. John Hall, the *Los Angeles
Times* sports columnist, reported that fans booed during a USC Trojans football game, "jeering the 433rd rerun of the animated commercial that had swallowed up, as is frequently the custom these
days, the glorious new Coliseum scoreboard." John McQuiston, a fan
from Riverside, California, was even more strident in his criticism
of the ARCO and American Airlines billboards. "Brilliantly lighted
and colorful, they detract from the potential information carried
by the boards themselves," McQuiston growled in a letter written to
the *Los Angeles Times*. "As well, they carry the implied message that
the Coliseum is no longer a public facility but a private one, for sale
to the highest bidder." McQuiston made his position on scoreboard
advertising clear: "Advertisements, however, do not belong on public
edifices."[15]

Aesthetic sensibilities were clearly different through most of the twentieth century. Yet, the changing nature of aesthetics is lost on architectural critics today. Paul Goldberger has become a leading voice among the legions of fans of the contemporary ballpark who has made a living criticizing what he calls the "concrete doughnuts" of the sixties and seventies. To Goldberger, Pittsburgh's Three Rivers Stadium was a "heavy handed concrete monolith," while the Houston Astrodome—hailed as the "Eighth Wonder of the World" when it opened in 1965—was "gargantuan and banal." Wagging his finger at the Dome's designers, Goldberger concludes that the stadium had a "windowless masonry facade with a whiff of mid-century modernist trim insufficient to make it look like anything more than a cylindrical version of a government building of the same era."[16]

Indeed, post-1990s ballpark enthusiasts solely rely on architectural aesthetics to assess stadium construction, ignoring the fact that such judgments are subjective and historically contingent. Using superficial and often inaccurate descriptors such as "multipurpose" and "suburban" to define the midcentury stadium and contrasting them with the supposedly more attractive "retro" or "jewel box" baseball facilities that were built in the 1990s, these critics do little more than reveal their preferences. The fetishizing of stadium design, contrasting "multipurpose" with "single-sport" stadiums, overlooks the fact that *all* stadiums, regardless of their design, must be multipurpose if they are to survive. A key component of stadiums—perhaps their essential component—is their accessibility to spectators. As the insightful stadium scholar Daniel Rosensweig has written, the so-called multipurpose suburban ballpark of the sixties and seventies was more inclusive than the "retro" stadiums built in the years after. "These parks," Rosensweig writes, "accommodated large degrees of social mixing merely gestured toward by historical baseball rhetoric. Cheap tickets, wide public concourses, and a lack of segregated seating enabled an unprecedented degree of fan diversity and mixing."[17]

The sixties and seventies were the high point of social urbanism, but the seeds of a new era of stadium design and sports advertising were planted then. Perhaps not surprisingly, franchises of the National Football League, a league that was gradually gaining a foothold in the American sports landscape, pushed the outer limits of what was deemed an acceptable form of corporate sponsorship. It wasn't until the early seventies, when pro football teams grew powerful enough to command the public to build their facilities, that football teams began to display advertisements in their own stadium. In 1973, the Dallas Cowboys agreed to a sponsorship deal with Pepsi that allowed the soft drink company to display an advertisement on the scoreboard of Texas Stadium, the team's new facility in suburban Dallas.

A more noteworthy development transpired that same year when the New England Patriots signed what is arguably the first stadium naming-rights agreement with the Schaefer Brewing Company. During the team's ten-year history, the Patriots, like the Kings basketball franchise years later, was a vagabond operation that struggled for survival. The team played home games at various venues, including Fenway Park and Harvard Stadium, neither of which was ideal for pro football. The club finally forged an agreement for a stadium to be built in the small town of Foxboro, but it needed funds to finance the deal. Schaefer stepped in and provided badly needed capital to make the new stadium possible. The Schaefer Stadium agreement was an outlier of sorts, a standalone case of a privately financed football facility in a period when most stadiums were funded and managed by the public. Unlike the corporate-named mega stadiums of the early 2000s, the Patriots' new facility was a cheaply constructed building that contained few amenities and fewer billboards. If the stadium's corporate name signaled the future of stadium construction, its Spartan design of backless bleachers and no protection from the elements made it very much like other football facilities during these years.[18]

By the mid-1980s, however, the era of the midcentury public facility with minimal advertising was coming to an end, and a new era of commercialism was beginning. The catalyst for this shift did not come from the world of professional sports. It came, ironically enough, from the sporting event that espoused amateurism more than any other:

the Olympics. It was the Los Angeles Olympic Organizing Committee (LAOOC) that unleashed new levels of commercialism previously unseen in the sports industry. When the International Olympic Committee (IOC) awarded Los Angeles the Games in 1978, LA was the only city left in the bidding process. With escalating costs and the recent history of terrorism that occurred at the 1972 games in Munich, few cities were interested in dancing with the IOC.

Los Angeles vowed not to rely on tax dollars to finance the Games, against the wishes of the IOC, which had previously stipulated that public funds underwrite the Olympics. But public money was not an option for the LAOOC because California was in the throes of the conservative "tax revolt" of the late 1970s, when conservative political forces convinced the public that the government was somehow excessively taxing them. The usage of public funds was coming under scrutiny, so devoting them to a sports venture was not politically viable. At the same time, the Olympic Movement suffered a major blow when the 1976 games in Montreal resulted in disastrous consequences for the host city. The Games left Montreal with an astronomical $1.6 billion debt, thirteen times the original estimated cost. There was simply no way Californians—or anyone—were going to publicly subsidize the Olympic Games in the late 1970s. However, desperation can trigger innovation, and the LA Olympic committee convinced the obstinate IOC that it could stage the 1984 Olympics without the usage of tax dollars.

To make it work, president of the LAOOC Peter Ueberroth needed the private sector to step up, and it did. Ueberroth, a travel executive, easily blew past any lingering distrust of commercialism in sports by going all in on corporate sponsorships to finance the Games. Though no billboards were displayed inside the venues that hosted Olympic events, the LA '84 Games enjoyed an unparalleled amount of corporate support. Indeed, corporate sponsorships and television rights were the main sources of financing. Ueberroth shrewdly secured an unmatched $225 million deal with ABC Sports for the rights to televise the event. Major national firms such as United Airlines, Fuji Film, McDonald's,

Coca-Cola, and 7-Eleven stepped up and lavished the committee with sponsorship money. No one had ever leveraged corporate sponsorships at this scale for a sporting event. The novelty of the effort gave the committee leverage in its dealings with all its partners, including the IOC. As a result, the Games generated an unheard of $232.5 million surplus, a feat that would not be replicated by subsequent host cities. The IOC learned its lesson well with the LA Olympics.[19]

One prominent contingent in Ueberroth's army of Olympic sponsors was Atlantic Richfield. Like other oil companies, such as Gulf and Union Oil, the company had previously engaged in broadcast rights sponsorships with the Oakland A's and the Los Angeles Lakers—and, of course, with the Los Angeles Memorial Coliseum Commission. The corporation also sponsored the ARCO Jesse Owens Games, an annual youth track-and-field competition named after the Olympic legend. In 1981, ARCO made its way into the LAOOC's "official" group of Olympic sponsors by pledging $9 million to finance the installation of new tracks at the LA Coliseum and at other fields in the region. No wonder the *Sacramento Bee* called the Kings' naming-rights deal an Ueberrothian endeavor, for he was the one who "made the Los Angeles Olympics a financial bonanza by auctioning the rights to virtually every venue to advertising-hungry corporations." The massive advertising activity generated by the '84 Olympics led writer L. Jon Wertheim to describe this period as one in which "sports was starting to make its transition from diversion to full-fledged industrial complex."[20]

In the fall of 1985, the sports-industrial complex continued to establish itself in yet another supposed amateur endeavor: college football. Going back to the advent of the Rose, Cotton, and, of course, Sugar Bowls, the sport's postseason bowl games had been conceived of as marketing tools for local businesses. However, it wasn't until 1985 when a company explicitly gained the right to attach its name to a bowl game. At that time, the Sunkist Growers Association signed an agreement with the Fiesta Bowl Committee in Phoenix. A year later, three more bowl-game naming-rights agreements were forged: the Sun Bowl

Association in El Paso, Texas, signed a naming-rights agreement with John Hancock Insurance; the Sugar Bowlers in New Orleans inked a deal with United States Fidelity and Guaranty to sponsor their annual New Year's classic; and Mazda Motors signed an agreement with the Gator Bowl in Jacksonville, Florida.[21]

Dave Lagarde, New Orleans *Times-Picayune* sports columnist, was one of many who decried the new trend in the sports industry. "If the public must be subjected to creeping corporate commercialism in bowl games, I suggest the bowls go about the task tastefully," he recommended. But, as Lagarde and many others feared, commercialism was not going away in the world of college sports. Over the next forty years, the number of college bowl games increased from eighteen games to over forty, and every single one had a corporate sponsor and a name that sounded ever more absurd. The Poulan Weed-Eater Independence Bowl, the Cheez-It Bowl, the GoDaddy.com Bowl are just a handful of examples of the tasteless practice of bowl-game naming-rights deals.[22]

In the years after Gregg Lukenbill achieved his dream of bringing pro basketball to Sacramento, the NBA embarked on a new era of expansion in order to cash in on the sport's rapidly rising popularity. NBA stars such as Earvin "Magic" Johnson, Larry Bird, Isaiah Thomas, and Michael Jordan; older stars Kareem Abdul-Jabbar and Julius Erving; and many other talents took the league to unprecedented levels of popularity and profitability. Under the leadership of Commissioner David Stern, the NBA finally was able to attract an ever-increasing segment of the American sporting public. Television money and advertising dollars filled the league's coffers. Existing franchises leveraged this popularity to forge new arena deals. In 1988, new arenas were constructed for the Detroit Pistons and Milwaukee Bucks; these arenas were technologically advanced and possessed greater potential revenue streams, such as luxury boxes for affluent spectators.

However, the NBA did more than persuade local and state governments to build new arenas. It saw that the time was right for league expansion as more cities clamored for professional basketball. In 1988, the Charlotte Hornets and the Miami Heat formed as new franchises.

One year later, two additional franchises were established in Orlando and Minnesota, followed by two more teams in 1995 when the league expanded into Toronto and Vancouver. After the Hornets moved to New Orleans in 2003, a new franchise was awarded to Charlotte one year later. Naturally, all these cities were required to build new facilities that adhered to the league's stipulations. Meanwhile, the National Hockey League embarked on its own process of expansion as ten cities were awarded new franchises during the 1990s. These cities, too, were required to build new facilities.

Suddenly, new basketball and hockey arenas were popping up at a dizzying rate in cities across the United States and Canada. During the 1980s, eleven indoor arenas were built for NBA and NHL franchises. During the 1990s, a staggering twenty-six indoor arenas were erected for NBA or NHL teams. After 2000, an additional twenty-three facilities opened for teams in these leagues. The numbers are astonishing considering that most of these arenas were shared between NHL and NBA teams, though some NHL teams expanded into other cities without basketball teams, which necessitated the building of their own ice palaces. The ability of basketball and hockey teams to cajole public officials to build new arenas indicated that pro basketball and pro hockey were approaching—and, in some cases, exceeding—the popularity of Major League Baseball. Basketball and hockey were now big-time players in the sports industry.

As these revolutionary changes in the business of sports were transforming the financing of stadiums and sports culture in general, another seismic shift in the world of stadium architecture occurred. If the revolution catalyzed by Greg Lukenbill's ARCO Arena is recognizable only in retrospect, another massive sea change in American stadium history was heralded when a new baseball stadium opened in Baltimore in 1992.

WHEN THE CAST-IRON GATES TO ORIOLE PARK AT CAMDEN YARDS were opened on April 4, 1992, the vast majority of fans, journalists, and architectural critics were enthralled. Touted as a "beautiful" ballpark even before it opened, the new building in downtown Baltimore did not disappoint. Critics raved about the stadium's "old style" design, the intimacy of the ballpark, the dramatic effect of the B&O Warehouse beyond right field, the asymmetrical field dimensions, the brick-and-steel facade, the cast-iron fence around the ballpark's perimeter, and other features designed to evoke the city's industrial past. All of it made fans feel like they were experiencing the beloved "classic" ballparks of the early part of the century, only with all the amenities of the 1990s. "With its asymmetrical field and set-back upper deck fashioned of steel trusses, Oriole Park is a fitting addition to the pantheon of green cathedrals that helped define their cities: Ebbets Field, Fenway Park, the Polo Grounds, Wrigley Field," Edward Gunts of the *Baltimore Sun* wrote weeks before it opened its doors. Gunts was one of countless journalists and architectural critics who lavished praise on the new old-time ballpark in Baltimore. The Orioles, he prophetically predicted, "have created a seminal building that will influence the way major-league sports facilities are designed from now on. It holds more lessons for combining sports and cities than the past five decades' worth of cookie-cutter stadiums that were passed off as people places. And Baltimore will be remembered as the city where they broke the mold."[23]

Oriole Park at Camden Yards was indeed a paradigm-shifting stadium. It did, in fact, signal that a new era of stadium construction was commencing. As many others have written, it brought an abrupt end to the era of multipurpose stadiums built to accommodate both baseball and football. "In one fell swoop," architectural critic and ballpark enthusiast Paul Goldberger wrote years later, "Baltimore had slain the multi-purpose dragon, the huge stadium that was made for both baseball and football and served neither adequately." The successful opening of the stadium in downtown instead of suburban Baltimore also signaled that stadiums were coming back to the city, where they would be inserted into the "urban fabric," designed to be part of the city as opposed to standing apart from it. Most stadiums and arenas constructed over the next thirty years would not capture the visual relationship between stadium and city that the Baltimore ballpark illustrated. Most would resemble giant spaceships or airplane hangars, overwhelming the surrounding landscapes. They were not as skillfully designed as Oriole Park, whether they were built in the city or the suburb. Still, over the next three decades, stadiums and arenas constructed in formerly dormant downtown areas were imagined less as civic monuments and more as engines of urban economic development, job creation, and tourist dollars.[24]

In the three decades after Oriole Park opened, a veritable stadium construction boom enveloped the United States. Fifty new "single-use" stadiums were built for MLB and NFL franchises. Many of these stadiums were constructed in previously abandoned "downtown" sections of cities, as politicians and developers successfully sold the public on the idea that stadiums could revitalize inner-city economies. Such messages proved quite persuasive, given that most cities in the United States had suffered through a decades-long period of postindustrial decline. Governmental neglect, the flight of many white Americans to the suburbs that led to a declining tax base, and rising crime rates left municipalities desperate for an infusion of private investment. Notwithstanding the claims of stadium developers, however, two decades of research has shown that sports facilities do not generate sustainable economic development for urban economies.[25] It is not coincidental that formerly industrial cities in the Midwest (Detroit, Pittsburgh, Cleveland, Cincinnati) and in Sunbelt cities (Atlanta, Nashville, Houston, Dallas, Denver, among others) were at the forefront of the stadium boom of the 1990s and 2000s. Ballparks like Oriole Park in Baltimore and Progressive Field (initially called Jacobs Field) in Cleveland catered to an affluent fan base returning to inner cities to consume experiences of urban nostalgia that the "retro" ballparks provided. Soon after, NFL franchises jumped on the stadium trend and more teams that reluctantly shared stadiums with baseball clubs compelled municipal and state authorities to build new stadiums for them, which escalated the costs of stadium construction.[26]

The opening of Oriole Park and Jacobs Field heralded a new type of stadium construction for Major League Baseball not prompted by a sudden desire for a new ballpark aesthetic. To be sure, fans enjoyed spectating in shiny new facilities, but there was no mass movement clamoring for more aesthetically pleasing sports stadiums. On the contrary, the campaign for new stadiums in the 1990s was orchestrated by sports leagues, politicians, and fellow travelers, including architects, sportswriters, and, eventually, real estate developers. Aesthetics and luxury guided the new stadium construction movement.

After the opening of Oriole Park at Camden Yards, suddenly every Major League Baseball franchise wanted their own "retro ballpark." Over the next thirty years, twenty-three baseball stadiums were built for Major League clubs, the vast majority of them financed with taxpayer dollars. With the multipurpose model widely discredited, pro football teams also convinced politicians to build new football-only stadiums. The days of sharing stadiums with baseball teams seemingly vanished overnight. Stadium construction for the NFL and MLB proceeded as rapidly as it had for the NBA and NHL. During the 1990s, eighteen new stadiums were built for MLB or NFL franchises. After 2000, thirty-four new stadiums opened for pro football or pro baseball teams. The effect of moving away from the supposedly unaesthetic multipurpose facility had major financial consequences. Whereas twenty-nine stadiums were built for NFL and MLB teams between 1960 and 1989, the vast majority were shared facilities. Fifty-two stadiums have opened since 1990, not including facilities built for minor league and college teams or the plethora of stadiums built or renovated as spring-training sites for Major League Baseball teams.

The new stadium-building craze ushered in a new community ritual: the ceremonial demolition of the previously enjoyed but widely derided midcentury stadium. As more stadiums and arenas were built, many of the older ballparks, stadiums, and arenas were demolished, often in highly ceremonial fashion. In cities throughout the country, fans gathered for detonation ceremonies to watch, cheer, and sometimes cry as the stadiums of the sixties and seventies were imploded.

Explosives were strategically placed throughout abandoned stadiums and fans watched the buildings turn into large clouds of dust and smoke. In other cases, old stadiums were left abandoned for years before they finally met the wrecking ball. The Silverdome, the home stadium of the Detroit Lions for only twenty-six seasons, was left to decay for sixteen years before being demolished in 2017. These demolitions were celebrated as rejections of the past, but they also reflect the wasteful spirit of the times.

If Gregg Lukenbill's ARCO Arena brought the Ueberrothian corporate sponsorship model to American pro sports, urban designer Janet Marie Smith's Oriole Park at Camden Yards brought stadium advertising back inside the stadium itself. "The advertising was a part of the architecture. It was never stuck on afterwards," she told author Peter Richmond in 1992. "It was thought of in terms of how it was part of the outfield fence, how it was part of the scoreboard. Now every marketing department will tell you you have to stick an ad where the camera will catch it—the catcher, the pitcher, and the ad. It wasn't thought about that way."[27] Paul Goldberger saw the return of billboards to outfield walls as a "charming reference to baseball's past."[28]

What Smith and her colleagues imagined as architectural accents became the dominant visual characteristic of the late-twentieth-century/early-twenty-first-century stadium. Beginning in the mid-1990s, virtually every major stadium or arena constructed for a professional sports franchise possessed a naming-rights deal. These deals were sometimes forged between local corporations and teams. Eventually, agreements were made with dominant national corporations that had no organic connections to the cities where the edifices were located. JPMorgan Chase, Staples, American Airlines, and State Farm Insurance, among other corporations, have had their names displayed at various stadiums and arenas across the country. Advertisements spread to almost every area of the stadium, not just the scoreboard. Naturally, they were placed in strategic locations where they could be seen by millions of television viewers: behind home plate, at courtside, and on the boards of hockey rinks. With the technological advancements of LED displays and virtual placement on screens, advertisements could be displayed almost continuously throughout the course of a game. In the forty years since the 1984 Olympics, corporations have poured money into sports advertising, and the stadium of today shows the effects of that investment in spades.

The designers of Oriole Park and their fans in the architectural world were inspired by the urban-preservationist ideas of Jane Jacobs, a staunch critic of midcentury mass architecture. However, retro-park enthusiasts harnessed her ideas not to preserve neighborhoods but to manufacture new ones in a new age of urban "revitalization," otherwise known as gentrification. Like other preservationists, they operated as agents of gentrification, apostles of urban beauty for the new affluent classes of the twenty-first-century American city. Indeed, the architect's fetish for the artistically crafted twenty-first-century baseball stadium has been overshadowed by the more common glass and concrete structures that loom over the surrounding urban landscape. As stadium construction has morphed into massive real estate developments, as was the case in Cobb County in suburban Atlanta, sports facilities are no longer standalone structures but anchoring monuments to a new form of territorial colonization.[29]

Lost on the legions of baseball fans and architectural critics who have made criticizing the midcentury stadium a cottage industry are the ways that the contemporary stadium has produced its own standardization and banality. In his hilarious rant against Major League Baseball, the comedian Chris Rock had a point when he cracked: "Every team is building a bullshit fake antique stadium that's supposed to remind you of the good old days." The "retro" craze was manufactured and carefully curated. As Rock pointed out, it was manufactured nostalgia for an affluent white fan base who were lured back to inner cities by municipal politicians and developers. What has been frequently said of the midcentury cookie-cutter stadium—that it had no sense of place—can also be said of the early-twenty-first-century stadium or arena regardless of its architectural style. The assaulting quality of corporate advertising actually creates a sense of no place. Indeed, whether one is watching on a screen or sitting in the stands, the stadium has become a nowhere land. Further, the skyrocketing cost of facility construction, which has been passed on to consumers and taxpayers, has made the twenty-first-century stadium into a monument to corporate welfare.[30]

This was made clear during the last years of Tiger Stadium, a beloved baseball cathedral that had stood in Detroit since 1912. In the 1990s, when Tigers owner Mike Ilitch first announced his desire for a new ballpark in the city's downtown district, a potent grass-roots movement sprang into action. Contrary to what Ilitch and Detroit mayor Coleman Young argued, the people insisted that Tiger Stadium was as historically significant as beloved Fenway Park and Wrigley Field, two facilities that escaped the fate of the wrecking ball. The group argued that Tiger Stadium should be preserved, yet renovated to respond to the desires of the sports industry of the twenty-first century. The Tiger Stadium Fan Club hired its own architect and proposed a renovation plan that was likely to cost less than the building of a new facility. Though the fan club was able to hold off the demolition of the beloved stadium for a decade, it ultimately failed to stop Ilitch from getting what he really wanted: a new ballpark as the centerpiece of a larger real estate development. The Tigers opened Comerica Park in 2000, and the old stadium at Michigan and Trumbull Avenues was demolished in 2008.[31]

The transfiguration of stadiums into corporate billboards in newly manufactured neighborhoods went hand in hand with their refashioning into playpens for the real and imagined VIP set. Nowhere was this more evident than in a neighborhood where another hallowed baseball stadium had been home to one of America's most iconic sports franchises.

EIGHTY-ONE TIMES A SUMMER, AND USUALLY A DOZEN OR MORE TIMES in the fall, large contingents of New York's urban and suburban gentry come barreling out of the Metro North commuter train stop and the nearby underground and elevated subway stations to worship at Yankee Stadium, the baseball shrine at 161st and River Avenue in the

Yankee Stadium, 2009. *Credit: Matt Boulton, Flickr*

Bronx. When the new version of the stadium opened in 2009, public funds had financed the creation of a new Metro North station to
accommodate the team's suburban rooters, who were being lured back
to the Bronx to watch the Yankees. Thousands of others endure the
gridlock that clogs the exit ramps off the Major Deegan Expressway
and surrounding streets that lead them to nearby parking garages.
They pay the steep parking fees to young black and brown men who
work at the parking facilities in the neighborhood.

As they stampede out of cars and trains, they resemble a conquer-
ing army arriving from Westchester County, Manhattan, or Brooklyn
wearing the navy-blue caps and pinstriped jerseys of the New York
Yankees. If they arrive early enough, they might grab a few beers at a
small number of neighborhood bars. Most, instead, opt to eat, drink,
and shop at the more plentiful establishments located inside the stadium. If the game is particularly consequential for the home team,
many will yell "Let's Go Yankees!" as their smartphone tickets are

scanned and they themselves are subject to security searches carried out by an army of black and brown security guards.

They walk through the main concourse past the many images of Babe Ruth, Lou Gehrig, Mickey Mantle, and other Yankee greats, grab their overpriced concessions, and make their way to their seats. First-time visitors might take note of the retro architecture that they would have read about before their arrival. Most ignore the architectural flourishes and instead spend their time watching the action on the diamond, looking at their smartphones, and being waited on by an army of black and brown concession workers.

When the old Yankee Stadium reopened in 1976 after a $100 million renovation, a new breed of working-class Puerto Rican fans was making its presence felt at the ballpark. They represented the millions of Puerto Ricans who had migrated to New York in the decades after World War II. They joined the multiracial crowd in the affordably priced outfield bleacher seats or the general admission sections of the upper deck, yelling "*Vamos, Vamos!*" (Let's go, let's go!) and cheered on their team.[32]

Decades later, the crowds that gather at the new Yankee Stadium are a different breed altogether. They are much whiter and more affluent. It often seems like the only nonwhite humans who congregate at the stadium are the underpaid concession workers, the security guards, and the better-paid ballplayers from Latin America, who labor on the field. Just as New Orleans's Tulane Stadium staged pageants of white supremacy during the Jim Crow era, so does New York's Yankee Stadium embody a subtler, more insidious form of racism in the twenty-first century.

The scene at today's Yankee Stadium is one that is replicated in many stadiums across the country, especially at baseball and football games. The crowds at basketball and soccer games—and music concerts—are likely to be more ethnically diverse, but they are still overwhelmingly composed of spectators of the affluent classes of gentrified America. During the 1990s and 2000s, stadiums were more numerous and more luxurious, and that's when they also became more inaccessible. The exclusiveness of the corporatized stadium is evident in seating designs. Just as airlines make room for first-class cabins on airplanes, stadiums have devoted increased real estate to luxury seating sections. Most new stadiums expanded luxury accommodations and retail space while reducing seating for historically significant working-class ("blue collar") fans. Ticket prices are beyond the reach of the vast majority of Americans.[33] Seating capacities were reduced in the name of enhancing intimacy between fans and players, but stadiums were, in fact, designed to prioritize space for luxury suites for corporate clients.

Moreover, new stadiums and arenas since the 1990s feature multiple tiers of luxury suites. Beginning with Minute Maid Park (formerly Enron Stadium) in Houston, luxury seating was transferred from the upper and mezzanine levels to the field level. These "club" or "premium" seating sections now dominate the first few rows of most stadiums, including older parks like Dodger Stadium. The fact that these sections have been literally sealed off from other sections makes visible the social hierarchies that architects inscribe on stadium design. These are the bread-and-butter designs of HOK Sport (subsequently renamed Populous), the architectural firm that designed Oriole Park at Camden Yards and many stadiums and arenas around the country. The firm has essentially taken the position of Osborn Engineering in the world of stadium design. However, whereas Osborn became known for its straightforward, solidly engineered structures, HOK/Populous has made the luxury stadium the hallmark of its designs.

Because the new stadium successfully appealed to white elite spectators, it had to be made safe for consumption, particularly for fans who were reared seeing images of dangerous inner cities. Such narratives, along with the security practices established following the terrorist attacks of September 11, 2001, provide the context for the emergence of private security companies, which became another distinguishing feature of the corporate privatized stadium. Contemporary Services Corporation (CSC) has been a conspicuous presence in stadiums across the United States. Created in 1967 in Los Angeles by Damon Zumwalt, the company is one of the largest security providers for a host of events in stadiums across the United States and Canada. The company's client and event lists are extensive, including more than 150 stadiums and arenas, over 100 universities and colleges, more than 30 convention centers, and numerous clients within the professional leagues of MLB, MLS, NBA, NFL, NHL, and NASCAR. CSC also provides services for a number of sporting mega events, including collegiate bowl games, NCAA Final Four tournaments, the Ryder Cup, the Presidents Cup, the US Open Tennis Championships, 33 Super Bowls, 10 Olympic Games, 4 presidential inaugurations, 3 papal visits, and 2 FIFA World Cups, among other major events. As Zumwalt claims on the company website: "I grouped together young athletes from various ethnic communities. These young men were all champions from different sports, physically impressive and leaders in their communities. They were also in the same age group as the patrons attending the rock and roll shows. Thus, we coined the phrase 'peer group security.'" Zumwalt's concept of "peer group security" is particularly revealing, illustrating the ways the company facilitates self-regulation of the crowds at these events. The enormous scope of the company's operations illustrates the investments and profits private security companies can make. Moreover, this corporation's reliance on workers "from various ethnic communities" parallels a similar dynamic by which black and brown workers make up significant portions of the correctional workforce in recent decades. At the twenty-first-century stadium, the black and brown working class finds itself in the ironic position of being custodians of a social hierarchy that marginalizes them.[34]

At the end of the twentieth century and in the first two decades of the twenty-first, the American stadium gentrified. Its remaking into an enclave of exclusivity thwarts and in some ways undoes the social gains America's marginalized groups made during the freedom struggles of the sixties, seventies, and eighties. Because the stadium construction boom of the mid-twentieth century dove-tailed with the civil rights, feminist, and gay liberation movements, the stadium became a place of unprecedented social mixing and political expression. The fact that the majority of facilities were publicly controlled ensured that the stadium maintained its historic civic character, even when many of those facilities were built in suburban locations.

During the past thirty years, however, the vast majority of facilities have remained under public control, but the triumph of the sports industry and the corporate world transformed the stadium into a hypercommodified monument to social exclusion. At Yankee Stadium in the Bronx and at many other facilities across the country, social class differences became more racially defined. The spectating class became whiter and the army of concession workers, security guards, and performers became blacker and browner. By the second decade of this century, the gaps in these widening social hierarchies had contributed to a rapidly combustible political culture. While the affluent classes enjoyed their craft beers, their sushi rolls, and their fuku sandwiches in plush premium seating, the American stadium became a social powder keg. As one space where Americans of different backgrounds converge, it is not surprising that the stadium became a place where social conflicts were bound to break out.

In fact, that is precisely what transpired in the second decade of the century. Weeks after Freddie Gray, a twenty-five-year-old African American, died in the custody of the Baltimore Police Department, a crowd of protesters converged on the beloved Oriole Park at Camden Yards—to express their anger about the circumstances of Gray's death. As they approached the ballpark on April 25, 2015, they were greeted by police officers standing guard in front of the stadium's antique-looking iron gates. Hours later, when that evening's baseball game ended, city officials ordered fans to remain in the ballpark so they would avoid clashing with protesters still in the area.

There it was for all to see. The sight of thousands of predominantly white baseball fans in a stadium sealed off from groups of mostly black protesters outside—in a majority-black city—revealed how the ballpark had become, as sports critic Dave Zirin noted at the time, a "fortress . . . a barrier erected on the foundations of racial and economic inequality dressed in the trappings of spectacle and sports."[35] Oriole Park was not the quaint antique ballpark of yesteryear. It was exposed as a monument to political and social exclusion disconnected from the communities that surrounded it.

The Freddie Gray protests in 2015, like the outbursts in Ferguson, Missouri, a year earlier, would become a recurring scenario in the coming years. As protests for racial justice and Black Freedom flared up in the twenty-first century, the American stadium, even if it had been gentrified, would once again serve as a venue where America's dispossessed made their voices heard.

CHAPTER EIGHT

WAR AND DEMOCRACY AT THE BALLPARK

I
t was a routine NFL preseason contest between the San Diego Chargers and the San Francisco 49ers at Qualcomm Stadium on August 31, 2016. The game was one of the increasing number of exhibition contests league owners scheduled before the regular season to extract as much value as possible from their players. It was also routine because the game provided the occasion for the Chargers' annual Salute to the Military promotion, which was one of the many military appreciation nights that have occurred at stadiums across the country since the terrorist attacks of September 11, 2001. Indeed, the Chargers have been organizing military promotions since the late 1980s in a city whose relations with the US Navy date back to the early twentieth century.

On this evening, the Chargers planned a robust program honoring service members. Fans in attendance enjoyed pregame entertainment provided by the Marine Band San Diego and the Frog-X Parachute Team, which featured retired Navy SEALs landing on the field of Qualcomm Stadium. Two hundred and forty sailors, marines, and soldiers presented an oversized US flag and service emblems from all branches of service. Color guards from the Navy, the Marine Corps, and the Army were also part of the flag presentation. The national anthem was performed by Petty Officer 1st Class Steven Powell from the US Navy. At halftime, the Chargers honored six Vietnam War veterans with a patriotic fireworks show. At the start of the third quarter, Petty Officer 1st Class Powell returned to the field to sing "God Bless America."

While fans were anticipating the military promotion, they were also wondering if another event that was not part of the planned military appreciation ceremony was going to transpire that night. As it turned out, the most noteworthy aspect of the evening was not the patriotic pageantry but a silent act of dissent by Colin Kaepernick, the start-ing quarterback of the visiting 49ers. In a previous preseason game, Kaepernick departed from the custom of players and coaches standing and saluting the flag during the anthem by sitting on the bench. "I'm not going to stand up to show pride for a country that oppresses Black people and people of color," he told the press days before the game.[1] The summer of 2016 was a period of high-profile police shootings of unarmed African Americans. Police violence against black people was a centuries-old phenomenon, but since the early 2010s, the killings of Trayvon Martin and Michael Brown, the death of Sandra Bland while in police custody, and other instances of black deaths at the hands of the police or vigilantes had galvanized the emergence of the Black Lives Matter movement. That summer, Alton Sterling and Philando Castile joined the long list of black men who had been shot and killed by police or civilians.

The crowd stood in the forty-nine-year-old stadium that was clum-sily adorned with the customary corporate advertisements tacked up all around the facility. The building was originally known as San Diego Stadium before "Qualcomm," the name of a cell phone company, was slapped onto it in the 1990s. The corporate amenity machine was an imperfect fit for San Diego's version of the midcentury facility. It turned out to be difficult to refurbish buildings designed for accessi-ble assembly into exclusive playgrounds for the real and aspiring VIP crowd. This incongruence was a big reason why the Chargers would eventually break the hearts of fans and leave town for a fancier facility in Los Angeles after the end of that season.

But that was a story for another day. On that summer night at "the Q," as locals came to call it, the Chargers were doing their part to honor the military. After consulting with former player and military veteran Eric Boyer before the game, Kaepernick decided to make what he perceived to be a more respectful gesture. As Petty Officer Powell sang "The Star-Spangled Banner," the quarterback and his teammate Eric Reed took a knee rather than standing to salute the flag along with their teammates. Their gesture was once again an expression of solidarity with black people and other people of color who were victims of racism and police violence. The move was powerfully resonant. Many fans booed Kaepernick, some cheered, and everyone, it seemed, noticed.

The man who was once a darling of the football world for his outstanding play leading the 49ers to the 2013 Super Bowl suddenly became a pariah. Kaepernick's protest was amplified by the fact that it was a presidential election year between the Republican blowhard right-wing candidate Donald Trump and the Democratic nominee Hillary Clinton. The sport and conservative media punditry opined frequently, while right-wing politicians portrayed him as the poster child of the ungrateful anti-patriotic black American, to be ridiculed and despised by the riled-up crowd of aggrieved white people.

The media frenzy made Colin Kaepernick the most visible athlete to explicitly identify with the revitalized Black Freedom movement. After the murder of Trayvon Martin in 2012, prominent athletes had engaged in symbolic stands against the resurgence of police violence. However, Kaepernick's vilification occurred because it disrupted the most sacred ritual at the American stadium, one that had become ever more sanctified in the decades since the terrorist attacks of September 11. As the sportswriter and critic Howard Bryant has written: "Not only did America seem to be in lockstep in honoring the military, but the cultural pressure against dissent was so strong, opponents didn't dare speak out against fifty thousand flag-wavers." Kaepernick was but one of an increasing number of athletes who had enough of fifteen years of blind obedience to a state of perpetual war. Enough with

the elevation of the police to the status of military heroes, a conflation that was a legacy of 9/11. And enough with the unjustified use of
violence against African Americans. Other athletes followed suit, and
the American stadium once again served as a public square where the
country's marginalized and dispossessed took a stand for justice.

Colin Kaepernick joined the long-standing tradition of black athletes speaking out against injustice, a phenomenon Howard Bryant has
called "the heritage."[2] Like Jackie Robinson, Bill Russell, Muhammad
Ali, Tommie Smith, and John Carlos, among others from previous
generations, he decided to use his stature as a prominent black athlete
to highlight the persistence of racism in America. Kaepernick's action
was reminiscent of Smith's and Carlos's Black Power salute on the
medal stand in the Estadio Olímpico Universitario at the 1968 Olympic Games in Mexico City. Like Smith and Carlos, he chose to stage
his silent gesture in the amplifying environment of the stadium itself.
Simply taking a knee on a field of play in front of the television cameras
and tens of thousands of people amplified the message of the movement for racial justice. The subsequent virulent response to his action
exemplified the magnifying power of the stadium. From the minute
Smith and Carlos stepped off the medal stand on that fateful night in
Mexico City, they, too, had faced an enormous backlash that essentially destroyed their careers. In the late sixties, the United States was a
polarized society. However, the environment that Kaepernick and his
contemporaries faced during the past decade has been equally, perhaps
more, polarized.

The quarterback took his knee at a time when stadiums were less
likely to be places of dissent. Protests at the ballpark have never been
welcomed by the vast majority of fans or the sports industry. Beginning in the 1990s, as the freedom struggles of midcentury were pushed
into the realm of the distant past, the sports industry has championed
the notion that the stadium space—and sports in general—should be
removed from politics. In a period of illusionary prosperity, stadiums
were imagined as places where highly paid athletes and performers
entertained the American public. There was no need to agitate for

political and social change at the stadium, or so it seemed. Indeed, the Cold War was over and the battles waged by the freedom movements of the sixties, seventies, and eighties had been won. Americans could now sit back and be avid consumers. The argument for the apolitical stadium became particularly resonant as the stadium's spectators became whiter and more affluent and the people who worked for and entertained them got blacker and browner.

After 9/11, however, the United States waged war against enemies at home and abroad, and the government politicized stadiums in a sustained and perhaps unprecedented manner. Over the last two decades, sports franchises have partnered with the US military to make stadiums into stages for elaborate jingoistic rituals to shore up allegiance to the military and law enforcement. At the same time, right-wing nationalism, once seen as a fringe element in US society and politics, has also become increasingly influential in determining the meaning and practice of American patriotism. The military and the police elevated themselves to the status of national heroes who sacrifice themselves for the cause of a nebulously defined "freedom," even as most of the freedoms Americans enjoyed were being circumscribed by those very same institutions. The police and the military were often portrayed in these celebrations as one and the same. Indeed, aside from the colors of the uniforms, these previously distinct realms of the US government have often been indistinguishable. The same tactics used to defeat enemies in Afghanistan and Iraq have been employed to silence political dissenters and maintain the widening inequities in American society.[3]

In 2016, when Colin Kaepernick and fellow athletes took their solidarity with the Black Lives Matter movement to the stadium, many white fans, politicians, and members of law enforcement were able to argue with straight faces that politics had no place in sports even as they continued to fiercely advocate for the necessary worship of the police and glorification of the military. But Kaepernick's and others' protests became increasingly hard to discredit as calls for racial justice intensified in the wake of the election of Donald Trump in 2016 and especially after the murder of George Floyd by Minneapolis police and the onset of the COVID-19 pandemic.

The early-twenty-first-century stadium has become more important not only because it was remade into an arena of entertainment for affluent fans based on the exploited labor of people from marginalized communities but also because it has arguably become the country's most visible theater of militarized nationalism. In the two decades since the terrorist attacks, the American stadium has been one of the few collective spaces where Americans are summoned to rally behind the flag or, rather, behind the wars it waged in Afghanistan and Iraq. Militarized patriotism has become deeply entrenched in big-time American sporting culture, and in American society in general.

But much to the dismay of the NFL establishment, many football fans, and the media punditry, Kaepernick's and others' protests were only the beginning. As they were in the sixties and seventies, the ballpark and the arena have once again become battlegrounds for the struggle for racial justice. By the summer of 2016, black activists had

Colin Kaepernick and Eric Reid, Qualcomm Stadium, September 1, 2016.
Credit: Michael Zagaris/San Francisco 49ers via Getty Images

persisted in highlighting ongoing racist violence against black people by police officers and vigilantes for four years after the murder of Trayvon Martin. In the years since, the resurgent Black Lives Matter movement continued to have a profound influence on the sports world.

Star black athletes, held up as exemplars of racial equality in the United States since the days of freedom movements at midcentury, shed their reluctance to speak out against racial injustice and to stand with those who were less fortunate in their communities. Their influence was most palpably felt in the summer of 2020, when the COVID-19 pandemic and an instance of yet another brutal police killing galvanized millions to take to the streets to stand against systemic racism. Notably, it was black women professional basketball players of the Women's National Basketball Association (WNBA) who took athlete activism a step further when they actively campaigned against Kelly Loeffler, one of the league's owners who was running to hold her US Senate seat. In a sense, the upheavals of the past two decades resemble the battles of the 1930s and the 1960s, when America's social movements made the stadium a place where the struggles of the oppressed would be fought over and redefined.

THE STADIUM HAS LONG BEEN THE VENUE WHERE AMERICANS WERE rallied to causes championed by the United States government. It has been a place for staging US national identity since its earliest incarnations, though "The Star-Spangled Banner" has not always been a part of stadium performance culture. The first recorded instance of Francis Scott Key's anthem being performed at a stadium occurred when a live brass band played the song during the opening of the Union Grounds in Brooklyn on May 15, 1862. The song was periodically performed at various baseball and college football games during the late nineteenth century, but it was not until World War I that it was performed frequently. Not surprisingly, it was at Griffith Stadium in Washington, DC, on Opening Day in 1917 when the assistant secretary of the Navy Franklin D. Roosevelt led the raising of the flag while "The

Star-Spangled Banner" was played. After Key's tune officially became the US national anthem in 1931, it still wasn't regularly performed at stadiums until World War II. In addition to more frequent performances of the anthem, stadiums staged patriotic ceremonial war reenactments at large stadiums like the Los Angeles Memorial Coliseum.[4]

During the Vietnam era, Richard Nixon, perhaps more than any other president, actively sought to promote compliant American patriotism through sports. Nixon seemingly showed up at every consequential sporting event during his presidency to make athletes into exemplars of the loyal Americans he needed to continue the war in Southeast Asia. He was especially fond of using football to promote traditional values and reactionary politics in the face of insurgent radical political movements and the counterculture. The National Football League and the college football world became willing participants in this form of Nixonian statecraft. However, the NFL's willingness to support the war in Vietnam had begun even before Nixon took office, when Commissioner Pete Rozelle started the practice of jet flyovers during the singing of the national anthem before Super Bowl II at Miami's Orange Bowl in January 1968. The growing popularity of televised sports also contributed to the government's efforts to delegitimize political dissent and promote US policies on Vietnam. Over time, the Super Bowl became a mega sporting event where bellicose forms of nationalism were staged in front of millions of people watching on television around the world.[5]

After the Vietnam War and the Watergate scandal, a widespread suspicion of the government led to a toned-down version of US patriotism. Color guards were still called upon to carry flags during pregame ceremonies at major sporting events, but the military was far less prominent. The patriotic pageantry of the pregame ceremonies of the Super Bowl, Major League Baseball's All-Star Game, and the World Series during America's bicentennial in 1976 is a quaint cultural artifact compared to what would unfold in subsequent decades. At the Super Bowl in Miami's Orange Bowl that year, for example, Up with People, the squeaky-clean performance group, performed their repertoire of hokey songs during the halftime show, as they would four more times during the late 1970s and early 1980s. This was a far cry from the inaugural Super Bowl flyover that occurred at the height of the Vietnam War in that same stadium eight years earlier.[6]

Marvin Gaye's memorable performance of "The Star-Spangled Banner" at the 1983 NBA All-Star Game in the Forum in Los Angeles illustrates the ways society allowed Key's tune to be converted into a sultry R & B tour de force.[7] Aside from the customary appearance of color guards, the presence of the military during patriotic rituals at stadiums was minimal. In a way, the performances of the national anthem in the post-Vietnam years exemplify a society that was more confident in its professed beliefs and its institutions, even in the aftermath of a polarizing war that the United States did not win. As the seventies gave way to the eighties, it was unnecessary, and perhaps politically counterproductive, for the government to bang Americans over the head with the deadening beat of war drums and patriotic songs at every turn.

Still, militarism crept back into stadiums and arenas following the Gulf War, which revived the confluence of militarized patriotism and sports. At the 1991 Super Bowl, for instance, a crowd of more than seventy-three thousand in Tampa Stadium waving miniature US flags was awash in red, white, and blue as Whitney Houston gave her stirring rendition of "The Star-Spangled Banner." In a sense, the performance foreshadowed a recurring scenario at stadiums and arenas after 9/11: here was the pop star, often a black woman celebrity like Houston, charged with rallying the nation behind a war effort amid stone-faced military officers guarding American flags and precisely executed jet flyovers.[8]

The Gulf War signaled a change in American sporting culture, but it wasn't until the crashing of the four planes on September 11 that the days of innocuous milquetoast Up with People performances were supplanted by a bellicose American nationalism that sought to enforce a culture of blind compliance. "Post-9/11 America killed the neutral sporting event," Howard Bryant has correctly observed. Though sports and the ballpark have never been neutral, all pretenses of neutrality were discarded over the past few decades. As a result, there has been little tolerance for dissent in a period when the US government engaged in a two-decades-long war against terrorism. Taking cues from Nixon and from his father George H. W. Bush, George W. Bush and the US military unabashedly used sport to legitimate the war against terrorism abroad. What is more, at stadiums and arenas across the country, the government and sports world tried to make police officers among the heroes of 9/11. When clear evidence of police killings of black and nonwhite Americans came to public attention in the 2010s, a virulent culture of obedience sought to discredit and silence any efforts to speak out for racial justice and equality. The American stadium had become hyperpoliticized, celebrating militarism and conservatism, even as the government and sports leagues insisted that it was not a place for protest or politics.[9]

YET, THE TWENTY-FIRST-CENTURY BRAND OF MILITARIZED AMERIcan patriotism at the ballpark did not emerge out of the ashes of the Twin Towers, the Pentagon, or the field in Somerset County, Pennsylvania. In some ways it began years before in the front offices of struggling sports franchises in San Diego, California, the same city where Kaepernick first took a knee in September 2016. The reaction to 9/11, and the Bush administration's subsequent War on Terror, certainly played a decisive role. But the militaristic ballpark patriotism of recent decades actually took shape as a marketing gimmick by two sports franchises looking to make a buck. And the team that in many ways pioneered this marketing strategy was not unlike Gregg Lukenbill's Sacramento Kings, a sports franchise that needed an infusion of new revenue. In 1995, the San Diego Padres was a struggling National League baseball team trying to regain its footing. Since the team's creation as an expansion franchise in 1969, the Padres was a mediocre outfit on the field and at the box office, with the exception of a few winning seasons in the 1980s. The team routinely had the lowest attendance figures in the National League. By 1994, San Diego's base-ball franchise had hit rock bottom, finishing in last place in the division and last in the league in home attendance. Moreover, the MLB players' strike in 1994, which led to the cancellation of the season, further alienated the team's fan base.

While the strike continued into the winter months, a new owner-ship group bought the Padres. Software giant John Moores and Larry Lucchino, the former president of the Baltimore Orioles and a driving force in the construction of Oriole Park at Camden Yards, were among the investors. Lucchino was a lawyer and protégé of Edward Bennett Williams, the longtime owner of the Washington Redskins. The task of the new ownership group was to build a winner, aggressively market their team, and join the new ballpark craze by getting out of the multipurpose facility recently rebranded as Qualcomm Stadium by persuading the local government to build a new baseball-specific stadium—in short, to do what the Orioles had done in Baltimore.

Over the next six years, Moores and Lucchino achieved all these objectives. The team turned into a winner on the field, making the postseason twice in four years, including a trip to the 1998 World Series. More importantly, they pushed the city of San Diego into footing most of the bill for a new stadium called Petco Park, which, not unlike Oriole Park, was hailed as a "successful" retro baseball stadium after it opened in 2004, even though the financing of the $453 million facility was not as successful as the team and the city have claimed over the years.[10]

The Padres club was an innovator on the marketing front. During the late seventies and early eighties, the team was associated with its immensely popular mascot, the San Diego Chicken, and its McDonald's-themed brown, gold, and orange uniforms. But when the Padres hired Jack Ensch, a retired naval officer, to be the team's liaison with the Navy and Marine Corps in November 1995, the team was looking to cultivate a new identity. Ensch's job was to market the franchise to the area's 450,000 active-duty and retired service members and their families. "We bill ourselves as the military's team," Ensch bluntly told the *San Diego Union-Tribune* in 1998. During the sixteen seasons that he was in the employ of the Padres, Ensch developed an elaborate marketing plan that included providing complimentary and discount tickets to military personnel, creating an annual Military Opening Day, holding reenlistment ceremonies at the ballpark, and having Navy SEAL parachuters land on the field before games, among other activities. Some of these promotions had already been adopted by the San Diego Chargers, the local NFL franchise, which began to hold military appreciation nights in the late 1980s, but the Padres took military marketing to another level long before other professional sports franchises did. The team could not honor the military enough, it seemed, especially after the United States waged wars in Afghanistan and Iraq. The Padres have held various military-themed promotions, including Military Spouse Appreciation Day, Salute to the Military Child, and Salute to Military Veterans.[11]

The Padres was the first pro sports team to create military-themed uniforms for players. A year before the terrorist attacks of September 11, Ensch suggested the team begin wearing a special camouflage uniform on Military Opening Day to honor America's service members. The uniform received mixed reviews but eventually became a regular part of the team's uniform rotation, evolving through various iterations over the years, from an Army "Woodland Design" to a Navy SEAL "Desert Version." Fans could fantasize about hitting home runs and shooting down terrorists as the Padres donned camouflage unis. Though some criticized the uniforms on aesthetic grounds and others wondered about the ethics of the Padres regularly advertising the military, most fans loved these promotions and became accustomed to equating war with sporting competitions. There was no reason to discontinue the tradition because the camouflage uniforms sold well among fans and they were widely adopted by other franchises. Patriotism was turning a profit for the Padres.[12]

As part of the larger trend of hypercommercialization that has overwhelmed the country over the past few decades, this new form of patriotism originated with marketers rather than arising from a genuine spirit of patriotic zeal. In the same way that the Sacramento Kings owners' business decisions altered the stadium and arena environment in the 1980s, so, too, was it transformed by the profit-seeking activities of San Diego's local professional sports franchises in the 1990s. The team that had once been known for its San Diego Chicken mascot and loud brown, gold, and orange uniforms had remade itself into the baseball team of the American military. Other teams would copy the Padres' formula, and the aftermath of the terrorist attacks provided the perfect context to cash in on militarized patriotism. The conversion of the ballpark into a site of recurring military pep rallies in many ways began at Qualcomm Stadium in San Diego.

US PRESIDENTS HAVE THROWN CEREMONIAL FIRST PITCHES AT Major League Baseball games since the early twentieth century. At the dawn of the twenty-first century, on the night of October 30, 2001, at Yankee Stadium in the Bronx, the forty-third president of the United States found himself embarking on this tradition in an unprecedented circumstance. Only seven weeks after the terrorist attacks of September 11, George W. Bush strode to the pitcher's mound on that late-October evening before the third game of the 2001 World Series. At the time, the nation was still reeling from the trauma of 9/11, and it seemed that another attack could occur at any moment. That fall, an anthrax scare also kept the nation on edge. A heavily securitized stadium greeted the crowd of over fifty-five thousand that was feeling especially skittish.

It is easy to forget that during much of the first year that Bush was in office, "Dubya" was still not seen as a legitimate president by a large portion of the American public. After all, it wasn't until the Conservative-majority Supreme Court stopped the contested Florida recount in the *Bush v. Gore* case that he was declared the winner of the bitterly contested 2000 presidential election. His inarticulate, folksy, malapropos speech obscured his extraordinary wealth and privilege, and it led many to rightly wonder whether he was fit to be president.

The terrorist attacks of September 11 further discredited his regime in many corners, but any criticism of the government's culpability in the attacks was overrun by the rush to rally around the flag and support the president. From a purely political standpoint, 9/11 turned out to be the best thing that happened to Bush, and it was a boon to New York City mayor Rudolph Giuliani, whose ruthless treatment of the New York working classes and his condoning of police violence against black people were quickly forgotten after the planes crashed into the Twin Towers in lower Manhattan. Baseball season resumed after a temporary pause, and Bush and Giuliani made the ballpark the place where both sought to reestablish their legitimacy in the eyes of the public.

On October 30, 2001, in Yankee Stadium, one of the most hallowed stadiums in America, Bush staged a remarkable bit of political theater. "Ladies and Gentlemen," the Yankees' legendary public address announcer Bob Sheppard announced during the pregame ceremonies, "please direct your attention to the area in front of the pitcher's mound for tonight's ceremonial first pitch." The sellout crowd of 55,820 roared as the president of the United States emerged from the Yankees dugout wearing a navy-blue FDNY jacket. When he reached the pitcher's mound, he raised his right arm and gave the crowd a thumbs-up sign. Then he stepped on the pitching rubber and threw a perfect strike to the catcher. The crowd unleashed a thunderous roar before chanting: "USA! USA!" repeatedly.[13]

Weeks before, Bush had told the nation that the time for grieving was over. Americans had a duty to show the terrorists that they were ready to move forward and get on with their lives. "Get on board. Do your business around the country," he encouraged the nation. "Fly and enjoy America's great destination spots. Get down to Disney World in Florida. Take your families and enjoy life, the way we want it to be enjoyed."[14] The government would take care of the terrorists, he insisted. To enjoy life also meant to go back to the ballpark, where fans would not only enjoy sporting events but also be reminded again and again that they were in a state of war. This was an unprecedented moment of presidential statecraft that redefined the meaning of the stadium and sporting cultures in American life.

Bush's first pitch before Game 3 of the 2001 World Series refashioned American nationalism, but the signs of the new sporting culture were already becoming evident when sports returned to the field of play a week after 9/11. Stadium rituals would rapidly shift from expressions of grief for those who died on that horrifying day to unabashed elevations of those the government in Washington, DC, and New York deemed to be the true heroes of 9/11: the first responders who sought to rescue the thousands trapped in the World Trade Center, the EMS workers, and especially firefighters and police officers. When baseball resumed, the elevation of police officers and firefighters was already underway. Sports franchises and politicians encouraged Americans to blindly root for new home teams, the police, and the fire departments.

The unveiling of new team affiliations was made clear when the New York Mets faced off with the Atlanta Braves on September 21 at Shea Stadium. It was a powerful moment for New Yorkers, one in which they were able to collectively grieve the still unfathomable losses of 9/11. Still, the pregame ceremony enacted a script that would narrow the range of those who were to be remembered and those who were not. Even though only 23 of the 2,763 people who died at the World Trade Center were police officers, they were deemed to be the most heroic *and* victimized by the terrorist attacks.

On that night at Shea Stadium, members of the Mets donned NYPD, FDNY, and Port Authority police caps. A color guard of officers from these units took the field, and a group of midshipmen from the Merchant Marine Academy unfurled a large US flag.[15] Even at that moment, loss turned into a commodity as FDNY and NYPD caps became—and still are—a popular tourist collectible associated with New York. Law enforcement officers and firefighters, not the seventy-three workers at the Windows of the World restaurant on the 107th floor of the North Tower who perished that day, for example, were honored and remembered. At stadiums and arenas in other parts of the country, local police departments were honored and elevated as the real heroes of America, even when they had no role in the efforts to save lives on that fateful day.

There were new uniforms to wear at the ballpark—that of firefighters and the police—and there were new rituals to be adopted. And yet again, it was the San Diego Padres, the team with an established practice of promoting militarized patriotism, that made yet another contribution to the new stadium environment after 9/11. John Dever, a member of the team's public relations staff, tried to figure out how to help create a more appropriate ballpark environment that was sensitive to the somber national mood. He wondered if it made sense to replace "Take Me Out to the Ballgame," the cheery anthem that was traditionally played during the seventh-inning stretch, with another more solemn song. He proposed replacing the tune with Irving Berlin's "God Bless America." The proposal was forwarded to Larry Lucchino, who liked the idea so much that he relayed it to Bud Selig, MLB commissioner. Soon after, a new stadium ritual was born at MLB ballparks. "God Bless America" was the new song to be performed at every Major League Baseball stadium across the country during the seventh-inning stretch.[16]

As new patriotic ceremonials took shape at Major League ballparks, other teams and leagues joined the race to be the most patriotic. Following the pattern of the Mets and Yankees, on September 23 the players of the Giants and Jets, New York's two NFL franchises, wore caps with NYPD and FDNY logos as they took the field to face the New England Patriots at Foxboro Stadium. During the pregame ceremonies, former Marine and Massachusetts state trooper Dan Clark fired up the crowd with a jingoistic retelling of an earlier moment when the "nation was at war": the scene of the Battle of Fort McHenry that inspired Francis Scott Key to pen "The Star-Spangled Banner" in 1814. The crowd was whipped into a frenzy as Clark ceased beating his war drums and sang the anthem himself. The man who has become known as the "Singing Trooper" would go on to a twenty-year career performing bellicose versions of the national anthem. As a state trooper and a veteran, Clark was the perfect embodiment of the post-9/11 conflation of the military and law enforcement.[17]

Scenes of this sort occurred at stadiums all over the country. At Dodger Stadium a few days earlier, the team had honored members of the Los Angeles Police Department during the 9/11 pregame observance. Fans were encouraged to forget the LAPD's well-documented history of corruption, abuse, and racist policing. During a pregame ceremony before the Dodgers faced the Padres on September 18, after fans observed a moment of silence for those who lost their lives on September 11, legendary broadcaster Vin Scully encouraged the somber crowd to look at their "own backyard, to honor the men and women who put their own lives in danger to protect and preserve the people of Los Angeles." The Dodgers and LAPD thought it was the appropriate occasion to award the Medal of Valor, the LAPD's highest honor, to Mark Miriles and David Orozco. Miriles and Orozco had acted bravely in the line of duty, but their particular acts of heroism had no connection whatsoever to the events of September 11. This was an opportunistic attempt at reputation rehabilitation by a department with a long history of terrorizing the city's populations of color, including the brutal beating of Rodney King. It was yet another moment when the police and their partners converted the traumas of 9/11 into rituals of forgetting.[18]

Those early patriotic ceremonies in the immediate aftermath of the terrorist attacks set the parameters for how 9/11 would be publicly remembered at stadiums and arenas across the United States. There could have been—and have been—multiple ways to remember the horror of that day. The civilians who jumped from the towers to their death, the hundreds of other clerical workers from the city's working class who were trapped in the incinerating fires, the heroes who died trying to stop Flight 93 from becoming another missile—though many have been remembered at 9/11 memorials, their stories have been overshadowed by official accounts peddled by the state. Law enforcement and the military became the faces of the national trauma. At stadiums and arenas across the country, "the police and the military and the flag across the expanse of the field [became] permanent additions to the game day roster."[19]

Over the next two decades, stadiums nationwide would present the military and law enforcement as the heroes of 9/11. As the wars in Afghanistan and Iraq raged on into the second decade of the century, stirring up support for the troops and for law enforcement became routine at American stadiums and arenas. A coterie of "Singing Trooper" figures performed "The Star-Spangled Banner" and "God Bless America." Oversized flags were regularly unveiled by stone-faced soldiers and police officers, commemorative NYPD and FDNY caps were donned by players, camouflage uniforms were created and sold, and jet flyovers became recurring parts of pregame ceremonies. Teams and leagues copied the Padres' and the Chargers' military marketing schemes by creating a wide array of military appreciation promotions and adding new law enforcement appreciation rituals.

With the endless wars in Iraq and Afghanistan, honoring veterans became yet another stadium ritual. In the early 2010s, MLB conducted elaborate ceremonies for veterans showcasing the league's Welcome Back Veterans program for soldiers returning from war. Family reunification ceremonies pulled at the heartstrings of a public that might have wondered how long US troops would be at war. The deadening beat of the war drums at stadiums, game after game, year after year, normalized war and helped the US government defeat whatever was left of the American anti-war movement. Though there was a massive movement against the Bush administration's effort to link Saddam Hussein to the terrorist attacks, overall the anti-war activity of the 2000s was not equivalent to the powerful anti-war movement of the Vietnam era.

And yet, there was a good reason why militarized patriotism became ubiquitous at the American stadium. In theory, there is nothing inherently wrong with honoring military service members. But in reality, the performances of soldier recognition were a continuous effort to generate support for the war machine. Seemingly kind acts of recognition were in fact products of a business transaction between the

Department of Defense and professional sports teams. Capitalist commodification was at the heart of militarized patriotism at the ballpark. In 2015, Arizona senators John McCain and Jeff Flake unveiled the *Tackling Paid Patriotism* report that exposed the fact that the military paid $6.8 million to sports teams to manufacture acts of patriotism at the stadium. The militarized rituals that were routinely organized at NFL, MLB, NBA, NHL, NASL, and other stadiums and arenas were actually paid for with taxpayer money and orchestrated by teams and the Pentagon. NFL teams received $6 million of those funds. The military cut checks to teams to carry out heartwarming displays of honoring wounded veterans and surprise homecomings, to have soldiers sing "God Bless America," and to conduct on-field enlistment ceremonies, among other acts portrayed as voluntary expressions of gratitude and patriotism. Teams reciprocated with promises of player appearances, tickets to games, access to luxury suites, and other VIP perks for soldiers and military officials. The report, authored by two pro-military Republican senators, provided clear evidence that ballpark patriotic displays were in fact hoaxes. In short, honoring the military was a little side hustle for professional sports franchises and the Defense Department.[20]

During this same period, the refashioning of police officers into selfless heroes in effect sanctioned them to wage another kind of war within the boundaries of the United States. Law enforcement appreciation promotions held at stadiums and arenas all over the country contributed to the glorification of police. These promotions have multiplied in recent years, even after police came under increasing scrutiny for shooting unarmed civilians. However, terrorists would not be the targets of a new kind of domestic war. Rather, multitudes of black and brown people have been the primary targets of police violence and mass incarceration.[21]

WEEKS BEFORE COLIN KAEPERNICK KNEELED DURING THE ANTHEM at Qualcomm Stadium, on July 9, 2016, three days after the murder of Philando Castile, players for the Minnesota Lynx WNBA franchise came out of their locker room at the Target Center in Minneapolis wearing new warm-up shirts. Team cocaptain and legendary All-Star Maya Moore, cocaptain Rebekah Brunson, and their teammates Seimone Augustus and Lindsay Whalen wore CHANGE BEGINS WITH US: JUSTICE AND ACCOUNTABILITY on the front of their black T-shirts and the names PHILANDO CASTILE and ALTON STERLING and BLACK LIVES MATTER on the back. They held an impromptu gathering with the press to announce that they were speaking out against racism and police violence. "Tonight, we will be wearing shirts to honor and mourn the losses of precious American citizens and to plea for change in all of us," Brunson said. "Racism and unjust phobic fear of black males, and disregard of black females is very real." Though their message was one of unity between civilians and police officers, it was clear that they were foregrounding the concerns of black communities. This was not lost on four off-duty police officers, who reacted to the players' actions by refusing to provide security that night at the Target Center. In the era of police glorification, even pleas for accountability were deemed unacceptable by police unions and their supporters.[22]

The next night, players for the New York Liberty WNBA franchise conveyed a similar message to the public. They took the floor at Madison Square Garden wearing warm-ups with the words BLACK LIVES MATTER and DALLAS 5 printed on their shirts in response to the Sterling and Castile killings and the retaliatory shooting of five Dallas police officers by a black veteran. "We do need people to stand up and understand and express that black lives are just as important as any other lives in America, and right now that's not being seen," Liberty guard Tanisha Wright told the press. WNBA league officials initially responded to the protests by fining players for wearing unsanctioned uniforms, a violation of league policies. Wearing uniforms with corporate sponsors was acceptable. Donning gear displaying messages of social justice was not. The league eventually saw the illogic of its policies and rescinded the fines a few weeks later. More demonstrations and protests followed that summer and into fall during the NFL season, which turned out to be Kaepernick's last in professional football. A movement against racist policing was taking shape among prominent black athletes who insisted on expressing their demands inside the confines of the American stadium.[23]

By taking their outrage to the virtual world and the streets, the movement known as Black Lives Matter catalyzed by Alicia Garza, Patrice Cullors, Opal Tometi, and thousands of other black activists exposed the lies of police heroism. This twenty-first-century version of the Black Freedom movement emerged in the wake of the murders of Trayvon Martin in Sanford, Florida, and Michael Brown in Ferguson, Missouri. Like the civil rights organizers of the sixties, who skillfully used the television cameras to amplify their message, their twenty-first-century descendants used the smartphone and social media to make their voices heard. The #BlackLivesMatter hashtag gave an existing movement greater influence through the channels of social media. The killings of Eric Garner, Tamir Rice, and others by law enforcement triggered more activism and protests. Police brutality against black people has existed since the earliest days of slavery in the Americas, and activists have been calling it out for generations. Angela Davis was one of a number of activists who have challenged police repression and political imprisonment for decades. As activists in recent years have shown, police brutality goes hand in hand with the massive imprisonment of black people and other nonwhite men and women.[24]

As public awareness of police violence grew in the early 2010s, privileged black athletes could no longer look away. Taking their cues from activists, black athletes used the stadium to amplify the demands of the movement against racist policing. By wearing Black Lives Matter T-shirts and by speaking out against racism, they challenged the prevailing wisdom of race in the sports world since the civil rights era. After Jackie Robinson broke the color line in professional baseball, and as black and Latino athletes went on the fields and courts of play, sports symbolized the triumphs of the civil rights movement. The prominence of black athletes has bolstered the myth of American meritocracy, that Americans from any background, no matter how marginalized, could make it in the United States. The stadium and the arena were imagined as spaces where racism no longer mattered, where meritocracy and cross-racial interaction were the norm. This was not mere mythology, especially as player salaries in major professional sports skyrocketed in the seventies, eighties, and nineties. Black fans came through turnstiles; congregated outside the ballpark to hawk tickets, programs, and souvenirs; and became an inextricable part of the stadium scene.

Even as the possibilities of upward mobility for Americans dwindled during the 1990s and early 2000s as class stratification sharpened, sports still symbolized the apparent breakdown of racial and class barriers. The Magic Johnsons, the Michael Jordans, the Tiger Woodses, and the vast majority of black athletes followed a version of the template laid out by O. J. Simpson during the seventies: Achieve adoration and fame through success on the field and make commercials that help corporate America make more money. Engage with marginalized communities through philanthropy, not political activism. Help the less fortunate by setting up foundations, running sports camps, and holding golf tournaments. Follow the formula of the rich white men who signed your checks. Now, the Maya Moores and the Colin Kaepernicks of the world were flipping the script, no longer content to achieve fame, fortune, and the adoration of their white bosses and fans. They stood with the dispossessed and called upon society to address racism and inequality, and they dared to do so within the confines of the stadium itself.

It is not surprising that black women athletes in the WNBA were at the forefront of the athletic version of the Black Lives Matter movement. What makes the twenty-first-century Black Freedom movement unique is the prominence of black women and queer and transgender activists in organizational leadership and in the definition of the movement's platforms. Black women activists have put a wider spectrum of the dispossessed at the forefront of the struggle. The movement found a fertile base among the women who labor in the WNBA. The professional basketball league has been in existence since 1996, but despite showcasing the skills of many talented women, players were routinely underpaid and undersupported. They performed before small but loyal crowds in arenas they shared with NBA teams. Women's pro basketball was shackled by the sexism embedded in the sports world. And yet it was these players who transformed the message of the Movement for Black Lives in the sports world.[25]

Soon, athletes' support for the Black Lives Matter movement ran headlong into the giant wall of reactionary patriotism that had been built at the American ballpark since the start of the War on Terror. Although many Americans praised the public stands politicized athletes took, most virulently reacted in the manner that they always had against political dissenters. The chorus of criticism of Kaepernick on social media was echoed by the fans who burned his jersey and booed him, and it intensified as more and more players took a knee and raised fists during the national anthem during the 2016 and 2017 sports seasons. "He's oppressed making $126 million!" a fan ranted in a Facebook video before torching Kaepernick's jersey. Well-paid professional athletes had no right to complain, the argument went. They simply need to "shut up and dribble" and be grateful.[26]

As the calendar turned to 2020, the forces pushing back against the movement seemed to be prevailing. Donald Trump's election suggested that a sizable part of the American public had little interest in addressing police brutality and systemic racism. Though Kaepernick and protesting athletes clarified over and over again that they were not taking a stand against the military, politicians and their pundits in the Fox News world continued to mischaracterize the protests. Despite the praise and adulation he received from supporters throughout the country and from some sectors of corporate America that sought to capitalize on black activism, Kaepernick never entered a stadium as a professional football player again after the 2016 season. NFL owners, many of them donors to Republican causes, ensured that his playing days in the NFL were over. Other players who had actually committed crimes such as sexual assault could make a living playing pro football, but there was no roster spot for a player who stood for justice in the post-9/11 age. The claim that the Black Lives

Matter movement was "disrespecting the flag" and the "troops" continued to prevail.

Still, the Movement for Black Lives transformed the American stadium from an arena of compliant patriotism to a space of contestation. The 2010s was a decade of polarization akin to the 1930s and the 1960s. It wasn't the boxing ring or the baseball diamond that took center stage. This time, it was the gridirons of the National Football League, the lord of spectator sports in the United States. The stadium and the arena staged a contest of militarized patriotism and law enforcement glorification versus social justice and democracy. Players refused to remain silent and displayed various protest gestures during the national anthem in the 2017 season, while Kaepernick was shut out of the league. Fans booed and jeered as players took a knee, raised their fist, or stood armlocked during the national anthem. Donald Trump inflamed the situation and delighted his followers by imploring team owners to "get that son of a bitch off the field right now." Finally, owners, including Jerry Jones, kneeled with players in an attempt to mollify and control the protests.

Though many supporters of Kaepernick and the Black Freedom movement continued to raise their voices against racial injustice, the political environment at stadiums and arenas seemed to settle to a lower simmer of discontent and tension. As the 2010s drew to a close, the athlete activist movement in the NFL was effectively neutralized by corporate dollars earmarked for social justice work, but in reality these donations were designed to silence ballpark protests. Team owners and league officials continued to act as ventriloquists for right-wing politics by rehearsing the argument that stadium protests during performance of the national anthem were unpatriotic. And yet, it was when the stadium was suddenly emptied of fans that its social and political significance became most apparent.

In March 2020, the unthinkable happened. America, and many other parts of the world, was shut down by the rapid spread of the

COVID-19 virus. Congregation spaces, such as stadiums and arenas, were ideal environments for the spread of an infectious respiratory disease. It was soon discovered that social distancing and masking were the only viable ways to manage the spread of the disease during the prevaccine era of the pandemic. Arenas that housed professional and collegiate sports closed their doors. College sports were canceled, and professional leagues were halted indefinitely. The games would not go on for several weeks. A grim, horrifying reality of disease and death descended upon the country at a dizzying rate as hospitalizations and deaths skyrocketed in the first months of the pandemic in the United States. When pro hockey, basketball, baseball, and football finally resumed later that year, they did so in empty stadiums. Without a cure or a means of reliable treatment, aside from a mask, leagues were forced to conduct games without fans in the seats.

The effects of the COVID-19 pandemic were devastating, and so was another round of violence against black people. In March, Breonna Taylor was shot and killed by police barging into her home in Louisville, Kentucky, during a botched police raid. Ahmaud Arbery was shot and killed by white civilians in Glynn County, Georgia, after they were convinced the black man jogging in their neighborhood was a criminal. And the life was drained out of George Floyd's body by Derek Chauvin's knee on a Minneapolis street.

George Floyd's death was the last straw. Millions of people flooded the streets to express their outrage, and, as iconographic parts of the urban landscape, stadiums were ideal places to come together. In Brooklyn, crowds converged on the Barclays Center, the home arena of the Nets NBA franchise. The arena had been a divisive development project. Over the years, the ocular-shaped plaza outside the arena had been used for a variety of purposes, including protests against the arena project itself.[27] In the summer of 2020, thousands descended on the arena to express their outrage at the most recent round of police killings. They grieved, they protested, and they organized. For many who had been isolated in their homes because of the pandemic, it was a cathartic experience. Organizers, well versed in twenty-first-century activist techniques, used familiar mechanisms, such as the smartphone and social media, to coordinate demonstrations. However, now these techniques rallied thousands and millions of others, including many white Americans. Americans from all racial backgrounds who had been cooped up in their homes for months took to the streets to march, scream, and take a knee. It was the summer of redemption for Colin Kaepernick, even though he wasn't in need of any redemption.

Soon, athletes joined the movement, including many who had not spoken out against racial injustice. At that point, something remarkable happened. When Drew Brees, the veteran white quarterback of the New Orleans Saints, was asked about the possibility of players protesting in the upcoming NFL season, he regurgitated the old lie of equating protest with antipatriotism. "I will never agree with anyone disrespecting the flag of the United States of America," he roared during a Yahoo! Finance interview.[28] The interview went viral, but so did the response from a group of prominent NFL stars who took it upon themselves to craft an open letter, of sorts, to their league. They positioned themselves, not the owners, as representatives of the National Football League. After they explicitly identified with those who died at the hands of police, the players asked:

> So on behalf of the National Football League, this is what we the players would like to hear you state: We, the National Football League, condemn racism and the systemic oppression of black people. We, the National Football League, admit wrong in silencing our players from peacefully protesting. We, the National Football League, believe black lives matter.[29]

Brees apologized soon after, but the more noteworthy reaction came from the NFL. Two days later, Commissioner Roger Goodell responded to the video by condemning systemic racism and admitting the league was wrong in attempting to silence players' protests. Using the script provided to him by the players, he stated: "We, the National Football League, believe Black Lives Matter." Just like that, the spell of militarized patriotism was broken. Except, as players would soon discover, there was a price to pay for demanding league support. Still, the extraordinary speed by which Americans acquired a literacy on racism—previously seen as the problem of individual bigots, now seen as "systemic racism"—was astonishing. For the remainder of that summer, team and league officials stepped back and let players engage in activist work.[30]

It was at this moment when the NBA and WNBA "bubbles" that were created in Florida became the center of gravity in the American sports world. Their seasons would resume not in their home arenas but on the grounds of the ESPN Wide World of Sports Complex and at the IMG Academy in Bradenton. To prevent the creation of superspreader events, only players, league personnel, and select members were allowed into the bubble. Fans were not permitted into the carefully controlled environment. The absence of fans freed players in both leagues to use their shortened seasons as platforms to speak out against systemic racism. Both leagues unveiled uniforms with a variety of Black Lives Matter slogans. The WNBA dedicated its season in the bubble to promoting racial justice.

In the context of the pandemic-induced bubbles, athletes became further emboldened. Kelly Loeffler, then a US senator and owner of the Atlanta Dream WNBA franchise, condemned the league's decision to promote the cause of racial justice. Loeffler, a rich white businesswoman turned politician, had been a basketball enthusiast and team owner since 2010. However, once Georgia governor Brian Kemp appointed her to replace Johnny Isakson as senator in December 2019, she quickly embraced the Trumpian brand of white grievance politics. In 2020, Loeffler ran to hold onto her Senate seat. The Republican politician in the age of Trump quickly turned the Black Lives Matter movement into right-wing talking points. "The truth is, we need less, not more, politics in sports. In a time when polarizing politics is as divisive as ever, sports has the power to be a unifying antidote," Loeffler wrote. Taking pages from the right-wing playbook of anti-black racism, Loeffler declared, "I adamantly oppose the Black Lives Matter political movement, which has advocated for the defunding of police, called for the removal of Jesus from churches and the disruption of the nuclear family structure, harbored anti-Semitic views, and promoted violence and destruction across the country."[31]

Players condemned Loeffler's remarks, but they also had another surprise in store. On August 4, 2020, players on the Dream and other teams in the league boldly showed up at the gyms at IMG Academy wearing VOTE WARNOCK T-shirts, in support of Raphael Warnock, Loeffler's opponent in that year's Senate race in Georgia. The unprecedented protest—of players openly engaging in a political campaign against a league owner—was a major boost to Warnock's senatorial campaign. The players' campaigning for Warnock had a significant impact on the race. Before the Dream debuted their VOTE WARNOCK shirts, the Democratic candidate was polling at only 9 percent. After the players campaigned for Warnock, his profile increased dramatically. In subsequent weeks, players worked hard not only on behalf of Warnock's campaign but also on behalf of voter turnout across Georgia and in other parts of country. Athlete activism in the bubble was directly translating into influencing formal politics.[32]

There was more that summer. Yet another high-profile police shooting triggered more bold protest actions in the basketball bubbles, which spilled over to other sports, including the normally conservative worlds of Major League Baseball and NASCAR. The shooting of Jacob Blake in Kenosha, Wisconsin, on August 26, 2020, prompted an unprecedented work stoppage by the Milwaukee Bucks and Orlando Magic, who announced that they would not take the floor for that night's playoff game. Once again, the players highlighted the absence of police accountability. "When we take the court and represent Milwaukee and Wisconsin we are expected to play at a high level, give maximum effort and hold each other accountable," Bucks guard George Hill read during yet another impromptu press conference. "We hold ourselves to that standard, and in this moment, we are demanding the same from our lawmakers and law enforcement." The Bucks players were essentially making the same points that the Lynx players had made four years earlier. This time, however, they did it as part of their rationale for refusing to play. Here again, players courageously challenged the myths of police heroism built over the previous two decades.

Teams in the WNBA, MLB, and other sports leagues followed suit. The players of the New York Mets and the Miami Marlins staged their own refusal to play at Citi Field. Team management nervously looked on as players from both teams lined up in front of their dugouts, paused for forty-two seconds of silence, before walking off the field, leaving a Black Lives Matter T-shirt at home plate. After three days of intense discussion among themselves and with former president Barack Obama and basketball legend Michael Jordan, the NBA players returned to the court only after receiving pledges of support from the league and from some public officials that action would be taken to address the ongoing problem of racist policing.[33]

Suddenly, the American stadium was rebranded as an arena of social justice. However, it took the form of what everything has since the 1990s—a corporate advertisement. Taking their cues from the

Black Lives Matter in the NBA bubble. *Credit: Kevin C. Cox/Getty Images*

basketball bubbles in Florida, teams installed Black Lives Matter–inspired signage at baseball, football, and soccer stadiums and even at NASCAR racetracks. Gigantic BLACK LIVES MATTER slogans appeared on stadium facades, fields, courts, and scoreboards across the country. Slogans like SAY HER NAME were imprinted on uniforms. BLM virtual advertisements appeared alongside ads for Goya Foods, whose CEO had donated money to the Trump campaign.

In the summer of 2020, the American stadium was dramatically converted into a monument to social justice, even if for just a brief time. Black players and their allies repudiated the gospel of "stick to sports" that deterred athletes from speaking out against injustice. In subsequent weeks and months, player activism, in partnership with enlightened members of the sports management world, refashioned the stadium yet again into a vehicle of something equally as consequential.

As THE NATIONWIDE PROTEST MOVEMENT GATHERED STEAM IN JUNE 2020, the management of the Atlanta Hawks decided to try to make a difference. "It struck me that if nothing came out of these protests to create change, then we would have failed," Hawks CEO Steve Koonin told the press. "I thought the most accessible change was getting more people to vote." So, management went to work, not on their normal tasks as workers for a pro basketball franchise. They went about the business of learning how to make democracy work. Prompted by its own players, coaches, and employees, the team donated the use of the arena, along with hundreds of hours of staff time, for in-person voting in the upcoming election. With stadiums empty because of the pandemic, the team rightly saw the moment as an opportunity to address the needs of the community. "We are more than a basketball team," Koonin insisted.[34]

Koonin was one of a number of team executives who were moved to action by the protests. However, the idea of stadium voting had already been discussed in the wake of the 2016 election. The Ross

Initiative in Sports Equality (RISE), a coalition of players, team executives, and public officials, was one of a plethora of civic engagement groups that formed to address racial injustice in recent years. Jocelyn Benson, RISE's CEO, and Scott Pioli, assistant general manager of the Atlanta Falcons NFL franchise at the time, encouraged a conversation about making voting more accessible in a period when voter suppression was becoming more of a reality in black communities. Given the growing number of stadiums built in the United States and the enormous public resources required to construct and maintain them, they proposed using stadiums for pro-democracy efforts.

When the moment came to implement this idea, election administrators discovered that stadiums and arenas were ideal sites to carry out elections. They are large, usually publicly owned buildings that are accessible to transportation, with adequate parking, and they are equipped with operations staff to handle large crowds. All these traits became major assets as state and county officials were faced with the enormous challenge of finding safe voting spaces during the days of the prevaccine pandemic.

Unbelievably, teams shed their reluctance to engage in the political sphere and answered the call for change. Sports franchises from all the major sports leagues, but especially the NBA and WNBA, participated in the effort to create voting centers at stadiums and arenas. Forty-eight stadiums and arenas were converted into polling stations during the 2020 elections. The vast majority of them were used as early voting sites. With normal game operations suspended, teams had the staff, the energy, and the resources to compete with each other to turn out the most voters. The Hawks operations staff set up voting machines all over the arena, including in the concourses and on the floor where the basketball court was typically set up. After a technical snafu caused delays on the first day of early voting on October 12, 2020, elections officials and Hawks poll workers worked incredibly well. The average time it took for Atlantans to vote at the arena was twenty-six minutes, a much shorter time than typical for voters in the city. The arena was used in that year's primaries, the general election, and the Senate runoff race. An estimated fifty thousand people voted at the arena during the historic 2020 election.

Similar partnerships took shape in cities all over the country. In Los Angeles County, nearly all the major sports facilities were used as polling stations. At Dodger Stadium, the region's temperate climate made it possible for voters to vote in the outdoor concourses. Voters encountered a festive atmosphere, with mariachi bands providing entertainment. In Boston, voters cast their ballots in the concourses of the historic Fenway Park. In Charlotte, the local NFL and NBA arenas were voting stations. Similar outcomes transpired all over the country. Buildings that have since the 1990s been widely thought of merely as sport and entertainment buildings were returning to their original function as civic institutions. While these efforts were made possible by the temporary shutdown of sports by the pandemic, franchises and election officials realized that versions of the voting program could happen with proper planning in the future. During the 2022 midterm elections, some of the same facilities were used again as voting stations, and plans for remounting the sites in the 2024 election are unfolding. A period of polarization, war, and death unexpectedly yielded to glimpses of the revitalization of American democracy.[35]

DURING THE FIRST TWO DECADES OF THE TWENTY-FIRST CENTURY, the American stadium was a social and political powder keg. An institution that had played an important role in American society and politics was somewhat suddenly remade into a platform for militarism and a culture of compliance that suffocated anyone who voiced any political dissent. The wave of militarized patriotism, which emerged during the Gulf War in the early nineties, was catalyzed by the reaction to the terrorist attacks of 9/11. As the Bush and Obama administrations waged their wars in Afghanistan and Iraq, sports teams were among the most visible institutions called upon to legitimize the war effort. The sports industry, now the de facto ruler of the American stadium, used its overwhelming political influence to make it into a recruit-ment station for the American military. An institution that had pro-vided space for political expression became a repressive environment of blind obedience.

In recent years, however, the modern Black Freedom movement has pushed back and made the stadium into a major arena of contes-tation. The notion that sports should be removed from politics and that stadiums are merely palaces of pleasure was definitively repudi-ated. Such a position was harder to sustain as black communities were being brutalized by hypermilitarized police forces and the majority of Americans were experiencing their freedoms taken away by the very institutions that demanded blind obedience. The 2020 elections in some ways marked a turning point in the two-decades-long period of social and political warfare in the United States. The crisis generated by the COVID-19 pandemic and the ongoing crisis of police violence had somehow created the conditions for a reinvigorated civic life in which the American stadium played a substantial role. It remains to be seen whether the early-twenty-first-century movement for social jus-tice and political democracy can preserve the important interventions that have been made in recent years. The stadium, as it has for more than a century, will act as a barometer of the state of democracy and the fate of the nation in the years to come.

CONCLUSION

I n the summer of 2020, when millions of people took to the streets declaring "Black Lives Matter" after George Floyd's murder, it seemed everyone was talking about systemic racism. The spell of nearly two decades of blind compliance to militarized patriotism and the concurrent glorification of police was broken, or so it seemed. Nationwide, activists prompted a larger reevaluation of the various ways structural racism persists in the United States, and a long-standing odious racist tradition in sports was finally toppled. On June 18, 2020, the George Preston Marshall monument that stood outside RFK Stadium in Washington, DC, was vandalized. Overnight, someone had drawn the words CHANGE THE NAME in dripping bright-red paint on the fading burgundy and gold statue. The very next day, which happened to be Juneteenth, the long-standing black American tradition of emancipation celebration, Events DC, the public entity that managed the site, decided to remove the statue. "This symbol of a person who didn't believe all men and women were created equal and who actually worked against integration is counter to all that we as people, a city and nation represent," Events DC said in a statement. "Removing this statue is a small and an overdue step on the road to lasting equality and justice."[1] The monument to the man who had been hailed as a pro football pioneer and a Washington, DC, legend that had stood on federal property for decades was mercifully gone.

A month later, the Washington NFL franchise that Marshall founded finally announced that it would discontinue the use of the name "Redskins." Seven years earlier, the widely disliked team owner

Daniel Snyder had proclaimed to the world: "We will never change the name of the team." Suddenly, Snyder was forced to change his tune. The calls for a reckoning with systemic racism prompted previously indifferent corporate sponsors to finally call upon Snyder to change the name. The activists of 2020 had given voice to a demand that many Native American groups had been making for decades. A year later, the team rebranded itself as the Commanders. A long-standing tradition of Native mascotry had finally ended. The Cleveland MLB franchise, which had stubbornly clung to its team name and mascot traditions, followed suit and eventually changed its name to the Guardians. Other teams persist in keeping their Native names, but the renaming of these teams was a rare occasion when the desires of the sports industry did not override those of a substantial portion of the public.[2]

The defacing and removal of the Marshall monument was one of a number of reckoning moments with American history that have transpired since 2020. Not surprisingly, as a prominent monument to the past and present, the stadium was one of the prime locations where monuments to white supremacy were being toppled across the United States. At the same time that George Preston Marshall was removed from public memory, another former historically significant figure with roots in the history of Washington sports vanished from sight. In Minneapolis, activists successfully compelled the Minnesota Twins to remove a statue of longtime owner Calvin Griffith that had been erected outside Target Field, the team's stadium. Griffith had taken over the management of the franchise from Clark Griffith when it was the Washington Senators and moved it to Minnesota in 1961. Years later, he crowed to local fans during a speech at a Lions Club event that he moved the franchise because he was attracted to the "good hard-working white people" of Minnesota as opposed to the predominantly black population of Washington, DC. Griffith's comments, well-known for decades, suddenly came to the surface during the rapidly changing atmosphere of 2020. Whereas Griffth's statue was targeted by activists, the statue to beloved Twins legend Kirby

Puckett, which also was located outside the stadium, was not, despite his well-documented history as a perpetuator of domestic violence. A national racial awakening did not always translate into a larger recognition of other forms of oppression.[3]

As the stadium became a place where symbols of racial injustice appeared to be falling by the wayside, it also turned out to be an institution that helped safeguard US democracy. Poll workers carried out the labor of democracy at forty-eight arenas and stadiums across the country. During the 2020 election, arenas and stadiums were ground zero for democracy work. Even as election workers were fanatically harassed and intimidated by right-wing supporters of Donald Trump, they nevertheless painstakingly counted votes in arenas in Phoenix, Atlanta, and elsewhere, proving a Biden triumph.

And yet a sobering reality has surfaced since those heady days of 2020. A moment of racial reckoning and democratic renewal gave way, once again, to hyper-commodification and a resumption of the oppression that provoked the social and political turmoil in the first place. Stadiums continue to be stages of spectacular athletic and artistic feats that enable Americans to forget about the continuing crisis that afflicts this country and the larger world. The stellar performances of today's established and emerging star athletes, such as Patrick Mahomes, Nikola Jokic, and Caitlin Clark, and legendary performing artists, such as Beyoncé, among countless others, keep spectators coming through the stadium doors over and over again.

However, a climate of social and political polarization lingers and continues to show up at the stadium and the arena, whether spectators like it or not. The jet flyovers and the jingoistic performances of American patriotism continue at stadiums and arenas across the country, even if they have toned down just a bit. These displays are now part of an institutionalized and formulaic rotation of stadium advertisements where Black Lives Matter and watered-down "End Racism" slogans coexist with celebrations of law enforcement and the military and ads for State Farm Insurance. The wars in Afghanistan and Iraq have ended, but militarism relentlessly grinds on. So far, the Great Racial

Awakening of 2020 has produced little more than a wider awareness of a well-rehearsed script of perfunctory anti-racist declarations. And yet even this unsatisfying outcome has come under attack by the seemingly unstoppable train of right-wing political mobilization that continues unabated even after Donald Trump's defeat and the failed coup attempt of January 6.

Still, as unprecedented as the current social and political crisis seems to be, in some ways, it is just the latest instance of a longer history of struggle that has been carried out at stadiums and arenas for generations. Governments and corporate elites will undoubtedly approach the stadium as a platform to preserve the social and political status quo. Yet, social movements that have widened our understanding of the lives and struggles of vulnerable and dispossessed Americans are likely to continue to remind the country of its unfulfilled promises of freedom and democracy. Because stadiums and arenas are inextricable parts of American social, political, and cultural life, this will be a recurring pattern that is likely to persist in years to come.

AS WE HAVE SEEN, THE STADIUM HAS NEVER BEEN *MERELY* A SPORTS facility. The association between stadiums and sports is understandable. Americans have gathered at these facilities to watch and participate in sporting events, concerts, the circus, and a host of other cultural events for more than a century. They have congregated outside these facilities to tailgate, sell tickets, hawk merchandise, and sell food. Like cathedrals, these places are where rituals take place on and off the field. However, the stadium has also been an institution with a more substantial role in American life. Throughout its history, it has been much more than a place to root for the home team. It has been a place where community desires have been expressed. It has been a place where national and local aspirations have been created and performed in front of large audiences. It has also been a place of statecraft, politics, and resistance. It continues to fulfill these functions, even as it has been dressed up as a temple of worship to the corporate gods of the twenty-first century. Looking back at the ways athletes, activists, and social movements have used the stadium to publicly demand justice in the distant and recent past makes this abundantly clear.

In the 1870s, when New Yorkers turned out to P. T. Barnum's Grand Roman Hippodrome to behold the wonders of the acrobatic feats of talented circus performers, they also saw reenactments of the conquest of the American West and received the subtle and not-so-subtle messages that those who were not white were to be derided and even ridiculed. In the Jim Crow South, white southerners came to Tulane Stadium in New Orleans to see the toughness, strength, and speed of football players on the gridiron while also witnessing pageantry and spectacles conveying the belief that the white supremacist order promised by the (failed) Confederacy lived on in the twentieth century. At the height of the polarized 1930s, Nazi sympathizers packed Madison Square Garden more than once to declare their allegiance to an Aryan Nation.

And yet, at those same venues, and at many others, Americans committed to the vision of a nation for all pushed back and showed up at America's public square—the stadium—to project their own visions of a just society. Isadore Greenbaum courageously emerged from the crowd of hostile antisemites to disrupt the rally of fascist hate organized by the German American Bund. Thousands of other New Yorkers, from labor and Communist activists to political leaders from the city's immigrant classes, such as Fiorella LaGuardia, joined the anti-fascist cause and barged through the Garden's doors to reject the fascist message that was spreading across the Atlantic to the United States in the 1930s. During the Second World War, the Garden became an important stage for the Black Freedom movement when thousands of New Yorkers turned out to the annual Negro Freedom Rallies to declare that victory against the Nazis abroad would mean nothing without victory against racism at home.

The Negro Freedom Rallies at the Garden during the 1940s were precursors to the great social movements of the mid-twentieth century.

During the 1960s, civil rights activists used stadiums and arenas all over the country to convince Americans that the odious system of Jim Crow segregation had to end. They protested outside RFK Stadium in Washington, the Memorial Coliseum in Los Angeles, Kezar Stadium in San Francisco, and at other venues to demand that George Preston Marshall's segregationist charade end. They partnered with white allies to organize rallies at the Sports Arena in Los Angeles, Cobo Hall in Detroit, and Soldier Field in Chicago to demand that the federal government put an end to Jim Crow in the South and housing, job, and educational discrimination in the North. And a few years later, over a hundred thousand people turned out to the Los Angeles Coliseum to commemorate the 1965 Watts uprising, to sing and dance to the sounds of the talented musicians of Stax Records, and to unabashedly declare that Black Freedom meant little without genuine black community empowerment.

Native American activists and second-wave feminists also approached the stadium as an arena to make their concerns known. For decades, Native Americans objected to the odious practice of Native mascotry perpetuated for more than a century by sports institutions. In the early 1970s, the American Indian Movement targeted the Washington Redskins franchise, among other sports teams, demanding it halt its long-standing tradition of Native American denigration. For decades, AIM protested at stadiums across the country. Their efforts slowly moved the needle on the question of Native mascots, eventually compelling many teams to abandon their faux Native names and mascots. In 2020, the Washington pro football franchise finally retired its name. Meanwhile, second-wave feminists took their struggles to the American stadium. In addition to fighting for opportunities on the field of play, women were eager to break into the sportswriting profession. Their fight to gain access to places of work at the stadium, namely, the press box and the locker room, altered the gender landscape of the sports world in the 1970s. Their activism continued for years thereafter.

Gay liberation activists carried the protest traditions of previous decades into the 1980s when they built from scratch the Gay Games movement in San Francisco. The event was more than a declaration of gay rights. It responded to the anti-gay rights crusade galvanized by Anita Bryant and others not only by contesting homophobia but also by doing what social movements have often done best—putting forth a vision of society that reflected their values and aspirations. To be sure, the Gay Games of the 1980s were an exhibition of athletes who had been excluded by the homophobic culture of American athletics. However, they were much more than an argument that gays and lesbians were athletes, too. Like the historic Wattstax concert, the Gay Games were a community celebration that reflected the best of what the American stadium has offered throughout its history. As the opening and closing ceremonies at Kezar Stadium powerfully illustrated, the Gay Games were a showcase of a marginalized community in all its fullness. Even though they assembled in a decaying structure that was only a few years away from the wrecking ball, the simple design of the facility—stands rising around a performative stage—allowed spectators and participants to feel a sense of affirmation. It was an athletic event, a political rally, and a party all at the same time, and it was made possible by the fact that its organizers, like those who organized the Wattstax concert, had access to a public institution with a mandate that was broader than merely serving as a facility for professional sports.

A few examples reveal how the freedom movements of the mid-twentieth century creatively repurposed stadiums to demonstrate what the United States could be when its marginalized and dispossessed people could freely express their desires and aspirations in a public forum. This freedom has been much more circumscribed during the past few decades, as stadiums have become less accessible as a result of their exclusionary designs and their high costs of admission. Unlike the Black Freedom movement of the sixties and seventies, which could access the stadium to organize events, today's Movement for Black Lives has been told in no uncertain terms that it is not welcome in the American stadium. More than two decades of remaking stadiums into supposed apolitical platforms for corporate advertisement and militarized nationalism have actually curtailed the freedoms Americans enjoyed in previous decades. Yet, this is precisely why a revisiting of the history of the American stadium is in order.

The claims of an apolitical stadium made by the sports industry notwithstanding, the American stadium will continue to play a major role in the social and political lives of the nation if only because Americans can't help but build more of them. In addition to traditional sports franchises' ongoing new-stadium lobbying efforts, the steady growth of professional soccer in the United States has meant that soccer leagues have joined the race to build new stadiums. Unlike the mega soccer stadiums in Europe, these smaller venues resemble the intimate environments of baseball, basketball, and football facilities of earlier generations, but they are slowly becoming resource-sucking, corporatized entities themselves. Universities have also joined in the stadium-building craze of the past three decades, either building new facilities or retrofitting the 1920s-era constructions as newly hyper-commercialized spaces. More damaging are sports franchises' constant demands that the public finance the construction of new facilities even when there is no need for them. The shelf life of stadiums is decreasing as sports franchises argue that 1990s-era stadiums are now obsolete. In Atlanta, a new stadium was built for the Falcons NFL franchise only twenty-five years after its previously deemed state-of-the-art facility was built. Similar cases of accelerated stadium building have occurred in other parts of the country.[4]

Even when an argument for a new stadium can persuasively be made, public officials do not capitalize on those occasions to push for better stadium deals. Indeed, the amount of public subsidies devoted to stadium construction continues to rise. In March 2022, New York State governor Kathy Hochul and Erie County pledged $850 million in taxpayer subsidies to a new facility for the Buffalo Bills NFL franchise. Meanwhile, ballpark proponents such as Larry Lucchino and

Paul Goldberger and even former stadium critics such as Andrew Zim-balist stump for stadium builders. In Kansas City, the home of HOK/Populous, the architectural firm that has profited the most from the stadium-building wave of the past thirty years, the Royals MLB fran-chise is pushing for a new stadium. Kauffman Stadium, long cited as a model baseball stadium and the team's home for the past five decades, is now seen as out-of-date because of its suburban location. Even Ori-ole Park at Camden Yards, the building that kicked off the post-1990s stadium-building craze, is being declared obsolete and in need of ren-ovation. Politicians continue to devote enormous amounts of public subsidies to stadium projects, promising economic revitalization even as economists have repeatedly shown that stadiums do not generate sustainable economic development.[5]

The current era of stadium building has been slightly disrupted by an emerging anti-Olympics movement. Anti-Olympics activists have achieved some success in slowing down the mega-event jugger-naut that is the International Olympic Committee. In 2015, a strong grassroots movement in Boston helped defeat Olympic boosters' attempts to bid on hosting the Olympics. Similar movements have emerged in Tokyo and Los Angeles, and it remains to be seen whether they can steer Olympic planning into a model that is more just and sustainable.[6]

One logical response to the sports-industrial complex's unre-lenting campaigning for new stadiums is for governments to refuse to commit any public subsidies to construction. This is a compelling argument that many have made for decades. In the early 1990s, the province of Ontario, Canada, was hemorrhaging money while man-aging the Skydome, Toronto's brand-new stadium. Like all stadiums, it had opened to much fanfare and praise, but public officials soon confronted the undeniable reality that their shining new toy was a money pit. Only a few years after it was built, they addressed the prob-lem by returning to the model of stadium financing that existed in the late nineteenth and early twentieth centuries: private ownership. The brilliant sports scholar and former athlete Bruce Kidd led this effort, arguing that public subsidies should not support venues whose primary constituency is corporate elites. Kidd's privatization position is backed by the undeniable evidence that stadiums have rarely been financially solvent. Why not return the stadium to what it was in the days when Tex Rickard ran Madison Square Garden as a private and profitable operation? Indeed, the boxing impresario opened the building to civic and political affairs, which was one reason why it became an important political gathering place in the decades after Rickard's death.[7]

The role of sports and stadiums in American life is much more deeply intertwined with civic and political institutions today than when the sports industry was in an embryonic stage of development in the 1920s. In many communities, sports franchises have made themselves into local institutions that cultivate strong local and regional affiliations. Americans remain attached to their stadiums, even today's generic temples named after corporations. Moreover, even the privately financed venues rely on some form of public subsidy, which usually provides the land or transportation infrastructure that make stadiums possible.

Still, the time for Americans to halt the ability of the sports industry to saddle municipalities with bad stadium deals is long overdue. The logic that each major sports team should have facilities tailored to its sport has led to the quadrupling of stadium construction during the past thirty years. Contrary to the claims of sports franchises and their political supporters, communities seldom, if ever, need to build new stadiums, especially if stadiums are designed primarily for profit maximization and their vision of civic engagement is confined to providing a platform for jet flyovers and law enforcement appreciation promotions. What communities can use are what stadiums have long provided—large spaces for commonalities to be formed through collective rituals. In an age when social interaction is almost always mediated by digital technologies, the stadium is one of a dwindling number of spaces of in-person human interaction. These interactions are often powerful if temporary experiences of communion.

More substantial commonalities can be forged not only by cheering for favorite performers at sports events and concerts but also by participating in a wide array of activities together. Political rallies organized by mainstream political parties and local activist organizations can be coupled with traditional civic engagement programs to reestablish multiple channels of political expression. The possibilities for common community experiences to be forged in the confines of the stadium are multiple.

If stadiums will continue to be part of the American landscape, then communities must insist their elected officials ensure that these buildings produce more tangible public benefits. At best, stadiums provide a social value and a recognizable space of local identification, though the practice of corporate naming rights tends to obliterate the local identity of many facilities. Even the retro ballpark design is formulaic. In addition to community benefits agreements, which in theory are supposed to guarantee job and housing creation, politicians need to insist on greater community control over the usage of stadium spaces. The Los Angeles Memorial Coliseum Commission operated in this manner for several decades. From 1945 until the early 2010s, the commission managed the city's iconic stadium, successfully balancing the desires of multiple sports teams with a stated commitment to community access. The commission faded into virtual nonexistence after it turned over the stadium's operations to the University of Southern California, but there is no good reason new forms of community stadium control cannot be envisioned.

Alternative designs and uses can be more aggressively pursued. Recently constructed college football stadiums, some of which include in their design substantial space for students and faculty and other academic affairs, provide examples of what a reimagined stadium space could look like. Moreover, the advent of stadium voting in 2020 provides a glimpse of what such arrangements can look like on a recurring basis. Sports franchises have shown that they are willing to support civic engagement and devote their operations teams to democracy work. The success of stadium voting in 2020 indicates that political leaders should insist that days on the stadium calendar be devoted to voting and other forms of civic engagement. The myth that stadiums must be sports specific obscures the fact that all stadiums are multiuse in practice, and they should be designed as such.[8]

With community control and multiple uses should come new models of stadium design. Stadium architects have gotten good at refashioning stadiums for corporate constituents. For the past three decades, luxury seating and various forms of privatized spectating and socializing have been at the core of architectural firm HOK/Populous's stadium designs. Yet other models exist. Though it was ultimately defeated by the political machinations of local officials, in the 1990s the Tiger Stadium Fan Club argued for community involvement in the redesign of the city's aging but beloved stadium. The club hired architects, and the designs the Tiger Stadium Fan Club commissioned in the 1990s were innovative plans for renovating the stadium into a venue that could survive in the twenty-first century. If Wrigley Field and Fenway Park could be renovated for modern life, why couldn't Detroit's beloved baseball cathedral? After nine years of struggle, however, the endeavor failed to halt the demolition of the old facility and the building of a new one. However, the fan club's efforts can inspire community-engaged stadium planning that foregrounds open access rather than exclusivity for the VIP crowd.[9]

The question of the twenty-first-century stadium is tied to a larger question that looms over American life: How can citizens make corporations, including sports franchises, more accountable to a wider public? For three decades, sports franchises have spun tales of stadium-driven neighborhood revitalization. Listening to today's team executives rehash long disproven orthodoxies about the benefits of stadium construction is akin to hearing the "wah wah" sounds of faceless adults in Charles Schulz's *Peanuts* animated television specials. Nonsensical talking points are only understandable to those who want to believe them. The stadium has seldom been a financially profitable endeavor. Stadiums are costly to build and expensive to maintain, and always have been. The repackaging of the stadium into an engine of economic revitalization during the 1990s has enriched developers and sports franchises at the expense of the local communities. The repeated evidence of stadiums running in the red show that their value does not translate into a metric.

The long history of the American stadium suggests that it plays the role of a public institution irrespective of the nature of its ownership. Investing in a stadium is best understood as a commitment to a public good, akin to budgeting for public parks and other public institutions that facilitate community cohesion. These were the arguments that midcentury stadium builders made to taxpayers in the period when facilities were coming under public control. Ultimately, the stadium needs to recognized, and perhaps actively cultivated, as the multifaceted institution that it has always been in American life.

ACKNOWLEDGMENTS

This book was a long time coming. It began, as it does for many of us who are fascinated by the stadium environment, when my father took me to sporting events in the late 1970s. As a New York native, my first stadium experiences were attending baseball games at Yankee and Shea Stadiums. On a cool night in April 1979, we were part of a small but boisterous crowd who watched the lowly San Francisco Giants face the lowlier New York Mets in a meaningless regular-season game at Shea. But, as a young black/Latino Caribbean American, the experience was far from meaningless. I was completely taken by the sight of Vida Blue, the black American star pitcher, firing his fastball and looking stylish in his vibrant orange and black Giants uniform with white cleats, orange socks, and high stirrups. Seeing black and Latino athletes perform in front of racially integrated crowds at Shea, Yankee, and Madison Square Garden and other venues during those years made a profound impression, and it signaled to me that the stadium belonged to *us* as much as it did to everyone else. Thank you to my parents, Francisco and Amparo Guridy, for introducing me to the stadium experience.

Whether it was a sporting event, a concert, or the circus, I never ceased to be fascinated by the stadium atmosphere: the cheering, the booing, the exhibition of different spectating cultures by that diverse crowd of Puerto Ricans, black Americans, the many variations of people called "white" in New York (Jews, Irish, Italians, and WASPs), and fans from all over the world. There was always a sense of anticipation and excitement and sometimes danger when fans would get out of hand, as they often did then. I now see in retrospect that I came of age in the years after the great freedom movements of the sixties and seventies helped make the stadium, like many other institutions, accessible to as wide a swath of Americans as it has ever been.

These formative experiences at stadiums as a spectator became even more impactful when I became a student of the Black Freedom struggle and the struggles of colonized people elsewhere. I vividly recall watching the massive rally at Yankee Stadium that was part of Nelson Mandela's glorious tour of the United States after his release from prison in 1990. I did not have the chance to attend the rally in person, but I will never forget the experience of watching on television the late Harry Belafonte as the emcee, rousing speakers, and musical acts such as the Mighty Sparrow, Judy Collins, and Sweet Honey in the Rock on that memorable night. Even though I was just starting to grasp the significance of the anti-Apartheid struggle in South Africa, the rally delivered the unmistakable message that a powerful social movement was responsible for a momentous occasion in world history.

This book, like all publications, has been a collective endeavor. Like all historians, I am deeply indebted to all the archivists who make it possible for us to do our work. Thank you to the archival staffs at the Williams Research Center of the Historic New Orleans Collection, the Tulane University Archives, the People's Archive of the District of Columbia Public Library, the New York Public Library, the Huntington Library, the LA84 Foundation, and the library at Occidental College.

Enormous thanks to my agent, Jill Marr, and my editor, Michael Kaler, for believing in this project and for offering insights that made this a better book. Thanks also to Kyle Gipson, who was an early supporter of this book when it was first in formation. Thank you to the rest of the Basic Books team for their talents and expertise.

I am indebted to my dear colleagues and friends Amy Bass, Brenda Elsey, and George Chauncey for taking time from their busy schedules to read and comment on all or parts of the manuscript. I am truly blessed to have outstanding graduate students at Columbia University who have taught me so much over the years. Special gratitude goes to Evan Brown, Juliana DeVaan, and Amanda Hardin, who carefully read the entire manuscript and gave me insightful feedback. I am grateful to my wonderful research assistants, Evan Brown and Claudia Wolff, who helped me track down information in various archives. Big thanks also to Vayne Ong, who provided invaluable assistance in the latter stages of the project. I am also enormously grateful to the many students I have had the privilege of teaching in my "Sport and Society in the Americas" class at Columbia. Their insights and enthusiasm and feedback sharpened my thinking on the stadium's place in society in the past and in the present.

Heartfelt gratitude to the following colleagues and friends for the various ways they helped make this book possible: Rosanne Adderley, Mila Atmos, Howard Bryant, Craig Calcaterra, Peter Carry, Annie Coleman, Amira Rose Davis, Bill Deverell, Nicole Dewey, Nancy Faust, Sharla Fett, Chris Gaffney, Farah Jasmine Griffin, Steve Hindle, Kellie Jones, Adam Kosto, Priscilla Leiva, Melissa Ludtke, Lawino Lurum, Shawn Mendoza, Lawrie Mifflin, Lincoln Mitchell, Mae Ngai, Alex Puerto, Marla Stone, John Tofanelli, Tova Wang, and Mabel Wilson. I must express a special note of gratitude to the late Margaret Farnum, the longtime general manager at the Los Angeles Memorial Coliseum, whom I had the pleasure of getting to know during the last years of her life. When I showed up at her doorstep in 2013 as a total stranger, Margaret welcomed me into her home and shared with me her recollections of the Coliseum scene during the days when it was at the center of Angeleno sport and civic life. It was a delight to get to know her and her son Bill, who has always been warm and generous with me over the years.

Thank you to my daughter, Zaya, for her endless patience while her dad was hustling to write this book. Thanks also for giving me the opportunity to be your softball coach. Being a part of our regular old-school-style neighborhood youth team reminds me how, despite all of the problems produced by the hypercompetitive and overly professionalized world of youth sports, something magical can happen when people come together to do something collectively just because they love it. Watching you develop as an athlete, artist, and person never ceases to be gratifying.

Last, but not least, I want to express my profound love and gratitude to my Beloved, the incredibly gifted poet, scholar, and writer Deborah Paredez. This book would not have been possible without her love, encouragement, and expertise. Even as she was working on her own book and managing her many other professional commitments, she always took the time to help me clarify my thinking about stadiums and why they matter, proofread countless drafts, and offered insights on the joys and challenges of the writing life. Thank you, *mi Amor,* for sharing with me a commitment to social justice and the passion of beholding live performance at the stadium, the arena, and the theater. I am profoundly grateful to you for our twenty years of life partnership, and I am eagerly looking forward to many more adventures with you in the years to come.

NOTES

INTRODUCTION

1. Andy Newman, "How a Once-Loathed Brooklyn Arena Became a Protest Epicenter," *New York Times*, June 16, 2020.

2. Norman Oder, "No, Mikhail Prokhorov Doesn't 'Own' the Barclays Center," City and State New York, April 19, 2018, www.cityandstateny.com/opinion/2018/04/no-mikhail-prokhorov-doesnt-own-the-barclays-center/178550/.

3. Newman, "How a Once-Loathed Brooklyn Arena."

4. Stephen G. Miller, "The Greek Stadium as a Reflection of a Changing Society," in *A Companion to Sport and Spectacle in Greek and Roman Antiquity*, eds. Paul Christesen and Donald G. Kyle (Chichester, West Sussex, UK: Wiley Blackwell, 2014), 287–294.

5. Katherine E. Welch, *The Roman Amphitheatre: From Its Origins to the Colosseum* (Cambridge: Cambridge University Press, 2007).

6. Engin Akyürek, *The Hippodrome of Constantinople* (Cambridge: Cambridge University Press, 2021); David M. Perry and Matthew Gabriele, "What the Medieval Olympics Looked Like," *Smithsonian Magazine*, July 20, 2021, www.smithsonianmag.com/history/what-medieval-olympics-looked-180978232/.

7. Michael T. Friedman and Jacob Bustad, "Sport and Urbanization," in *The Oxford Handbook of Sports History*, eds. Robert Edelman and Wayne Wilson, chap. 9, Oxford Handbooks (New York: Oxford University Press, 2017), https://doi.org/10.1093/oxfordhb/9780199858910.013.3; Juan Luis Paramio, Babatunde Buraimo, and Carlos Campos, "From Modern to Postmodern: The Development of Football Stadia in Europe," *Sport in Society* 11, no. 5 (2008): 517–534; Sigrid Brandt, Jorge Haspel, Ralph Paschke, and John Ziesemer, eds., *Das modern Erbe der Olympischen Spiele* [The Modern Heritage of the Olympic Games] (Berlin: ICOMOS, 2021).

8. Steven Reiss, *City Games: The Evolution of American Urban Society and the Rise of Sports* (Urbana: University of Illinois Press, 1989), 203–227.

9. Philip B. Kunhardt, *P. T. Barnum: America's Greatest Showman* (New York: Knopf, 1995); George L. Chindahl, *A History of the Circus in America* (Caldwell, ID: Caxton Printers, 1959).

10. Colleen Aycock and Mark Scott, *Tex Rickard: Boxing's Greatest Promoter* (Jefferson, NC: McFarland and Company, 2012).

11. Reiss, *City Games*, 219; Bruce Kuklick, *To Everything a Season: Shibe Park and Urban Philadelphia, 1909–1976* (Princeton, NJ: Princeton University Press, 1991).

12. Lawrence S. Ritter, *Lost Ballparks: A Celebration of America's Legendary Fields* (New York: Viking Studio Books, 1992); Paul Goldberger, *Ballpark: Baseball in the American City* (New York: Knopf, 2019); Richard G. Weingardt, "Frank Osborn: Nation's Pioneer Stadium Designer," *Structure Magazine*, March 2013, 61–63, www.structuremag.org/?p=930.

13. Ronald A. Smith, "Far More Than Commercialism: Stadium Building from Harvard's Innovations to Stanford's 'Dirt Bowl,'" *International Journal of the History of Sport* 25 (2008): 1453–1474.

14. "Coliseum Throng Views Tableau of War Scenes," *Los Angeles Times*, October 28, 1945.

15. N. D. B. Connolly, *A World More Concrete: Real Estate and the Remaking of Jim Crow in South Florida* (Chicago: University of Chicago Press, 2014).

16. Philip J. Deloria, *Playing Indian* (New Haven, CT: Yale University Press, 1998); J. Gordon Hylton, "Before the Redskins Were the Redskins: The Use of Native American Team Names in the Formative Era of American Sports, 1857–1933," *North Dakota Law Review* 86, no. 4 (2010): 879–930.

17. Geri Strecker, "The Rise and Fall of Greenlee Field: Biography of a Ballpark," *Black Ball* 2, no. 2 (2009): 37–67.

18. On the importance of the developments of the 1950s, see Neil Sullivan, *The Dodgers Move West* (New York: Oxford University Press, 1987), and Benjamin Lisle, *Modern Coliseum: Stadiums and American Culture* (Philadelphia: University of Pennsylvania Press, 2017).

19. Goldberger, *Ballpark*, 171–195; Lisle, *Modern Coliseum*; Daniel Rosensweig, *Retro Ball Parks: Instant History, Baseball, and the New American City* (Knoxville: University of Tennessee Press, 2005), 84–85.

20. Gary Gerstle, *The Rise and Fall of the Neoliberal Order: America and the World in the Free Market Era* (New York: Oxford University Press, 2022).

21. Sean Dinces, *Bulls Markets: Chicago's Basketball Business and the New Inequality* (Chicago: University of Chicago Press, 2018).

22. Roger G. Noll and Andrew Zimbalist, eds., *Sports, Jobs, and Taxes: The Economic Impact of Sports Teams and Stadiums* (Washington, DC: Brookings Institution, 1997); Kevin J. Delaney and Rick Eckstein, *Public Dollars, Private Stadiums: The Battle over Building Sports Stadiums* (New Brunswick, NJ: Rutgers University Press, 2003)—these are just two examples of the vast literature that illustrates the unprofitability of stadium-led economic development.

23. Howard Bryant, *The Heritage: Black Athletes, a Divided America, and the Politics of Patriotism* (Boston: Beacon Press, 2018).

24. Dave Zirin, *The Kaepernick Effect: Taking a Knee, Changing the World* (New York: New Press, 2021).

CHAPTER ONE: PALACES OF PLEASURE, ARENAS OF PROTEST

1. Nancy MacLean, *Behind the Mask of Chivalry: The Making of the Second Ku Klux Klan* (New York: Oxford University Press, 1994).

2. Robert Keith Murray, *The 103rd Ballot: The Legendary Democratic Convention That Forever Changed Politics* (New York: Harper & Row, 1976).

3. Murray, *The 103rd Ballot*, 151.

4. Camille Kaminski Lewis, "'I Come from Georgia': Andrew Cobb Erwin's Resistance to the Ku Klux Klan," *Rhetoric & Public Affairs* 23, no. 2 (2020): 331–365; Murray, *The 103rd Ballot*, 153–164.

5. Murray, *The 103rd Ballot*, 252–256.

6. Sven Beckert, *Monied Metropolis: New York City and the Consolidation of the American Bourgeoisie* (Cambridge, MA: Harvard University Press, 2001), 18–19; Robert Greenbaugh Albion, *The Rise of the New York Port, 1815–1860* (Boston: Northeastern University Press, 1984).

7. Tyler Anbinder, *City of Dreams: The 400-Year Epic History of Immigrant New York* (Boston: Houghton Mifflin Harcourt, 2016), 493; Suzanne Hinman, *The Grandest Madison Square Garden: Art, Scandal, and Architecture in Gilded Age New York* (Syracuse, NY: Syracuse University Press), 3; Michael T. Friedman and Jacob Bustad, "Sport and Urbanization," in *The Oxford Handbook of Sports History*, eds. Robert Edelman and Wayne Wilson, Oxford Handbooks (Oxford: Oxford University Press, 2017); Steven Reiss, *City Games: The Evolution of American Urban Society and the Rise of Sports* (Urbana: University of Illinois Press, 1989).

8. Reiss, *City Games*.

9. Miriam Berman, *Madison Square: The Park and Its Celebrated Landmarks* (Salt Lake City, UT: Gibbs Smith, 2001), 14; John Thorn, *Baseball in the Garden of Eden: The Secret History of the Early Game* (New York: Simon & Schuster, 2012).

10. Paul Goldberger, *Ballpark: Baseball in the American City* (New York: Knopf, 2019), 3–48.

11. Philip B. Kunhardt, *P. T. Barnum: America's Greatest Showman* (New York: Knopf, 1995); George L. Chindahl, *A History of the Circus in America* (Caldwell, ID: Caxton Printers, 1959); Janet M. Davis, *The Circus Age: Culture and Society Under the American Big Top* (Chapel Hill: University of North Carolina Press, 2002).

12. Kunhardt, *P. T. Barnum*, 242–243.

13. Goldberger, *Ballpark*, 24; Joseph Durso, *Madison Square Garden: 100 Years of History* (New York: Simon & Schuster, 1979), 18.

14. "Miscellaneous: Mr. P. T. Barnum's Show," *New York Times*, October 21, 1873; Durso, *Madison Square Garden*, 13–18.

15. "Barnum's Roman Hippodrome," *New York Times*, April 28, 1874.

16. Houston Sports Association, *Inside the Astrodome* (Houston: Houston Sports Association, 1965); Charles Maher, "Cooke Says He'll Build the Forum in Inglewood," *Los Angeles Times*, July 2, 1966.

17. "Musical and Dramatic: Gilmore's Concert Garden," *New York Times*, May 30, 1875; Durso, *Madison Square Garden*, 19.

18. Suzanne Hinman, *The Grandest Madison Square Garden: Art, Scandal, and Architecture in Gilded Age New York* (Syracuse, NY: Syracuse University Press), 72–85.

19. "A Place of Amusement," *New York Times*, October 30, 1887; Hinman, *The Grandest Madison Square Garden*, 89.

20. *Madison Square Garden Hall of Fame* (New York: Robert W. Kelly, 1967), 9.

21. Hinman, *The Grandest Madison Square Garden*, 305–315.

22. Frank Andre Guridy, *The Sports Revolution: How Texas Changed the Culture of American Athletics* (Austin: University of Texas Press, 2021).

23. Randy Roberts, *Papa Jack: Jack Johnson and the Era of Great White Hopes* (New York: Free Press, 1985); Geoffrey Ward, *Unforgivable Blackness: The Rise and Fall of Jack Johnson* (New York: Vintage, 2006).

24. Colleen Aycock and Mark Scott, *Tex Rickard: Boxing's Greatest Promoter* (Jefferson, NC: McFarland and Company, 2012), 136; Arne King, "Re-visiting the Walker Law of 1920 Which Transformed Boxing," Sweet Science, March 27, 2020, https://tss.ib.tv/boxing/featured-boxing-articles-boxing-news-videos-rankings-and-results/63847-re-visiting-the-walker-law-of-1920-which-transformed-boxing.

25. Randy Roberts, *Jack Dempsey: The Manassa Mauler* (Urbana: University of Illinois Press, 2003), 130–144.

26. Murray, *103rd Ballot*, 96–97; Robert Pruter, "Yesterday's City: Chicago's Other Coliseum," *Chicago Magazine of History* 38 (2012): 44–65.

27. Durso, *Madison Square Garden*, 123–128; "Hoover Declares for Dry Law Enforcement, Pledges Farm Aid," *San Francisco Examiner*, August 12, 1928; Paul Michael Peterson, *Chicago Stadium* (Charleston, SC: Arcadia Publishing, 2011), 58–59.

28. "Garden Hears Last Roars of Gay Crowds," *New York Times*, May 6, 1925.

29. "Garden Opens in a Blaze of Color," *New York Times*, December 16, 1925.

30. "New Rickard Arena Work Is Under Way," *New York Times*, January 10, 1925.

31. "New Rickard Arena Work Is Under Way"; J. A. Sessler, "The New Madison Square Garden," in Historical Book issued at the Opening Events of the Madison Square Garden, Eighth Avenue and 50th Street, New York City (New York, 1925); "Madison Square Garden Opens in New Home," *New York Times*, November 29, 1925.

32. Goldberger, *Ballpark*, 76–127; Stew Thornley, *Land of Giants: New York's Polo Grounds* (Philadelphia: Temple University Press, 2000); Robert Weintraub, *The House That Ruth Built: A New Stadium, the First Yankees Championship, and the Redemption of 1923* (New York: Little, Brown, 2011).

33. Richard A. Johnson and Brian Codagnone, *The Boston Garden* (Charleston, SC: Arcadia Publishing, 2002).

34. Robert Wimmer, *Detroit's Olympia Stadium* (Chicago: Arcadia, 2000); Don Hayner, *The Stadium, 1929–1994: The Official Commemorative History of Chicago Stadium* (Chicago: Performance Media, 1993); William Houston, *Inside Maple Leaf Gardens: The Rise and Fall of the Toronto Maple Leafs* (Toronto: McGraw-Hill Ryerson, 1989).

35. Durso, *Madison Square Garden*, 170.

36. David Clay Large, *Nazi Games: The Olympics of 1936* (New York: W. W. Norton, 2007), 69–109.

37. "20,000 Pledge Fight on Fascist Regimes," *New York Times*, November 29, 1934; Pellegrino Nazzaro, "Modigliani's Visit to the United States and the Origins of the American Labor Party," *Rivista di Studi Politici Internazionali* 52 (Aprile–Giugno 1985): 241–278.

38. Alan M. Shore, "Arena of Protest: The Staging of Jewish-Christian Discourse at Madison Square Garden in the Nazi Era" (PhD diss., University of California, Berkeley, 2016); Anbinder, *City of Dreams*, 493.

39. Harvey Klehr, *The Heyday of American Communism* (New York: Basic Books, 1984); Michael Denning, *The Cultural Front: The Laboring of American Culture in the Twentieth Century* (London: Verso, 1996).

40. "Crowd Overflowing the Garden Hears Leaders," *New York Times*, March 28, 1933.

41. "20,000 Nazi Friends at a Rally Here Denounce Boycott," *New York Times*, May 18, 1934.

42. "NY and Boston Cops Make Savage Attack on Workers Marching in Anti-Nazi Protest," *Daily Worker*, May 19, 1934; Arnie Bernstein, *Fritz Kuhn and the Rise and Fall of the German-American Bund* (New York: St. Martin's Press, 2013), 37–49.

43. Dorothy Thompson, "Miss Thompson Issues Statement on Bund Rally," *New York Herald Tribune*, February 21, 1939, quoted in "The German American Bund Meeting," *Contemporary Jewish Record*, March 1, 1939, 55–56.

44. German American Bund, *Free America!: The German-American Bund at Madison Square Garden, February 20, 1939* (New York: A.V. Pub. Corp., 1939), 15.

45. Arnie Bernstein, *Swastika Nation: Fritz Kuhn and the Rise and Fall of the German-American Bund* (New York: St. Martin's Press, 2013), 2.

46. *Free America!*, 6–7.

47. *Free America!*, 18. Emphasis in the original.

48. *Free America!*, 20.

49. "20,000 Jam Madison Square Garden as Throng Battles Police Outside," *Washington Post*, February 21, 1939; Bernstein, *Swastika Nation*, 179–180, 186–187; "Bund Foes Protest Policing of Rally," *New York Times*, February 22, 1939.

50. "20,000 Jam Madison Square Garden"; *A Night at the Garden*, directed by Marshall Curry (Field of Vision, 2017); "20,000 Hear Browder on 'Daily,' C.I. Anniversaries," *Daily Worker*, February 28, 1939.

51. David Margolick, *Beyond Glory: Joe Louis vs. Max Schmeling and a World on the Brink* (New York: Knopf, 2005), 283–309.

52. "Joe Louis Odds-on Favorite to Stop Simon and Bias," *People's Voice*, March 28, 1942.

53. "Freedom Rally Star Studded," *People's Voice*, June 23, 1945; Martha Biondi, *To Stand and Fight: The Struggle for Civil Rights in Postwar New York City* (Cambridge, MA: Harvard University Press, 2003), 8–10; Farah Jasmine Griffin, *Harlem Nocturne: Women Artists, Progressive Politics During World War II* (New York: Basic Civitas, 2013); "Rally Speeches," *People's Voice*, June 30, 1945.

CHAPTER TWO: AMERICA'S SUGAR BOWL

1. "Greatest Crowd of Visitors Seen for Bowl Game," *Times-Picayune* (New Orleans), December 15, 1940.

2. Charles H. Martin, *Benching Jim Crow: The Rise and Fall of the Color Line in College Sports, 1890–1980* (Urbana: University of Illinois Press, 2010).

3. Martin, *Benching Jim Crow*, 42–45; Jerry Nason, "Leahy Lauds Montgomery," *Boston Globe*, January 22, 1941; "Lou Montgomery, Former Boston U Star, Still Bitter over 1940 Bowl Ban," *The Afro-American*, January 28, 1956.

4. Chad Seifried and Donna Pastore, "Analyzing the First Permanent Professional Baseball and Football Structures in the United States: How Expansion and Renovation Changed Them into Jewel Boxes," *Sport History Review* 40 (2009): 170–171.

5. On black college football in the South, see Michael Hurd, *Black College Football, 1892–1992: One Hundred Years of History, Education, and Pride* (Virginia Beach, VA: Donning Co., 1993); Derrick White, *Blood, Sweat, and Tears:*

Jake Gaither, Florida A&M, and the History of Black College Football (Chapel Hill: University of North Carolina Press, 2019).

6. Michael Oriard, *King Football: Sport and Spectacle in the Golden Age of Radio and Newsreels, Movies and Magazines, the Weekly and the Daily Press* (Chapel Hill: University of North Carolina Press, 2001).

7. Charles H. Martin, "Integrating New Year's Day: The Racial Politics of College Bowl Games in the American South," *Journal of Sport History* 24, no. 3 (1997): 358–377.

8. Richard Campanella, *Time and Place in New Orleans: Past Geographies in the Present Day* (New Orleans, LA: Pelican Publishing, 2002), 134.

9. Charles Gayarré, "A Louisiana Sugar Plantation of the Old Régime," *Harper's New Monthly Magazine* 74 (December 1, 1886): 606–621.

10. Gayarré, "A Louisiana Sugar Plantation of the Old Régime," 606–621. For one of countless examples, see "Roamin' on the River," *Times-Picayune* (New Orleans), December 29, 1974.

11. Cécile Vidal, *Caribbean New Orleans: Empire, Race, and the Making of a Slave Society* (Chapel Hill: University of North Carolina Press, 2019).

12. Jackson Faulkner, "Tulane Cannot Ignore Its Historical Roots to Slavery," *Tulane Hullabaloo*, May 18, 2019, https://tulanehullabaloo.com/50267 /views/tulane-cannot-ignore-its-historical-roots-to-slavery/.

13. Philip D. Curtin, *The Rise and Fall of the Plantation Complex* (Cambridge: Cambridge University Press, 1990); Khalil Muhammad, "The Barbaric History of Sugar in America," *New York Times*, August 14, 2019.

14. Marty Mulé, *Sugar Bowl: The First Fifty Years* (Birmingham, AL: Oxmoor House, 1983), 7.

15. Joe Frederickson, *The Tournament of Roses: The First 100 Years* (Los Angeles: Knapp Press, 1989).

16. "New Year Tilt Called 'Sugar Bowl Classic,'" *Times-Picayune* (New Orleans), July 25, 1934. Miami civic boosters would name their game the Orange Bowl, and the creators of the postseason game in Dallas called their game the Cotton Bowl.

17. Chad Seifried, Kasey Britt, Samantha Gonzales, and Alexa Webb, "The Development of Tulane Stadium: From Rise to Raze," in *New Orleans Sports: Playing Hard in the Big Easy*, ed. Thomas Aiello (Fayetteville: University of Arkansas Press, 2019), 96.

18. See files on DeBlanc, Digby, and Poche in Series I, Subseries 7, Sugar Bowl Collection, the Historic New Orleans Collection, New Orleans, LA.

19. Anthony J. Stanonis, *Creating the Big Easy: New Orleans and the Emergence of Modern Tourism, 1918–1945* (Athens: University of Georgia Press, 2006), 38–39.

20. Stephen H. Norwood, "The Sugar Bowl: Manhood, Race and Southern Womanhood, 1935–1965," in Aiello, *New Orleans Sports*, 155; "Tulane, Temple Bands Practice for Sugar Bowl," *Times-Picayune* (New Orleans), January 2, 1935; Charles L. Dufour, "Tulane 20, Temple 14: Greenies Rally to Win," in Digby, *The Sugar Bowl*, 17–18.

21. "Quaint and Romantic Old New Orleans," *The 1st Annual Sugar Bowl Classic*, January 1, 1935 (program), 41, Series IV, Subseries 1, Sub-sub-series 2, Folder 1: Individual Football Programs, Sugar Bowl Collection (SBC hereafter), the Historic New Orleans Collection (THNOC hereafter).

22. American Sugar Cane League, "Louisiana's Second Crop," *Official Program of the Fifth Annual Sugar Bowl Classic*, January 2, 1939, 29, in Series IV, Subseries 1, Sub-sub-series 2, Folder 5; "The All-American Sugar Bowl Line," *22nd Annual Sugar Bowl Classic*, January 2, 1956 (program), 18, in Series IV, Subseries 1, Sub-sub-series 2, Folder 17: Individual Football Programs, SBC, THNOC.

23. Patricia Minnigerode, "Sugar Bowl Prospers," *New York Times*, November 14, 1937.

24. Ronald A. Smith, "Far More Than Commercialism: Stadium Building from Harvard's Innovations to Stanford's 'Dirt Bowl,'" *International Journal of the History of Sport* 25 (2008): 1453–1474.

25. "Stadium Sites," Living New Deal, https://livingnewdeal.org/new-deal-categories/parks-and-recreation/stadiums/; Charlton W. Tebeau, *The University of Miami: A Golden Anniversary, 1926–1976* (Coral Gables, FL: University of Miami Press, 1976), 176–177.

26. Clarence L. Mohr and Joseph E. Gordon, *Tulane: The Emergence of a Modern University, 1945–1980* (Baton Rouge: Louisiana State University Press, 2001), 163–180.

27. "Minutes of Specially Called Meeting of the Executive Board of the New Orleans Mid-Winter Sports Association Held May 18, 1937," box 1, minute book 2, February 1935–January 1939, SBC, THNOC.

28. Christopher Thomas Gaffney, *Temples of the Earthbound Gods: Stadiums in the Cultural Landscapes of Rio de Janeiro and Buenos Aires* (Austin: University of Texas Press, 2008), 20.

29. Martin, *Benching Jim Crow*, 81.

30. Blain Roberts, *Pageants, Parlors, and Pretty Women: Race and Beauty in the Twentieth Century South* (Chapel Hill: University of North Carolina Press, 2014), 193.

31. "Minutes of Specially Called Meeting of the Executive Board of the New Orleans Mid-Winter Sports Association Held October 25, 1951," box 3, minute book 6, December 1949–April 1954, SBC, THNOC.

32. SugarBowlClassic, "1955 Sugar Bowl—Navy vs. Ole' Miss," YouTube video, 35:35, April 2, 2020, www.youtube.com/watch?v=4tIsAOLgJDs&t=1162s; "From A to Z with Sam Lacy," *The Afro-American*, January 15, 1955.

33. Clarence A. Laws to Rufus Harris, November 29, 1941, box 12, New Orleans Midwinter Sports Assoc. History, Sugar Bowl, 1940–1959 folder, Tulane University Archives.

34. "Bowl Segregation Is Hit," *New York Times*, December 22, 1954.

35. "Sugar Bowl Race Ban Sidestepped by Navy," *The Afro-American*, January 1, 1955; Norwood, "The Sugar Bowl," 166.

36. Norwood, "The Sugar Bowl," 169.

37. Martin, "Integrating New Year's Day," 358–359.

38. Martin, *Benching Jim Crow*, 59–67.

39. "Big Classics Draw 400,000," *Times-Picayune* (New Orleans), January 1, 1955; Martin, *Benching Jim Crow*, 80–81. Grier was entertained by black New Orleanians from Dillard University during his stay (Oral history interview with Bobby Grier, June 14, 2014, MSS 630.10.1, THNOC).

40. Charles A. Raynard, "Legislation Affecting Segregation," *Louisiana Law Review* 17, no. 1 (December 1956): 121; "Mixed Race Sports Ban Signed," *Times-Picayune* (New Orleans), July 17, 1956.

41. "Athletic Ban to Be Studied," *Times-Picayune* (New Orleans), June 17, 1956; "Mixed Race Sports Ban Signed," *Times-Picayune* (New Orleans), July 17, 1956; "Minutes of Regular Executive Committee Meeting of the New Orleans Mid-Winter Sports Association, Held on Thursday, July 12, 1956," box 3, minute book 7, May 1954–June 1959, SBC, THNOC.

42. "Don't Let Hysteria Replace Reason," *Times-Picayune* (New Orleans), July 15, 1956.

43. Examples from the voluminous scholarship on the civil rights movement are Manning Marable, *Race, Reform, and Rebellion: The Second Reconstruction and Beyond in Black America, 1945–2006*, 3rd ed. (Jackson: University Press of Mississippi, 2006); Taylor Branch, *Parting the Waters: America During the King Years, 1954–1963* (New York: Simon & Schuster, 1989); Barbara Ransby, *Ella Baker and the Black Freedom Movement: A Radical Democratic Vision* (Chapel Hill: University of North Carolina Press, 2003).

44. Martin, *Benching Jim Crow*; Frank Andre Guridy, *The Sports Revolution: How Texas Changed the Culture of American Athletics* (Austin: University of Texas Press, 2021); Dave Dixon, *The Saints, the Superdome, and the Scandal* (New Orleans, LA: Pelican Publishing, 2008).

45. Adam Fairclough, *Race and Democracy: The Civil Rights Struggle in Louisiana, 1915–1972*, 2nd ed. (Athens: University of Georgia Press, 2008), 335–336; "Decision Desegregates Municipal Auditorium," *Times-Picayune* (New Orleans), July 2, 1963.

46. "Minutes of Regular Executive Committee Meeting of the New Orleans Mid-Winter Sports Association Held on Thursday, March 2, 1961," box 3, minute book 8, June 1959–February 1963, SBC, THNOC.

47. "Minutes of Regular Executive Committee Meeting of the New Orleans Mid-Winter Sports Association Held on Thursday, September 12, 1963," box 3, minute book 9, February 1963–April 1968, SBC, THNOC.

48. Norwood, "The Sugar Bowl: Manhood, Race and Southern Womanhood"; "LSU Defense Defeats Syracuse on Late Field Goal, 13–10," *Washington Post Times Herald*, January 2, 1965.

49. Guerry Smith, "Trailblazers: Four Black Players Who Integrated Tulane's Football Team in 1971 to Be Honored Saturday," *Times-Picayune* (New Orleans), October 29, 2021, www.nola.com/sports/tulane/article_33b4edc2 -38f0-11ec-86fe-075f1a52bca4.html; Mohr and Gordon, *Tulane*, 191–242; Martin, *Benching Jim Crow*, 219–220.

50. College Football Historian, "1970 Sugar Bowl Ole Miss vs Arkansas ABC (1969 Season) Manning," YouTube video, 3:12:40, March 13, 2023, www.youtube.com/watch?v=Pe7xieyxDXY&t=187s.

51. Guridy, *The Sports Revolution*, 95, 348–349.

52. Virgil Moody, "1972 Sugar Bowl Oklahoma vs Auburn 1972 1971 Season," YouTube video, 2:25:36, www.youtube.com/watch?v=8wWT0YusByc&t=2878s; Don Yaeger, *Turning of the Tide: How One Game Changed the South* (New York: Center Street, 2006).

53. "Grambling Dumps Southern Before 76,753," *Los Angeles Sentinel*, November 28, 1974.

54. "Farewell Celebration: Tulane Sugar Bowl Stadium, November 18, 1979," Stadium Vertical File, Tulane University Archives.

CHAPTER THREE: NATION TIME AT THE COLISEUM

1. Unless otherwise noted, all concert information in text is drawn from Mel Stuart's *Wattstax* film, originally released in 1973. All endnotes referencing the concert cite the re-released 2004 version on DVD: *Wattstax*, directed by Mel Stuart (Burbank, CA: Warner Home Video, 2004).

2. Danny Widener, *Black Arts West: Culture and Struggle in Postwar Los Angeles* (Berkeley: University of California Press, 2010); Josh Sides, *LA City Limits: African American Los Angeles from the Great Depression to the Present* (Berkeley: University of California Press, 2006).

3. Neil Sullivan, *The Dodgers Move West* (New York: Oxford University Press, 1987); Frank Andre Guridy, *The Sports Revolution: How Texas Changed the Culture of American Athletics* (Austin: University of Texas Press, 2021).

4. Sullivan, *The Dodgers Move West*; Neil Sullivan, *The Diamond in the Bronx: Yankee Stadium and the Politics of New York* (New York: Oxford University Press, 2001).

5. St. Claire Drake and Horace Cayton, *Black Metropolis: A Study of Negro Life in a Northern City* (Chicago: University of Chicago Press, 2015), 102.

6. Derrick White, *Blood, Sweat, and Tears: Jake Gaither, Florida A&M, and the History of Black College Football* (Chapel Hill: University of North Carolina Press, 2019), 8.

7. Michael Hurd, *Thursday Night Lights: The Story of Black High School Football in Texas* (Austin: University of Texas Press, 2017).

8. Rob Ruck, *Sandlot Seasons: Sport in Black Pittsburgh* (Urbana: University of Illinois Press, 1993), 156–158.

9. Larry Lester, *Black Baseball's National Showcase: The East-West All-Star Game, 1933–1953* (Lincoln: University of Nebraska Press, 2002).

10. Neil Lanctot, *Negro League Baseball: The Rise and Ruin of a Black Institution* (Philadelphia: University of Pennsylvania Press, 2008).

11. John W. Harshaw Sr., *Cincinnati's West End* (Create Space Independent Publishing Platform, 2011), 83.

12. Dave Parker and Dave Jordan, *Cobra: A Life of Baseball and Brotherhood* (Lincoln: University of Nebraska Press, 2021), 12.

13. Kareem Abdul-Jabbar and Peter Knobler, *Giant Steps: The Autobiography of Kareem Abdul-Jabbar* (New York: Bantam Books, 1983), 290.

14. On black fans and workers in Atlanta, see Clayton Trutor, *Loserville: How Professional Sports Remade Atlanta—and How Atlanta Remade Professional Sports* (Lincoln: University of Nebraska Press, 2022).

15. On stadiums and suburbanization, see Benjamin D. Lisle, *Modern Coliseum: Stadiums and American Culture* (Philadelphia: University of Pennsylvania Press, 2017).

16. Burr Snider, "MC Hammer Nails Down Rap," *San Francisco Chronicle*, September 24, 1989.

17. Dave Anderson, "Dancing Harry and Earl the Pearl," *New York Times*, January 6, 1973; Earl Monroe with Quincy Troupe, *Earl the Pearl: My Story* (Emmaus, PA: Rodale Books, 2013).

18. "Dr. King's Freedom Rally Draws Crowd of 25,000," *Los Angeles Times*, June 19, 1961.

19. "125,000 Walk Quietly in Record Rights Plea," *Detroit Free Press*, June 24, 1963; Liam T. A. Ford, *Solider Field: A Stadium and Its City* (Chicago: University of Chicago Press, 2009), 202–213; "Huge Mass Protest," *San Francisco Examiner*, April 16, 1967.

20. White, *Blood, Sweat, and Tears.*

21. E. G. Robinson to Rix Yard, March 9, 1965, box 31, Athletics: Dr. Rix Yard, Director, 1963–65, Herbert Longenecker Papers, Tulane University

Library. The school finally relented in 1974, when Grambling played Southern in the first Bayou Classic.

22. Michael Hurd, *Collie "J": Grambling's Man with the Golden Pen* (Haworth, NJ: St. Johann Press, 2007).

23. William N. Wallace, "60,811 See Morgan State Win Here, 9–7," *New York Times*, September 29, 1968.

24. *1st and Goal in the Bronx: Grambling vs. Morgan State 1968*, documentary, CBS Sports Network, aired September 28, 2011; William C. Rhoden, *Forty Million Dollar Slaves: The Rise, Fall, and Redemption of the Black Athlete* (New York: Three Rivers Press, 2006), 20.

25. Sides, *LA City Limits*, 36–56.

26. Brad Pye Jr., "It's Official: Grambling Battles Alcorn Here," *Los Angeles Sentinel*, August 21, 1969.

27. Jack Hawn, "Grambling Favored by 7 in Freedom Classic," *Los Angeles Times*, September 8, 1973.

28. Bill Graham, *Bill Graham Presents: My Life Inside Rock and Out* (Cambridge, MA: DaCapo Press, 2004).

29. The concert was the subject of the acclaimed documentary *Summer of Soul*, directed by Ahmir "Questlove" Thompson (United States: Onyx Collection, 2021).

30. Unlike Wattstax, the Fania concert was brought to a premature end when the crowd stormed the field and destroyed the sound equipment.

31. Gerald Horne, *Fire This Time: The Watts Uprising and the 1960s* (Charlottesville: University Press of Virginia, 1995).

32. On black cultural movements and black politics in Los Angeles in this period, see Horne, *Fire This Time*; Sides, *LA City Limits*; Scot Brown, *Fighting for US: Maulana Karenga, the US Organization, and Black Cultural Nationalism* (New York: New York University Press, 2003); Daniel Widener, *Black Arts West: Culture and Struggle in Postwar Los Angeles* (Berkeley: University of California Press, 2010), 90–218; Joshua Bloom and Waldo E. Martin Jr., *Black Against Empire: The History and Politics of the Black Panther Party* (Berkeley: University of California Press, 2014), 139–148, 216–225.

33. Bruce M. Tyler, "The Rise and Decline of the Watts Summer Festival," *American Studies* 31 (1990): 61–81.

34. Rob Bowman, *Soulsville USA: The Story of Stax Records* (New York: Schirmer Trade Books, 1997), 202.

35. Bowman, *Soulsville USA*, 268; Judy Speigelman, "And They Did Come in Their Multitudes," *Soul*, October 9, 1972, 1.

36. Robert Gordon, *Respect Yourself: Stax Records and the Soul Explosion* (New York: Bloomsbury Press, 2013), 297–298. On Willie Davis and Schlitz, see Davis, *Closing the Gap: Lombardi, the Packer Dynasty and the Pursuit of Excellence* (Chicago: Triumph Books, 2012), 293–306.

37. Judy Spiegelman, "Black Moses Leads 100,000 to Wattstax," *Soul*, October 9, 1972. One of the cameramen who worked on the film was Larry Clark, the pathbreaking filmmaker associated with the LA rebellion movement during the 1970s. Clark collaborated with Ted Lange, who acted in *Wattstax*, to make the fascinating underground film *Passing Through*. See Widener, *Black Arts West*, 134–136.

38. The Stax–Wolper–Summer Festival relationship parallels the dynamics behind the making of the Watts Writing Workshop. See Widener, *Black Arts West*, 91.

39. "Minutes of the Regular Meeting of the Los Angeles Memorial Coliseum Commission," July 5, 1972, 69, Los Angeles Memorial Coliseum Commission Meetings Collection, 1933–2022, Digital Library Collections, LA84 Foundation, https://digital.la84.org/digital/collection/p17103coll13/id/621/rec/946.

40. Stephen Gee, *Iconic Vision: John Parkinson, Architect of Los Angeles* (Los Angeles: Angel City Press, 2013), 138.

41. Woody Strode, *Goal Dust: The Warm and Candid Memoirs of a Pioneer Black Athlete and Actor* (Lanham, MD: Madison Books, 1990), 100.

42. Kenneth Hahn, "Keeping the Coliseum Public," *Los Angeles Times*, September 27, 1987.

43. "Statement by Supervisor Kenneth Hahn, Vice President of the Coliseum Commission," February 25, 1966, folder 6.2.1, Kenneth Hahn Collection, Huntington Library, Art Collections, and Botanical Gardens, San Marino, CA.

44. On the "invisible walls of steel," see Lonnie G. Bunch, "The Greatest State for the Negro: Jefferson L. Edmonds, Black Propagandist of the California Dream," in *Seeking El Dorado: African Americans in California*, eds. Lawrence B. de Graaf, Kevin Mulroy, and Quintard Taylor (Los Angeles: Autry Museum of Western Heritage; Seattle: University of Washington Press, 2000), 143.

45. On Mahalia Jackson at the Coliseum, see "40,000 Hear Mahalia Jackson at Festival," *Los Angeles Sentinel*, July 31, 1958. On Martin Luther King's speech at the Sports Arena, see "Dr. King's Freedom Rally Draws 25,000," *Los Angeles Times*, June 19, 1961. On the King memorial at the Coliseum, see "Negro and White Congregation: 20,000 Pay Tribute to Dr. King at Coliseum," *Los Angeles Times*, April 6, 1968.

46. "Minutes of the Regular Meeting of the Los Angeles Memorial Coliseum Commission," April 1, 1970, 27, Los Angeles Memorial Coliseum Commission Meetings Collection, 1933–2022, Digital Library Collections, LA84 Foundation, https://digital.la84.org/digital/collection/p17103coll13/id/955/rec/889.

47. "Coliseum's Black Progress," *Los Angeles Sentinel*, May 20, 1971.

48. "Watts Summer Festival," Minutes of the Regular Meeting of the Los Angeles Memorial Coliseum Commission, August 2, 1972, 84–86, Los Angeles Memorial Coliseum Commission Meetings Collection, 1933–2022, Digital

Library Collections, LA84 Foundation, https://digital.la84.org/digital/collection/p17103coll13/id/623/rec/951.

49. DLW 130-023, "Feature Film," David L. Wolper Collection, David L. Wolper Center for the Study of the Documentary, University of Southern California, Los Angeles (subsequently abbreviated as DLWC).

50. Komozi Woodard, *A Nation Within a Nation: Amiri Baraka (Leroi Jones) and Black Power Politics* (Chapel Hill: University of North Carolina Press, 1999), 209.

51. On Hayes's chain suit, see Saul, "What You See Is What You Get," and Emily Lordi, "How Isaac Hayes Changed Soul Music," *New Yorker*, October 1, 2019, www.newyorker.com/culture/cultural-comment/how-isaac-hayes-changed-soul-music.

52. Thanks to performance historian Juliana DeVaan for making me aware of this fact.

53. See "Show Schedule," box 131, folder 1, DLWC.

54. Spiegelman, "Black Moses Leads 100,000 to Wattstax."

55. "Wattstax '72 Praise in Senate," *Los Angeles Sentinel*, November 23, 1972.

56. "Get Yourselves Together," *Soul*, October 23, 1972, 17; "Wattstax Concert at Coliseum," *Los Angeles Times*, August 22, 1972.

57. Philip Elwood, "The Man Behind All That Jazz," *San Francisco Examiner*, November 5, 1982.

58. For other examples of placemaking in Los Angeles, see Natalia Molina's *A Place at the Nayarit: How a Mexican Restaurant Nourished a Community* (Oakland: University of California Press, 2022). On "spatial entitlement," see Gaye Theresa Johnson, *Spaces of Conflict, Sounds of Solidarity: Music, Race, and Spatial Entitlement in Los Angeles* (Berkeley: University of California Press, 2013); Widener, *Black Arts West*; Priscilla Leiva, "Just Win Baby! The Raider Nation and Second Chances for Black and Brown LA," in *Black and Brown in Los Angeles: Beyond Conflict and Coalition*, eds. Josh Kun and Laura Pulido (Berkeley: University of California Press, 2014), 346–372; Scott Saul, "What You See Is What You Get: *Wattstax*, Richard Pryor and the Secret History of the Black Aesthetic," Post 45, August 12, 2014, https://post45.org/2014/08/what-you-see-is-what-you-get-wattstax-richard-pryor-and-the-secret-history-of-the-black-aesthetic/#identifier_14_5149.

59. Bowman, *Soulsville USA*, 317–371; Tyler, "The Rise and Decline," 71–79; "Watts Festival Concert Ends on Bad Note," *Los Angeles Times*, August 23, 1973; "Disappointment Brings 1974 Festival to Close," *Los Angeles Times*, August 22, 1974.

60. Local activists in Los Angeles have challenged this oft-touted claim. See Jules Boykoff, *NOlympians: Inside the Fight Against Capitalist Mega-Sports in*

Los Angeles, Tokyo and Beyond (Nova Scotia: Fernwood Publishing, 2020); Max Felker-Kantor, *Policing Los Angeles: Race, Resistance, and the Rise of the LAPD* (Chapel Hill: University of North Carolina Press, 2018).

CHAPTER FOUR: SETTLER STADIUM

1. Jack Walsh, "Redskins Keep It Up, Whip Cards," *Washington Post Times Herald*, October 1, 1962.

2. Philip J. Deloria, *Playing Indian* (New Haven, CT: Yale University Press, 1998).

3. Chris Myers Asch and George Derek Musgrove, *Chocolate City: A History of Race and Democracy in the Nation's Capital* (Chapel Hill: University of North Carolina Press, 2017).

4. Kevin Bruyneel, *Settler Memory: The Disavowal of Indigeneity and the Politics of Race in the United States* (Chapel Hill: University of North Carolina Press, 2021), xiii.

5. Asch and Musgrove, *Chocolate City*, 5–46.

6. Brad Snyder, *Beyond the Shadow of the Senators: The Untold Story of the Homestead Grays and the Integration of Baseball* (New York: McGraw-Hill, 2003), 4.

7. "Baseball Notes," *Washington Post*, June 27, 1904.

8. Snyder, *Beyond the Shadow of the Senators*, xi–xiii.

9. J. Gordon Hylton, "Before the Redskins Were the Redskins: The Use of Native American Team Names in the Formative Era of American Sports, 1857–1933," *North Dakota Law Review* 86, no. 89 (2010): 879–930; Jennifer Giuliano, *Indian Spectacle: College Mascots and the Anxiety of Modern America* (New Brunswick, NJ: Rutgers University Press, 2015).

10. Joseph B. Oxendine, *American Indian Sports Heritage*, 2nd ed. (Lincoln: University of Nebraska Press, 2016); Hylton, "Before the Redskins," 889.

11. Linda Waggoner, "On Trial: The Washington R*dskins Wily Mascot Coach William 'Lone Star' Dietz," *Montana: The Magazine of Western History*, Spring 2013, 24–47; Thomas G. Smith, *Showdown: JFK and the Integration of the Washington Redskins* (Boston: Beacon Press, 2011), 1–17; Andrew O'Toole, *Fight for Old DC: George Preston Marshall, the Integration of the Washington Redskins, and the Rise of a New NFL* (Lincoln: University of Nebraska Press, 2016), 22–23.

12. Robert H. Boyle, "All Alone by the Telephone," *Sports Illustrated* 15, no. 15 (October 16, 1961): 38.

13. Corinne Griffith, *My Life with the Redskins* (New York: A. S. Barnes & Company, 1947), 92.

14. Griffith, *My Life with the Redskins*, 39.

15. Smith, *Showdown*, x.

16.   "Minutes of the Semi-Annual General Membership Meeting of the New Orleans Mid-Winter Sports Association Held on Thursday, August 13, 1942," box 2, minute book 4, Sugar Bowl Collection, Historic New Orleans Collection, New Orleans.

17.   Shirley Povich, "This Morning," *Washington Post*, November 29, 1937.

18.   Mark Dyreson, "If We Build It, Will They Come? The Plans for a National Stadium and American Olympic Desires," *International Journal of the History of Sport* 25, no. 11 (September 2008): 1475–1492; District of Columbia Armory Board, *District of Columbia Stadium: History, Financing, Construction* (Washington, DC: District of Columbia Armory Board, 1961), 9–10.

19.   Neil J. Sullivan, *The Dodgers Move West* (New York: Oxford University Press, 1987); Benjamin Lisle, *Modern Coliseum: Stadiums and American Culture* (Philadelphia: University of Pennsylvania Press, 2017).

20.   Sullivan, *The Dodgers Move West*, 42.

21.   "Eisenhower Signs Bill to Authorize Stadium," *Washington Post Times Herald*, September 8, 1957.

22.   O'Toole, *Fight for old DC*, 102–110.

23.   "100 Picket Kezar in Protest," *San Francisco Examiner*, September 18, 1961; "Pickets Keep Vigil While 'Skins Lose," *Washington Post Times Herald*, October 2, 1961.

24.   Smith, *Showdown*; O'Toole, *Fight for Old DC*, 153–167.

25.   Edwin Shrake, "To Be Seen Seeing the Redskins," *Sports Illustrated* 23, no. 14 (October 4, 1965): 61; Bob Considine, "Days of Griffith, Old Park Recalled," *Washington Post Times Herald*, April 10, 1962.

26.   District of Columbia Armory Board, *District of Columbia Stadium*.

27.   Benjamin D. Lisle, *Modern Coliseum: Stadiums and American Culture* (Philadelphia: University of Pennsylvania Press, 2017).

28.   District of Columbia Armory Board, *District of Columbia Stadium*, 2.

29.   "Where Else Can You March at 28?" *Washington Post*, September 29, 1969; Sally Quinn, "Watching 40 Pairs of Legs Kick for the Joy of the Game," *Washington Post*, November 23, 1969; Laura A. Kiernan, "Redskinettes Enjoy Accolades at RFK," *Washington Post*, November 7, 1972.

30.   Shrake, "To Be Seen Seeing the Redskins," 61.

31.   Frank Andre Guridy, *The Sports Revolution: How Texas Changed the Culture of American Athletics* (Austin: University of Texas Press, 2021), 171–182.

32.   Shrake, "To Be Seen Seeing the Redskins," 52.

33.   Daniel Rosensweig, *Retro Ball Parks: Instant History, Baseball, and the New American City* (Knoxville: University of Tennessee Press, 2005), 84–85.

34.   Thom Loverro, *Hail Victory: An Oral History of the Washington Redskins* (Hoboken, NJ: Wiley, 2006).

35.   Richard King, *Redskins: Insult and Brand* (Lincoln: University of Nebraska Press, 2016), 95.

36. Vine Deloria Jr., *Behind the Trail of Broken Treaties: An Indian Declaration of Independence* (New York: Delacorte Press, 1974).

37. "'Redskins' Target of Movement," *Washington Evening Star*, January 19, 1972.

38. Shelby Coffee III, "Indians Open War on Redskins," *Washington Post*, March 30, 1972.

39. "Redskins Keep Name, Will Change Lyrics," *Washington Post Times Herald*, July 18, 1972.

40. "Braves Mascot Defends His Role," *Washington Star and Daily News*, August 13, 1972.

41. Courtland Milloy, "Redskins Rally Sounds Different to Indians," *Washington Post*, January 8, 2000.

42. Joelle Rostkowski, *Conversations with Remarkable Native Americans* (Albany: State University of New York Press, 2012), 14.

43. Ken Denlinger, "Protest of 'Redskins' Draws 2,000 at Stadium," *Washington Post*, January 27, 1992.

44. Lewnwdc, "Washington Redskins Crush Dallas Cowboys in Final Game at RFK Stadium, 12-22-96." YouTube video, 2:45:16, www.youtube.com /watch?v=eILOnI29490&t=708s.

CHAPTER FIVE: THE INNER SANCTUMS

1. Dave Zirin, "Sportswriting Trailblazer Melissa Ludtke," Edge of Sports podcast, *The Nation*, November 24, 2020, www.thenation.com/podcast/society /sportswriting-trailblazer-melissa-ludtke/.

2. Zirin, "Sportswriting Trailblazer Melissa Ludtke."

3. Jean Hastings Ardell, *Breaking into Baseball: Women and the National Pastime* (Carbondale: Southern Illinois University Press, 2005).

4. Susan Ware, *Game, Set, and Match: Billie Jean King and the Revolution in Women's Sports* (Chapel Hill: University of North Carolina Press, 2011).

5. *Let Them Wear Towels: Behind Closed Doors Were Closed Minds*, directed by Ricki Stern and Anne Sundberg (ESPN Home Entertainment, 2013).

6. Ronald A. Smith, "Far More Than Commercialism: Stadium Building from Harvard's Innovations to Stanford's 'Dirt Bowl,'" *International Journal of the History of Sport* 25, no. 18 (2008): 1453–1474.

7. Murry Sperber, *Shake Down the Thunder: The Creation of Notre Dame Football* (New York: Henry Holt, 1993), 271.

8. Steel Heilpern, "Journalists Inspect New Press Box Before Varsity Practice at Stadium," *Michigan Daily*, September 23, 1956.

9. Los Angeles Memorial Coliseum Commission, *The Story Behind the Largest and Finest Stadium in America* (Los Angeles: Los Angeles Memorial Coliseum Commission, 1952).

10. Mike Carey with Jamie Most, *High Above Courtside: The Lost Memoirs of Johnny Most* (Champaign, IL: Sports Publishing, 2003); interview with Lawrie Mifflin, August 18, 2022.

11. *New York Herald Tribune*, October 18, 1924.

12. Roger Kahn, *The Era, 1947–1957: When the Yankees, the Giants, and the Dodgers Ruled the World* (Lincoln: University of Nebraska Press, 2002), 71–72; Jerome Holtzman, *On Baseball: A History of Baseball Scribes* (Champaign, IL: Sports Publishing, 2005).

13. Ardell, *Breaking into Baseball*, 201.

14. Richard Lapchick, "Sports Media Remains Overwhelmingly White and Male, Study Finds," ESPN.com, September 22, 2021, www.espn.com/espn/story /_/id/32254145/sports-media-remains-overwhelmingly-white-male-study-finds.

15. David Halberstam, *October 1964* (New York: Fawcett Books, 1994), 172–181; Bryan Curtis, "No Chattering in the Press Box," Grantland, May 3, 2012, https://grantland.com/features/larry-merchant-leonard-shecter-chipmunks -sportswriting-clan/.

16. Jim Bouton with Leonard Shecter, *Ball Four: My Life and Times Throwing the Knuckleball in the Big Leagues* (New York: World Publishing, 1970); Roger Angell, "Sharing the Beat," *New Yorker*, April 9, 1979, 78.

17. James R. Hines, *Figure Skating in the Formative Years: Singles, Pairs, and the Expanding Role of Women* (Urbana: University of Illinois Press, 2015), 94–108.

18. Frank Andre Guridy, *The Sports Revolution: How Texas Changed the Culture of American Athletics* (Austin: University of Texas Press, 2021), 212, 258.

19. "Dieter Ruehle: A Part of Incredible Dodgers History," Think Blue LA, https://thinkbluela.com/2017/11/dieter-ruehle-newest-member-of-dodgers -remarkable-history/.

20. Nancy Livingstone, "The Little Blonde Behind Home Plate," *Chicago Tribune*, June 4, 1972; Tonya Malinowski, "How Nancy Faust and Her Organ Set the Tone for America's Pastime," ESPN.com, April 4, 2021, www.espn.com/mlb /story/_/id/29705268/how-nancy-faust-organ-set-tone-baseball.

21. Doris O'Donnell, "Cleveland Girl Had Fun Trying to Crash Press Box," *Boston Globe*, May 22, 1957.

22. Joanne Lannin, *Who Let Them In? Pathbreaking Women in Sports Journalism* (New York: Rowman & Littlefield, 2022), 1–8.

23. Natalie Weiner, "The Girl in the Huddle," SB Nation, February 4, 2020, www.sbnation.com/2020/2/4/21119144/elinor-kaine-penna-giants-jets-sports writer.

24. Elinor Kaine, "Quill Flashback: Women's Right to Write," *Quill Magazine*, March 3, 2009, www.quillmag.com/2009/03/03/quill-flashback-womens-right -to-write/.

25. Weiner, "The Girl in the Huddle."

26. Floyd Sullivan, ed., *Old Comiskey Park: Essays and Memories of the Historic Home of the Chicago White Sox, 1910–1991* (Jefferson, NC: MacFarland & Company, 2014), 7–8; "Girl Scribe Starts Ward Fan Club," *Chicago Tribune*, August 23, 1964; David Condon, "In the Wake of the News," *Chicago Tribune*, April 21, 1972; Cooper Rollow, "Lynda 'Out' Trying to Cover Sox," *Chicago Tribune*, April 20, 1972.

27. Ruth Rosen, *The World Split Open: How the Modern Women's Movement Changed America* (New York: Penguin, 2006).

28. Joan Steinau Lester, *Fire in My Soul: The Life of Eleanor Holmes Norton* (New York: Atria Books, 2003), 149–150; Lynn Povich, *The Good Girls Revolt: How the Women of Newsweek Sued Their Bosses and Changed the Workplace* (New York: PublicAffairs, 2012).

29. Phil Rosenthal, "Jeannie Morris, Chicago Author and Pioneering Sports Broadcaster, Dead at 85," *Chicago Tribune*, December 16, 2020.

30. Diane K. Shah, *A Farewell to Arms, Legs, & Jockstraps: A Sportswriter's Memoir* (Bloomington, IN: Red Lightning Books, 2020), 27–32.

31. Madeline Blais, "Hot Sox Give Cool Reception to Female Sportswriter," *Boston Globe*, September 16, 1972.

32. Charles Maher, "Women in the Press Box," *Los Angeles Times*, November 4, 1975.

33. Angell, "Sharing the Beat," 60.

34. Marcelle St-Cyr, "In the Locker Room with the Guys," Radio-Canada, November 26, 2018, https://ici.radio-canada.ca/sports/podium/55/podium-marcelle-st-cyr-journaliste-hockey-lnh-vestiaire-femmes; Robin Herman, "All Stars of Wales Win," *New York Times*, January 22, 1975; Robin Herman, "Reporter's Notebook: A Look at Equal Rights and Hockey," *New York Times*, February 9, 1975.

35. St-Cyr, "In the Locker Room"; *Let Them Wear Towels* documentary.

36. Herman, "Reporter's Notebook."

37. Angell, "Sharing the Beat," 83, emphasis in original.

38. Angell, "Sharing the Beat," 89.

39. Angell, "Sharing the Beat," 86.

40. Shah, *A Farewell to Arms, Legs, and Jockstraps*, 117–118.

41. Tom Friend, "The Natural," *ESPN the Magazine* 3, no. 14 (February 17, 2003), https://a.espncdn.com/magazine/vol3no14stevenson.html; Julius Erving with Taro Greenfeld, *Dr. J: The Autobiography* (New York: HarperCollins, 2013), 336.

42. Samantha Stevenson, "Confessions of a Female Sportswriter: Hanging with the Jocks," *Oui* 7, no. 5 (August 1978): 78.

43. Stevenson, "Confessions of a Female Sportswriter," 80.

44. Stevenson, "Confessions of a Female Sportswriter," 80.

45. Charles Bricker, "'Power Mom' Behind Teen's Quick Rise," *Sun-Sentinel* (Fort Lauderdale, FL), June 30, 1999.

46. "Oral History Interview with Melissa Ludtke, 1994," Washington Press Club Oral History Collection, Washington Press Club Foundation.

47. Zirin, "Sportswriting Trailblazer Melissa Ludtke."

48. Tomiko Brown-Nagin, *Civil Rights Queen: Constance Baker Motley and the Struggle for Equality* (New York: Pantheon Books, 2022).

49. Red Smith, "Another View on Equality," *New York Times*, January 9, 1978.

50. Melisa Ludtke Lincoln, "Locker Rooms: Equality with Integrity," *New York Times*, April 15, 1979.

51. Barbara Howard, "40 Years Ago, Female Reporters Won Right to Locker Room Access," *All Things Considered*, WGBH.org, September 25, 2018, updated August 1, 2023, www.wgbh.org/news/national/2018-09-25/40-years-ago-female -reporters-won-the-right-to-locker-room-access.

52. *Ludtke v. Kuhn*, 461 F Supp. 86 (SDNY 1978).

53. Lannin, *Who Let Them In?*, 35–36.

54. Susan Fornoff, *Lady in the Locker Room: Adventures of a Trailblazing Sports Journalist*, 2nd ed. (Oakland, CA: GottaGoGolf, 2014).

55. Lannin, *Who Let Them In?*, 28–31; Mike Freeman, "*Herald* Reporter Harassed; Club Warns Players," *Boston Globe*, September 21, 1990.

CHAPTER SIX: OUT AT THE BALLPARK

1. Allen White, "Gay Games Wind Up," *Bay Area Reporter* 12, no. 36 (September 9, 1982): 1, 2.

2. Wayne Friday, "Politics and Poker," *Bay Area Reporter* 12, no. 35 (September 2, 1982): 14.

3. "Bee Gees Concert History," Concert Archives, www.concertarchives .org/bands/bee-gees--2; Alice Echols, *Hot Stuff: Disco and the Remaking of American Culture* (New York: W. W. Norton, 2010).

4. Gary Deeb, "Deejay Goes on Record: Disco Is a Disease," *Chicago Tribune*, July 5, 1979.

5. Deeb, "Deejay Goes on Record."

6. Gillian Frank, "Discophobia: Antigay Prejudice and the 1979 Backlash Against Disco," *Journal of the History of Sexuality* 16 (May 2007): 293–297.

7. SoxDrawer, "Disco Demolition Night 30 Years Later," YouTube video, 7:58, July 16, 2009, www.youtube.com/watch?v=97lgR41qZC8&t=160s.

8. Tim Lawrence, *Love Saves the Day: A History of American Dance Music* (Durham, NC: Duke University Press, 2003); Frank, "Discophobia," 297–298.

9. Paul Dickson, *Bill Veeck: Baseball's Greatest Maverick* (New York: Walker & Company, 2012).

10. Virtually the entire telecast of the game by Chicago television station WSNS, along with clips of local news coverage, can be seen on YouTube. See Classic MLB1, "1979-07-12 Tigers at White Sox (Disco Demolition)," YouTube Video, 3:27:16, April 26, 2017, www.youtube.com/watch?v=LZaXq338HN4&t=6698s; Museum of Classic Chicago Television, "Super Disco Demolition: The 40th Anniversary Compilation," YouTube video, 1:39:19, July 12, 2019, www.youtube .com/watch?v=kqDkBM9vxw8&t=334s.

11. Steve Dahl with Dave Hoeksbra and Paul Natkin, *Disco Demolition: The Night Disco Died* (Chicago: Curbside Splendor, 2016); Gimlet, "Disco Demolition Night," *Gimlet Undone* podcast, November 14, 2016, https://gimletmedia.com /shows/undone/39h27b.

12. Dahl, Hoeksbra, and Natkin, *Disco Demolition*; Micah Salkind, *Do You Remember House? Chicago's Queer of Color Undergrounds* (New York: Oxford University Press, 2019); Echols, *Hot Stuff*, 208–215.

13. Martin S. Jacobs, *Kezar Stadium: 49ers Fans Remember* (San Francisco: Martin S. Jacobs, 2020).

14. Susan Stryker and Jim Van Buskirk, *Gay by the Bay: A History of Queer Culture in the San Francisco Bay Area* (San Francisco: Chronicle Books, 1996), 64–65; Winston Leyland, ed., *Out in the Castro: Desire, Promise, Activism* (San Francisco: Leyland Publications, 2002).

15. Andrew Maraniss, *Singled Out: The True Story of Glenn Burke* (New York: Philomel Books, 2021), 192–196; John D'Emilio, "Gay Politics, Gay Community: San Francisco's Experience," in *Making Trouble: Essays on Gay History, Politics, and the University*, ed. John D'Emilio (New York: Routledge, 1992), 74–95; Stryker and Van Buskirk, *Gay by the Bay*, 51–84; Leyland, *Out in the Castro*.

16. D'Emilio, "Gay Politics, Gay Community"; Lincoln A. Mitchell, *San Francisco Year Zero: Political Upheaval, Punk Rock, and a Third-Place Baseball Team* (New Brunswick, NJ: Rutgers University Press, 2019).

17. Tom Waddell, with Dick Schaap, *Gay Olympian: The Life and Death of Dr. Tom Waddell* (New York, 1996), 38; Mark Brown, *Gay Games I: The True Story, the Forgotten Man* (Conneaut Lake, PA: Page Publishing, 2020).

18. Waddell and Schaap, *Gay Olympian*, 28.

19. Waddell and Schaap, *Gay Olympian*, 125–129.

20. Waddell and Schaap, *Gay Olympian*, 151–152; Caroline Symons, *The Gay Games: A History* (London: Routledge, 2010), 55–56.

21. "Olympics Choose Kezar," *Bay Area Reporter* 11, no. 8 (April 1981): 35.

22. Jennifer Foote, "Dr. Tom Prescribes Gay Games as an Antidote to Stereotypes," *San Francisco Examiner*, August 26, 1982.

23. Susan K. Cahn, *Coming on Strong: Gender and Sexuality in Women's Sport*, 2nd ed. (Urbana: University of Illinois Press, 2015), 185–206; Tom Waddell, "Gay Athletic Games '82: Details and Information," *Bay Area Reporter* 12, no. 3 (January 21, 1982): 25.

24. Waddell and Schaap, *Gay Olympian*, 153–155; Symons, *The Gay Games*, 47.

25. Waddell and Schaap, *Gay Olympian*, 145–148.

26. Scott Treimel, "Gay Athletic Games Open to Cheers," *Bay Area Reporter* 12, no. 35 (September 2, 1982): 2.

27. Zane Blaney, "1982 Gay Games Opening Ceremony," Zane Blaney Collection of the GLBT Historical Library, Internet Archive, https://archive.org/details/glbths_2016-18_002_sc; Treimel, "Gay Athletic Games Open to Cheers."

28. Blaney, "1982 Gay Games Opening Ceremony," https://archive.org/details/glbths_2016-18_002_sc; Treimel, "Gay Athletic Games Open to Cheers"; Stephanie Salter, "Jubilation at Gay Games," *San Francisco Examiner*, August 29, 1982.

29. "Women at the Games: Six Behind the Scenes Volunteers," *Bay Area Reporter* 13, no. 34 (August 26, 1982): 42.

30. Symons, *The Gay Games*, 50; Judy Davidson, "The Early Gay Games: The Bay Area Years," in *San Francisco Bay Area Sports: Golden Gate Athletics, Recreation, and Community*, eds. Rita Liberti and Maureen M. Smith (Fayetteville: University of Arkansas Press, 2017), 237.

31. Zane Blaney, "1982 Gay Games Closing Ceremony," Zane Blaney Collection of the GLBT Historical Library, Internet Archive, https://archive.org/details/glbths_2016-18_014_sc; Allen White, "Gay Games Wind Up," *Bay Area Reporter* 12, no. 36 (September 9, 1982): 1, 2.

32. "A Message About AIDS for the Male Athletes and Visitors to Gay Games II," *Bay Area Reporter* 16, no. 32 (August 7, 1986): 13.

33. Stryker and Buskirk, *Gay by the Bay*, 85–116; Emily K. Hobson, *Lavender and Red: Liberation and Solidarity in the Gay and Lesbian Left* (Oakland: University of California Press, 2016), 155–186; Waddell and Schaap, *Gay Olympian*, 185–186; Rick Thoman, "Let's Celebrate! Tom Waddell on the Joy of Participation and Gay Games II," *Bay Area Reporter* 16, no. 32 (August 7, 1986): 67.

34. Roy M. Coe, *A Sense of Pride: The Story of Gay Games II* (San Francisco: Pride Publications, 1986), 9–11; Symons, *The Gay Games*, 57–58.

35. Coe, *A Sense of Pride*, 22.

36. "Get Your Tickets Now," *Bay Area Reporter* 16, no. 32 (August 7, 1986): 10.

37. Symons, *The Gay Games*, 71.

38. "Letters: Glitz, Glam, and Gym Bunnies," *Bay Area Reporter* 16, no. 33 (August 21, 1986): 8; "Eight Magic Days," *Bay Area Reporter* 16, no. 35 (August 28, 1986): 8.

39. "This Is About People Dying: The Tactics of Early ACT UP and Lesbian Avengers in New York City: An Interview with Maxine Wolfe by Laraine Sommella," in *Queers in Space*, eds. Gordon Brent Ingram, Anne-Marie Bouthillette, and Yolanda Retter (Seattle: Bay Press, 1997), 421; James Wentsy, "Storytellings: Maxine Wolfe (Shea Stadium)," Vimeo video, 7:03, January 20, 2017, https://vimeo.com/200388124.

40. "This Is About People Dying," 421–422.

41. ACT UP Oral History Project, "043: Maxine Wolfe," video, 4:03:44, February 19, 2004, https://actuporalhistory.org/numerical-interviews/043-maxine-wolfe; *United in Anger*, directed by Jim Hubbard (New York: United in Anger, 2012).

42. "This Is About People Dying," 423.

43. Sarah Schulman, *Let the Record Show: A Political History of ACT UP New York, 1987–1993* (New York: Farrar, Straus and Giroux, 2021), 5.

44. M. J. Murphy, "Putting Pressure on Religious Right," *Bay Area Reporter* 19, no. 30 (July 27, 1989): 41, 53.

CHAPTER SEVEN: CORPORATE TEMPLES OF EXCLUSION

1. "Sacramento Group Buys NBA's Kansas City Kings," *San Francisco Examiner*, June 8, 1983.

2. "$5 Million Ad Deal Puts Arco's Name on Kings Arena," *Sacramento Bee*, August 21, 1985.

3. Roger G. Noll and Andrew Zimbalist, eds., *Sports, Jobs, and Taxes: The Economic Impact of Sports Teams and Stadiums* (Washington, DC: Brookings Institution, 1997); Kevin J. Delaney and Rick Eckstein, *Public Dollars, Private Stadiums: The Battle over Building Sports Stadiums* (New Brunswick, NJ: Rutgers University Press, 2003)—these are just two examples of the vast literature that illustrate the unprofitability of stadium-led economic development.

4. Edward Achorn, *The Summer of Beer and Whiskey: How Brewers, Barkeeps, Rowdies, Immigrants and a Wild Pennant Fight Made America's Game* (New York: PublicAffairs, 2013).

5. Robert Weintraub, *The House That Ruth Built: A New Stadium, the First Yankees Championship, and the Redemption of 1923* (New York: Little, Brown, 2011).

6. Nathan M. Corzine, "American Game, American Mirror: Baseball, Beer, the Media and American Culture, 1933–1954" (master's thesis, University of Missouri, Columbia, 2004), 76.

7. "We're Backing the Braves," *Sporting News*, April 1, 1953; Chris Foran, "That Time Miller Brewing Picked Up the Tab for the Stadium's Scoreboard," *Milwaukee Journal Sentinel*, December 12, 2017, www.jsonline.com/story /life/green-sheet/2017/12/12/time-miller-brewing-picked-up-tab-stadiums -scoreboard/941663001/.

8. "Name of Busch Stadium Follows Tradition," *Sporting News*, April 22, 1953; "Frick Cries over Beer, So Cards Name Park for Busch and Budweiser Goes Down Drain," *New York Times*, April 11, 1953.

9. James Edward Miller, *The Baseball Business: Pursuing Pennants and Profits in Baltimore* (Chapel Hill: University of North Carolina Press, 1990).

10. Classic Baseball on the Radio, "1964 4 17 First Game at Shea Stadium Mets vs. Pirates Murphy, Kiner, Nelson," YouTube video, 2:38:49, April 22, 2017, www.youtube.com/watch?v=JVkQc1-ZNeM&t=325s.

11. Robert Lipsyte, "'Fabulous' Stadium Delights Fans," *New York Times*, April 18, 1964.

12. Prescott Sullivan, "A Boon for One and All!," *San Francisco Examiner*, September 19, 1966; Ed Levitt, "Concrete Goddess," *Oakland Tribune*, September 11, 1966.

13. Leonard Koppett, "Pirates Open Their New Park, but Reds Celebrate 3-2 Victory," *New York Times*, July 17, 1970; Roy Blount Jr., "Curtain Up on a Mod New Act," *Sports Illustrated*, April 19, 1971, 33.

14. "Coliseum Scoreboard Approved," *Los Angeles Times*, December 15, 1971.

15. John Hall, "What's the Score?," *Los Angeles Times*, October 2, 1972; "Scoreboard Complaint," *Los Angeles Times*, August 5, 1972.

16. Paul Goldberger, *Ballpark: Baseball in the American City* (New York: Knopf, 2019), 181, 185–186.

17. Daniel Rosensweig, *Retro Ball Parks: Instant History, Baseball, and the New American City* (Knoxville: University of Tennessee Press, 2005), 84–85.

18. Harold Kaese, "Name Stadium for Schaefer," *Boston Globe*, August 27, 1970; Jerry Nason, "Schaefer Big Boston Booster," *Boston Globe*, September 12, 1970.

19. Stephen R. Wenn, "Peter Ueberroth's Legacy: How the 1984 Los Angeles Olympics Changed the Trajectory of the Olympic Movement," *International Journal of the History of Sport* 32 (2015): 157–171; Wayne Wilson, "Sports Infrastructure, Legacy and the Paradox of the 1984 Olympic Games," *International Journal of the History of Sport* 32 (2015): 144–156.

20. "Facts About ARCO and the 1984 Olympics," box 139, folder 10, Tom Bradley Administration Papers, Charles Young Research Library, UCLA; "ARCO to Renovate Coliseum, Build 7 Olympic Tracks," *Los Angeles Times*, December 5, 1980; Tom Jackson, "Grand Opening," *Sacramento Bee*, October 5, 1985; L. Jon

Wortheim, *Glory Days: The Summer of 1984 and the 90 Days that Changed Sports and Culture Forever* (Boston: Houghton Mifflin Harcourt, 2021), 54.

21. "Cash-Kissed Bowl," *Los Angeles Times*, December 29, 1985.

22. Dave Lagarde, "Sun Bowl Latest to Be Sacked by Corporate Rush," *Times-Picayune* (New Orleans), July 1, 1986.

23. Edward Gunts, "This Diamond Is a Cut Above," *Baltimore Sun*, March 22, 1992.

24. Goldberger, *Ballpark*, 222; Dan Moore, "The Baseball Stadium That 'Forever Changed' Professional Sports," The Ringer, August 4, 2022, www.theringer.com /mlb/2022/8/4/23288546/camden-yards-30th-anniversary-baltimore-influence?r =9kig9.

25. See Roger G. Noll and Andrew Zimbalist, eds., *Sports, Jobs, and Taxes: The Economic Impact of Sports Teams and Stadiums* (Washington, DC: Brookings Institution, 1997); Kevin J. Delaney and Rick Eckstein, *Public Dollars, Private Stadiums: The Battle over Building Sports Stadiums* (New Brunswick, NJ: Rutgers University Press, 2003); John Charles Bradbury, Dennis Coates, and Brad R. Humphreys, "Public Policy Toward Professional Sports Stadiums: A Review," *Journal of Policy Analysis and Management* (January 30, 2023): 1–39, http://dx.doi.org/10.2139/ssrn.4340483.

26. Rosensweig, *Retro Ball Parks*; Robert C. Trumpbour, *The New Cathedrals: Politics and Media in the History of Stadium Construction* (Syracuse, NY: Syracuse University Press, 2007).

27. Peter Richmond, *Ballpark: Camden Yards and the Building of an American Dream* (New York: Simon & Schuster, 1993), 177.

28. Goldberger, *Ballpark*, 216.

29. John Charles Bradbury, "Sports Stadiums and Local Economic Activity: Evidence from Cobb County, Georgia," *SSRN Electronic Journal*, January 2021, 1–34, https://papers.ssrn.com/sol3/papers.cfm?abstract_id=3802875.

30. Stereo Williams, "Preach, Chris Rock: Why Black People Can't Get into Baseball," *Daily Beast*, April 14, 2017, www.thedailybeast.com/preach -chris-rock-why-black-people-cant-get-into-baseball.

31. Michael Betzold, John Davids, Bill Dow, John Pastier, and Frank Rashid, *Tiger Stadium: Essays and Memories of Detroit's Historic Ballpark, 1912–2009* (Jefferson, NC: McFarland, 2018), 129–165.

32. Murray Schmach, "Yankees' Biggest Fans Shouting 'Vamos!'" *New York Times*, September 27, 1976.

33. Sean Dinces, "The Attrition of the Common Fan: Class, Spectatorship, and Major League Stadiums in Postwar America," *Social Science History* 40, no. 2 (2016): 339–365.

34. CSC, website, https://csc-usa.com/about/overview/, accessed September 30, 2023.

35. Dave Zirin, "Camden Yards and the Baltimore Protests for Freddie Gray," *The Nation*, April 27, 2015.

CHAPTER EIGHT: WAR AND DEMOCRACY AT THE BALLPARK

1. Steve Wyche, "Colin Kaepernick Explains Why He Sat During the National Anthem," NFL.com, August 27, 2016, www.nfl.com/news/colin-kaepernick -explains-why-he-sat-during-national-anthem-0ap3000000691077.

2. Howard Bryant, *The Heritage: Black Athletes, a Divided America, and the Politics of Patriotism* (Boston: Beacon Press, 2018).

3. Kathleen Belew, *Bring the War Home: The White Power Movement and Paramilitary America* (Cambridge, MA: Harvard University Press, 2018).

4. Mark Clague, *O Say Can You Hear: A Cultural Biography of "The Star-Spangled Banner"* (New York: W. W. Norton, 2022), 115–144; "Mighty 'Battle' Thrills 100,000 at Coliseum," *Los Angeles Times*, June 9, 1944.

5. Nick Sarantakes, *Fan in Chief: Richard Nixon and American Sports, 1969–1974* (Lawrence: University of Kansas Press, 2019).

6. Doug Williams, "When Up with People Dominated Halftime," Fandom ESPN Playbook (blog), ESPN.com, January 31, 2013, www.espn.com/blog /playbook/fandom/post/_/id/17649/when-up-with-people-dominated-halftime.

7. "Marvin Gaye Sings the United States National Anthem at the 1983 NBA All-Star Game," video, 2:55, Classic Motown, https://classic.motown.com/video /marvin-gaye-sings-the-u-s-national-anthem/.

8. Danyel Smith, "The Story of Whitney Houston's Epic National Anthem Performance at the 1991 Super Bowl," ESPN.com, February 11, 2022, www .espn.com/nfl/story/_/id/29846571/the-story-whitney-houston-epic-national -anthem-performance-1991-super-bowl.

9. Bryant, *The Heritage*, 213.

10. Steven P. Erie, Vladimir Kogan, and Scott A. MacKenzie, "Redevelopment, San Diego Style: The Limits of Public-Private Partnerships," *Urban Affairs* 45 (2010): 644–678.

11. James W. Crawley, "Ensch on Deck for Padres," *San Diego Union-Tribune*, August 17, 1998. The Chargers first announced a Salute to the Military preseason promotion in 1989. "Neil Morgan," *San Diego Union-Tribune*, August 9, 1989; Bill Center, "Retired Navy Captain and Anchor for Padres," *San Diego Union-Tribune*, January 24, 2011; "Padres Bringing Back Brown for Five Dates in 2015," *San Diego Union-Tribune*, January 29, 2015.

12. Michael J. Clark, "Military Appreciation Sunday and the Padres Legendary Camo Uniforms," *East Village Times*, www.eastvillagetimes.com /military-appreciation-sunday-the-padres-legendary-camos/.

13. 30 for 30 Shorts, "First Pitch," vol. 3, episode 12, directed by Angus Wall, aired September 11, 2015 (ESPN Films, 2015).

14. "At O'Hare, the President Says 'Get on Board': Remarks by the President to Airline Employees, O'Hare International Airport, Chicago, Illinois," press release, the White House of President George W. Bush, September 27, 2001, https://georgewbush-whitehouse.archives.gov/news/releases/2001/09/20010927 -1.html.

15. Ron Briley, "'God Bless America': An Anthem for American Exceptionalism and Empire," in *Sports and Militarism: Contemporary Global Perspectives*, ed. Michael L. Butterworth (New York: Taylor and Francis, 2017), 115–128.

16. Paul Lukas, "Exclusive: The Man Who Brought 'God Bless America' to MLB Ballparks," Uni Watch, April 23, 2019, https://uni-watch.com/2019/04/23 /exclusive-the-man-who-brought-god-bless-america-to-mlb-ballparks/.

17. Bart Simpson, "2001 Jets @ Patriots," YouTube video, 2:35:04, November 10, 2020, www.youtube.com/watch?v=r5e-V8N7Zz4.

18. Stephen's Baseball Archives, "San Diego Padres vs. Los Angeles Dodgers, September 17, 2001," YouTube video, 4:23:27, August 16, 2021, www.youtube .com/watch?v=NsraUBJ7g7g; Jill Leovy, "2 Police Officers Awarded LAPD's Medal of Valor," *Los Angeles Times*, September 6, 2001; Max Felker-Kantor, *Policing Los Angeles: Race, Resistance, and the Rise of the LAPD* (Chapel Hill: University of North Carolina Press, 2018).

19. Bryant, *The Heritage*, 119.

20. Burgess Everett, "Pentagon Spent Millions on 'Paid Patriotism' with Sports Leagues," *Politico*, November 4, 2015, www.politico.com/story/2015/11 /pentagon-contracts-sports-teams-215508.

21. City News Service, "Dodgers to Hold Law Enforcement Appreciation Night," NBC4, April 2, 2019, www.nbclosangeles.com/news/dodgers-to-hold -law-enforcement-appreciation-night/136275/.

22. Alysha Tsuji, "Minnesota Lynx Wear Warmup Shirts in Honor of Philando Castile, Alton Sterling, and Dallas PD," *USA Today*, July 9, 2016, https: //ftw.usatoday.com/2016/07/minnesota-lynx-honor-philando-castile-alton -sterling-dallas-pd; Des Bieler, "Off-Duty Cops Quit Security for WNBA Game After Players Wear Black Lives Matter Shirts," *Washington Post*, July 12, 2016, www.washingtonpost.com/news/early-lead/wp/2016/07/11/off-duty-cops-quit -security-for-lynx-game-after-players-wear-black-lives-matter-shirts/.

23. Seth Berkman, "Liberty Show Solidarity with Black Lives Matter in Rare Public Stance," *New York Times*, July 10, 2016, www.nytimes.com /2016/07/11/sports/basketball/liberty-show-solidarity-with-black-lives-matter -in-rare-public-stance.html; Merrit Kennedy, "WNBA Rescinds Fines Against Players Wearing Shirts Supporting Shooting Victims," NPR, July 24, 2016, www.npr.org/sections/thetwo-way/2016/07/24/487237380/wnba-rescinds-fines -against-players-wearing-shirts-supporting-shooting-victims.

24. Michelle Alexander, *The New Jim Crow: Mass Incarceration in the Age of Colorblindness* (New York: New Press, 2010).

25. Barbara Ransby, *Making All Black Lives Matter: Reimagining Freedom in the Twenty-First Century* (Oakland: University of California Press, 2018).

26. Cindy Boren, "Colin Kaepernick Protest Has 49ers Fans Burning Their Jerseys," *Washington Post*, August 28, 2016, www.washingtonpost.com/news/early-lead/wp/2016/08/28/colin-kaepernick-protest-has-49ers-fans-burning-their-jerseys/; Emily Sullivan, "Laura Ingraham Told Lebron James to Shut Up and Dribble; He Went to the Hoop," NPR, February 19, 2018, www.npr.org/sections/thetwo-way/2018/02/19/587097707/laura-ingraham-told-lebron-james-to-shutup-and-dribble-he-went-to-the-hoop; Bryant, *The Heritage*, 8–9.

27. Norman Oder, "Brooklyn's Accidental New Town Square," Bklyner, June 10, 2020, https://bklyner.com/brooklyns-accidental-new-town-square/.

28. Daniel Roberts, "Drew Brees on Potential Return of Kneeling Protests: I Will Never Agree with Anyone Disrespecting the Flag," Yahoo! Finance, June 3, 2020, www.yahoo.com/video/drew-brees-on-potential-return-of-nfl-kneeling-protests-i-will-never-agree-with-anybody-disrespecting-the-flag-172424082.html.

29. Mike Florio, "Players Produced Powerful Video Demanding Clear Messages from the NFL," NBC Sports.com, June 4, 2020, https://profootballtalk.nbcsports.com/2020/06/04/players-produce-powerful-video-demanding-clear-messages-from-nfl/.

30. Jourdan Rodrigue and Lindsay Jones, "Inside NFL Players' Black Lives Matter Video, and How It Forced Goodell's Hand," *The Athletic*, June 6, 2020, https://theathletic.com/1857643/2020/06/06/inside-nfl-players-black-lives-matter-video-and-how-it-forced-goodells-hand/.

31. Sopan Deb, "WNBA Owner Clashes with Players on Protests," *New York Times*, July 9, 2016.

32. Angele Delevoye, "The WNBA Influenced the Georgia Senate Race, New Research Finds," *Washington Post*, November 30, 2020; Candace Buckner, "WNBA Players Helped Oust Kelly Loeffler from the Senate. Will She Last in the League?," *Washington Post*, January 7, 2021.

33. Jerry Beach, "Mets, Marlins Walk Off Field in Social Injustice Protest," AP News, August 27, 2020, https://apnews.com/article/6bdbf9d765de7f385d4ad8436e1548b7.

34. Stephen Deere, "Fulton County Elections Board Adds 11 New Voting Sites," *Atlanta Journal-Constitution*, June 29, 2020.

35. Civic Responsibility Project, *Voting in 2020: Professional Sports Stadiums & Arenas as Polling Places* (Washington, DC: Civic Responsibility Project, 2022), www.civicresponsibility.org/resources.

CONCLUSION

1. "DC Monument to Redskins Founder Is Vandalized, Removed," NBCWashington.com, June 19, 2020, www.nbcwashington.com/news/local/dc-monument-to-redskins-founder-is-vandalized-removed/2338545/.

2. Mandy Bell, "New for '22: Meet the Cleveland Guardians," MLB.com, July 23, 2021, www.mlb.com/news/cleveland-indians-change-name-to-guardians.

3. Alex Prewitt, "We Weren't Welcome When This Guy Was Around; So Now He's Not Welcome When We're Around," *Sports Illustrated*, June 19, 2020, www.si.com/mlb/2020/06/19/calvin-griffith-statue-minneapolis-black-lives-matter; George Dohrmann, "The Rise and Fall of Kirby Puckett," *Sports Illustrated*, March 17, 2003, https://vault.si.com/vault/2003/03/17/the-rise-and-fall-of-kirby-puckett-the-media-and-the-fans-in-minnesota-turned-the-twins-hall-of-famer-into-a-paragon-of-every-virtueand-that-made-his-human-flaws-when-they-came-to-light-all-the-more-shocking.

4. Dana Rubenstein and Ken Belson, "New York City Reaches Deal to Build Soccer Stadium in Queens," *New York Times*, November 15, 2022, www.nytimes.com/2022/11/15/nyregion/soccer-stadium-nycfc-willets.html; Corey Kilgannon and Andrew Salcedo, "How the Immigrant Dream in an Automotive Shantytown," *New York Times*, December 18, 2019, www.nytimes.com/interactive/2019/12/18/nyregion/willets-point-development-queens.html; Phil Rogers, "Rangers Saying Goodbye to a Beautiful Ballpark After Only 26 Years," *Forbes*, June 11, 2019, www.forbes.com/sites/philrogers/2019/06/11/rangers-saying-goodbye-to-beautiful-ballpark-after-only-26-years/?sh=9b6937a24f3d.

5. Luis Ferré-Saturní, "Buffalo Bills Strike Deal for Tax-Payer Funded $1.4 Billion Stadium," *New York Times*, March 28, 2022; Victor Matheson, "I've Studied Stadium Financing for Over Two Decades and the New Bills Stadium Is One of the Worst Deals I've Ever Seen," *The Conversation*, April 15, 2022, https://theconversation.com/ive-studied-stadium-financing-for-over-two-decades-and-the-new-bills-stadium-is-one-of-the-worst-deals-for-taxpayers-ive-ever-seen-180475; Neil deMause, "The Stadium Scam Goes Minor League and It Has an Unlikely Ally," *Deadspin*, September 18, 2018, https://deadspin.com/the-stadium-scam-goes-minor-league-and-it-has-an-unlik-1828896356; Kevin Collison, "Downtown Ballpark for Kansas City Royals Now Makes Sense, Speaker Says," *Flatland*, January 31, 2020, https://flatlandkc.org/news-issues/downtown-ballpark-for-kansas-city-royals-now-makes-sense-speaker-says/.

6. Abby Elizabeth Conway, "USCO, Local Olympic Organizers Drop Bid to Bring 2024 Olympics to Boston," WBUR.com, July 27, 2015, www.wbur.org/news/2015/07/27/usoc-pulls-boston-olympic-bid; Jules Boykoff, *NOlympians: Inside the Fight Against Capitalist Mega-Sports in Los Angeles, Tokyo, and Beyond* (Nova Scotia: Fernwood Publishing, 2020).

7. Bruce Kidd, "Toronto's Skydome: The World's Greatest Entertainment Centre," *Sport in Society* 16 (2013): 388–404.

8. Margaret Fosmoe, "Curtain Rises on Notre Dame Stadium Renovations," *South Bend Tribune*, August 12, 2017, www.southbendtribune.com/story/news /local/2017/08/12/curtain-rises-on-notre-dame-stadium-renovations/45805867/.

9. Michael Betzold, John Davids, Bill Dow, John Pastier, and Frank Rashid, *Tiger Stadium: Essays and Memories of Detroit's Historic Ballpark, 1912–2009* (Jefferson, NC: McFarland, 2018), 129–165.

INDEX

Frank Andre Guridy is an award-winning historian and the author of three books. He is a professor of history and African American studies and the executive director of the Eric H. Holder Initiative for Civil and Political Rights at Columbia University. He lives in New York City.